The Origins of Reasonable Doubt

JAMES Q. WHITMAN, 1957-

The Origins of
Reasonable Doubt,

THEOLOGICAL ROOTS OF
THE CRIMINAL TRIAL

Yale University Press
New Haven
& London

Set in by Sabon type by Keystone Typesetting, Inc., Orwigsburg, Pennsylvania.
Printed in the United States of America.

Library of Congress Cataloging-in-Publication Data
Whitman, James Q., 1957–
The origins of reasonable doubt : theological roots of the criminal trial /
James Q. Whitman.
p. cm.
Includes bibliographical references and index.
ISBN 978-0-300-11600-7 (cloth : alk. paper)
1. Burden of proof—Moral and ethical aspects—Europe—History. 2. Evidence,
Criminal—Europe—History. 3. Judgments, Criminal—Europe—History.
4. Religion and law—Europe—History. I. Title.
KJC9601.W45 2007
345.4'06—dc22
2007033384

A catalogue record for this book is available from the British Library.

The paper in this book meets the guidelines for permanence and durability of the
Committee on Production Guidelines for Book Longevity of the Council on
Library Resources.
10 9 8 7 6 5 4 3 2 1

Contents

Illustrations

Acknowledgments

Versions of this book have been presented in seminars at a number of institutions, including the École des Hautes Études en Sciences Sociales, Yale Law School, Harvard Law School, New York University Law School, Cornell Law School, Università di Roma III, the University of Illinois College of Law, and Amherst College. I am grateful to participants at all of these venues for their comments. I am also particularly grateful to individual scholars who provided me with critical comments and other aid: Bernadette Meyler, Mirjan Damaska, Charles Donahue, Thomas Gallanis, Antoine Garapon, James Gordley, R. H. Helmholz, Andrew Huxley, Baber Johansen, Waltraud Kozur, John Langbein, Susanne Lepsius, Richard Ross, Sara McDougall, Antonio Padoa-Schioppa, Heikki Pihlajamäki, Hugh Scogin, and Yan Thomas.

Unless otherwise noted, all translations are by the author. I have generally quoted biblical passages in the King James Version, in the expectation that it is the King James Version with which my readers will be most familiar. Where the King James Version is likely to be misleading, though, I have used one of the other standard translations.

Introduction

No person in the United States of America can be convicted of a crime unless that person's guilt is proven with certainty. Mere probability of guilt is not enough: if the accused does not willingly plead guilty, all the essential elements of guilt must be proven to a jury, and they must be proven "beyond a reasonable doubt."[1] It would be hard to name a doctrine more familiar, or more basic to the American sense of justice. Indeed, the requirement of proof "beyond a reasonable doubt" is so fundamental that the Supreme Court has read it into our constitutional law, even though the phrase "reasonable doubt" appears nowhere in the Constitution.[2] The Court's interpretations of the Constitution are often controversial, but there is no controversy about this one: everyone seems to agree that American criminal law would be unimaginable without the reasonable doubt standard of proof, regardless of what the text of the Constitution may or may not say.

Yet behind this fundamental and universally familiar doctrine lies a troubling mystery—the mystery that is my point of departure in this book. "Beyond a reasonable doubt" is among the most majestic phrases in our law; but in practice it is vexingly difficult to interpret and apply. There is always *some* possible uncertainty about any case. Exactly what kind of uncertainty counts as a legal "doubt"? Exactly when are legal "doubts" about the guilt of the accused "reasonable" ones? Jurors are sometimes understandably baffled.[3]

Even some of the most sophisticated members of the legal profession find the question too difficult to answer.[4] Indeed, there is a considerable corpus of case law in which judges flounder unhappily over the definition of "reasonable doubt." According to the traditional common law rule, still in force in many states, judges are forbidden to explain the meaning of the phrase.[5] No matter how much jurors may beg for guidance, under the traditional rule they are on their own in interpreting "reasonable doubt."[6] Even in those states where judges are permitted to define the standard, they are often not required to do so.[7] Nor has the Supreme Court been much help. The Court has made it clear that an error in defining "reasonable doubt" is never harmless;[8] the rule is too fundamentally important for that. At the same time, though, the Court has simply abandoned any effort of its own to define the standard.[9] "Attempts to explain the term 'reasonable doubt,' " the Court once dryly observed, "do not usually result in making it any clearer to the minds of the jury."[10]

All this makes for an unsettling spectacle. The reasonable doubt standard is undeniably fundamental to the American sense of justice. Weighty decisions about the fate of real people depend upon it: Once a jury has determined a person to be guilty "beyond a reasonable doubt," that person's fate is almost always sealed: the common law system makes it very difficult to appeal a criminal conviction. Yet a majority of our judiciary seems to have come to the conclusion that the phrase "reasonable doubt" can be assigned no definitive meaning. A cynic or postmodern philosopher might point to this situation, whether in despair or in glee, as evidence for the deep incoherence of the most basic propositions of the law. A moral philosopher might question our authority to punish fellow citizens on the basis of a rule that does not seem to make sense.

It is not my purpose in this book to offer a cynical or postmodern account. We *can* make sense of our law of reasonable doubt. But in order to make sense of it, we sometimes have to dig deep into its history. As this book aims to show, the reasonable doubt formula seems mystifying today because we have lost sight of its original purpose. The origins of reasonable doubt lie in a forgotten world of premodern Christian theology, a world whose concerns were quite different from our own. Our modern law is the product of a deep transformation, in the course of which some of the old religious foundations of the criminal trial were forgotten.

This is a book about the forgotten theological roots of the criminal trial. The reasonable doubt rule, this book aims to show, is the last vestige of a vanished premodern Christian world. At its origins, this familiar rule was not intended to perform the function we ask it to perform today: It was not primarily intended to protect the accused. Instead, it had a significantly different purpose. Strange as it may sound, the reasonable doubt formula was originally concerned with protecting the souls of *the jurors* against damnation.

In the Christian past, as we shall see, there was more at stake, in a criminal trial, than the fate of the accused. The fate of those who sat in judgment was at stake at well. The famous injunction of Saint Matthew — *Judge not lest ye be judged!* — had a concrete meaning: convicting an innocent defendant was regarded, in the older Christian tradition, as a potential mortal sin. The reasonable doubt rule was one of many rules and procedures that developed in response to this disquieting possibility. It was originally a theological doctrine, intended to reassure jurors that they could convict the defendant without risking their own salvation, so long as their doubts about guilt were not "reasonable." "Beyond a reasonable doubt" was originally a rule for anxious Christians, living in an age haunted, as our world no longer is, by the fear of damnation. This means that if we wish fully to understand our contemporary law, we must leave modern legal doctrine behind and dive deep into the waters of medieval Christian moral theology. Indeed, we must dive into the anthropology of premodern law much more broadly: the medieval Christian world was simply typical of premodern societies all over the world, in which the act of judging was often seen as full of menace, both for the judge and for the witnesses who gave testimony against their neighbors.

The task of this book is to trace this premodern religious history, a history much older than the common law, and covering a world much wider than England or America. As we shall see, medieval and early modern Christians experienced great anxiety about the dangers that acts of judgment presented for the soul. As all readers of Dante know, medieval officeholders faced the risk of damnation if they committed sin in the course of their official acts. Those risks confronted judges just as they faced every other official. Indeed, medieval church lawyers were especially fascinated by the dangers of judging, to which they devoted considerable attention. As they saw it, any sinful misstep committed by a judge in the course of judging "built him a mansion in Hell,"[11] and rules had to be developed to shield judges from the consequences of their own official acts. This was especially true any time a judge imposed "blood punishments" — that is, execution and mutilation, the standard criminal punishments of pre-nineteenth-century law.

And when it came to inflicting blood punishments, premodern Christian theology turned in particular on the problem of "doubt." Doubt about the facts presented a real danger to the soul of the individual judge. Doubt was the voice of an uncertain conscience, and in principle it had to be obeyed. Such was the rule laid down in particular by the standard "safer way" school of

Christian moral theology, which grew up during the central Middle Ages: "In cases of doubt," as the safer way formula ran, "the safer way is not to act at all."[12] For Christians living in an age of fear and trembling, any "doubtful" act was full of danger, and this applied to judging just as it did to all other acts involving the individual conscience. As a typical French "dictionary of conscience" explained the standard Christian law in the eighteenth century, "In every case of doubt, where one's salvation is in peril, one must always take the safer way. . . . A judge who is in doubt must refuse to judge."[13] A judge who sentenced an accused person to a blood punishment while experiencing "doubt" about guilt committed a mortal sin, and thus put his own salvation in peril.

The story of the reasonable doubt rule is simply an English chapter in this long history of safer way theology, a history in which Christian theologians worried for centuries over the nature of judging, over the problems of doubt, and over the dangers of what a famous seventeenth-century English pamphlet called "the Guilt of *Blood.*" Common law jurors were Christians, and they were Christians who engaged in acts of judgment. This meant that to be a juror was potentially to "build yourself a mansion in Hell" — "to pawn [your] Soul," as the same pamphlet put it.[14] There is plenty of evidence that English jurors took this quite seriously, especially at the end of the eighteenth century. As the moral philosopher William Paley described the situation in 1785, around the time that the reasonable doubt rule first established itself in England, jurors experienced "a general dread lest the charge of innocent blood should lie at their doors."[15] Jurors simply did not want to convict, Paley complained: In their "weak timidity," they held it "the part of a *safe* conscience not to condemn any man, whilst there exists the minutest possibility of his innocence."[16] It was in response to such juror "timidity" and "dread" that the reasonable doubt standard introduced itself into the common law. English Christian jurors of the 1780s, following the standard precepts of centuries-old safer way theology, often wished to take the "surest side"[17] or the "safer way,"[18] refusing to convict the accused where they experienced "any degree of doubt."[19] The reasonable doubt rule arose in the face of this religiously motivated reluctance to convict, taking its now-familiar form during the 1780s. It is still with us today, a living fossil from an older moral world.

Such is the story this book tells. As it suggests, the "beyond a reasonable doubt" standard was not originally designed to make it more difficult for jurors to convict. It was designed to make conviction *easier*, by assuring jurors that their souls were safe if they voted to condemn the accused.[20] In its original form, it had nothing to do with maintaining the rule of law in the sense that we use the phrase, and nothing like the relationship to the values of liberty we ascribe to it today. It was the product of a world troubled by moral anxieties that no longer trouble us much at all. This makes it unsurprising that our law should find itself in a state of confusion today. We are asking the reasonable doubt standard to serve a function that it was not originally designed to serve, and it does its work predictably badly.

Some preliminary words are in order before diving into the details. The topic of this book is not new. The problem of the origins of reasonable doubt has attracted a number of first-rate scholars, most notably Barbara Shapiro, James Franklin, Anthony Morano, Steve Sheppard, and John Langbein.[21] Some of them, especially Shapiro and Franklin, have come tantalizingly close to resolving the mystery of the rule. I shall draw gratefully on the work of all these historians. Yet in the end, as I shall argue, these scholars have not gotten the history right. In one way or another, all of them have conceived of the reasonable doubt rule as a rule of factual proof, as a heuristic for determining the truth in cases of ignorance, akin to the rules of factual proof in natural science. They have not recognized that the rule was bound up with the fate of those who sat in judgment. As we shall see, this has prevented them from fully understanding the dynamic of the past. More important, it has prevented them from appreciating the dilemmas of the present. If we do not grasp the depth of the theological problem that haunts the history of the reasonable doubt rule, we will not understand how our law arrived at the unsettling state of confusion it is in today. We need a new account.

The new account that this book offers inevitably ranges widely over western European history. The history of reasonable doubt is really just an English episode in a much larger Christian history. Doctrines closely akin to it were applied to judges in every part of western Christendom, from Spain to Germany, from Italy to England. Accordingly, this is a book that ventures well beyond the conceptual limits of the common law, and well beyond the geographical limits of the world of eighteenth-century England and America. This may seem strange to readers who are used to thinking of the common law as an invention of a purely Anglo-American world. Nevertheless, there is an important lesson in it for all Americans who care about their legal system. As legal scholars like Richard Helmholz, Charles Donahue, Harold Berman, Mike MacNair, and George Fisher have shown, the history of the common law is inextricably bound up with the general Western history of Christianity: The law of England has to be seen against the broader background of the law and traditions of western Christendom;[22] we will simply never understand our law if we pretend that it is the product of a narrowly Anglo-American legal tradition. Indeed, as I shall argue, the Christian story itself is only one episode in a larger human history: Anxieties about the dangers of judging were widespread, if not universal, in the premodern world, and Christianity itself must be seen in a larger comparative and anthropological context. All of this has its place in the history of reasonable doubt.

Accordingly, the book begins, in chapter 1, by assembling some comparative and anthropological evidence, to show how widespread premodern anxieties about judging and punishing were. It also begins by developing a basic distinction: the distinction between procedures that aim at *factual proof*, and procedures that aim at what I shall call *moral comfort*. As I hope to show, the distinction between factual proof and moral comfort is fundamentally important for understanding the original meaning of the reasonable doubt rule, and indeed for understanding premodern law more broadly.

Factual proof procedures, as the name suggests, aim to achieve proof in cases in which the truth is unknown. Moral comfort procedures, by contrast, aim to relieve the moral anxieties of persons who fear engaging in acts of judgment — persons such as early modern criminal jurors. As chapter 1 will argue, premodern law was much more concerned with moral comfort than is our law today, and it was much less concerned with factual proof. Indeed, the transition from an emphasis on moral comfort to an emphasis on factual proof is one of the master themes in the making of modern law: One of the features that makes our law modern is our relative lack of anxiety about judging others. As chapter 1 argues, moral comfort procedures and factual proof procedures are easily confused. Yet unless we distinguish these two functions carefully, we cannot fully grasp the history of criminal procedure. Nor can we grasp the dilemmas of modern American law. Those dilemmas have to do precisely with the fact that our system, deeply attached to tradition, has held on to numerous premodern institutions; the American common law has preserved many premodern moral comfort procedures in an age when the problems of criminal justice are primarily problems of factual proof. "Reasonable doubt" is one of them.

From there, the book turns to the specifics of Christian history, exploring the peculiar theology of premodern Christian efforts to provide judges with moral comfort. This involves a long Western history that starts in antiquity and only slowly reaches the England of the eighteenth century. The theology and jurisprudence of doubt and blood punishments developed principally in Continental Europe. It began developing in late antiquity, especially in the theology of Saint Augustine, my topic in chapter 2. It came to its first maturity during the twelfth century, particularly during the great campaign against the judicial ordeal.

The medieval judicial ordeal figures especially prominently in this book.

Historians have long recognized that jury trial first emerged as an alternative to the judicial ordeal. Strange as it may sound, our law began to take shape when the church set out to abolish the painful and frightening ordeals of the hot iron and the cold water. This means that the religious history of jury trial begins with the religious history of the ordeal, and my central chapters make the ordeal their focus. Thus chapter 3 will ask the reader to venture deep into the meaning of the medieval ordeal, while chapter 4 will investigate the Continental theology of judging that grew up as the ordeal went into decline, and chapter 5 will give an account of how jury trial emerged in England. Chapters 6 and 7, finally, will trace the ultimate rise of the law and theology of reasonable doubt in the seventeenth and eighteenth centuries. These chapters will involve the investigation of a great deal of Christian theology — not only the theology of doubt but also questions concerning the judge's use of his "private knowledge," and the nature of Catholic confession and its Calvinist alternatives.

All of this makes for a long but essential journey. We cannot really understand the reasonable doubt rule until we have worked through these centuries of religious anxiety. More broadly, we cannot really understand the modern predicament of the criminal law. The seas of religion have receded, after many centuries. But the landscape of the law still includes many of its older diluvian features, and we will not be able to keep our footing unless we know its history. Modern law is the product of a deep moral transformation. Our ancestors were afraid to judge, at least sometimes. Certainly they were more afraid than we are. If they were Christians, they brought a sense of their own sinfulness to the task of judging, doubting their own authority to condemn. At least some of the time, they took Matthew's *Judge not, lest ye be judged!* in real earnest, and their legal doctrines reflected that fact.

The making of the modern world has destroyed that attitude. Modern secularization has brought the decline of the fearful religiosity of the past. This is true even of avowedly pious people; none of us experiences the depth of daily fear that our ancestors experienced. In many aspects of life this is a good and liberating thing: Humans who no longer quake and tremble are humans who live richer lives in many ways. But in criminal justice this modern liberation has had consequences that are sometimes troubling, and not only because we convict accused persons under a reasonable doubt standard that we do not understand. The larger truth is that we have slowly been losing the capacity to gaze into our own breasts and ask ourselves hard questions about when and how we have the right to punish others.

Of Factual Proof and Moral Comfort

Israel ex. cum Priuil Reg.

Ceux qui pour obeir a leur mauuais Genie   Ne se plaisent quau mal violent la raison ;   Produisent dans le Camp mil sanglans vacarmes
Manquent a leur deuoir, vsent de tyrannie ;   Et sont les actions plenes de trahison   Sont ainsi chastiez, et passez par les armes .   12.

Judge not, lest ye be judged!
— *Matthew 7:1*

The Search for Moral Comfort

"Judge not lest ye be judged!" is hardly more than a pretty piety for us. In past centuries, though, this injunction and others like it carried a positive threat — a threat taken very seriously, and one that had a significant impact on the shaping of the criminal trial.

Legal procedures in the premodern world were not like legal procedures today. They did not always aim only at achieving certainty in cases where the guilt of the offender was unknown. Nor did they aim only at providing procedural safeguards for the accused. Instead, they were often designed to help relieve the judge's own anxieties about the act of judging. As James Fitzjames Stephen, the pioneering nineteenth-century historian of the criminal law, put it, premodern judges often dreaded "the responsibility — which to many men would appear intolerably heavy and painful — of deciding . . . upon the guilt or innocence of the prisoner."[1] Indeed they did. They dreaded this responsibility so much that they avoided entering verdicts if at all possible, or else sought to diminish their personal responsibility in other ways. Premodern judges were often assailed by anxieties. In consequence, they often were not seeking *factual proof* so much as they were seeking *moral comfort*.

Not all the dangers that premodern judges faced were spiritual. Sometimes they were legal: medieval Islamic jurists, for example, held that judges who falsely convicted an accused person should suffer exactly the same punishment they had inflicted.[2] There were comparable rules in the West, too. In medieval Italy, for example, judges were subject to civil and criminal liability for incorrect judgments.[3] English jurors faced similar legal threats until 1670.[4] On a grosser level, the physical well-being of a judge was sometimes threatened in the past, just as it is still occasionally threatened today. In particular, as historians have demonstrated, medieval judges sometimes had to reckon with the possibility of clan vengeance. A medieval judge who voted to convict an ac-

Figure 1. The firing squad, punishment for soldiers who flee in battle. In Jacques Callot's 1633 representation we see troops firing in standard early seventeenth-century formation, obliged to kill one of their own. Jacques Callot, *L'Arquebusade*, etching no. 12 in the series *Les misères de la guerre*. Collection of the author.

cused man, even a manifestly guilty one, might find himself the target of a blood vendetta by that man's relatives. If you adjudged a man guilty, in a world dominated by the rules of clan vengeance, you had his blood on your hands, and his relatives were pledged to avenge him.[5] The same was of course true of witnesses: in vengeance cultures, a witness, as medieval theologians observed, "may easily run the risk of death."[6]

But lives and livelihoods were not all that was at stake in a premodern trial. It is especially important to recognize that our ancestors dreaded, as Stephen implied, the *moral* and *spiritual* responsibilities of judgment. This was particularly true where capital punishment was concerned. Even where there is no immediate threat of clan vengeance, having blood on your hands can be a frightening business. It is not just clansmen who exact vengeance. God too, or the fates, may also be committed to avenging blood.[7] "God," as Adam Smith was still putting it in the eighteenth century, administers punishments because he is "the great avenger of justice."[8] Indeed, as anthropologists and historians of religion have shown, anyone in the premodern world involved in the killing of another person subjected himself to the risk of bad luck, bad karma, bad fate, of some kind of vengeful divine retribution;[9] and when it comes to capital cases, judges are, after all, persons who can be thought of as lending their hands to the killing of another human being. Might not God, or the fates, come after the judges themselves?

This may sound bizarre to the modern reader. We are accustomed to the idea that the judge's professional identity puts him or her in a moral position different in kind from that of a person "cooperating in a killing"; modern judges succeed in maintaining a psychic distance from the raw results of the judgments they enter, as Robert Cover argued in a celebrated article with the evocative title "Violence and the Word."[10] But the capacity to maintain that kind of psychic distance developed only very slowly. Judges were not by any means always clearly exempted from the risk of spiritual responsibility for the killings over which they presided, whether in the Western or the non-Western worlds, and they sometimes displayed considerable anxiety.

To illustrate this, it is helpful to begin with a non-Western example, which will provide a useful foil for the Christian tradition. This example is drawn from the world of the Theravada Buddhist tradition of Burma, as described by Andrew Huxley. It involves judging and "kamma," the Pali word for karma, and it features the infant who, in a later life, would be reborn as the Buddha. The future Buddha, in this tale, has been born as the son of a just king:[11] "In the Temiya Jataka the future Buddha at one month old, sitting with the king, his father, in court, witnesses his father sentencing criminals to death [and other horrible punishments]. Instantly he remembers that in a past life he too condemned men to death, and that as a result he burned in hell for 80,000 years. To escape inheriting the throne, the Future Buddha pretends to be unable to walk, speak or hear. In the face of this canonical warning that inflicting punishment can damage your kamma, the devout Buddhist prince should refuse to become king."[12]

This passage offers us a paradigmatic example of the moral anxieties attached to judging in the premodern world. Judging is dangerous — not just to the accused but also to the judge. It is dangerous to the judge regardless of the merits of the case. There is no suggestion here that the king was condemning *innocent* persons to death. On the contrary, the story begins by declaring that he ruled "justly." The dangers to his kamma were dangers presented by *any* act of condemnation. As Huxley observes, this was an attitude that pushed Theravada Buddhists toward a radical antinomianism, which at the limit preached a collapse of all social institutions. As late as the mid-nineteenth century, according to one observer, Burmese Buddhists familiar with this passage warned against serving as a judge.[13]

Western Christian thinkers were never quite so radically antinomian: Western fears have mostly involved condemning the innocent, not the guilty. Nevertheless, Christianity had its own antinomian streak, and its own anxieties about the afterlife, and there are closely related passages and practices in western law as well, passages and practices that betray a real anxiety about the spiritual risks associated with judging. *Beware the act of judging*, declared theologians all through the Middle Ages: *You risk making yourself into a murderer.*[14] Or as the most famous text on jury trial of the seventeenth and eighteenth centuries, Sir John Hawles's *The Englishman's Right*, put it, echoing the medieval theological tradition: Let the conscientious juryman "tremble," lest he be "guilty of [the defendant's] Murther."[15] If most of us have forgotten these anxieties, they were still very much alive for our medieval and early modern ancestors.

So how can you judge in a capital case without becoming a "murtherer" yourself? The response given by the Temiya Jataka offers essentially no hope: Judging, according to this Theravada tale, is quite simply synonymous with killing. But the Western Christian tradition has typically taken a more forgiving approach, creating institutions that allow judges to condemn offenders to death without suffering crippling personal anxiety. Indeed, throughout Western legal history we find many procedures designed to ease or eliminate the burden of moral responsibility for judges, soldiers, executioners, or persons who join in a group killing from necessity. These are what I shall call *moral comfort procedures*, procedures designed to guarantee that judges in capital cases, and people like them, can take away with them a necessary dose of moral comfort, even while participating in a death.

There is nothing strange in the idea that trial procedures might some-times have more to do with easing the moral burdens of the judge than with proving the guilt of the accused. We all know that trial sometimes serves such a moral comfort function. After all, it is not the case that we only hold trials where there is meaningful ignorance about the guilt of the ac-cused. Even when the guilt of the accused is entirely obvious, we still feel an obligation to convict according to the proper procedures. Indeed, we would feel profoundly uneasy if we sentenced obviously guilty defendants to a severe punishment without having first dotted and crossed all the procedural i's and t's. Procedure in such cases does not serve a proof function: It does not aim to eliminate our ignorance about the facts. Instead, it aims to reassure those of us who act as judges. It offers us a kind of moral safe harbor in administering punishment, by allowing us to declare that the accused was convicted accord-ing to impersonal procedures, and not according to our own individual whim. Procedure, in such cases, serves to diminish the anxiety we feel in punish-ing others.[16]

That sort of anxiety certainly still exists in our trials. Nevertheless, it used to be much more sharply felt, and the moral comfort function of procedure loomed much larger in the premodern world than it does today. That does not mean that premodern trials were never concerned with factual proof. Of course they sometimes were. Nor does it mean, to say it again, that modern procedures never offer moral comfort. Procedure in any legal system some-times serves both of these functions. But the mix has changed. Moral comfort used to matter much more than it does today, and the shape of premodern procedure reflects that fact.

Indeed, as we turn back to the premodern world, we find a striking range of moral comfort procedures — procedures used not only in the setting of the trial but in any setting involving a collective killing. Many of those procedures were directed at executioners, or other ordinary killers from necessity, such as sol-diers.[17] There are some examples of such premodern procedures that are still familiar to modern readers. We all know, for example, how firing squads work. One member of the squad is chosen to receive a blank, but no member of the squad is permitted to know precisely which of them is the chosen one. This procedure, which is presumably very old, seems at first glance exceedingly odd.[18] But its purpose is not all that difficult to fathom: As legal scholars well understand, firing squad procedure is intended to relieve the individual squad members of a burdensome sense of moral responsibility, by allowing each one to doubt that it was he who fired the fatal shot. It offers, as we might say, a kind of spiritual safe harbor for the conscience of each individual fusilier.[19]

Another example still familiar to modern readers is the traditional procedure for cannibalism among shipwrecked sailors—the procedure that was rejected in the famous 1884 English case of *Regina v. Dudley and Stephens*. According to this traditional procedure, starving seamen could kill and eat one of their number, but only provided that they drew straws to determine which of them would be the victim.[20] This is the procedure immortalized in the cheery French children's song "Il Était un Petit Navire," some versions of which turn the question into a standard French debate over cuisine:

> They drew the short straw
> They drew the short straw
> To know who, who, who would be eaten
> To know who, who, who would be eaten.
>
> Fate chose the youngest
> Fate chose the youngest
> So it was he who, who, who was designated
> So it was he who, who, who was designated.
>
> Now they tried to decide with what sauce
> Now they tried to decide with what sauce
> The poor child, child, child should be eaten
> The poor child, child, child should be eaten.
>
> Some thought he should be fried
> Some thought he should be fried,
> Others preferred, -ferred, -ferred a fricassee
> Others preferred, -ferred, -ferred a fricassee.

As all first-year law students know, the *Dudley and Stephens* court, in condemning cannibalism as a form of unjustifiable homicide, denied that there was any sense in this procedure of drawing straws, which it dismissively described as "somewhat strange."[21] Yet this "somewhat strange" procedure ought to make intuitive sense to all of us. Drawing straws makes it possible to assert that God, or fate, or chance has made the decision to kill, thus lifting the moral responsibility from the participants in the killing.[22] Indeed, when it comes to cannibalism, we can all grasp the reassuring spiritual logic of this sort of procedure: Any of us driven to cannibalism would be glad for the chance to claim that the decision had been made by chance or God, not by ourselves. In past centuries, the same procedure was used in other contexts, too, in which one member of a group had to die so that the others might live. If one must die for all, we draw lots, allowing chance to make the fatal decision.[23]

There are many other examples of such procedures, which aim in one or way or another to soothe the worries of participants in collective killings. The last one that I would like to cite comes from Richard Lee's 1979 anthropological study of the !Kung: "[A !Kung] man named /Twi had killed three other people, when the community, in a rare move of unanimity, ambushed and fatally wounded him in full daylight. As he lay dying, all the men fired at him with poisoned arrows until, in the words of one informant, he looked like a porcupine. Then, after he was dead, all the women as well as the men approached his body and stabbed him with spears, symbolically sharing the responsibility for his death."[24] In effect, this is yet another example of a premodern moral comfort procedure — in this case, procedure having to do with the very collective character of a collective killing. If everybody stabs, everybody can disclaim a measure of moral responsibility.

In the premodern world, these same sorts of procedures were also used to comfort judges faced with the anxieties of judging. We do not ordinarily think of judging as an act that resembles serving on a firing squad, cannibalizing one's starving boat mate, or joining in a collective orgy of communal stabbing; but our ancestors did, and they developed a variety of procedures that offered judges their own sorts of moral safe harbors. To borrow the language of Guido Calabresi and Philip Bobbitt, judges often sought some way to make themselves into "aresponsible" decision makers.[25] Some of the relevant procedures were little different from the procedures in literal collective killings. Jury trial itself is a collective proceeding, like the !Kung communal execution described by Lee; and it too is one that requires unanimity. Like that communal execution, jury trial (and other forms of collective judging) may serve partly to diminish the individual sense of moral responsibility. If we all vote to convict, none of us is fully responsible: We have all stabbed, as it were. *Collectivizing* is thus one form of moral comfort procedure.

Another is *randomizing*. If we want to avoid feeling responsible, we can leave the decision to execute to chance or the intervention of the gods, just as the traditional rule on cannibalism depended on chance or the intervention of the gods. In traditional Chinese law, for example, prisoners were selected for capital punishment in the way that allowed everyone involved to disclaim personal agency, even while attempting to manipulate the result. A British observer of the late nineteenth century describes the procedure:

[The list of criminals subject to the death sentence is] written on a large sheet of paper thus:

```
A. C. D. E. F.  G. H. I.
K. Z. M. N. O. P. Q. R.
S. T. U. V. W. X. Y. Z.
A. B. C. D. E. F. G. H.
I. J. K. L. M. N. O. P.
Q. R. S. T. U. V. W. X.
Y. Z. A. B. C. D. E. F.
G. H. I.  J. K. L.  M. N.
```

not alphabetically, or by chance, but so that the names of those prisoners who are, in the opinion of the Board, less guilty than the others are placed either at the corners or in the centre. The list is then submitted to the Emperor, who, with a brush dipped in vermilion, makes a circle on it at seeming, and to some extent real, hazard, and the criminals whose names are traversed by the red line are ordered for execution. The others remain on the list until the next year, but, if they escape the vermilion pencil for three years, their sentences are then commuted.[26]

The drama here too — the drama of a "seeming, and to some extent real, hazard" — involves nothing other than the universal fear of human responsibility for death, a fear at work even in systems with a highly bureaucratized machinery of capital punishment. Rabelais memorably caricatured the mentality involved, in the person of his fictional Judge Bridoye, who decided cases by the throw of the dice. When you let difficult questions be decided by a chance, as Rabelais explained in half-mock sympathy with Judge Bridoye, there is no evil in it. Instead, "the divine will" manifests itself to "man in his anxiety and doubt."[27] Rabelais was echoing Saint Augustine, who said the same thing without any trace of jesting. Deciding matters by chance is nothing evil, declared the great saint; instead, it is a way of seeking out "the divine will" in the face of "human doubt."[28]

When obliged to judge, we seek succor in our anxiety and human doubt: *collectivizing* and *randomizing* are two ways of comforting us. Alongside those two, we can identify two other principal classes of moral comfort procedures that have played especially prominent roles in the Western tradition. First, there are *responsibility-shifting* procedures — rules that aim to comfort the judge by forcing some other agent to assume all or part of the responsibility for making the final judgment. Stephen, the great nineteenth-century historian of criminal law, interpreted jury trial in exactly this way: "It is hardly necessary to say that to judges in general the maintenance of trial by jury is of more importance than to any other members of the community. It saves judges from the responsibility — which to many men would appear intolerably heavy and painful — of deciding simply on their own opinion upon the guilt or innocence of the prisoner."[29] The structure of jury trial, as Stephen interpreted it, was such that each of its two actors, judge and jury, could shift some of the responsibility for judgment over to the other, thus diminishing the sense of responsibility for both.

The same observation was made, in considerably more dramatic language, by our seventeenth-century pamphleteer Hawles, who described the dynamic of jury trial this way: "[T]he Guilt of the *Blood* or *ruin* of an Innocent man [is] *Bandyed* to and fro, and *shuffled off* from the Jury to the Judge, and from the Judge to the Jury, but really *sticks fast to both,* but especially *on the Jurors.*"[30] To Hawles, jury trial was something akin to a children's game, in which judge and jury each tried to see to it that the other ended up "it." Many premodern procedures took such forms; premodern judges feared "the Guilt of *Blood*" and were eager to "shuffle it off" onto some other actor. The medieval ordeal offers a striking example of a procedure that could serve such a guilt-shuffling, children's-game-like purpose: As we shall see in chapter 3, ordeals were often inflicted on persons whose guilt was already obvious. The ordeal, in such cases, did not serve as a means of factual proof. Instead, its purpose was to force God to make the decision to convict the accused, thus shuffling what Peter Brown calls "the odium of human responsibility" off the shoulders of the community and onto the shoulders of the Almighty himself.[31] *Let God be the one who makes the decision to kill him!* Mature medieval law, as we shall see, pursued a similar strategy. In order to protect the judges, the law both in England and on the Continent aimed to shuffle all the moral responsibility off the shoulders of the judge and onto those of the witnesses.[32]

Alongside collectivizing, randomizing, and guilt-shuffling, we can, finally, identify a fourth, and especially important, approach to easing the judge's sense of moral responsibility. This is what we may call *agency denial.* Agency denial procedures allow the judge to disclaim meaningful personal agency even while entering a capital verdict. A fine example of such agency denial, as we shall see, is the law of evidence that developed on the medieval Continent. Medieval canon lawyers insisted that the judge should convict the accused pursuant to a highly rule-bound heuristic. By so doing, they aimed to guarantee that the judge would incur no personal moral responsibility: in a perfectly rule-bound system, declared the canonists, it was *the law* that made the decision, not *the judge.* Or, to quote the starker language of the great twelfth-century canonist Gratian:[33] In a perfectly rule-bound system, "it is the law that kills him, not you [lex eum occidit, non tu]."[34] This idea too would reappear among English jurors: As one of the leading moral theologians of the seventeenth century described it, jurors were eager to avoid the moral "agency" for judgment by declaring, "*It is the Law that doth it, and not we.*"[35] Agency denial of this kind still survives, of course, in our own attitudes toward procedure.

Moral Comfort and Factual Proof: A Troubling Historical Relationship

Moral comfort procedures, in short, were a universal and multifaceted feature of premodern law. Today, moral comfort plays a much less prominent role. Our modern legal systems are much more strongly oriented toward problems of factual proof. Indeed, if we were hunting for a grand generalization about the history of procedure, we might venture the following: *Moral comfort has been playing a steadily declining role in procedure over the past two centuries, while factual proof has grown steadily more important.* This is one of the master themes in the making of modern law.

The relative decline of moral comfort, and the relative rise of factual proof, reflect our changing historical circumstances. Religious anxiety has diminished over the past couple of centuries, and so we have felt a decreasing need for moral comfort. We simply do not worry, in the way our ancestors did, that a judge might suffer damnation. Nor, for that matter, do we often worry that the relatives of the defendant will come after us seeking vengeance. The old cultures of vengeance are as dead as the old cultures of piety. At the same time, urban communities have grown larger and more complex. Living in modern urban communities, we have felt a growing need for factual proof; there are simply many more cases in which there is uncertainty about guilt and innocence than there used to be. Nowadays, in a modern city, we are often in the dark when we try a criminal case. This was less true two or three centuries ago, when crimes were often committed in small, often intimate, communities. Anonymous urban crime was certainly not absent in the premodern world, but it played a far smaller role than it does today.

There is yet another important reason why factual proof has become more important in modern trials: because of the rise of plea-bargaining. In the pre-nineteenth-century world, there was no plea-bargaining. It was expected that every case would go to trial — even ones in which there was no uncertainty whatsoever about the facts. This meant that the face of the trial was quite different from what it is in modern America. Today, patently guilty persons rarely undergo a full-scale trial. Before the mid-nineteenth century, by contrast, the dockets were heavy with cases in which the guilt of the accused was entirely obvious to everybody in the courtroom. When criminal courts were in session, one manifestly guilty offender after another was paraded before the court for ceremonious condemnation. As a result, trials did not routinely present the kind of difficult problems of factual proof that they present today.[36]

For all these reasons, trials presented a different picture in the premodern world. Today, we reflexively think of a criminal trial as a fact-finding event. In our world of urban crime and plea-bargaining, we are used to imagining the criminal trial as a proceeding that takes place when there is a mystery about what happened — an unsolved, or at least unproven, crime. We do not know whether the defendant committed an alleged act, so we hold a trial in order to determine the truth. For us, the criminal trial is, as it were, the last step in a detective process that begins with a police investigation and ends with a determination by the jury, which is charged with definitively finding the facts.

The past was different. Factual proof simply loomed less large to our ancestors than it does to us. Instead, they often thought of the trial as a solemn event in which the court and the community formally took responsibility for inflicting punishment on a defendant who was fairly clearly guilty. That is how Blackstone, for example, described his own eighteenth-century world. It was the purpose of jury trial, Blackstone wrote, to make sure that "every accusation" against the defendant "should afterwards be confirmed by the unanimous suffrage of twelve of his equals and neighbours."[37] At trial, as Blackstone imagined it, neighbors judged neighbors. It was frequently the case that the defendant was manifestly guilty; really difficult factual puzzles were much less common than they are today. The job of those who sat in judgment was to "confirm" what everybody already knew, or strongly suspected, was true. Certainly there were occasionally factual puzzles that the jurors had to solve. But frequently the toughest question in such a trial was whether the defendant's neighbors would be willing to take the momentous step of giving their formal, unanimous, "confirmation."

That world is gone. Our trials are no longer events in which Christian neighbors make the morally difficult decision to "confirm" accusations against members of their community. We live in an age of less moral discomfort and more factual mystery. Yet if moral comfort no longer seems as centrally important to us as it once did, the old moral comfort procedures have nevertheless survived in the American common law. Indeed, it is the thesis of this book that many of our American "proof" procedures — most importantly the reasonable doubt standard — were not originally intended as factual proof procedures at all. They are institutional survivals from an earlier age. They are premodern moral comfort procedures that have been converted, often clumsily and unsuccessfully, into modern factual proof procedures. The world has changed, but the institutions of the American common law have not changed with it. The result is a dilemma, and indeed sometimes a very serious moral dilemma, in American criminal law.

To understand this dilemma, we must begin by recognizing the truth of two propositions about the relationship between factual proof and moral comfort:

1. Any good factual proof procedure does more than just provide proof. It also provides a measure of moral comfort; *but*
2. many good moral comfort procedures do not function at all well as factual proof procedures.

Let me begin with the first of these. By "factual proof procedures" I mean procedures that are well designed to aid in the discovery of the truth in cases of uncertainty. These are what philosophers of science call "heuristic" procedures, procedures that are crafted to guide us in the dispassionate search for truth.

There are many such procedures in modern legal systems. Take, for example, the treatment of uncorroborated confessions. Suppose the defendant confesses to a crime, but there is no other evidence that directly implicates him in that crime. Should we trust his confession? Almost every legal system in the modern world (outside the Anglo-American common law) says no. In almost every modern legal system outside the common law world, there is a rule holding that a confession by the accused cannot support a conviction unless that confession is corroborated by independent evidence.[38] The reason for this rule is clear. As lawyers have recognized for centuries, uncorroborated confessions are inherently unreliable; people make false confessions with disturbing frequency.[39] This means that, in the absence of a rule against uncorroborated confessions, we are likely to make some serious mistakes, convicting innocent persons. The heuristic rule requiring courts to disregard uncorroborated confessions is thus a classic factual proof rule. There are of course many other examples of such heuristic rules, from rules requiring proper authentication of evidence, to rules about the credibility of documents or other non-oral evidence, to, most recently, rules mandating DNA testing.

Such rules are factual proof rules, and they are factual proof rules *by design:* They are structured in such a way as to aid the court in the search for the truth in cases in which there is real uncertainty about the guilt of the accused. Yet they do not only serve the end of factual proof. Well-designed factual proof rules always also provide a measure of moral comfort. This is for the simple reason that the pursuit of the truth can always serve as a means of easing the sense of moral responsibility: If we can convince ourselves that our decision was dictated by the truth, we can diminish our sense of personal responsibility for making it. We can say something like what the medieval church lawyers said about their highly rule-bound procedures: that *the law* made the decision. We can declare ourselves to be simple servants of the truth, rather than judges with undiluted moral responsibility. For this reason, a system strongly oriented toward the discovery of the truth will always be a system that leaves judges with a relatively easy conscience.

Well-designed factual proof rules thus always also serve a moral comfort purpose. But not all moral comfort procedures are well-designed factual proof rules. Indeed, the moral comfort procedures that I described in the previous section — collectivizing, randomizing, responsibility-shuffling, agency denial — are all examples of procedures that are, at best, factual proof procedures by unintentional accident. These procedures are not factual proof procedures by design, and they typically do little to aid in the determination of the truth in cases of significant factual uncertainty.

To be sure, our desire for moral comfort may sometimes arise out of a species of uncertainty about the facts: there *are* occasions when we fear to convict because we are not absolutely certain that the accused is guilty in fact. Nevertheless, moral comfort procedures are not identical with factual proof proceedings. First of all, as we shall see repeatedly in this book, humans often feel a need for moral comfort even when they are faced with no factual uncertainty whatsoever. But even in cases in which there is some factual uncertainty, moral comfort procedures embody a deeply different attitude toward the process of fact-finding — most especially when it comes to the problem of doubt. When we search for factual proof, we are able to dismiss some doubts as relatively unimportant. We aim to take the attitude of a scientific investigator: Hunting for the truth dispassionately, we are willing to weigh probabilities and discount minor doubts on the road to certainty. We are willing to draw conclusions even when our evidence is imperfect. When we search for moral comfort, by contrast, we are anything but dispassionate. We fear for ourselves, and correspondingly we lay far greater weight on even our most minor doubts than any scientific investigator would. As the moral philosopher Paley put it in 1785, the judge in search of moral comfort may suffer from "weak timidity . . . whilst there exists the minutest possibility" that the accused is innocent. "Minute possibilities" matter little in scientific investigation. But for the anxious judge they may pose insuperable obstacles. The slightest doubt may seem overwhelming, if we are uneasy about our own potential responsibility for the act of judgment.

Moral comfort procedures are about that kind of uneasiness. Instead of being addressed to the dispassionate scientific investigator, they are addressed to the simmering inner fears of the anxious judge. Instead of offering a sober algorithm for assessing factual probabilities, they offer the judge a means of calming himself down. Such moral comfort procedures played a fundamental role in the pre-nineteenth-century world, when trials presented fewer mysteries and religious belief was stronger and more widespread. Yet in American law, these premodern moral comfort procedures have often survived into the present, where they are used as clumsy and ineffective factual proof procedures.

Take, for example, the rule of jury unanimity. American law (with a few exceptions) ordinarily requires jury unanimity to convict or acquit.[40] This rule creates many difficulties for our legal system, since it opens up the possibility of hung juries. Why do we maintain the rule of unanimity? At first glance it may seem to be a rule intended to protect the accused. Yet it is clearly not well designed for that purpose. After all, the rule requires unanimity to acquit as well as to convict. So can we describe it as a factual proof rule? Americans often do exactly that. As Stephen Garvey and Paul Marcus put it, it is part of the "folk wisdom" of American criminal law that jury unanimity and the beyond a reasonable doubt standard hang together: the state must prove the elements of a substantive offense "beyond a reasonable doubt and to the satisfaction of every juror."[41] The purpose of the unanimity rule is thus, according to this folk belief, to aid in the discovery of the truth.

But is the unanimity rule really a well-designed proof rule? In fact, as thoughtful professional lawyers recognize, it is not. Why, after all, would the search for truth require perfect unanimity among twelve observers? Other legal systems do not have such a rule. French law, for example, a system that is strongly oriented toward careful determination of the truth, does not require unanimity.[42] Instead, it requires a supermajority to convict.[43] The same is true of German law.[44] This may sound sinister to the average American, but the French and German rule is easy to defend. It is much the same as the rule used in natural science. In science too we look for supermajorities, not unanimity. Consider our standards of truth in a field like astrophysics. If there were only twelve astrophysicists, and ten or eleven of them believed in the truth of the Big Bang, we would be prepared to discount the dissent of the eleventh or twelfth. Indeed, standard philosophy of science tells us that *near*-unanimity is the appropriate standard of truth in the scientific community, not unanimity. Why should we not discount the views of a couple of foolish scientists — or, for that matter, the views of a couple of foolish jurors?

So why does American law require unanimity? The answer is that the American common law, with its characteristic conservatism, has maintained a very old institution that originally served a different purpose. The unanimity rule dates far back into the Middle Ages. As we shall see in chapter 5, it grew up in early jury trials over landed property. Landed property mattered immensely in the Middle Ages, and there was great reluctance to award a disputed piece of property to one of two disputants unless twelve members of the community would agree to share the responsibility for the decision. As we shall also see, there was no sense that these twelve decision makers had any particular gift for divining the truth about mysterious facts. Yet today we insist that requiring unanimity is a good way of figuring out what really happened. Nevertheless, requiring unanimity is not a proof procedure *by design*, and no amount of declaring it to be a good proof procedure will make it into one. We can turn the medieval unanimity rule into a modern factual proof rule only by twisting and forcing it.

There are many other such examples in the American common law as well. Consider, for example, the American treatment of uncorroborated confessions. As we have seen, almost every modern legal system has a rule requiring courts to disregard confessions if there is no corroborating evidence to prove the defendant's guilt, since the experience of centuries has taught us that such confessions are unreliable. Yet modern American law[45] (like modern English law)[46] rejects this nearly universal factual proof rule! These common law systems *do* allow convictions to be based on confessions uncorroborated by direct proof of the defendant's guilt. Why? Why do the modern common law systems reject a rule regarded as fundamentally important in the search for factual truth in every other part of the modern world?

The answer, I suggest, here as so often, is that the common law developed in a world in which the search for factual truth was less important than it is today. In the premodern world, it was often regarded as essential that the accused confess. This was indeed in part because confessions had evidentiary value — but only in part. Requiring confessions did not have to do only with the pursuit of truth. Requiring condemned persons to confess was also a way of compelling them to take responsibility for the judgment passed upon them, thus lifting the responsibility from the shoulders of their judges. In prerevolutionary France, for example, confessions were regarded as having deeply problematic value, and the law discounted them as evidence.[47] Nevertheless, as leading legal historians have remarked, a confession was regarded as desirable because it served, at least in part, "to soothe the conscience of the judges."[48] It is far easier to send people to their death when they have acknowledged their guilt. Indeed, in the early modern period, an accused person was often obliged to confess *after* he had already been convicted, "begging forgiveness from God, the King and justice for the crime he has committed."[49] The common law rule on confessions emerged in this world, in which confessions were regarded as having value both as evidence *and* as conscience soothers. Other systems have been modernized since the eighteenth century, and their procedures are now firmly oriented toward fact-finding. The old conscience-soothing function of confession has been dropped outside common law jurisdictions. The common law, by contrast, has never fully moved on into the modern world.

Similar things can be said, most broadly, of the very structure of jury trial itself. Jury trial is well designed to serve a moral comfort function, as we shall see. To the extent that the use of the jury serves to "shuffle the guilt of Blood and ruin" from the shoulders of the judge to the shoulders of the jurors, it serves to ease the judge's sense of responsibility. Such indeed is the function it served, at least in part, in the Middle Ages. Yet Americans treat it as an institution designed to aid in the search for truth. In particular, American law declares the jury to be a "lie detector": it claims that lay jurors are especially good at finding the truth, because they have a peculiar talent for distinguishing true testimony from false testimony. Yet in fact, as scholars have amply shown, jurors do a poor job of sorting out true testimony from false. The idea of the jury as lie detector, as George Fisher has elegantly argued, is a relatively recent historical invention.[50] Jury trial, like the use of uncorroborated confessions, is an institution that originally arose primarily to serve a moral comfort function. In modern American law, it has been converted, very uneasily, into a factual proof institution.

In short, we live with a system of justice that has preserved a range of old moral comfort institutions, twisting and forcing them in order to make them serve the modern purpose of taking factual proof. This reflects the conservatism of the common law, which resists abolishing old institutions, always preferring to turn them instead to new uses. Of course there are some beauties in such institutional conservatism. Yet the old institutions in question are often poorly designed for the job to which we put them, and using them sometimes brings us to a morally dubious pass.

It is important to make one last observation about the relationship between factual proof and moral comfort before turning to the details of the theological history that is my subject in this book. The desire for factual proof and the desire for moral comfort have something important in common. They both tend to raise the bar against conviction. If the truth of the allegations against the accused must be adequately proven, it is of course more difficult to convict. By the same token, if judges are reluctant to judge, that reluctance too may make it more difficult to convict. Indeed, as we shall see, conviction rates in the premodern world were often quite low, precisely for that reason. In this sense, both the commitment to finding the truth and the urge to avoid moral responsibility for judgment can lie at the foundation of a system of procedural protections for the accused.

Conclusion

Factual proof and moral comfort stand in an uneasy and historically troubling relationship, and there are deep dangers in confusing these two purposes of procedure — dangers to which modern American law is very much prey. They are dangers we can avoid only if we recognize the importance of moral comfort, and keep a sharp eye on the distinction between institutions primarily designed to serve the ends of factual proof and institutions primarily designed to ease the judge's sense of personal responsibility.

Yet scholars have too often neglected these distinctions, regarding criminal procedure as a business having to do too exclusively with factual proof. Scholars have too often tended to regard American criminal procedures as though they were factual proof procedures *by design*, intended to aid in the discovery of the truth. Modern evidence scholars often take such an approach: they treat the rules of evidence like rules of science, intended to guide the investigator in the search for the truth.[51] Judges and prosecutors typically make the same assumption when they try to explain "reasonable doubt" to jurors. For example, prosecutors sometimes make use of the so-called jigsaw puzzle analogy: finding facts under the beyond a reasonable doubt standard, so goes their explanation, is like solving "a thousand piece puzzle" where "some of the pieces . . . were lost."[52] Historians, for their part, also speak in the same terms — most important, for my purposes, historians of reasonable doubt. They often start from the supposition that trials take place because we do not know not what happened and conclude that procedures are designed to help us determine what happened.[53]

And in some cases, these historians are clearly right: there are indeed some procedures that are manifestly designed primarily to uncover the truth. Some procedures *are* factual proof procedures by design. Yet in other cases they are just as clearly wrong, and wrong in ways that lead us into important errors in our interpretation of the law. In particular, our historians have not rightly understood the origins of the rule of reasonable doubt. To understand those origins, we must dig deep into Christian theology and the Western European tradition of moral comfort. It is to that theology that I now turn.

The Christian Judge and the Taint of Blood:
The Theology of Killing in War and Law

*As everyone knows, bad people kill good people whenever they like;
whereas good people are not permitted to kill bad people except through
public wars and legal judgments. This is one of the mysteries of God,
which it is not given to Man to understand.*

— *Agobard of Lyons (769–840),* Liber contra Judicium Dei

To our premodern ancestors, criminal trial was about one thing above
all: shedding blood. Let the conscientious juryman "tremble," lest he be "guilty
of [the defendant's] Murther." So wrote Sir John Hawles in his *Englishman's
Right*.[1] In a trial, "the Guilt of the *Blood* or *ruin* of an Innocent man [is]
Bandyed to and fro, and *shuffled off* from the Jury to the Judge, and from the
Judge to the Jury."[2] Hawles's pamphlet, first published in 1680, was perhaps
the most widely circulated piece of writing on the subject of jury trial in the
eighteenth century — one of those works that belonged in the library of every
liberty-minded American in the age of the Revolution. When Thomas Jefferson
was asked in 1789 to recommend books on jury trial for use by the French
revolutionaries, for example, he picked Hawles, along with a few others, as a
representative of the American understanding of the value of adjudication by
"12 honest jurymen."[3] In Hawles we discover how jury trial was viewed in the
great era of Anglo-American revolutions that ran from the 1680s through
the 1780s.

What we discover is, in part, a Christian theology of bloodshed that reached
back more than a thousand years. Hawles's ugly warning — the warning that
the Christian who judged his fellow might thereby make himself a "murderer"
— had indeed been sounded for many centuries. Saint Augustine, for example,
had insisted on the danger that the judge might make himself a murderer a
millennium earlier. The same alarm was raised by the medieval church lawyers: a judge who did not follow correct criminal procedure in condemning a
man to death, they held, committed the mortal sin of murder. Christian thinkers were indeed deeply worried about the salvation of the judge from an early
date in the development of Christian theology, and most especially about the
salvation of the judge who imposed blood punishments.

The claim that premodern Christians were uneasy about inflicting blood

Figure 2. "He beareth not the sword in vain: for he is the minister of God, a revenger to execute
wrath upon him that doeth evil." Saint Paul, portrayed in a thirteenth-century manuscript with
his traditional attribute, the sword. *St. Paul.* Paris, Bibliothèque Mazarine, MS 9, f. 417 verso,
vue 2 (mid-thirteenth century).

punishments may seem surprising. After all, we are accustomed to thinking of the premodern world, Christian or not, as far more ferocious than our own. The premodern world, for us, is a world of the Spanish Inquisition, of *autos da fè*; in general, it is a world of a kind of merciless and egregiously bloody justice. And indeed, there is no doubt that Christian texts sometimes seem to encourage a real ferocity in judging. The most important of these texts was recently discussed by one of the most prominent of American Catholics, Associate Justice Antonin Scalia, in a lecture that has stirred considerable controversy. Justice Scalia correctly cites the leading New Testament text on the theology of judging. This famous passage, Justice Scalia observes, sounds unconditionally harsh to modern ears:

> St. Paul had this to say (I am quoting, as you might expect, the King James version):
>
>> Let every soul be subject unto the higher powers. For there is no power but of God: the powers that be are ordained of God. Whosoever therefore resisteth the power, resisteth the ordinance of God: and they that resist shall receive to themselves damnation. For rulers are not a terror to good works, but to the evil. Wilt thou then not be afraid of the power? Do that which is good, and thou shalt have praise of the same: for he is the minister of God to thee for good. But if thou do that which is evil, be afraid; for he beareth not the sword in vain: for he is the minister of God, a revenger to execute wrath upon him that doeth evil. Wherefore ye must needs be subject, not only for wrath, but also for conscience sake. (Romans 13:1–5)
>
> This is not the Old Testament, I emphasize, but St. Paul. One can understand his words as referring only to lawfully constituted authority, or even only to lawfully constituted authority that rules justly. But the *core* of his message is that government — however you want to limit that concept — derives its moral authority from God. It is the "minister of God" with powers to "revenge," to "execute wrath," including even wrath by the sword (which is unmistakably a reference to the death penalty).

"These passages from Romans," continues Justice Scalia, "represent the consensus of Western thought until very recent times. Not just of Christian or religious thought, but of secular thought regarding the powers of the state."[4]

In this lecture, intended to demonstrate that Christianity does not condemn the death penalty, Justice Scalia gives voice to a widespread assumption: we all tend to think that the old Christian world was a harsh world, up to and including the age of our own American Revolution. And of course, in many ways it was. Justice Scalia is by no means foolish in saying what he says in his lecture. The passage that he quotes is the right one: Romans 13 does indeed lie at the foundation of the Western Christian theology of judicial bloodshed. The conclusion that he draws is not false: Christian theology did justify the death penalty for many centuries—though, contrary to Justice Scalia's assertion, Paul's reference to "the sword" was not just a reference to the death penalty. As we shall see, it was also a reference to mutilation, a very common punishment among our ancestors. In the early stages of the common law, for example, Christian judges sentenced offenders to have their eyes gouged out, or their feet or testicles cut off.[5] (Indeed, even in the era of the American Revolution, our Founding Fathers still spoke casually of punishments of life *or limb*, and Thomas Jefferson did not hesitate to propose mutilation punishments.)[6] At any rate, the older Christian teachings were indeed often ferocious; and there remains plenty of Christian authority in favor both of executing people and of mutilating them. The Justice is perfectly correct in saying so.

But for all that, Justice Scalia does not do justice to the anxieties and the subtleties of the Christian tradition—or, for that matter, to the "consensus of Western thought." Premodern Christian judges did wield the sword of vengeance, but they did not find it easy to do so. On the contrary: they struggled mightily with the moral duties of judging; and trials often resulted in acquittals. If Justice Scalia quotes Saint Paul correctly, he nevertheless misses much of what was most Christian about the theology that grew out of Romans 13, and that eventually found its way into Revolution-era pamphlets like that of John Hawles.

This chapter traces the history of that Christian theology. Like Justice Scalia, I begin with Saint Paul's theology of the sword. It will not do to stop with Saint Paul, though: we must follow developments during the subsequent centuries of Christian thought. Out of Paul's theology, the great Latin church fathers, Saints Ambrose, Jerome, and Augustine, developed a complex teaching about the relationship between judging and bloodshed. Like Saint Paul, they held that judges were "ministers" of the law. Like Saint Paul, moreover, they held that judges were empowered to shed the blood of wrongdoers. Indeed, they regarded judges quite literally as shedders of human blood: they routinely linked the figure of the judge with the figure of the soldier. Law and war went together, in the minds of premodern Christian theologians: both were ways of killing people. Correspondingly, the moral theology of judging was linked with the moral theology of war: as the Carolingian archbishop of Lyons, Agobard, put it in the early ninth century, "good people" were permitted to kill "through public wars and legal judgments." Consequently, as we shall see, the theology of just judging was essentially identical with the theology of just war. Law, to Christian theologians, was a way of making war on the world.

Yet if premodern theologians regarded the judge as a killer, akin to the soldier, they were not unreservedly bloody minded. On the contrary, the writings of the church fathers displayed a real uneasiness about judicial bloodshed, and they often called upon their Christian flock to show mercy. These teachings never died: they remained alive during the early Middle Ages and were revived in forms both subtle and influential during the great renaissance of Christian law and theology of the period 1050–1250 — the period that saw the birth of the common law. In particular, by about 1200 Christian authors had arrived at the conclusion that the judge could keep himself safe from mortal sin only by strictly following procedures — by killing, as the canon lawyers put it, "iuris ordine servato," while "observing the proper procedures of the law." These doctrines of judicial killing had a marked influence on the structure of early jury trial, as we shall see, and they were still exerting their influence in the early years of the American Republic.

The Beginnings of the Christian Moral Theology of Judging: The Horror of Blood, the Just War, and the Just Judge

When we hunt for the religious roots of modern trial, we find ourselves focusing on one period in particular: the formative and dramatic centuries between about A.D. 1000 and A.D. 1250. This was the period when both the common law of England and the civil law of Continental Europe first emerged, and as we shall see it was the period when the basic theological structure of jury trial took shape. It was also the period during which the mature Christian theology of judicial killing emerged. Most especially it was the period of the decline of the judicial ordeal, the most important event in the religious history of jury trial. Accordingly, the period A.D. 1000–1250 will be my main focus in the next few chapters.

Before turning to that formative period, though, we must begin with the early development of the Christian theology of judicial bloodshed, a theology that dates far back into antiquity. It was in antiquity that the basic terms of the Western Christian moral theology of judging were established, in particular by Saints Jerome and Augustine. These late antique saints built a remarkable body of theological thought, one that connected the act of judging directly to acts of war.

As we saw in the first chapter, theological concern about the fate of the judge is widespread in the human world. Christianity is no exception. Like other religious systems, premodern Christianity developed a theology that addressed the dangers inherent in the act of judging. Nevertheless, Western Christian theology developed its own peculiar doctrines, on the basis of its own fundamental commitments and ideas.

In particular, as it emerged in antiquity, the Christian moral theology of judging revolved around one ritually charged problem: the problem of bloodshed. This was a concern that Christians inherited from Judaism. Blood and bloodshed play a central role in Jewish ritual: biblical law includes many ritual regulations involving contact with blood. Thus the rules of *kashrut* require that Jews avoid consuming blood.[7] Menstruating women are of course also taboo in the Jewish tradition, and those who have come into contact with them must be cleansed.[8] The women themselves must be ritually cleansed at the end of their menstrual period. Jewish tradition also includes the important story of the murder of Abel, whose blood "cried up" from the earth that had been compelled to swallow it.[9] Similarly, the book of Numbers tells us that soldiers who returned from battle had to absent themselves from camp for seven days while they purified themselves.[10] There are also two particularly important Old Testament passages on bloodshed: Genesis 9:6: "Whoso sheddeth man's blood, by man shall his blood be shed: for in the image of God made he man"; and, of course, the familiar Fifth (or by the alternative reckoning Sixth) Commandment, "Thou shalt not kill."[11]

Now, it is important to emphasize that these Old Testament passages on blood are largely rules about pollution, not guilt. Concepts of pollution, as anthropologists like Mary Douglas have observed, are associated with dirt and impurity. A person polluted through contact with a substance like blood is a person who must be cleansed, who must be purified.[12] Concepts of pollution are different from concepts of guilt. Concepts of guilt typically turn on intent, and on the assignment of responsibility for acts that are defined as "bad." Persons who have committed a guilty act are persons who must be punished, not cleansed. Conversely, mere contact with a polluting substance like (in these Old Testament passages) menstrual blood, carries no necessary implication of guilt. That does not mean that questions of guilt or intent play no role in the Jewish tradition, of course. It means only that questions of pollution figure heavily in the biblical texts, in ways that proved important for later Christian interpreters.

For the Jewish ritual focus on blood was indeed inherited by its daughter religion, Christianity, as well: the "Guilt of *blood*," to quote once more John Hawles, continued to play a central role in Christian theology. But as the Christian tradition developed, it took different approaches.

In part the Christian tradition differed in the sense that some of the old Jewish taboos vanished. In particular, the ritual prohibitions on the consumption of blood, and the ban on contact with menstruating women, were abandoned. Nevertheless, blood continued to play a fundamental role. In one respect, that role was strikingly positive: the blood of Christ was treated as sacred. Indeed, in communion, Christians were actively directed to consume Christ's blood[13] — presumably a repellant injunction for the Jewish hearer. At the same time, though, Christians continued, in some respects, to regard blood with horror, just as Jews did. In particular, the old Jewish blood taboo survived in one limited form: as we shall see, Christians were enjoined to avoid shedding the blood of others.

The Christian tradition also differed from its Jewish predecessor in another critical respect. It tended to shift the orientation away from pollution and toward guilt. Indeed, the history of the Christian theology of warfare and judging can be understood as the history of a gradual decline of pollution ideas and a gradual rise of familiar ideas of moral responsibility. The early Christian sources, following in the line of the Jewish tradition, continued to speak of contact with blood as a form of contamination that required cleansing. But in the late fourth and early fifth centuries, the great Western church fathers Saints Ambrose, Jerome, and Augustine began to plead for an approach oriented more toward ideas of guilt. The influence of those Latin church fathers continued during the Middle Ages. Pollution ideas certainly did not vanish before the late medieval period. Nevertheless, gradually — very gradually — the pollution-oriented ban on contact with blood became a guilt-oriented ban on intentional bad acts.

We find the Christian theology of blood in two related theories in particular, the theory of just war and the theory of just judging. The ancient Christian theology of war and judging was founded on a variety of scriptural texts, from both the New and Old Testaments. Some of the key Jewish texts remained key Christian ones — notably the story of Cain and Abel. In the Christian tradition, though, these Jewish texts were joined by important passages from the New Testament. One especially important passage was 1 John 3:15. "Whosoever hateth his brother," declared this passage, alluding in an obvious way on the tale of Cain and Abel, "is a murderer: and ye know that no murderer hath eternal life abiding in him." The theology that called judges potential murderers would often cite this text. The New Testament also included a number of other texts specifically about judging. The passage that I have quoted so often, "Judge not, lest ye be judged," is one.[14] Another is Pontius Pilate's attempt to wash his hands of the blood of Christ.[15] Even the famous imprecation of Matthew 26:52 — "They that take the sword shall perish with the sword" — was directly relevant to judging, since Saint Paul made it clear, in Romans 13:4, that judges "bore the sword," just as soldiers did.

On the basis of such texts, and a few others as well, ancient theologians built a Christian doctrine characterized by a "horror of blood": "Ecclesia abhorret a sanguine," as the Christian formula ran, "the church recoils from blood."[16]

The shedding of human blood, even in a just cause, was condemned. But in the early Christian tradition, it was distinctly condemned as a form of pollution. What this meant, in the early Christian context, was that the shedding of blood rendered its perpetrator unfit for communion. Thus Saint Isidore of Pelusium declared, in the fifth century, that anyone who shed human blood had been polluted and had to undergo purification.[17] Clergy in particular were enjoined to avoid shedding blood. A council at Valence in A.D. 374 declared that any cleric polluted by the commission of a "mortal crime" must be removed from orders.[18] Or as the Council of Lerida declared in the early sixth century, for example, clergy who shed blood, "even in a case of necessity," were to abstain from communion for two years.[19]

As many readers will know, the theology of just war applied these doctrines to soldiers. That theology, in its early phases, was very much colored by pollution concepts, in a way typical of early Christianity. Early church fathers held that there were Christians soldiers who fought in just causes, shedding blood legitimately. Yet the fact that soldiers shed blood legitimately did not change the disturbing fact that they had polluted themselves. On the contrary, "even killings committed in war are not exempt from reproach, and must be purified."[20] Accordingly, for many theologians, though soldiers could fight, they needed to undergo purification.

Thus, taking a standard Christian approach, leading early Christian authors held that the purification of soldiers could only be achieved through exclusion from communion for a time. In a much-cited passage, Basil the Great declared that Christians who killed, even as legitimate soldiers, had to abstain from communion for three years.[21] Cyprian of Carthage, for his part, reversed the argument. Those who had taken communion had to avoid the shedding of blood afterward. Any killing of human beings was a mortal sin, just like adultery and fraud; accordingly, Christians who had held the Eucharist could not "stain their hands with the sword and gore."[22] For early church fathers, the problems of bloodshed in war thus remained what problems of blood had mostly been in the Jewish tradition: they were largely problems of pollution, which had to be dealt with through ritual purification. It is only when we come to the Latin church fathers of late antiquity, and in particular to Saint Augustine, that we find a theology of just war that focuses entirely on the *justness* of the war, and not on the risk of blood pollution faced by combatants.

We see the same pattern of development in the early history of the theology of judging; it too experienced a movement from a focus on pollution to a focus on justness, as defended most forcefully by Saint Augustine. Indeed, in ancient and medieval Christian thought, the doctrine of just war was closely linked with the doctrine of just judging, as scholars of just war have occasionally recognized.[23] This was for a simple reason: in criminal matters, judges routinely ordered "blood punishments." Indeed, such "blood punishments" — execution and mutilation — were the ordinary prescribed forms of punishment everywhere in the Western world until the eighteenth century, at least for low-status persons.[24] This meant that the law was as much about the business of bloodshed as war. So it was that Saint Paul declared that the ruler "bears the sword" as "God's servant, an agent of wrath to bring punishment on the wrongdoer."[25] (Indeed, in traditional Christian iconography, Paul himself was portrayed with a sword.) Like soldiers in a just war, judges took the sword in hand. To serve as a judge was, as it were, to make war on the world.

But by making war on the world, did judges pollute themselves? This was the question faced by the great Latin church fathers of the late fourth and early fifth centuries, Saints Ambrose, Jerome, and Augustine. After some struggle, they gave the same answer with regard to judging that they gave with regard to war: the issue was not one of pollution but one of the justness of the judge's action.

Judging and Bloodshed in the Western Mediterranean: Ambrose, Jerome, Augustine

To follow the ancient debates over the theology of judging, we must focus upon the western Mediterranean, and especially Italy, in the late fourth century. The Western Christian legal tradition began to take shape in late antiquity, as the western half of the Roman Empire moved steadily out of the orbit of the centers of Roman power in the Greek-speaking East. Among the leading figures in the formation of the Western tradition were two great bishop-judges of the late fourth and early fifth centuries: Saint Ambrose, who became bishop of Milan in A.D. 374, and Saint Augustine, the follower of Saint Ambrose who, after a period of time in Italy, became bishop of Hippo, in North Africa, in 396. Other figures too grew out of the same Italian milieu, including Pope Saint Damasus and Saint Jerome. It is in the works and lives of these leading Christians that we can trace the rise of a distinctive Western theology of judging.

These were men who knew about the dilemmas of judging from firsthand experience. Ambrose and Augustine, in particular, lived at a time when Christian bishops were increasingly engaged in the business of government. During the early centuries of Christianity, Christianity was, of course, not a state religion; and Christian doctrine did not really contemplate the possibility of a Christian wielding high governmental powers. But over the course of the fourth century this changed: Christians, and especially Christian bishops, began to assume powers of judging and administration.[26] Ambrose and Augustine belonged to this world, in which Christians were acquiring unfamiliar, and potentially treacherous, forms of secular authority. Ambrose, who had been a high Roman official before his election as bishop, was the de facto governor of Milan and a man of empirewide power. Augustine too was a judge, and sometimes in effect ruler of his community. Both men were confronted with the hard realities of practical judging, and as we follow their writings and their careers, we see both of them groping their way toward a theology that would ease the conscience of the Christian judge.

As we have seen, early Christian theology treated soldiering as a polluting activity. This was not only true of the Greek East. The same theology was very much alive in the western empire in the late fourth century, when Ambrose and Augustine arrived on the scene: councils of the western church held that clerics who had shed blood must purify themselves.[27] That same doctrine was also applied to judges. In developing their theology, Ambrose and Augustine had to confront directly the belief that judging was a polluting activity, just like soldiering.

Indeed, in late fourth-century Italy, many Christians, the heirs of centuries of exclusion from government, believed that judging was a polluting activity, one that required strenuous purification. We have various pieces of evidence for the existence of this belief. One is an official document of the church: a letter written, probably by Pope Saint Damasus, in 374, the year that Ambrose became bishop. That letter, addressed to the bishops of Gaul, laid down a strict rule. Anyone who had served in a position of secular power was excluded from holy orders: such persons "used the sword," wrote Damasus, "handed down unjust judgments, and inflicted torture." They could not serve as ministers of God.[28] This was a significant declaration, since former government officials, like Ambrose, must not infrequently have been recruited into the episcopacy. Damasus was making a declaration of almost daring public policy significance when he held that those who had shed blood as part of the work of government could not serve as officers of the church.

The pope was not the only Western Christian of the time to take such an attitude. Indeed, it was not just a matter of official church doctrine; we know that there was an unofficial popular Christian culture that held the same belief. Here our evidence comes primarily from the well-documented career of Saint Ambrose. First of all, we have a remarkable story told by Ambrose's secretary and biographer, Paulinus of Milan. The story concerns Ambrose's election as bishop. It is a famous story indeed, one of the great tales of ecclesiastical history.

Ambrose was the child of an extremely powerful Roman bureaucrat, one of the most highly placed officials in the Roman world. Following in his father's footsteps, Ambrose himself entered government service as a young man. By 374, he too was a man of great power, charged with the administration of Milan, one of the most important cities in the empire. As the famous tale of Ambrose's life goes, this powerful man had no desire to enter the service of God at all. Events, however, overtook him. After the death of the bishop of Milan, Ambrose attended the gathering of the congregation called to elect a successor. He attended in his official capacity, simply in order to guarantee the maintenance of order (or so, at least, his biographer insisted). However, it came to pass that a child suddenly cried out, "Ambrosius Episcopus!" "Bishop Ambrose!" To Ambrose's surprise and distress, the Milanese congregation immediately joined in, chanting the same phrase, and so acclaiming him its bishop.

It was impossible for a Christian to refuse such an election. Nevertheless, Ambrose resisted; and it is in the story of his resistance that we discover how deeply Italian Christians regarded judging as an activity tainted with blood. Paulinus, Ambrose's secretary, describes what followed in a biography of Ambrose, which Paulinus composed for Augustine. Immediately after his acclamation as bishop, Ambrose tried to disqualify himself by polluting himself with blood: "Having left the church, he had a tribunal readied for him. Forsooth, he who was soon to rise to the bishop's throne ascended to the seat of judgment! Then, contrary to his custom, he ordered several persons to be tortured. Yet when he had done this, the people nevertheless acclaimed him, saying 'Thy sin be upon us!' [A reference to Matthew 27:24–25: 'Pilate . . . took water and washed his hands in the sight of the crowd, saying, "I am innocent of this man's blood. Look to it yourselves." And the whole people said in reply, "His blood be upon us and upon our children" ']."[29]

This is a striking, not to say disturbing, story. Ambrose took it for granted that a judge would be regarded as too polluted by blood to serve as bishop, and he was willing to go so far as to torture a few sorry victims in order to disqualify himself in the eyes of the people; but the Milanese congregation responded by taking his pollution upon itself. This story surely cannot be true in any simple sense: it is all too obviously seen through a distorting theological lens. Nevertheless, its author clearly assumed that his reader knew that belief in the impurity of judges was widespread, and that his reader would see nothing strange in a judge casually ordering torture. Judging was simply understood to be a bloody business; and we can gather from this story that in the western empire, at least in late fourth-century Italy and perhaps in Gaul,[30] there was a popular Christian belief that it was a polluting activity.

At any rate, Ambrose did become bishop of Milan. But popular Christian belief that judges were tainted with blood did not vanish. We know this from a last piece of Ambrosian evidence, a letter that Ambrose wrote around A.D. 386, twelve years after his ascension to the episcopacy and in the same year that he converted Augustine to Christianity. The letter in question is addressed to a late fourth-century Italian judge named Studius. This Christian judge was anxious about his duties, and he sought Ambrose's counsel about taking communion after inflicting capital punishment. Ambrose responded by observing that many Christian judges experienced the same anxiety about the death penalty that Studius did: Indeed, "many [judges] abstain from communion of their own volition [sponte], and are praised for it."[31] Moreover, noted Ambrose, there was at least one heretical sect that simply shut all judges out of communion.[32] The popular Christian culture that deemed the act of judging to be tainted by the "horror of blood" was thus still alive, and Christian judges were taking it seriously.

And what was Ambrose's attitude to this popular Christian culture? Strikingly, he did not fully reject it. Instead, he offered a mixed response. He refused to condemn the desire of Christian judges to abstain from communion in order to purify themselves. Nevertheless, he held that such acts were not obligatory. Thus Saint Ambrose, like Justice Scalia almost two thousand years later, quoted Saint Paul, the sword-bearing apostle: "He who judges, bears the sword for good reason"; since God is an avenger against those who do evil.[33] This meant that judges did not need to approach communion in a spirit of excessive rigor. "If you do take communion," wrote Ambrose, "you can be excused. But if you do not, you deserve praise."[34] The most important thing for a judge, he concluded, was to show mercy.[35] In the end, Ambrose thus still lingered in the spiritual world of his theological predecessors. He still accepted the idea that judges, as bearers of the sword, were persons in possible danger of pollution.

Saint Augustine and Saint Jerome, two younger followers of Ambrose, went further, setting out to push Western theology decisively away from pollution and toward guilt. They took kindred approaches, rejecting any sort of extreme fear of blood pollution that would make the administration of criminal justice impossible. Indeed, these church fathers did not speak the language of pollution at all. Instead, they adopted a different kind of moral language. Killing, explained Jerome and Augustine, while always morally troubling, was nevertheless sometimes justified. What was true of just war was true of just judging: what mattered was whether judges acted justly; and acting justly meant acting pursuant to "the law."

Thus Saint Jerome, the translator of the Bible into Latin, spoke of some killings, following Saint Paul, as "the ministry of the laws." In particular, he held, there was no ban on fiercely punishing criminals or those guilty of sacrilege. Such punishments, insisted Jerome, did not really amount to shedding blood at all: "To punish murderers, those who commit sacrilege, and poisoners, is not to shed blood. It is the ministry of the laws."[36] There was no danger to the purity of just judges: in effect, they had not shed blood at all. This text was frequently quoted by Jerome's Christian successors looking for moral comfort in the execution of the criminal law in subsequent centuries. As for Augustine, in his Commentary on the Ten Commandments, he too used a phrase that would be repeated for centuries: "Cum homo juste occiditur, lex eum occidit, non tu," "When a man is killed justly, it is the law that kills him, not you."[37] Like Jerome, Augustine thus held that the just judge effectively did not shed blood at all.

It was Augustine, who had been converted and baptized by Ambrose himself, who offered the classic account of this argument, in his early fifth-century tract *On the Free Will*.[38] Judges, explained Augustine once again, were akin to soldiers. Both killed. This was disturbing on its face. Yet it had to be understood that both judges and soldiers were permitted to kill. How so? In justifying the special license to kill of this anomalous pair, the judge and the soldier, Augustine first offered an argument from ordinary language: Neither the soldier nor the judge, he noted, was ordinarily called "a murderer."[39] Second, Augustine emphasized once again that judges and soldiers, unlike true murderers, killed pursuant to the law. Augustine's tract is framed as a dialogue between himself and his interlocutor, Evodius:

> *Evodius.* If murder means killing a man [Si homicidium est hominem occidere], nevertheless sometimes this may happen without sin: after all, a soldier can kill an enemy; and a judge, or the judge's minister, can kill a malefactor. Or again a person may unintentionally let his spear fly from his hand. These do not seem to me to sin when they kill a man.
>
> *Augustine.* I agree. But they are not ordinarily called murderers. But in that case tell me: Suppose somebody kills his master, because he is afraid of being punished brutally. Do you think he should be counted among those who kill a man in such a fashion as not to deserve the name "murderer"?
>
> *Evodius.* His case seems to me to be very different indeed: after all, the others kill pursuant to the law, or at least not against the law; whereas his misdeed is not approved by any law.[40]

Rebellious slaves certainly had no legal license to kill; but judges and soldiers did. A few pages later, Augustine elaborated by explaining that those who killed pursuant to the law did not sin, because they killed without personal interest or passion, "libido." Indeed, the absence of personal interest or passion was what distinguished the just government from the unjust one: "Now a soldier killing the enemy is a minister of the law, because he can easily perform his office without any passion. . . . Those who repel the forces of the enemy with equal force in order to keep the citizenry safe, are capable of obeying the law, by which they are commanded to act, without passion; and the same can be said of all ministers who are properly subject to the powers that be."[41] Avoiding "passion" was critically important: the just state was one whose officials always acted as impersonal ministers of the law, never yielding to passion or personal interest. In this we can see, clearly enough, the influence of Stoic philosophy on Augustine.[42] Only dispassionate officials, operating in the inveterate Stoic spirit of the Roman governing classes, could be certain of avoiding the name of "murderer." Indeed, we can usefully think of Augustine as addressing the challenges of Christian ritual theology by drawing on the resources of the Roman philosophy of good government.

Western Christian bishops, men of great power and responsibility, thus began to build a theology that would transform Christian debate by the end of the Middle Ages. Ignoring the dangers of blood pollution, they instead asked whether judges had played a responsible role as just ministers of the law. It was this approach that permitted these great church fathers to avoid the Buddhist radicalism of the Temiya Jataka. Burmese Theravada Buddhists, as we saw in the previous chapter, feared any act of judging: even the just judge was inevitably damned. By contrast, these church fathers, who were beginning to take over the reins of Roman government, developed a Christian theology that permitted judges to lend their efforts to killing criminals, without themselves suffering the loss of eternal life as "murderers." In effect, this approach allowed Christians to deny their own meaningful personal agency: they could declare themselves to be acting not in their own persons but merely as "ministers of the law."

The Central Middle Ages

It took many centuries for Christian authors to embrace fully the teachings of Jerome and Augustine. Their writings were certainly not forgotten during the early Middle Ages. Christian writers continued to repeat the basic doctrines of the Latin church fathers. The law of judging and the law of war continued to be linked; we may quote again Agobard, the Carolingian bishop of Lyon, who stated the standard view in the early ninth century: "As everyone knows, bad people kill good people whenever they like; whereas good people may not kill bad people except in public wars and legal judgments. This is one of the mysteries of God, which it is not given to Man to understand."[43] Public wars and legal judgments were two related permissible ways of killing bad people. In discussing both these ways of killing, Carolingian authors continued to quote Jerome and Augustine.[44]

Nevertheless, early medieval Christian writings did not follow the lead of the Latin church fathers with any consistency or rigor, and even in the thirteenth century pollution ideas remained strong. As we read the medieval sources, we find an indiscriminate mix of pronouncements, some of which focus on the pollution associated with bloodshed, some of which focus on the "justice" or the "ministry" of the law.

Many early medieval texts emphasized the risk that blood could bring pollution, especially for clergy. Thus in the seventh century councils forbade priests to serve as judges in cases that could result in death or mutilation.[45] Similarly, early medieval penitentials required that those who had shed blood purify themselves through a fast or penitence of forty days.[46] A striking example of the same attitude comes from the Pseudo-Isidorean Decretals, a ninth-century forgery intended to buttress the position of bishops. Clerics, declared the forger, could not appear before secular courts. After all, he claimed, the very word "court" ("curia") was etymologically derived from "blood" ("cruor"): "No cleric or deacon or priest shall enter any court in any case, nor presume to plead before any judge who has officially taken the bench, for 'courts' come from 'blood' and the idolatrous making of sacrifices."[47] *Curia a cruore*, so ran the folk etymology: Courts shed blood; and clergy, who must remain pure, should have nothing to do with them. This idea remained current throughout the early Middle Ages, as it had been in antiquity. We must turn to a much later period to discover a sustained and reflective revival of the ideas of Jerome and Augustine. Even in the thirteenth century, pollution ideas remained powerfully present. The movement away from pollution logic, and toward guilt logic, was gradual and inconclusive.

We can trace this gradual and inconclusive movement in two different sets of sources: First, the texts surrounding the Peace of God movement; and second, the developing literature of canon law. I begin with the Peace of God, a much-studied religious movement that played a striking role in the early establishment of European legal order.

Carolingian authority collapsed by the middle of the ninth century, and from roughly 850 to 1000 the western fringe of Europe was at its poorest and most barbaric. This was the period par excellence when inhabitants of the centers of world civilization would have regarded western Europe as a tract of remote, insignificant, and contemptibly savage border regions. There was certainly "law" in some sense during this period, as anthropologically minded legal historians have insisted. Nevertheless, it is clear enough that rule of law, as we understand it today, was desperately weak. Developed judicial institutions, and especially trained judicial personnel, were relatively rare, particularly north of the Alps. In many parts of Europe, especially regions that had witnessed the collapse of Carolingian governmental institutions, predatory local magnates established a reign of unchecked domination that lasted for generations.[48] Local magnates also exercised control over churches, which were staffed by illiterate, venal, and sexually active clerics. Justice in this world was haphazard and often differed little from the naked application of force. Justice also often made use of the judicial ordeal in various forms.

Only toward the very end of the tenth century did inhabitants of these comparatively chaotic regions begin to erect the institutions of the basic order that would characterize the Western world in later centuries. From the late tenth century onward, though, changes steadily accumulated. By 1250 or so, the European world had been dramatically transformed: embryonic governmental institutions had made significant progress in the monopolization of violence, the Catholic Church had undergone a period of strenuous reform, and the great legal traditions of England and the Continent had emerged. Where developed judicial institutions were rare in the year 1000, two hundred and fifty years later they had become relatively common. The period 1000–1250 was thus an age when a recognizable European order — including, among other institutions, jury trial — emerged out of profound disorder.

In this and the following chapters I shall present a variety of aspects of the legal transformation of this period. Here I start with a brief account of the Peace of God (later Truce of God) movement. In the early decades of this remarkable period, the Peace of God/Truce of God movement played a fascinating, if not entirely easy to interpret, role.

The Peace of God movement appeared in southern France toward the end of the tenth century, as a religious effort to put some kind of a check on the endemic violence of the time. These early Peaces of God were limited affairs, aiming to put a stop to violence only when it targeted clergy and unarmed persons. Some historians associate the Peace movement with the millenarian enthusiasm that seized many Europeans with the approach of the year 1000. As the millennium neared, ecstatic crowds, led by clerics, gathered in open fields, where they were sworn upon holy relics to honor moratoria on violence. However, the movement faded somewhat in importance in the years immediately after 1000.[49] By the middle of the eleventh century, though, the Peace of God revived, and evolved into something more ambitious: the so-called Truce of God, the *Treuga Dei*. The Truce of God aimed to forbid all violence, at least during certain holy periods of the week and the year. It also provided for standing institutions to enforce a kind of rule of law.[50] From the middle years of the eleventh century onward, this movement took wing, as what was variously called the "Peace" or "Truce" of God was established in many parts of Europe, sponsored both by the church and by secular authorities. Over subsequent centuries, the Peace/Truce continued to play a part in the making of new legal systems. It became associated in various ways with the "Peace" of the King, or with treaty-based "peaces" established by cities, lending a color of holiness to European efforts to create good legal order.[51]

We should be careful not attribute too much to the Peace of God movement. The Peace was not the only force tending to create rule of law in the chaos of these centuries, and it did not introduce itself everywhere. Its impact on the technical doctrines of Western law was limited: although canon lawyers developed a law of the Peace, that law was of relatively minor importance in later centuries. Moreover, the theology of the Peace was primitive by the standards of later periods. It would be wrong to point to the Peace as the single great force in the making of legal order in Europe. Nevertheless, for purposes of the history of judging, the movement is of immense interest: it tells us a great deal about the religious presuppositions that were in the wind in western Europe as judicial institutions began to form.

In particular, it tells us a great deal about the importance of the theology of bloodshed, and of the persistence of both pollution and guilt logics in the formative centuries of European law. It also tells us how close the role of the judge seemed to that of the soldier. In part, the theological focus of the Peace movement was upon the shedding of blood. Thus the Council of Narbonne, which established the basic doctrines of the peace in 1054, declared, "Qui christianum occidit, sine dubio Christi sanguinem fundit," "Whoever kills a Christian, without a doubt sheds the blood of Christ."[52] This was an idea with deep roots. It was ultimately drawn from Genesis 9:6: "Whoso sheddeth man's blood, by man shall his blood be shed: for in the image of God made he man." But it was more immediately founded on theological texts of the ninth century. A number of ninth-century authors had declared that bloodshed was forbidden because man was made in the image of God. As they often repeated: "Whoever spills human blood, His blood is spilled as well: For man is made in the image of God."[53] In preaching the dangers of bloodshed, the makers of the Peace movement spoke, much of the time, a language of blood pollution — a language that echoed the Christian theology of Cyprian and Basil; in particular, they spoke of the "blood" or the "sword and gore" that made Christians unfit for communion.[54] This was true of the Council of Narbonne in 1054, and it remained true thereafter. The Peace was about excluding "pravi homines,"[55] "depraved men," from the community of those fit to partake in Christian ritual.

At the same time, though, the theory of the Peace also drew on the "justice"-oriented theology of Augustine. This was already true in 1054. In a sentence too rarely quoted by historians, the Council of Narbonne declared that the purpose of the Peace was simply to guarantee that "the law" would correct those who killed "injuste," "unjustly."[56] Canon lawyers continued to embrace an Augustinian style of reasoning thereafter: in standard canon law doctrine, the law of the Peace was treated simply as an aspect of the law of just war.[57] Indeed, the doctrines of the Peace lay at the foundation of the law of just war, just as they lay at the foundation of just judging.[58] The judge and the soldier continued to share a conceptual kinship, just as they had in antiquity. The problem of the Peace was the problem of determining when blood could "justly" be shed, by the two figures who had the authority to bear the sword: the soldier and the judge, two doers of violence.

For the Peace indeed authorized the use of violence. This deserves some emphasis: the Peace was not about eliminating all violence but about suppressing the wrong kinds of violence. Modern readers may find this easy to misunderstand. This is because modern readers will naturally tend to think of the Peace of God in Hobbesian or Weberian terms, as the product of a felt need to "control . . . appalling violence."[59] Indeed, Europe around the year 1000 may seem the classic setting for a collective effort to monopolize violence. Where would the movement for a state monopolization of violence be more at home than in the chaotic and desperately violent European border regions of that date?

To think in such terms is, however, anachronistic, and quite misleading if we wish to understand the Peace's theology of law. It is true that the Peace movement can be understood as the first step in a long process by which European states gradually monopolized violence. But it was a tentative first step. The Peace movement was not yet inspired by a full-scale Hobbesian or Weberian ideology. It presupposed not an unalloyed horror of all violence (something we hardly find in the Western world before the nineteenth century) but an uneasiness about the ritual consequences of the shedding of blood, as well as a conviction that killing had to be done "justly."

This helps us to understand the significance of the Peace for both soldiers and judges. With regard to the former, historians have emphasized the link between the Peace and the Crusades, which was first preached in 1095. As they have observed, the Crusades were in important ways the other side of the coin of the Peace. It was the ambition of the movement not to eliminate violence among magnates but to redirect that violence against infidels. "The many provisions of the Peace of God resolutions against breakers of the peace amounted to nothing less than a new form of war, one provided for this time by the Church itself."[60] This was true not only of crusaders but also of judges. Judging was still understood to be a bloody business, just as it was in the time of Saint Ambrose. With regard to them too, the Peace brought a "new form of war," as we shall see when we look more closely at canon law.

Indeed, it is important, before turning to the development of canon law, to emphasize that Peace theology placed heavy moral burdens on its judicial personnel — those charged with the duty of killing "justly." The Peace established itself largely by imposing religious obligations through oath. Those obligations were imposed on all participants, judicial personnel included. Accordingly, as the Peace/Truce developed in the eleventh century and after, it introduced to many parts of western Europe new classes of sworn judicial officers — "illi," as the leading church reformer Ivo of Chartres called them around 1100, "qui iusta iudicia se facturos de pace iuraverunt," "those who have sworn an oath that they will give just judgments under the Peace."[61] The workings of the Peace everywhere depended on such "juratores" or jurors. This deserves some emphasis, perhaps, for Anglo-American readers. We like to associate medieval "jurors" more or less exclusively with the common law, but there were many such officers on the Continent as well.[62] Here, as in many other regards, the common law cannot be seen in isolation from broader Western developments.[63]

These "sworn" officers of the Peace faced disquieting moral challenges.[64] As the French historian Robert Jacob has vigorously argued, the new judges of the Peace assumed a new kind of judicial role, one that carried a heavy moral burden. The oaths they took were intimidating. Like participants in the early Peaces, they would be sworn on holy relics around the year 1000 — an awe-inspiring business.[65] Later on, they might, like English jurors, also be sworn to judge in light of "conscience": as the Peace of Valenciennes declared in 1114, the "iurati pacis," the "jurors of the Peace," were to give a "just judgment," and they were to do so "according to God and conscience and right reason and according to their best intellect."[66] Oaths were taken seriously in this age, and they put the souls of these judges to a real test: in the words of a Norman formula to which I shall return, judges who had sworn an oath under the Peace faced the fearsome risk "that your souls will be damned in perpetuity, and your bodies will be exposed to shameful abuses in a gaping Hell."[67] This Peace movement thus brought with it a new kind of judicial officer, charged with a new kind of moral anxiety.

The Revival of Late Antique Moral Theology

During the same period, canon law developed rapidly. Indeed, the period of the triumphs of the Peace movement coincides with a great revival of the ancient theology of judicial bloodshed, which we can trace through all of the leading canon texts of the period. It is in those texts that we find a sustained revival of the ideas of Jerome and Augustine — and at the same time an enduring belief in the capacity of blood to pollute those it touched.

Canon law is the law of the Christian church, but it is not limited to church matters. It is a body of law that purports to cover all aspects of life. It is made up of pronouncements by church councils, as well as decisions of the popes and their officials and other Christian texts. These materials were gathered by medieval canonists, whose compilations served as the principal source for canon law.

In the early Middle Ages, the law of the church was to be found in scattered and unorganized sources. From about A.D. 1000 onward, though, various scholars and church leaders set about the task of assembling and organizing the law.[68] There were important canon collections produced during the eleventh century, notably by two figures, Burchard of Worms, working early in the century, and Ivo of Chartres, working toward the end of the century. But the great leap came in the mid-1100s, with the so-called Decretum of Gratian, whose complex genesis has been traced by Anders Winroth.[69] Finally, toward the end of the twelfth century, the wisdom of the new canon law was brought together in the "summae," the compendia, of scholars like Bernard of Pavia and Raymond de Peñafort, who wrote during the critical decades when the common law and the civil law of the Continent took shape.

All of these early canonists, working during the first formative age of post-antique Western law, were concerned with the classic problems of blood guilt addressed centuries earlier by Jerome and Augustine. In particular, they worried over the question that had worried Augustine: What was it that could make a man a "homicida," a "murderer"? Like Augustine before them, they believed that the dangers of becoming a murderer were subtle and difficult to evade. One did not have to pull the actual trigger to acquire guilt. "They deceive themselves perilously," declared Burchard, "who believe that the only murderers are those who kill a man with their own hands." On the contrary, anyone who counseled or exhorted murder was guilty too, just as the Jews made themselves guilty when they cried, "Crucify him!"[70] Burchard's passage was adopted by his successors, too;[71] the risk of contamination by "murder" was very much present in the minds of these early canonists.

But Burchard's successors went further, returning to the moral theology of the Latin church fathers. Thus Ivo cribbed from Augustine's *Free Will*, endorsing the distinction between "murderers," on the one hand, and soldiers and judges on the other. The great difference was that judges, like soldiers, followed "the law" and acted without "passion."[72] At the same time, Ivo, like others, also quoted the folk etymology from the Pseudo-Isidorean Decretals: "curia a cruore," " 'court' comes from 'blood.' "[73] The text of Gratian, which definitively initiated the modern tradition of canon law some fifty years later, also quoted the classic texts of Augustine. Gratian edited the ideas of

Augustine down to a pithy and powerful statement: "If 'murder' means killing a man, nevertheless sometimes a killing can be done without sin: After all, a soldier can kill an enemy; and a judge, or the judge's minister, can kill a malefactor. Or again a person may unintentionally let his spear fly from his hand. These do not seem to me to sin when they kill a man. Nor indeed are they ordinarily called 'murderers.' When a man is killed justly, it is the law that kills him, not you."[74] *It is the law that kills him, and not you.* As we shall see in chapter 4, this passage was rapidly embraced by canon lawyers eager to create a moral theology of judging. Within a few years after Gratian wrote, his borrowing from Augustine would become the basis of numerous canon texts.

We shall see more of those texts shortly. For the moment, let me close this chapter with three. Two reveal how deeply the canon lawyers reflected on the Augustinian tradition by the end of the twelfth century, and the third reveals how strongly pollution logic nevertheless survived, at a critical moment in the early thirteenth, when the church attempted an epochal reform: the abolition of the judicial ordeal.

First, two Augustinian texts. What did it mean to say, "It is the law that kills him, and not you"? By the end of the twelfth century, canon lawyers had a built a basic doctrine that answered this question. In part, it was a doctrine about killing without passion; in part, it was a doctrine about procedure. For the doctrine about killing, we can read Bernard of Pavia, who produced an important summa at the end of the twelfth century. Bernard laid out a teaching that distinguished four ways of bodily homicide. One of those was "by justice":

> There are four types of bodily homicide, since it can be done in four different ways: by justice, by necessity, by accident, and by free will. It is done by justice when a judge or minister kills a criminal who has been justly condemned. . . . With regard to homicide done by justice, we must make distinctions as follows. When a minister kills a criminal, it depends whether that criminal has been condemned or not condemned (i.e., to death); and where the criminal has been condemned, the minister kills him either out of love of justice or out of malice [livore]; and where he kills him out of love of justice, he does so either because he has been commanded to do so, or without having been commanded. If he kills someone who has not been condemned, he himself is guilty of homicide, since he rushed to judgment . . . ; if he kills the criminal out of malice, he is equally guilty of homicide . . . ; but if he kills a condemned criminal out of love of justice, and having been commanded to do so, he does not sin. Otherwise he sins.[75]

A judge could kill by justice, so long as he acted without "livor," without malicious passion. This was Bernard's elaboration on Augustine's doctrine of the avoidance of passion.

Raymond de Peñafort, a leading canon lawyer of the early thirteenth century, took the Augustinian tradition a step further. Killing by justice did not mean merely avoiding passion. It meant something that every lawyer could understand: following the correct procedures. As Raymond explained, following centuries-old tradition, secular justice involved killing — killing that was justified, to be sure, but that rendered a cleric unfit for holy orders.[76] Clerics must simply abstain from engagement in secular justice: curia a cruore, as tradition held. But what then of the secular judge? He was safe from mortal sin, explained Raymond — but only as long as he killed "iuris ordine servato," "keeping to the order [i.e., the procedures] of the law":

> Homicide is committed in four ways, to wit by justice, by free will, by necessity and by accident.
>
> *By justice,* when a judge or minister kills a criminal who has been justly condemned. If this homicide is done out of malice or the pleasure in shedding human blood, even if the criminal is justly killed, the judge commits mortal sin because of his corrupt intent. However, if it is done out of love of justice, the judge does not sin in condemning him to death and ordering his minister to kill him, nor is the minister condemned if he kills having been ordered to do so. Still, either of them will commit mortal sin if he does it without observing the procedures of the law [iuris ordine non servato].[77]

The judge must "observe the procedures of the law" when killing: this was the ultimate Augustinian conclusion of the canon lawyers around 1200. It marked out a path to safety for the judge that would be followed both in England and on the Continent: the salvation of the judge was to be found in the law of procedure.

If that Augustinian lesson became accepted in the literature of canon law, though, it did not entirely displace the old logic of pollution. Quite the contrary: in one of the most important pronouncements of the era, the church embraced an unmistakable pollution doctrine. That pronouncement was the canon known as "Judgments of Blood," the eighteenth canon of the Fourth Lateran Council of 1215. This was the canon that preached the abolition of the judicial ordeal, the topic of the next chapter. It spoke still in the old language of pollution, associating acts of judgment with other acts of bloodshed, such as surgery and warfare:

> No cleric may pronounce a sentence of death, or execute such a sentence, or be present at its execution. . . . Nor may any cleric write or dictate letters destined for the execution of such a sentence. Wherefore, in the chanceries of the princes let this matter be committed to laymen and not to clerics. Furthermore, no cleric may serve as a commander of marauders, archers, or other

such men devoted to the shedding of blood.[78] No subdeacon, deacon, or priest shall practice that part of surgery involving burning and cutting. Neither shall anyone in judicial tests or ordeals by hot or cold water or hot iron bestow any blessing; the earlier prohibitions in regard to trial by combat remain in force.[79]

In this canon, the church applied its teaching on judicial bloodshed to the judicial ordeal, an institution then in use everywhere in Europe. The danger of blood pollution was of course its principal motivation: Augustinian doctrine may have established itself among canon lawyers, but it was still far from wholly dominant in the church.

With this, we are ready to pass to the age of the birth of jury trial. The church's declaration that the judicial ordeal carried a blood taint set many of the terms for the moral theological development of the law both in England and on the Continent. To see how, we must look more deeply into the decline of the judicial ordeal and its consequences. That is my topic in the chapters that follow.

3

The Decline of the Judicial Ordeal:
From God as Witness to Man as Witness

The next three chapters are about the age of the birth of jury trial: the two and a half centuries from about A.D. 1000 to A.D. 1250. This was a remarkable and momentous period, during which the basic legal institutions of the Western world emerged out of a kind of chaos. At the beginning of this period, half a millennium after the collapse of Roman authority in the West, Europe was an impoverished and insignificant fringe region. The leading civilizations of the time were far away: they were in Islam, in Byzantium, in China of the Song dynasty, in the Hindu kingdoms of India. If visitors from any of those centers of high civilization had penetrated into transalpine Europe around the year 1000, they would have regarded the countries they found there as wretched, violent, and backward. Italy might have seemed more advanced to them — but only because it was a cultural outpost of Byzantium and Islam.

Two hundred and fifty years later, the contrast was immense. Europe was still a relatively peripheral border region in A.D. 1250. But it was a border region in the midst of a stunning and distinctive intellectual renaissance, notably in the university towns of Bologna, the leading center of the study of law, and Paris, the leading center of the study of theology. And two sophisticated legal systems had appeared: the common law of England, and the civil law of the Continent. These are the two legal systems that are in use in every part of the developed world today.

How did the common law and the civil law emerge out of the disordered, illiterate and violent societies that occupied the European fringe of Eurasia around A.D. 1000? And why did Europe produce not one but two different legal traditions? The answer is inevitably complex; historians have a great deal to say about how the societies of A.D. 1000 became the societies of 1250. Cities and trade were on the upswing. Nascent state apparatuses were growing in power. The church was in the midst of a wide-ranging institutional reform. Memories of Rome, still alive, played a galvanizing political role, both for German emperors and for Italian city-states. There were the ecstatic religious movements that produced the Peace of God, and more.

Nevertheless, in trying to explain the peculiar procedural structures of the two Western legal traditions, the common law and the civil law, historians have focused on one development in particular: the decline of the judicial

Figure 3. "Love justice, o Ye who judge the Earth!" In this thirteenth-century illumination of the opening words of the Book of Wisdom, we see Solomon, the doer of justice, handing the instrument of justice, the sword, to a knight. *Solomon handing a sword to a knight.* Paris, Bibliothèque Mazarine, MS 39, f. 119, vue 2 (circa 1230–1250).

ordeal. The illiterate and violent European societies of A.D. 1000, like relatively simple societies in many other parts of the premodern world, all made use of some form of the judicial ordeal. The most common forms used in Europe were the ordeal of the hot iron, by which an accused person was compelled to grasp a red-hot iron in his bare hand; and the ordeal of the cold water, by which the accused, naked and bound, was lowered into a pit of water. There were others too, all of them picturesque and most of them violent. These frightening proceedings were understood to be "judgments of God," efforts to induce God to decide the case by giving his "divine testimony." Alongside them came another form of the judgment of God, also in widespread use in Europe: trial by battle. This too was a frightening and violent business, which often resulted in death or maiming.

As Europe underwent the profound institutional transformation of the period 1000–1250, these judgments of God went into decline. They did not vanish entirely: their complete disappearance took centuries.[1] But after about 1100 the ordeals were under sustained attack from church reformers. These reformers charged the ordeal with two evils in particular. First, they argued that the ordeal "tempted God"; by this strange phrase they meant that the ordeal was an illicit attempt to induce God to perform a miracle. Second, they argued that the ordeal polluted those involved in it with blood.[2]

It was the second of these arguments that motivated the most important piece of church legislation on the ordeal: the famous eighteenth canon of the Fourth Lateran Council of 1215, known as "Judgments of Blood" — the canon quoted at the close of the last chapter. Ordeals required the blessing of priest to be effective. "Judgments of Blood" decreed that pronouncing such a blessing polluted clerics with blood, just as much as performing blood surgery did. The purpose of this canon was manifestly to safeguard the purity of the clergy, not to interfere directly with the administration of lay justice. Nevertheless, its implications for lay justice were radical. All throughout western Europe, systems of justice operated by using ordeals and trials by battle, at least some of the time. Without priests, those proceedings could not continue. The Fourth Lateran Council thus effectively decreed that European justice would have to be entirely restructured.

"Judgments of Blood" did not result in the immediate abolition of the ordeals. Its only immediate effect came in England, where the monarchy soon replaced the ordeal with a new institution: jury trial. In Continental Europe the canon was simply one important act among many in a continuing assault on the ordeal.[3] On the Continent too, though, the judicial ordeal was entering a period of accelerating decline in the thirteenth century, to be replaced by new forms of Continental procedure.

When scholars try to account for the emergence of the two great Western legal traditions in the period 1000–1250, they commonly pick out the assault on the ordeal as the single most important thread. The two new legal systems that emerged were both designed to replace the ordeal. To be sure, the two were different in character. The medieval common law replaced the ordeal with jury trial, shifting the burden of judgment from God to the twelve jurors: as scholars like to say, the common law substituted the *vox populi* for the *vox dei*, it replaced the voice of God with the voice of the people.[4] The Continent took a different route. Instead of replacing God by the jury, Continental law developed more exacting investigative methods of so-called "inquisitorial" procedure — methods that included judicial torture. In the mature form of Continental law, those exacting methods yielded a carefully crafted dossier, full of factual detail, which explained its judgments with scrupulous care. That dossier was assembled not by lay jurors but by persons with some formal education — priests or university-trained jurists.

These educated priests and jurists of the Continent were the ancestors of the trained lawyers and bureaucrats who manage Continental justice to this day. Indeed, we might say, with a little exaggeration, that where England replaced the voice of God with the voice of the people, the Continent moved toward replacing the voice of God with the voice of bureaucracy. Remarkably enough, by the thirteenth century, the fundamental differences between the common law and civil law traditions were already beginning to appear: the common law had already displayed its characteristic emphasis on lay justice and its weak bureaucratic tradition, whereas the civil law had already begun to opt for incipient forms of bureaucratic control of the law.

Nevertheless, both English jury trial, with its lay verdicts, and Continental "inquisitorial" procedure, with its ferocious investigative methods and its well-ordered bureaucratic dossiers, emerged as substitutes for the judicial ordeal. As historians like to observe, those are still the two systems, *mutatis mutandis*, which are now in use everywhere in the world today. The European campaign for the suppression of the judicial ordeal during the period 1100–1250 thus ultimately resulted in the creation of law that eventually spread from the once benighted European fringe of Eurasia to the entire modern industrialized world.

So Western law was born out of a religious attack on the judicial ordeal, and jury trial in particular was one of the Western forms that emerged in the wake of that attack. This means that if we want to understand the theological significance of jury trial, we must begin by understanding the history of the ordeal. Why did the ordeal go into decline, and what was the significance of the jury trial that replaced it? In trying to answer this question, we can look to two leading lines of scholarly interpretation. One of these lines of interpretation is correct, in my view, and the other is deeply misleading. Unless we choose the correct line, we will not understand the theological structure of jury trial as it emerged after 1100, which still haunts American law nearly a thousand years later.

The difference between the correct line of interpretation and the misleading one brings us back to the distinction developed in chapter 1, between factual proof and moral comfort. The mistaken line of interpretation supposes that the judicial ordeal was about factual proof. According to this line, which has been adopted by many, indeed most, historians, the strange and brutal ordeals that were in use around 1100 were fact-finding devices. As the pioneering medievalist Jacob Grimm put it, the ordeal was a "reverse oracle," an oracle that revealed hidden truths about the past rather than about the future. Leading scholars of the early common law take the same line: "Most ordeals," writes John Hudson, for example, "seem to have been in disputes where other methods of investigation had failed to establish guilt."[5] So does the standard Continental literature, which describes the ordeal as a "magical" way of finding facts.[6] What God revealed through his "divine testimony," in such ordeals as the hot iron or the cold water, was a hidden fact that could not be detected in any other way. In the words of a leading medievalist, the ordeal was "intended to reveal a specific fact; it was designed to deal with specific allegations when other evidence or proof was lacking."[7] The ordeal served as a kind of crystal ball, allowing truth to be picked out from behind clouds of uncertainty.

This line of interpretation has a dramatic implication about the great transformation of the centuries from 1000 to 1250: It implies that the rise of the two Western legal traditions was the rise of two new methods of acquiring factual knowledge about the world. If it is true that the judicial ordeal was a "reverse oracle," a "magical" means of determining hidden "specific facts," then the decline of the ordeal involved a change in the forms of Western perception. The strongest form of this argument treats the decline of the ordeal, and the concomitant rise of the common law and civil law, as the consequence of the rise of new forms of rationality. As one leading scholar summarizes the argument:

> Legal historians and ethnographers discovered long ago that there are two different attitudes towards the question of proof. There is a primitive, archaic system in which human enquiry, critical examination and reasoning play a small role, and where the courts are more eager to interrogate the elements of nature, such as water and fire, or spirits or divine beings, in order to elucidate the difficult question of guilt or innocence, right or wrong. We might call it the irrational approach. . . . The other approach, which we might call rational,

puts the burden squarely on the human mind and forces the courts to solve the riddle by all the means of enquiry and reasoning at the disposal of the human intelligence; interrogation of witnesses, direct observation, indirect information, examination of written documents, confessions, deductions from various indications and traces, the result of post-mortems and so on.[8]

According to this line of interpretation, the decline of the ordeal involved a shift in legal epistemology, a shift in mentalities about how to "solve the riddles" of crime: Western law, destined to spread to the entire world, developed as the magical approach to knowledge faded, and the rational or proto-scientific approach replaced it.

This interpretation is widespread, though scholars differ over the precise significance of this supposed revolution in the nature of fact-finding. Some do indeed view it as shift toward modern forms of rationality.[9] Others disagree that the ordeal is best described as an "irrational" form of fact-finding, arguing that there were perfectly rational reasons for the use of the ordeal to find facts.[10] But whether they think it was rational or not, these historians agree that its purpose was to determine facts in cases of uncertainty.

Yet there have always been a few scholars who doubted the claim that ordeals were oracles or magical fact-finding devices, including some very eminent figures; I am among the doubters.[11] I do not believe that ordeals were usually used as oracular or magical methods for divining specific facts in cases of unsolved crime. I think it is a mistake to treat the decline of the ordeal as an episode in the history of factual proof — a mistake that prevents us from understanding the nature of early jury trial. There is a better, and more correct, line of interpretation.

In fact, factual proof was not the issue at all, for the most part. What was primarily at stake was the moral responsibility for judgment. There was indeed a profound transformation during the period 1000–1250, a transformation that resulted in the emergence of Western legal systems. But what that transformation involved was not a revolution in legal epistemology but a revolution in governmental practice, which brought with it a great crisis in judicial and testimonial responsibility.

As I shall argue in the chapters that follow, ordeals were not used as "magical" means of discovering unknown facts. Indeed, as we shall see when we look more closely at the sources, there were plenty of cases in which there was no dispute about the facts whatsoever. Instead, what mattered most about the ordeals was their capacity to spare human beings the responsibility for judgment. An ordeal induced God to take the fearsome step of incriminating the accused person, thus allowing human beings to avoid the intimidating obligation of judging their fellows. As historian Peter Brown has acutely put it, the ordeal served to shift the "odium of human responsibility" to God.[12] Shifting the odium of responsibility to God was especially desirable from the point of view of potential witnesses. Testifying against one's neighbors was an exceedingly uncomfortable and risky business in the Middle Ages. The ordeal lifted that unpleasant obligation from the shoulders of the witnesses. Instead of resting judgment on human witnesses, an ordeal permitted judgment to be founded on the testimony of God, who was not subject to the ordinary risks of human life.

Now in a sense, of course, an ordeal held in order to acquire the testimony of God was about finding facts: it assumed that God did know what had happened. But it did not necessarily assume that *only* God knew what had happened. Much or most of the time the human witnesses too were perfectly well informed about the facts. The core problem, during the high age of the ordeal, was not that human witnesses did not know what had happened, so that some magical means of fact-finding was needed. The core problem was that the witnesses resisted declaring what they knew under oath. The fundamental conception of knowledge, in the world of these reluctant medieval witnesses, was no different from ours. Europeans of even this remote era shared our basic concept of factual proof. They too thought that knowledge of facts came from direct observation of the world, whether by God or by his human creatures.[13] Most important, they too thought of human testimony as the ordinary form of proof at law. They simply could not induce humans to speak honestly about what they had seen or heard, which meant that they had to turn to a different, incorruptible, Observer.

Why, then, did the ordeal go into decline, and with what consequences? The path to the right interpretation has been traced by historians Richard Fraher and (at least in some of his writings) Raoul van Caenegem.[14] As these scholars have emphasized, during the period beginning in the twelfth century the medieval church and medieval monarchies were making intensified efforts to monopolize violence — to take control of the process of justice, forcing Europeans to settle their conflicts in centralized court settings. Thus ecclesiastical and royal officials were making an initial effort to put a stop to local practices of clan vengeance. They were also slowly beginning to displace the jurisdiction of local feudal lords. During this period, officials from the centers of European power increasingly began to show up in European communities, insisting on their authority to dispense justice to a resentful and suspicious local population.

As these central authorities began to establish their presence, the comfortable and long-established practice of resorting to judicial ordeals went into a long and tense decline. Over the course of the twelfth and thirteenth centuries, church and royal officials gradually adopted a program that was deeply threatening to local society: they adopted a program of forcing local witnesses to testify. As we shall see, this happened only very slowly indeed. During the early part of the period 1000–1250, authorities remained content to allow judgments to be founded on the testimony of God. By the thirteenth century, though, human witnesses were being put under increasing pressure. This exposed two classes of persons to growing risks. First of all, witnesses, for in order to prosecute crimes like vengeance killings, officials had to compel ordinary people to take the unwelcome responsibility of testifying against their neighbors under oath. Second, judges, for the judges too faced peril in any system in which decisions could no longer be deferred to God.

The theological drama of the decline of the ordeal, it is my aim to show, was the drama of these judges and witnesses. So long as God gave judgment, no one else had to accept the "odium of human responsibility." Yet in the new worlds of Western law as it developed after the twelfth century, this would be longer be tolerated. The burden fell especially heavily on witnesses, most notably English jurors. Indeed, the shift from the testimony of God to the testimony of man put jurors in an extraordinarily delicate moral position. The jurors were twelve sworn witnesses, required by law to speak the truth. Worse yet, they were witnesses who acted as judges, being obliged to pronounce the judgment "guilty" in blood cases. This meant that their souls (and their bodies) were in substantial danger: they were compelled to take the moral responsibility that had previously been saddled upon God, courting the dangers of both vengeance and damnation.

As we shall see, they resisted. Indeed, the early history of jury trial is very much a history of monarchical efforts to compel sworn testimony and of witness efforts to resist. The birth of jury trial is thus an episode in the history of moral responsibility, not an episode in the history of mysteriously shifting modes of factual knowledge. And the structure of jury trial had to do with problems in the moral responsibility of judgment — problems that were still alive centuries later, when the reasonable doubt rule emerged.

This is a history that I shall tell in three chapters. This chapter presents the basic account of the workings of the ordeal, and of the aims of the medieval scholars and functionaries who attacked it. Chapter 4 presents the consequences of the decline of the ordeal in Continental Europe, where a new moral theology of judging and witnessing emerged as the foundation of a new style of Continental procedure. That procedure aimed to solve the dilemmas of the system of ordeals partly by compelling witness testimony and partly by compelling confession. It also aimed to protect the salvation of professional judges by the nasty expedient of placing all of the burden on the shoulders of the lay witnesses. The Continental system also involved the elaboration of a theology of "doubt," whose outlines chapter 4 will present. Chapter 5, finally, turns to the common law, with its peculiar, and morally challenging, deviation into jury trial. Accused persons were not compelled to confess in England. But the witnesses were put under especially severe pressure to testify under oath, with consequences that would be felt down into the eighteenth century.

The Ordeal: An Alternative to Oaths and Witness Testimony

The judicial ordeal was in use all over Europe in the early and central Middle Ages, just as it has been in use in many parts of the premodern world. The European judgments of God took numerous forms.[15] One was the same as that used by shipwrecked sailors driven to cannibalism: this was the ordeal by the drawing of lots.[16] There were many others, too, most of which subjected their victim — known as the "proband" — to some kind of test. For example, there were various "swallowing tests," such as one requiring the proband to swallow a dry portion of the Eucharist without choking. There was the ordeal of the cross, which required two disputants to stand before a cross, their arms outstretched, until one of them could hold the position no longer. There were others too, some of them magnificently evocative — like, for example, the test of the bier, which required a proband accused of murder to tread on the hand of the victim's corpse, in the expectation that the corpse would bleed if the proband was guilty. But the most common and most dramatic forms were the four mentioned by the Fourth Lateran Council: the ordeals of hot iron, cold water, hot water, and trial by combat.

All four were memorable, painful, and violent procedures. Trial by battle is the earliest form of the "judgment of God" that is widely attested in Europe, dating back to the very early Middle Ages. Trial by combat was generally restricted to very high-status persons; like its descendant, the duel, it was only for honorable people. Two such honorable persons would fight what was often a ferocious battle, lasting for many hours. If they chose not to fight themselves, they could often name a "champion" to fight for them. (By the central Middle Ages there were, in fact, professional champions-for-hire, who were well paid for their dangerous services.)[17] Death and maiming were not uncommon events in the course of trial by battle, so far as we can tell from the surviving records. The winner of the battle was the victor in the legal dispute.

The other judgments of God, by contrast, were generally reserved for low-status persons who did not qualify for trial by battle.[18] These low-status ordeals, which were widespread in early medieval Europe, were tests of the truthfulness of the proband — efforts to determine whether the proband had given true or false testimony. As medieval texts sometimes put it, they were proceedings in which the proband "took God as his witness."[19] This was usually done by subjecting the body of the proband to extremes of hot or cold. In the ordeal of hot iron, for example, the proband was obliged to grasp a red-hot iron, weighing from one to three pounds, and carry it for several feet. Thereafter, the proband's hand was bandaged. After three days, the bandages were removed from the hand, to see whether the burn wound was healing (taken as a sign that God declared the proband to be truthful) or suppurating and discolored (taken as the opposite). In the ordeal of the cold water, the proband was stripped naked, bound up in a fetal position, then slowly lowered into a body of cold water. A person who sank was regarded as having spoken the truth; one who floated had lied. In the ordeal of the hot water, the proband was made to extract a metal ring, or a piece of stone, from a boiling cauldron. Here again, the proband whose hand came through relatively unscathed was regarded as truthful.[20]

These judgments of God are riveting affairs, and they have stimulated a huge body of historical commentary. More than that: they have lodged themselves in the popular mind, as prime examples of the vivid barbarism of the Middle Ages. So much so that most readers may imagine that ordeals were a regular medieval occurrence. Nevertheless, it is important to emphasize that the judgments of God were never, so far as we can determine, the ordinary form of justice in any medieval period. Judgments of God, whether trial by battle or the low-status ordeals, took place only as kind of procedural last resort, after other means of decision had been exhausted. They were used only if four conditions were met: (1) No formal accuser came forward, (2) no witness testified, (3) the accused did not confess, and (4) the matter could not be resolved by the oath of a high-status, honorable person. It is essential that we understand all four of these conditions if we are to grasp the significance of the ordeal and its decline.

Let us begin with the first. The ordeal was administered only in cases in which no accuser was willing to make a formal accusation. From the point of view of medieval authors, the ideal proceeding began with a formal accusation. As Robert Bartlett explains, "Normal criminal procedure in the early Middle Ages hinged upon the appearance of an accuser, who brought the charge, offered to prove it, and took the consequences for failure to do so."[21] Those "consequences" were serious. An accuser might be obliged to prove his accusation by fighting a trial by battle to the death. Even accusers who did not face possible death, though, might face other consequences. "[A]t worst," as van Caenegem summarizes the law, "the accuser who failed to prove his case might undergo the punishment he had hoped to obtain for his opponent . . . at best he would suffer some minor penalty."[22] Bringing an accusation was a risky business.

Perhaps unsurprisingly, accusers did not always come forward. There were, however, also three other possibilities that would permit a decision without an ordeal. To begin with, sworn witness testimony could resolve a matter: if witnesses came forward, there would be no ordeal. Many local statutes stipulated that there was to be recourse to the ordeal only if human testimony could not be had.[23] Ivo of Chartres, the pioneer of canon law whom we encountered in chapter 2, stated the rule most concisely. Ivo, like other church reformers, was generally opposed to the ordeals. Nevertheless, he conceded that they could sometimes be necessary — but only if there were no witnesses: "[W]e must sometimes seek Divine testimony when . . . human testimony is wholly lacking."[24]

Witnesses, however, *were* often lacking. To quote Bartlett again, "The most characteristic situation in which the ordeal was employed [resulted from] the absence of witnesses, [where] the charge which was only a matter of general suspicion."[25] Ordeals, at least ordeals involving what we would call criminal matters, were generally administered in cases in which there was what canonists called ill-fame, "fama": "that is," as one great medieval criminal lawyer explained, "where there are rumors, and the voice of the public is saying that a person is guilty."[26] In such cases, it remained necessary to turn to God as the only available witness. The ordeals were thus typically held when the anonymous "voice of the public" declared someone's guilt but no individual witness or accuser was ready to come forward to incriminate the accused under oath.

So the ordeal could be avoided if there was an accuser or sworn witnesses. The same was also true in another circumstance: if the accused confessed. Indeed, standard medieval canon law declared that the very purpose of an ordeal was to "torture people into confessing," "confessionem extorqueri,"[27] and from an early date authorities declared that the threat of the ordeal was to be used to induce persons suspected of offenses to confess. If they did confess, the matter was ended. As a basic canon law text dating to the late ninth century explained, justice should ideally be done "through a spontaneous confession or through proof by witnesses of a publicly committed crime." Only failing that was a judgment of God in order: "Things that are hidden or unknown" were to be left to "the judgments of Him who alone knows the hearts of the sons of men."[28]

The ordeal was thus only conducted if three sorts of oral declaration were unavailable: no accusation, no witness testimony, and no confession. A fourth sort of oral declaration too could render any judgment of God unnecessary: a so-called purgative oath by a person of high social standing.

Early medieval law placed great value on the purgative oath — the oath by which an honorable, high-status person "purged" himself of an accusation or a challenge to his rights or veracity. Such an oath was, as it were, the opposite of a confession: it was a dispositive declaration of innocence. Oaths were invested with great religious meaning and were ordinarily taken upon holy relics. As standard medieval theology explained it, the oath taker resembled the proband in an ordeal: when he swore upon relics, he too "took God as his witness."[29] Indeed, Lodovico Muratori, the great Enlightenment Italian scholar and pioneer of the serious study of medieval institutions, regarded the oath as itself a form of judgment of God, and modern historians have agreed. Both the oath and the ordeal were sacral practices, by which individuals were forced to confront God in order to clear themselves of suspicion.[30]

The oath was taken in a variety of ways. Sometimes the oath takers swore as individuals. Sometimes they gathered supporters, so-called compurgators, whose sworn oath fortified their own. Sometimes they asked compurgators to swear in their stead, while themselves remaining silent.[31] Regardless of whether the oath was taken individually or collectively, it was closely associated with hierarchical social status. Bartlett explains the early medieval practice of oath taking: "The oath might be taken either alone or with oath-helpers, compurgators, and the choice between the two methods depended partly upon the nature of the offence but much more upon the status of the individual involved. The higher an individual's status, the more 'oath-worthy' he would be. Thus recourse to oath might be inappropriate in two situations: when the individual's own oath was no longer credible, or when the necessary number of compurgators could not be mustered."[32] Only persons of relatively high social standing and unimpeached reputation could clear themselves by oath. Like trial by battle, oath taking was fundamentally reserved to respectable, high-status persons.

The medieval sources reveal a strong preference for the resolution of disputes through such a purgative oath; if at all possible, a dispute should be resolved in that way. Yet an oath was not always available. Low-status persons could not clear themselves by oath at all; and high-status persons sometimes refused to do so. Consequently an alternative was needed.

The judgments of God served that end: they were alternatives to the purgative oath. Indeed, the sources present the judgment of God as a mere second-best solution — a functional replacement for the oath. This was equally true of high-status trial by battle and of the low-status ordeals of the hot and cold. Thus trial by battle took place only if the contestants refused to resolve their dispute by oath; and the battle that they fought was itself regarded as the functional equivalent of an oath. The loser in the battle was deemed a "perjurer," as though he had falsely sworn: "He whose champion succumbs," as an early eleventh-century text explained, "is the loser, as though his claim had been false witness given under oath."[33]

The same is true of the low-status ordeals of the hot and the cold. These proceedings were reserved to persons of problematic social standing, persons who were not oath-worthy, either because they were of low status or because their reputations had been tarnished in some other way. (If for some reason a high-status person had to undergo an ordeal, he might be permitted to substitute one of his servants or dependents.)[34] Yet they too were the functional equivalent of oaths. The ordeal allowed a person who was not oath-worthy to "take God as his witness," thus making his testimony trustworthy. Unlike their social superiors, non-oath-worthy persons could not take God as their witness simply through words; but they *could* do so by submitting themselves to pain and fear. Only after undergoing a painful and frightening test would a low-status person be deemed to have spoken honorably. The ordeal of hot or cold in a sense transformed a dishonorable person into an honorable one, allowing him to give "purgative" testimony. As Colin Morris has noted, there is a paradox in this that deserves emphasis: awful as it was, the ordeal actually conferred a procedural benefit on its low-status victims, allowing them to give testimony, with God as their witness, as though they were persons of high social standing.[35]

As an example of how Europeans followed these principles around the time of the Fourth Lateran Council, we may take the Burgesses' Assizes of Jerusalem, a legal text from a thirteenth-century court in the Crusader State of the Latin Kingdom of Jerusalem.[36] The Crusaders brought with them a distillation of European institutions, and this text shows us nicely how the judgment of God was generally conceived in the twelfth and thirteenth centuries.[37] The burgesses of Jerusalem were nonnobles, who did not resolve their dispute either through oath or through trial by battle. Instead, the Court of the Burgesses depended either on confessions or on witness testimony about publicly committed crimes, just as canon law decreed. In the absence of confession or witness testimony, the court turned to the ordeal of the hot iron.

To illustrate when the ordeal was appropriate, the Assizes of the Burgesses offered a pair of hypothetical homicide cases. In both, sworn witness testimony is not available; but in only one is there a confession. In the first of the cases in this pair, the accused admits to a killing. However, he claims a justification of self-defense: "If two or three men come before the court, bringing a dead man and also leading along a living man and say to the justice, 'Sir, we found this man dead in the street, all warm like one who has just been killed, and we found this man, whom we have brought here, near the corpse, going along the street; we went to him and asked him who had killed the man and he replied that the dead man attacked him in the street and that he had killed him in self-defense.' "[38] Here there are no eyewitnesses available to testify, but the accused has admitted to performing the act. In such a case, the accused was obliged to call upon God as his witness ["garant"], to prove the truthfulness of his claim: that is, he was to be subjected to the ordeal of hot iron. The use of the hot iron would effectively convert his plea of self-defense, otherwise inadmissible, into a dispositive oath of innocence. Note that there seems to be no notion here that the ordeal will reveal a hidden fact: there is no contested fact in this hypothetical case at all. The assumption is that the ordeal is a test of the truthfulness of the low-status accused person.

But what if there were no witnesses, and the accused did not admit the deed? The Burgesses' Assizes turn to this problem in their next provision. In this second hypothetical case, the accused is strongly incriminated by circumstantial evidence: he is found near a warm corpse, his sword dripping with fresh blood. However, he refuses to admit his deed. Brought before the assizes, he insists on his innocence. In such a case, "[t]he viscount must take him, and put him in prison for one year and one day, to see if any person will come forward during that period who wishes to accuse him of this murder, or to see whether he decides to carry the hot iron within one year and one day. But if no accuser comes forward within one year and one day, and he does not wish to carry the hot iron, the law judges that he must be delivered from prison as though he had been acquitted of the murder in question through trial."[39] If no witness or accuser came forward, and if the accused did not confess, it was impossible to proceed to trial or punishment. Only proper testimony, a legally valid oath, or a declaration of innocence fortified by an ordeal, would suffice. Absent that, the accused could only be imprisoned for a year and a day, presumably under harsh conditions. If he survived those harsh conditions without confessing, he was free. Here again there is hardly much doubt about the facts, in this second hypothetical case: the circumstantial evidence speaks volumes. The difficulties are created only by the absence of sworn testimony and the determination of the accused neither to confess nor to "carry the hot iron" in order to prove his veracity.

When the ordeal took place, it was generally surrounded with awe-inducing Christian ceremony. In this too it resembled the oath. Certain ordeals, like the test of swallowing the Eucharist and the ordeal of the cross, had obvious Christian significance. But the others were also Christianized affairs. Thus the person destined to suffer the ordeal would fast before it, spending time in prayer in church, dressed in the garb of a penitent. The ordeal itself was administered in a holy place, under holy supervision. English law, for example, declared that the ordeal was to be held "at an episcopal see, at a place desig-nated by a bishop, or at the very least in the presence of the bishop's minister and his clerks."[40] Many other texts too show ordeals being conducted in church. The ordeal was a religious event, which is why the ban ordered by the Fourth Lateran Council in 1215 had such importance.

The ordeal was also surrounded with Christian lore on the conflict between good and evil, right and wrong. It was conducted after a blessing pronounced by a priest, who invoked God "the just judge" of the Psalms.[41] Medieval libraries contained many texts of such blessings. These texts, like our other sources, revolve around the questions of witness testimony and confession. Many of them call upon God to chase away the devil, who has "hardened the heart" of the proband, preventing him from confessing. Others invoke a piece of religious lore to which we will return: the story of Susanna, who was falsely accused of illicit sex by two old men. "Just as You liberated Susanna from the false accusation," reads a blessing over the ordeal of cold water, addressed to God, "may You keep the proband safe if he is innocent."[42]

It was often a religious event in which God showed mercy. Most probands, our English evidence suggests, came through the ordeal unscathed.[43] Medieval authorities sometimes expressed frustration with this fact, complaining that God sometimes showed mercy, letting off accused persons who were obviously guilty. King William Rufus of England, for example, is quoted as declaring that God was no just judge, since he was in the habit of acquitting those known to be guilty.[44] Indeed, sometimes the English kings, and other officials as well, point-edly ignored the results of the ordeal, punishing accused persons despite the fact that they had passed. They took it for granted that those accused persons were guilty.[45] Indeed, the high rate of acquittals has led some scholars to conclude that the ordeal was deliberately rigged to show mercy.[46] We shall return to this aspect of the ordeal in chapter 5; as we shall see, what was true of the ordeal was also true of its successor, the early criminal jury, which displayed an inclination to acquit.

In what kinds of cases was the judgment of God used? Our records are spotty and unreliable. They are also distorted by various biases. We cannot be sure that we have any accurate sense of the real domain of the judicial ordeal. In the records that we do possess, though, we discover a limited number of categories. Sometimes the ordeal was used in matters that we would not re-gard as "legal" at all. For example, there are records of Christians who submit-ted to an ordeal in order to prove the superiority of the Christian or Catholic faith. One such record, from the very early Middle Ages, shows a Frankish deacon submitting to the ordeal of the boiling cauldron in order to prove that God favored the Catholic faith over the Arian.[47] Heretics too were often forced to undergo ordeals, in order to test whether God supported their form of Christian belief.[48]

As for the more "legal" cases, many were not what we today call "criminal." We have a large number of records of real property disputes, from all over Europe, that were determined by trial by battle.[49] As we shall see, the use of trial by battle to settle property disputes was common in Anglo-Norman England, for example. Married women whose fidelity had been challenged were subjected to ordeals[50] — including, famously, Empress Theutberga, tenth-century spouse of Emperor Lothar II. (She underwent two of them.)[51] Doubtful questions of the paternity of infants could also be settled in the same way.[52]

Finally, there were two important classes of cases that we would define as criminal: cases of theft and cases of homicide. There are many cases of theft,[53] including notably the theft of holy relics. Relics were often appropriated from the churches that held them, and some of our recorded instances of ordeals involve persons accused of stealing relics.[54] There are also many cases of homicide, of which we have seen examples from the Jerusalem Assizes above. Similarly, the ordinances of the Peace of God might require that persons accused of violent breaches of the Peace undergo an ordeal.[55]

Absence of Witnesses: Absence of Evidence?

Such were the ordeals, which have frequently been interpreted as "magical" fact-finding proceedings. But is it really possible that proceedings like "carrying the hot iron" were used to "solve a riddle," identify an unknown culprit, elucidate an unsolved crime in the absence of evidence? They seem to belong to a system in which evidence of the modern kind was not used to resolve cases at all. Instead, cases were disposed of by oath. On the face of it, the ordeals seem simply to be a means by which a low-status person could clear himself of an accusation by a form of oath, proving his veracity by subjecting himself to pain. Moreover, complaints like those of King William Rufus suggest that these low-status persons were often regarded as obviously guilty. So does the evidence of canon law. Why would canon law speak of "torturing people into confessing" unless it assumed that those accused were fairly clearly guilty? If the accused was clearly guilty, what were the "hidden facts" that needed to be cleared up?

Nevertheless, many important scholars insist that the ordeals were indeed meant as "magical" "methods of investigation," as oracular ways of solving factual mysteries involving not an accused whose guilt was obvious but an "unknown perpetrator" or a "hidden fact" for which evidence was lacking. These scholars include Hermann Nottarp, author of the standard text on the ordeal; and Robert Bartlett, the author of the most important recent book-length study. Bartlett, for example, declares that "trial by fire and water" was "intended to reveal a specific fact . . . when other evidence or proof was lacking."[56] He dismisses historians who do not believe that the ordeal was an oracular fact-finding device.[57] Medievalists like Charles Radding agree with Bartlett.[58] So do leading historians of the common law, like John Hudson, who views the ordeals as a "method of investigation."[59]

And it is true that some medieval texts sometimes seem to suggest as much: as the canon lawyers put it, the purpose of the ordeal was to achieve the revelation of "things that are hidden or unknown," through "the judgments of Him who alone knows the hearts of the sons of men."[60] Our sources do often say that the ordeal was meant to expose "occulta," "things hidden." Some of the cases do involve matters that were mysterious by their nature, like accusations of theft or disputes about paternity. Moreover, our sources tell us that the ordeal was used in cases in which no witnesses came forward to testify. Does this not imply that ordeals were "methods of investigation," used because no other means of determining the truth existed? Scholars have concluded exactly that. Indeed, our literature lays heavy emphasis on the fact that ordeals were only inflicted where no witness testimony was available.

Nevertheless, this line of interpretation is mistaken: it is seriously misleading to think of the ordeal as primarily a fact-finding institution — and misleading in ways that make it difficult to understand how the common law and the civil law first took shape.

Why would anybody interpret the ordeal as a proceeding intended to "reveal a specific fact . . . when other proof was lacking"? How did this line of interpretation attract so much support, from so many important scholars? To understand how this line of interpretation developed, we must take a brief excursion into the scholarly literature, in particular into the German literature.

The claim that the ordeal was about fact-finding dates back more than a century and a half. At its origin, it belongs to the tradition of German Romanticism. We can trace it back, in particular, to a founding father of medieval legal history: Jacob Grimm, known to all modern readers for the fairy tales he published with his brother Wilhelm. When Grimm looked upon the ordeals, working at the height of the early Romantic era in 1828, what he saw was primitive religion. At the time, German scholars were avidly studying pre-Christian rituals and myths, which had long been neglected by their Christian and Deist predecessors. Grimm's colleague Karl Otfried Müller, for example, writing in 1825, tried to recapture the pre-Christian mentality of the ancient Greeks, who had "a lively and natural form of belief," in which the divinity was "near, friendly — sat together with you at table."[61] Other scholars were piecing together the scraps of evidence for occult Greek practices at sites like Eleusis.[62]

Grimm, typical of this age of yearning for the lost world of primitive credulity, offered a characteristic early Romantic interpretation of the ordeal. Ordeals, he declared, were essentially a form of oracle, much like the oracles of ancient Greece and other pre-Christian cultures. However, whereas ordinary oracles concerned themselves with the future, ordeals concerned themselves with the past and the present.[63] When Grimm first ventured this claim in 1828, he made it cautiously; he did not yet maintain that ordeals were intended to reveal hidden facts. Indeed, he fudged noticeably on whether they were really about "obscure facts" or about "claims of right."[64] By 1835, though, when he published his magnum opus on primitive religion, his *German Mythology*, he felt no more doubt: ordeals were fact-finding devices, just like oracles, intended to clear up "events and actions in the past."[65] They were events in which the divinity reached down into daily life, to reveal things that men could not discover themselves.

Later scholars did not always literally repeat Grimm's particular argument that ordeals were a form of backward-looking oracle; that argument is hard to square with the medieval sources, which say pretty clearly that ordeals and oracles were two different things.[66] Nevertheless, especially in Germany, scholars often continued to follow the general line of Grimm's interpretation, holding that ordeals were meant to reveal hidden facts.[67] (I shall not trace the history of this long-lived Romantic interpretation in detail here.) Finally, after World War II, the claim that ordeals were meant to elucidate "obscure facts" was given its definitive modern statement by the highly influential Hermann Nottarp, who laid particular emphasis on a fact of undoubtedly capital importance: the fact that ordeals were held only if there was no witness testimony.

It is Nottarp whom we must read most carefully, and critically, if we are to understand how our modern ordeal literature has gone astray. Nottarp is the Grand Old Man of ordeal studies, universally cited by historians of the ordeal. His voluminous work *Gottesurteilstudien, Studies on the Ordeal,* first published in 1949, offers a magnificent collection of source material, and it has served as the standard work on the subject for the past fifty years. But the uncomfortable truth is that Nottarp's *Gottesurteilstudien,* despite being published after World War II, is a more or less unapologetically Nazi interpretation of the ordeal, one whose judgments offer very dubious versions of the old German Romantic line.

In fact, Nottarp's book was wholly in the Nazi spirit. Nottarp began his argument by focusing on the sheer physical brutality of the ordeals of the hot and cold. What could be the purpose of such horrible tests of physical endurance? Nottarp gave his fundamental answer in his opening pages: the ordeal was not a test of the fortitude of a low-status person declaring his innocence. Instead, the purpose of the brutal ordeal was to uncover "degenerate" ("entartete") members of the *Volk*.[68] In this, Nottarp explained, medieval law was no different from modern: "Today too, a-social and anti-social human beings have generally deviated from the path of normality . . . often showing characteristic signs of degeneracy in the form of their heads and faces."[69] Once the "degeneracy" of such weak and physically abnormal persons, unable to endure the pain and terror of the ordeal, had been revealed by the test of hot iron or cold water, they could be excluded from the medieval Teutonic community.[70] Seen in this light, argued Nottarp, the ordeals were indeed easy to understand. They were in fact well designed to ferret out a hidden truth. A healthy member of the Volk community, firm in the knowledge of his innocence, would have been able to withstand the rigors of the ordeal. Only weaklings would succumb. The "hidden fact" being revealed by the brutality of the ordeal was thus the degeneracy of the accused.[71]

If Nottarp had offered only this aggressively Nazi reading, his book might not have been so influential. But in defense of the claim that ordeals were a form of "investigation" of the facts, Nottarp did more. He embodied the diligence and immense learning that was characteristic of German scholars even during the Nazi period, and he did not rest his case solely on his assertions about the exclusion of "degenerates" from the community. He also added a further argument, drawn directly from the medieval sources, which has had lasting influence. He focused on a question that is indeed critical to the interpretation of the ordeal: the question of witness testimony.

As we have seen, the ordeal was ordinarily administered in cases in which "not only witnesses but even a specific accuser would be lacking."[72] To quote Ivo once again, ordeals were necessary because "we must sometimes seek Divine testimony, where human testimony is wholly lacking."[73] Nottarp regarded such texts as definitive evidence that the purpose of ordeals was to uncover hidden facts.[74] The absence of "human testimony," Nottarp held, implied the absence of *evidence*: ordeals were used because there was "no other means" of discovering the truth.[75] When "human testimony" was lacking, ordeals were used as a means of "criminal investigation," he explained, intended, "just like today," to identify "an unknown perpetrator."[76] In speaking of "unknown perpetrators" in this way, Nottarp was, we should note, again writing in a way typical of the 1930s and 1940s in Germany. German authors of that terrible time wrote a great deal about the crime problem—about the plague of unwitnessed crimes, committed in anonymous back alleys by shadowy "perpetrators" who had to be discovered and eliminated.

The world of the ordeal, for a Nazi author, was indeed a world of back alleys, a world like that of Peter Lorre's *M*, where degenerate persons committed hidden offenses that could be brought to light only through hard detective work. Imagining the world in this way led Nottarp to many peculiar conclusions, none of which has prevented subsequent scholars from relying on his work. Because Nottarp was certain that ordeals were a way of detecting hidden facts, for example, he denied that they could have been used to coerce confessions. Important medieval texts declared that the threat of the ordeal was used to induce accused persons to confess. As the standard canon law text put it, altogether unambiguously, ordeals were used to "torture people into confessing," "confessionem extorqueri."[77] Ordeals, the canon lawyers assumed, were frightening and painful affairs; they were inflicted on people who were fairly obviously guilty, but who would not confess; and it was hoped that the threat of them would be enough to induce the guilty to own up. Yet that account of the ordeal did not fit well with the thesis promoted by Nottarp, and he simply discarded it. The numerous authors who spoke in such terms, he explained blandly, had "a completely false image" of the ordeal.[78] They had "failed to understand the essence" of their own institutions.[79] The ordeal was a form of "criminal investigation" used in the absence of evidence, not a means of inducing confession in cases in which the truth about the guilt of the accused was already known. Accordingly, it was a mistake to think that ordeals had anything to do with torture.

Elsewhere too Nottarp simply discarded sources that did not fit with his interpretation. As we have seen, the proband was often acquitted, a fact about which figures like King William Rufus of England complained. William Rufus's complaint implied clearly that ordeals were used to acquit persons known to be guilty. Such complaints were of no use to Nottarp, since they offered no support for the idea that ordeals were "investigations" of "unknown perpetrators."[80] So he dismissed their importance, treating cases in which the ordeal was clearly not used as a "method of proof" simply as odd exceptions.[81] In the same vein, he downplayed the significance of the Fourth Lateran Council's condemnation of ordeals as "judgments of blood." That declaration, insisted Nottarp, was a minor effort to discipline clergy, not a major event in the history of the ordeal.[82] In particular, it had no bearing on the use of ordeals as a supposed "form of evidence" in secular courts.[83] After all, there was no sign that the council had any grasp of the "essence" of the ordeal: the idea that ordeals were "judgments of blood," as Canon 18 declared them to be, simply had nothing to do with their true nature as "criminal investigations."

Now, I hope it is manifest that the careful scholar should approach Nottarp's arguments with caution. Nevertheless, Nottarp's book has been quite influential in the postwar years, notably in the English-speaking world. For Anglophone readers, *Gottesurteilstudien* has the imposing feel of a great German tome, the product of a tradition of profundity and solidity unmatched west of the Rhine. It looks like exactly the sort of work that medievalists ought to consult, exactly the sort of work that justifies the requirement that graduate students in medieval history pass a German-language reading exam. And indeed Anglophone medievalists have consulted it eagerly — though I venture to guess that they have rarely read it through carefully.

Sometimes they have picked up on Nottarp's claim that the ordeal was a test of strength or consciousness of innocence. Sometimes they have picked up on some of his other minor interpretations of the "essence" of the ordeal. But the most important Anglophone medievalists have emphasized the strongest non-Nazi argument that Nottarp offered: the argument that in the absence of human testimony, ordeals were necessary to identify an "unknown perpetrator" or to discover an "unknown truth." This is the argument that has struck medievalists as founded on real mastery of the medieval sources.

Bartlett is a prime example. Early on in his much-admired book, Bartlett, like Nottarp, invokes the standard medieval rule that ordeals were administered when there was an absence of witnesses. On the next page, he alters his claim subtly, but significantly, in a way that tacitly endorses Nottarp's interpretation: ordeals were used, he says, in cases of "*the absence of evidence,* the absence of witnesses or even an accuser."[84] He thus takes it for granted that the absence of witnesses was the equivalent of an absence of evidence. Fifty pages later, when he returns to the same question, Bartlett simply drops any discussion of witnesses, and speaks only of evidence. "The ordeal," he declares, "was intended to reveal a specific fact; it was designed to deal with specific allegations when other evidence or proof was lacking."[85] By the close of his book, he treats the point as proven: ordeals were used, he declares, "at the clogged and tricky moment when neither testimony nor the oath offered a way forward." Not being able to get the truth from either testimony or oath, people turned to the ordeal to "shed light on obscure issues."[86]

This form of argument has now become standard. Following Nottarp, it has become the scholarly consensus that the medieval rule requiring an absence of *human testimony* before an ordeal could be administered was a rule requiring an *absence of evidence.* It has become the consensus that ordeals were, in Hudson's words, a "method of investigation" intended to provide proof of unknown facts in the absence of evidence.

Why Did the Witnesses Refuse to Testify?

Yet all along there have been a few leading scholars who doubted the very premise that ordeals were intended as "investigations" of hidden facts. The eminent ancient historian Peter Brown, for example, maintains that in the ordeal "God is revealing 'truth,' not any specific fact."[87] There are other leading scholars who agree with Brown, among them the leading French legal historian Jean Gaudemet.[88] A few other recent scholars have also weighed in — including law professor Trisha Olsen, in a learned and insightful article.[89] All these authors have rejected the notion that ordeals were methods of investigation.

And with good reason: "lack of human testimony" is not the same thing as lack of evidence. Early medieval law was not, for the most part, concerned with detecting "unknown perpetrators." Certainly it is sometimes the case that God was regarded as the only available "witness." But hardly as often as Nottarp imagined: there were few Peter Lorres lurking in the back alleys of medieval villages. A careful reading of the sources suggests that the ordeal was typically held *not* because "other methods of investigation" had failed but because the witnesses and the accusers refused to come forward and testify under oath. It is simply an error to assume that the absence of human testimony inevitably meant the absence of evidence — an error that makes it impossible to understand the moral theological significance of jury trial. Indeed, it is indispensable that we arrive at correct interpretation of the silence of the witnesses: the silence of the medieval witnesses is of fundamental importance for our understanding of the early procedures both of the common law and of the civil law.

Let us now face squarely the question of whether the judicial ordeal was designed as a fact-finding procedure used to "shed light on obscure issues."[90] As social historians have observed, it is inherently unlikely that "investigations" of the modern detective kind would ordinarily have been needed in many parts of Europe in the early and central Middle Ages. Many ordeals were inflicted in communities that were very small — villages of perhaps a few dozen persons. This implies, as two leading social historians noted some years ago, that there must frequently have been little uncertainty about the guilt or innocence of the proband: "Essentially, in all small-scale societies, people know what is going on; they know who is untrustworthy, who may be a thief, who has farmed his land, just as they know who is sleeping with whom. And that basic knowledge (generally accurate, although it may for the outcast, the weak or the unlucky, only be prejudice) underlies all the procedures, rational or irrational, of local dispute settlement, just as it is the basis too of collective judgment: the ordeal and the jury alike draw on it."[91] "In a peasant community . . . few things remained secret."[92] In very small societies, people usually have a pretty good guess as to whether the accused is guilty or innocent. Indeed, as we have seen, the standard medieval law of ordeals assumed exactly that: ordeals, medieval texts declared, were to be used when there was ill-fame, fama — when the voice of the people had already declared the accused to be guilty. These were small communities in which the kind of deep uncertainty that requires modern police investigations was much rarer than it is today. The ordinary situation was one in which the community experienced little doubt indeed about the facts, though they were unwilling to stand up and swear to them.

Of course, not all medieval communities were so small; and even in small communities there are mysteries. Moreover, there are offenses that are mysterious by their nature — matters like theft, accusations of adultery, and cases of contested paternity.[93] Theft is a particularly important example, as it is in the nature of thefts that they are committed in secrecy.[94] An ordeal conducted in order to determine who had committed a clandestine theft was in some sense an ordeal intended to clarify murky facts. In cases of theft, it may well be that God was sometimes the only witness. Nevertheless, even the cases involving theft are not free from ambiguity. In particular, we should remember that the ordeal was used in cases involving fama — cases in which the community had named a suspect. They were, by definition, not cases shrouded in utter mystery. Moreover, it is not necessary to suppose that medieval witnesses always knew the whole truth. It is easy to understand that they would have been reluctant even to testify to partial knowledge, if their testimony might result in criminal punishment.

Even more important, we should remember that the ordeal was used for many offenses that are *not* mysterious by their nature — offenses like homicide. Of course, clandestine homicides do take place. But in vengeance cultures, killings are typically performed publicly. Indeed, in the next chapter we shall examine a famous example of just such a public vengeance killing, which took place in the public square of the very large community of Bologna. Ordeals were used in such cases too; in a moment, I shall offer a number of examples of medieval cases in which there was no doubt about the facts whatsoever. The claim that ordeals were used only in cases of factual uncertainty — cases where investigation was needed — is simply unsupported by our sources.

Indeed, as the prominence of fama in sources suggests, the medieval judicial ordeal was not primarily a "method of investigation" of hidden facts at all. The ordinary case, the paradigm to which the ordeal was addressed, was not a case requiring sleuthing "just like today." It was a case in which the community was fairly sure of someone's guilt, but no one was willing to accuse and no one was willing to give sworn testimony to what he knew. It is thus entirely unsurprising that canon law characterized the ordeal as a method of forcing accused persons to confess.[95] The underlying assumption of the canon lawyers was that the guilt of the accused was already fairly certain, but that no sworn testimony was available to prove it. Historians who think otherwise are guilty of anachronism: they are imagining societies in which "perpetrators" were completely unknown much more frequently than was actually the case.

That does not mean that the voice of the people never made mistakes. Rumor is not a reliable source of truth, and innocent persons were undoubtedly convicted.[96] It means only that members of medieval communities did not imagine that undiscovered perpetrators were the primary problem that confronted their system of justice. They did not live in modern big cities, and most of the time they were pretty sure they knew who had done what. Their primary felt need was not for fact-finding procedures. It was for procedures that would allow them to accuse, and punish, a known malefactor, without taking full personal responsibility for doing so.

So why were the witnesses silent? The question is not hard to answer. In these societies, witnesses had many reasons for avoiding the responsibility of testifying, even when they knew the truth perfectly well. The same is true of the other forms of oral declaration that might have obviated an ordeal. Accusers had excellent reasons not to bring accusations. Accused persons, for their part, had good reason to refuse to clear themselves by oath, even if they were oath-worthy. And of course, sworn confessions carried great danger for the accused. In general, trustworthy oral declarations — whether accusations, witness testimony, confessions or oaths — were hard to come by.

It is easiest to understand why accusers would refuse to bring accusations. Bringing accusations was a dangerous business in the Middle Ages. As Bartlett himself observes, "Normal criminal procedure in the early Middle Ages hinged upon the appearance of an accuser, who brought the charge, offered to prove it, *and took the consequences for failure to do so.*"[97] Under ordinary circumstances, an accuser might well be obliged to prove his accusation by fighting a trial by battle to the death. It hardly needs to be said that this system provided a disincentive to bringing accusations. Unsurprisingly, we have good evidence that accusers hesitated. In one English ordeal narrative from the 1180s, for example, we read: "Afraid of having to undergo judicial combat at the request of the accused man, [the accuser] remained silent" in court.[98] Even accusers who did not undergo trial by battle might suffer the penalty prescribed for the crime they had alleged, or be subjected to a stiff fine.[99] Bringing an accusation was a potentially foolhardy undertaking.

So was serving as a sworn witness. It was inevitable that witnesses would resist testifying. Partly this was because of the norms of vengeance culture. As many scholars have argued, the societies of the early Middle Ages in Europe were ruled, in various ways, by the norms of vengeance.[100] Denizens of such cultures do not seek justice in court, at least not as a normal first resort. The norms of vengeance require self-help.[101] This is of obvious relevance in discussing cases of "murder." The alleged "murderers" in our records must, at least some of the time, have been persons who had committed feud killings. Local norms would have strongly discouraged witnesses from testifying before royal or church courts in such cases.

Moreover, in any case, testifying against any killers to outside officials would have courted vengeance from those killers' relations. Medieval authors were perfectly conscious of this deadly danger. One thirteenth-century French moralist, for example, described the following dilemma. Suppose a false accuser has made an accusation against someone. If a potential witness knows the accusation to be false, must he testify? In such a case, this author observed, the witness had good reason to hesitate. "If [the witness] betrays [the false accuser] . . . he may easily run the risk of death."[102] The reluctance of witnesses to testify was not just a matter of the risk of their own death, moreover. They also resisted testifying, the same author tells us, because they did not wish to take the guilt of the blood upon themselves. After all, giving testimony carried the possibility of causing the death of another: "If [the witness] betrays [the false accuser]," he wrote, "it may be the case that the accuser will be killed by the judge, or else by the relatives of the person against whom he wanted to bring the false accusation."[103] Serving as a witness courted blood guilt.

Not least, witnesses resisted testifying for a third, and critically important, reason: they did not wish to undergo the spiritually perilous business of taking an oath. Christian authors spoke constantly of the extreme "peril" involved in swearing oaths. We shall see many examples as we proceed. For the moment, consider a typical explication by the early thirteenth-century English moralist Thomas of Chobham. To swear an oath, he explained, was to take God as your witness. This was a solemn and dangerous business: "To take the name of God while declaring a falsehood is most evil, for God neither wishes to be, nor is capable or being, a false witness. He who makes God into a false witness in order to prove something thus does a great injury to Him. For it is perilous to invoke God as a witness to something about which man is not certain. Thus it said in the Decalogue: *Thou shalt not take the name of thy God in vain*."[104] "Perilous": the word appears again and again in discussions of sworn testimony. Christians could be expected to find swearing an intimidating business, and to resist swearing if possible.

Van Caenegem described these fears in a passage that deserves to be quoted. Medieval Europeans would feel fear, he writes, "when the priest was threatening God's wrath and the saint's relics were brought in. Even that great ruffian, Reynard the Fox, thought better of it when he saw the relics being brought in upon which he was supposed to swear his innocence, lost his nerve, and fled. . . . [H]ell was real enough to people of all walks of life. Thus we find the abbot and monks of Ely refusing money which the widow of a wicked knight brought them, because the abbot had seen his soul being carried to hell in a vision and he and his monks were frightened to touch the money of a damned man."[105] The dread of swearing on relics is also a theme upon which the medievalist R. W. Southern has written evocatively: medieval people were deeply intimidated by the relics upon which oaths were taken.[106] As we shall see, the dangers of the oath would continue to dog English jurors, the panel of twelve sworn witnesses whom English judges would charge "at the peril of their soul to say the truth."[107]

So it is no surprise that we have plenty of evidence that witnesses resisted giving sworn testimony. Much of that evidence comes from the practice of English government during the early years of the formation of the common law. The English kings and Norman dukes made sustained, and sometimes ferocious, efforts to compel persons of all social stations to testify under oath as "jurors" — a word meaning witnesses who were sworn by oath. We know that these "jurors" had to be threatened forcefully. Thus early thirteenth-century Norman jurors, after being obliged to swear on relics that they would tell the truth, were admonished in the following menacing terms: "Know ye by the faith and belief that you have in Lord Jesus Christ, and that you received in baptism, and upon these relics . . . that if you have lied or concealed the truth in this matter, your souls will be damned in perpetuity, and your bodies will be exposed to shameful abuses in a gaping Hell."[108] The Norman bailiffs who spoke in this way took it for granted that their witnesses resisted testifying truthfully under oath. Only coercion and threats could change that. The fundamental working assumption of the early common law was the same as the fundamental working assumption of the law on ordeals: the countryside was full of "witnesses" who knew the truth, but who would not testify unless coerced. The Crown confronted "wily villagers," as van Caenegem put it, who were all too likely to be "hiding a case of murder or another royal plea,"[109] and for good reason. Indeed, English records of the early twelfth century show that locals paid the king significant sums in order to be excused from the obligation to testify or judge — "100 pounds in order that they should no longer be judges or sworn witnesses."[110] People were willing to take a substantial financial loss in order to avoid giving sworn testimony (or judging); and the Crown was only willing to let them off in return for a substantial tax.

Indeed, the new common law of the late twelfth and early thirteenth century was revolutionary partly because it compelled witnesses to testify where they would previously have refused to do so. If, as Henry II declared in the later twelfth century, there were witnesses who "did not want or dare" to speak up, then twelve sworn jurors of the neighborhood would be forced to do so.[111] "The terror inspired by a royal master like Henry II," as van Caenegem puts it, summing up the dynamic of the situation, "would make them speak up."[112] Richard Fraher has observed that the same is true of the canon law of the thirteenth century. Fraher writes of Hostiensis, the great canon lawyer of the mid-thirteenth century: "Hostiensis explicitly rejected the conventional opinion of the canonists and the civilian jurists who taught that courts could not coerce witnesses to testify in criminal cases. The function of the witness, Hostiensis countered, is a public office. If jurists construed criminal accusations as merely private matters, and if courts could not compel witnesses to testify on behalf of an accuser, 'the innocent would be damned and the guilty would be absolved.'"[113] Much more evidence can be assembled to prove the same point. For example, a late twelfth-century English canonist already took the same view: witnesses had to be compelled to testify.[114] Witnesses in criminal matters simply did not want to give testimony, and so they had to be compelled. As the powerful king Frederick II of Sicily declared in 1231, the ordeals were to be abolished — and in their place witnesses were to be compelled to testify.[115] In the high age of the ordeal, before the revolution in government that began in the later twelfth century, it was not possible to coerce such witnesses. In the absence of coercion, as we might predict, they avoided the "perilous" business of giving sworn oral declarations.

Nor were witnesses the only ones who resisted giving sworn statements. So, revealingly, did another class of persons: high-status persons who could clear themselves by giving a purgative oath. Indeed, the use of trial by battle offers striking evidence of the extent to which high-status persons resisted taking oaths. As we have seen, trial by battle was reserved to high-status persons. Yet such persons were also oath-worthy: their disputes could have been settled by oath. This would have allowed them to avoid what the twelfth-century English text *Glanvill* calls the "uncertain issue" of trial by battle, which regularly resulted in death or maiming.[116] Of course, oath-worthy persons could often avoid battle by hiring champions. Even then, though, their chances depended on the capacities of their hired thug. Yet they chose trial by battle in cases in which they could have prevailed simply by swearing. Why? Why did such high-status persons ever choose battle, rather than swearing a purgative oath? The answer, for some times and places, is undoubtedly that persons strongly attached to their personal honor simply preferred a fight to the death. But we also have evidence that, in some times and places, disputants refused to swear because they did not want to face the temptation to perjure themselves. They preferred the risk of death, or (if they hired a champion) the risk of losing their claim, to the spiritual risk of taking an oath.

Thus a number of legal provisions from the earlier Middle Ages declare that trial by battle is appropriate because it permits the disputants to avoid the sore temptation to perjure themselves. Charlemagne declared as much, for example — even though he was programmatically opposed to the use of trial by battle. As the great emperor explained, in an ordinance directed to the Lombards, who were heavy users of trial by battle, "It is better that they should fight with clubs on the field of battle, rather than that they should commit perjury."[117] The underlying assumption is that swearing contests are more dangerous than trial by battle. If parties were obliged to swear oaths, they would risk committing perjury, which would have endangered their souls.

We find the same assumption elsewhere as well. For example, the so-called Law of the Family of Worms, promulgated by Burchard of Worms, the early eleventh-century canonist, offers a most interesting account of the nature and propriety of trial by battle. As bishop of Worms, Burchard was the feudal lord of a great domain, called his "family," whose affairs had to be regulated in detail. His regulations, which date to the 1020s, amount to a comprehensive early law code. They include the following prescription for trial by battle:

> If any member of the family should have a dispute with another member about any matter, whether about fields or vines or serfs or personalty, if it is possible to resolve the dispute through the testimonies of the two parties without oaths, this is to be preferred. If not, we desire that the following procedure be followed in order to avoid perjuries. Let each side declare their testimonies, and let their witnesses proclaim their approval joyously. Then let two be chosen to represent the aforesaid testimonies by fighting, so as to resolve the dispute through trial by battle. He whose champion succumbs, is the loser, as though his testimony had been false witness given under oath.[118]

This passage deserves some careful explication. It envisions a conflict between two of Burchard's more powerful vassals. Each of these disputants is powerful enough that he can expect to be supported by a number of "testes," witnesses. Such powerful men would normally have been oath-worthy, and could have resolved their differences without violence. Yet Burchard is eager to dispense them from the obligation of swearing oaths, "ut devitentur periuria." After all, a man swearing an oath in his own cause is all too likely to be tempted into perjury, if only as a result of the inevitable self-deception that afflicts many litigants; and perjury could bring damnation.

Burchard thus proposes that the contestants should resolve their disputes, if at all possible, through "testimonia" without an oath. These "testimonies," let us note, are not by any means clearly evidence about disputed facts. "Testimonia," in this passage, could easily be translated as "stories" or "claims of right" — claims of right to which the parties were not willing to swear. There is no reason to think that these "testimonia" were purely about facts: most likely they indiscriminately mixed disputes over facts and rights. Indeed, if we translate "testimonia" as "claims of right," we find the dynamic of trial by battle in Burchard's ordinance far easier to understand. It is difficult to grasp why anybody would think that trial by battle might shed light on uncertain facts. It is easy to understand why trial by battle might be used to settle claims of right.

At any rate, if the disputants cannot work out their conflicting claims without an oath, they are to gather their "witnesses," their supporters, around them. After these supporters "collaudunt" — that is to say, loudly declare their approval of their respective leaders — one supporter from each side is to step forward to engage in trial by battle. The two battlers are not to take oaths, any more than their masters did. But the master of the loser — most likely dead — is to be treated as a giver of "false witness," "as though he had committed perjury." Thus (as we have already seen) the issue of battle serves as the functional equivalent of oath-taking, in a setting in which all of the participants resisted taking an oath. Indeed, what stands out, in this passage, is the sheer reluctance of everybody involved to swear an oath. Like Charlemagne, Burchard prefers to encourage deadly battles, rather than demanding that his subjects swear oaths.

People avoided swearing oaths if they could. High-status disputants preferred trial by battle. Witnesses and accusers refused to come forward. These are facts of basic importance for understanding the "lack of human testimony" that was a prerequisite for the administration of the ordeal. Human testimony was not necessarily lacking because the truth was unknown or undetectable — though that was surely sometimes the case. In many instances, there must have been plenty of witnesses who were quite sure that they knew what had happened, as descriptions from our twelfth-century English sources clearly suggest.[119] Human testimony was lacking primarily because people refused to give it, and especially to give it under oath.

It is unsurprising, then, that our sources rarely seem to turn on any deep uncertainty about the facts. It is hard to find many narratives in which the ordeal is used as a species of divination, intended to detect undetected facts — especially outside the context of theft, paternity, and adultery cases. Sometimes medieval Europeans turned to the judgment of God in the sorts of cases assumed by the Law of the Family of Worms discussed above: cases in which there were conflicting claims of right. Sometimes they did so in cases of fama

— of the ill-fame of persons of whose guilt everybody in town was quite sure. Those conflicting claims of right, and instances of ill-fame, occasionally did involve disputed facts. But even when the facts were somehow in serious doubt, the sources do not present the ordeal as a method of factual detection. Instead, the sources present these cases as raising questions of personal honor, in which the "testimonies," the stories of the relevant parties, conflicted.

The judgment of God was not, in short, a test of truth, in such cases. It was exactly what it appeared to be: a test of truth*fulness*, of the veracity of the parties. It is true that our sources declare that the ordeal reveals "things that are hidden or unknown," through "the judgments of Him who alone knows the hearts of the sons of men."[120] But what those judgments reveal is not a fact that nobody knows. They reveal whether the human witnesses have "lied or concealed the truth." As the standard law on trial by battle declared, the loser is a perjurer, while the winner has spoken the truth. This is what God knows, in knowing "the hearts of the sons of men." Gaudemet put the point most crisply: the procedure that we are accustomed to, the procedure that developed after the decline of the ordeal, is oriented toward proof of facts. "The aim is to establish a fact, a crime, a purchase, a testament, etc." By contrast, in the system of ordeals "the aim is to say whether such-and-such a person is worthy of confidence, if we can put our faith in what he says."[121]

One last illustration, from late eleventh-century England, will help to make clear the dynamic of trial in the age of the ordeals, when the responsibility for testimony and judgment mattered much more than factual proof. We have a rich body of records from the last decades of the eleventh century. These records are never easy to interpret, especially since they often come from religious sources; but read carefully they give us a vivid sense of the ways of justice a century before the emergence of the English common law.

We possess the following narrative, for example, from a monastic historian, describing events that took place sometime between 1079 and 1083. This story helps us understand how a dispute between honorable persons was ideally to be resolved — and of how little the underlying assumptions of the late eleventh century resembled our own. It turns on a property dispute between Bishop Wulfstan of Winchester and Abbot Walter of Evesham, both of whom claimed control of certain villages. In a sense, this case involved a dispute over facts: the key question was which party had enjoyed rights over the property in question before the Norman Conquest. But our narrative does not treat that question as mysterious or difficult to answer. On the contrary: *all* of the witnesses in the narrative agreed, supporting the bishop. The drama in the narrative is entirely about the willingness of those witnesses to testify under oath, upon holy relics: "The bishop declared that he had lawful witnesses who had seen how things were in the time of King Edward. . . . Where-upon at the command of the king's justice and by the decree of the barons, judgment was reached. Since the abbot said that he had no witnesses against the bishop, the magnates gave judgment that the bishop should name his witnesses and produce them at the appointed day to prove under oath the words of bishop, whereas the abbot could bring in whatever relics he wanted." There is no meaningful dispute about the facts here. There are only witnesses (or at least willing witnesses) for one side. From an evidentiary point of view, the case is a slam dunk. It is also worth noting that the bishop, in this narrative, like the disputants in Burchard's Law of the Family of Worms, does not take an oath himself, instead leaving the oath to his witnesses, just as he might have left the fighting of trial by battle to a champion.

At any rate, the narrative goes on to describe the dénouement: "[On the day appointed for trial,] the abbot produced the relics, viz. the body of Saint Ecgwin. On the part of the bishop several trustworthy persons were present, prepared to swear the aforesaid oath. . . . When the abbot saw the sworn proof was ready and would certainly proceed if he was willing to receive it, he accepted his friends' counsel and renounced the oath in favor of the bishop."[122] Why was the abbot involved in this dispute at all, when he had (as we are told) *no* witnesses to support his claim? Why, to put it in contemporary American language, did this one ever go to trial? The answer is not that the facts were in any way subject to dispute. It is that the abbot hoped that the bishop's witnesses would refuse to swear upon a relic as imposing as the body of Saint Ecgwin — that they would be so intimidated by the awe of God and the saint that they would buckle. In the event, he proved wrong.

The case of the bishop of Winchester against Abbot Walter of Evesham shows us the eleventh-century system working as it was meant to work. It was a system for small communities, with sharply defined social hierarchies, in which deep mysteries about the facts were far less common than they are today. The law in these communities was not oriented toward the detection of uncertain facts, as modern urban law is. It aimed to guarantee that disputes over claims of right were resolved on the say-so of the local magnates, the powerful men in the society. Accordingly, resolution of conflict, in this system, hinged on the willingness of "lawful," "trustworthy" witnesses to give testi-mony under oath upon relics. Such witnesses, however, were not always avail-able. Giving oaths upon relics was an intimidating business. Moreover, high-status persons were, at least sometimes, reluctant to swear oaths in their own interest, since the temptation to commit the perilous act of perjury was strong. Lower-status persons could not give dispositive oaths at all. Their cases might be settled by witness testimony, though. In a pinch, the ordeals of hot iron, cold water, and the rest could effectively convert the testimony of low-status persons into testimony with the validity of a trustworthy oath. Through the ordeal, low-status persons could "take God as their witness," just as their superiors did by oath, demonstrating their commitment and fortitude by undergoing an ordeal.

Now, in offering this account of the workings of the judgment of God, I do not mean to suggest that there is nothing else to be said about it. The judgment of God was a complex social institution. We should not exaggerate the extent to which there was a "system" or well-worked-out "law" of ordeals that could be presented in some kind of nutshell. Medieval observers themselves were not always exactly sure when or why ordeals were used. Regional differences also deserve more investigation than I can give them.

My aim is only to insist on one thing that ordeals were usually not, and one thing that they usually were. Judgments of God were usually *not* investigations of facts that could not be discovered by "other methods." They usually *were* the functional equivalent of sworn oaths, in a world in which no person could be convicted except on the basis of sworn testimony. They typically took place not when no one had information about what had happened but when high-status persons were unwilling to swear under oath, witnesses were unwilling to testify, and accusers were unwilling to bring accusations. To put the point a bit differently, the system of ordeals made it unnecessary for unwilling witnesses and accusers to come forward.

This has a significant implication for the rise of jury trial, and of the new Continental law of the thirteenth century as well: there was only one means of compensating for the decline of the ordeal. If there were no judgments of God, witnesses would have to be *compelled* to testify; accusers would have to be *compelled* to bring accusations; and accused persons would have to be *compelled* to confess. As we shall see, this is exactly what happened in England during the twelfth and thirteenth centuries, and on the Continent somewhat later. Eliminating the judgment of God meant, above all, forcing human beings to swear oaths. The drama of the decline of the ordeal is thus the drama of the rise of compelled testimony, compelled accusation, and compelled confession.

The View from the Theologians

Let us now view the ordeal, finally, through the eyes of Christian theologians.

When theologians of the eleventh, twelfth, and thirteenth centuries looked upon the judgment of God, they saw a variety of dangers. They did not always condemn the judgment of God out of hand. But they worried about the moral dangers faced by two different actors. First and foremost, there was the danger that clerics would be polluted by bloodshed in pronouncing their blessing. This was the danger condemned by the Fourth Lateran Council in the canon "Judgments of Blood," with which I ended chapter 2.

But theologians worried about something else too, which did not appear in the text drawn up by the council. They were troubled by the moral dangers that confronted witnesses. The judgments of God were deeply implicated in the theology of sworn testimony. On the one hand, they were an alternative to "human testimony." They were a form of functional oath that did not require any honorable person to put his soul in peril. In consequence, they spared human witnesses the risk of perjury, a mortal sin. Yet this meant that if the ordeals were eliminated, witnesses would face a dangerous temptation to commit perjury. The same was true of accusers. It is in the light of these twin dangers — the dangers to clerics and the dangers of perjured testimony and accusation — that I shall now consider the theological literature.

Throughout the early and central Middle Ages, theologians were consistently hostile to the judgment of God to one degree or another. Much of the early hostility was toward trial by battle, for which the church tried to substitute the ordeal of the cross. The low-status ordeals also stirred hostility, though, as early as the ninth century, and the campaign against them continued thereafter, gathering particular steam in the later decades of the twelfth century.[123] The formal condemnation of 1215 was only the high-water mark of a long history of hostility.

Why did theologians object to the judgment of God? In part, they were concerned with scripture: theologians argued from an early date that the scriptural authority for ordeals was thin.[124] Some of their complaints had to do with the high acquittal rates associated with the judgment of God. As Fraher has shown, churchmen, like secular leaders, were concerned that too many crimes were going unpunished.[125] Sometimes they complained that the ordeals, especially in cases of alleged theft, resulted in the conviction of the innocent.[126] Finally, theologians made two particularly fundamental objections, whose importance was underlined in a famous article by John Baldwin forty years ago: first, they held that the ordeals "tempted God"; and second, they held that the ordeals involved clergy in bloodshed. These are the two objections that I shall emphasize as well; they are of prime importance for the theology of jury trial. The doctrine of the temptation of God spoke directly to the moral responsibility of witnesses, while the doctrine of clerical bloodshed spoke to that of judges.

Let us begin with the temptation of God. From an early date, theologians complained that ordeals tempted God, a complaint made with particular vigor during the twelfth and thirteenth centuries. What was "tempting God"? This phrase sounds very odd to our ears, but that is because the word "tempt" has shifted in meaning. The Latin "tentare" means (among other things) to "put somebody or something to a test," and when Saint Jerome translated the Hebrew Bible into Latin, he chose "tentare" as the Latin equivalent for the Hebrew "nasah," "to put to the test." Nasah is an important term in the Jewish tradition: in particular, the Jewish God sometimes puts Israel, or the wicked, to a test.[127] But in a few passages, the Old Testament reverses the customary roles of man and God. Instead of God putting man to the test, man puts God to the test, by asking for a miraculous sign. The famous passage of Isaiah said to prophesy the birth of Christ uses that phrase:

> [10] Again the LORD spoke to Ahaz, [11] "Ask the LORD your God for a sign, whether in the deepest depths or in the highest heights."
>
> [12] But Ahaz said, "I will not ask; I will not put the LORD to the test."
>
> [13] Then Isaiah said, "Hear now, you house of David! Is it not enough to try the patience of men? Will you try the patience of my God also? [14] Therefore the Lord himself will give you a sign: The virgin will be with child and will give birth to a son, and will call him Immanuel."

"Et dixit Ahaz non petam et non temptabo Dominum," as Jerome translated verse 7:12, "I will not importune and I will not tempt God." The New Testament too included a famous prohibition against tempting God, in Jesus' response to Satan: "Do not put the Lord your God to the test," "non temptabis Dominum Deum tuum."[128] To "tempt God" thus became a standard phrase, in the language of Latin Christendom, for asking for a miraculous sign.

The virgin birth was one example of a miraculous sign; and of course the successful judgment of God was another. The judgment of God was nothing other than a means of asking God for a sign. But why did theologians object to doing so? Here, as so often, we must read more deeply in Saints Augustine and Jerome. When twelfth-century theologians attacked "tempting God" through the ordeal, they did so on the basis of a passage from Augustine's commentary on Genesis. In that passage, the great saint, drawing on Jerome, condemned those who remitted matters to God's judgment in cases where men were capable of uncovering the truth themselves.[129] It was this argument upon which critics of the ordeal seized: ordeals were dangerous forms of tempting God — precisely because they were used, at least some of the time, when men were perfectly capable of determining the truth themselves.[130]

Thus the author of a French text of the early 1180s declared that ordeals were a "superstitious" evil — because they were applied in cases where the answer was already certain.[131] In fact, as Baldwin showed, the theologian, who denounced the ordeals did not denounce ordeals as a false means of fact-finding. Quite the contrary: for leading critics, the problem with ordeals was *not* their use as a method of investigation in the absence of evidence at all. Instead, they objected to ordeals precisely because they were inflicted where the guilt of the accused was already obvious, or could be readily discovered. These theologians simply took it for granted that matters of fama and the like were being turned over to the judgment of God, even though they could easily have been disposed of through human testimony. They assumed that other evidence *was* available.

I hope it is obvious that this theological complaint should be viewed against the background of the law of ordeals I have just sketched. It is a complaint that makes perfect sense when seen in the context of a world in which the truth was usually known to some or many, or easily determined, but the witnesses resisted giving testimony. The implication of the condemnation of "tempting God" was thus that humans would have to accept the responsibility involved in giving sworn testimony. Where divine testimony was declared out of bounds, human testimony would have to come in as a substitute. The implication, in short, was exactly the implication we have already traced: witnesses would have to be compelled to testify.

To say that was not to settle all theological questions, however. As theologians constantly emphasized, human testimony was full of "peril" for those who gave it. Here their favorite text was the story of Susanna, frequently invoked in the literature of the day. The story of Susanna is found in chapters of the book of Daniel that are now regarded as apocryphal. Medieval readers believed it to be authentic, though, and they used it as a basic narrative for the law of witness testimony. Susanna, a beautiful young virgin, was spotted, while bathing in her walled garden, by two elders. When she was alone, the elders approached her and demanded her sexual favors. They threatened that if she refused, they would testify that they had seen her fornicating with a lover. She refused them; they testified falsely against her; and her condemnation was imminent. At the last moment, though, the young Daniel thrust himself into the affair. He examined the two elders separately and found inconsistencies in their stories, and in this way saved Susanna.

The story of Susanna was a key text for medieval canonists, upon which they built in creating their law of procedure.[132] It provided, after all, a scriptural lesson on how to handle the pressing problem of witness testimony — and more narrowly, the pressing problem of *false* witness testimony. Medieval moralists inveighed constantly against false witnesses, of which the two lecherous elders were the prime examples. The dangers of the false witness were a staple of the ordeal texts, just as they were of other species of moral literature. Blessings over the ordeal frequently made reference to Susanna, whom God had "rescued from the false suspicion of crime."[133] At the same time, religious ordeal narratives featured the false accuser. This is true, for example, of one of the most frequently discussed English ordeal narratives: the case of Ailward. Ailward, falsely accused by the scurrilous Fulk the Reeve, was subjected to the ordeal of cold water in the 1170s. (He failed.)[134]

And indeed, false testimony must have been a constant danger, as royal and church courts tried to establish their jurisdiction in closed rural communities. False testimony is a perennial problem in societies with newly emerging court systems. In part this is because local witnesses will often feel pressure to lie in order to protect other members of their community, or indeed themselves. In part, it is because they will often feel tempted to lie in order to gain an advantage or vengeance. When courts first become available in relatively small, traditional societies, people often seize upon them, exploiting the opportunity to denounce those neighbors against whom they have a grudge, or whose possessions they covet. We have ample evidence of this danger from various periods in legal history. For example, historians have shown that the establishment of courts in colonial Spanish America led to massive litigation, as indigenous persons sued their neighbors in an effort to inflict pain on their local enemies.[135] Daniel Smail has recently documented the same phenomenon in medieval Marseilles.[136] In societies like these, new court institutions invite self-interested perjury. Not least, all litigants are subject to the temptation to shade the truth to their own advantage. It is thus no surprise if theologians believed that witnesses and accusers were likely to lie, despite the spiritual dangers involved. The countryside, theologians were convinced, was full of what the thirteenth-century English theologian John of Wales called "rabid dogs" — false accusers, eager to sink their teeth into their neighbors.[137]

Indeed, both accusers and witnesses would have faced a double temptation: on the one hand, the temptation to lie in order to protect themselves or their neighbors; on the other hand, the temptation to lie in order to profit from the opportunities courts offered them. Consequently, as Hans Fehr argued in an article eighty years ago, the specter of the perjured witness constantly shadowed discussions of adjudication as the ordeal fell into decline.[138]

The judgment of the God had always been an alternative to the oath — which meant that it had always helped forestall the dangers of perjury. The decline of the judgment of God thus inevitably meant the dangers of perjury were magnified. Witnesses would have to testify, but it was expected that they might often lie, at great peril to their souls. The decline of the ordeals brought with it a shift in the responsibility for judgment, and a disturbing one. It meant compelling witnesses to testify at their inevitable spiritual peril.

The decline of the ordeal would also involve another disturbing shift in the responsibility for judgment: a shift to a new burden for judges.

As we have just seen, the Fourth Lateran Council condemned clerical participation in the ordeal, and reiterated previous condemnations of trial by battle. Clerics who blessed the judgment of God, the council declared, polluted themselves with bloodshed. They were no different from, and no better than, clerics who served as captains of "marauders, archers, and men devoted to bloodshed." Nor were they different from, or better than, surgeons who cut into human flesh, spilling human blood. They must be forbidden to lend their ministry to the ordeal.

This ban was in some ways entirely unsurprising. The ban on clerical participation in judgments of God was simply typical of a theology that reached far back into antiquity, as we have seen. But it had a significant implication that is not obvious at first glance. If there were to be no ordeals, then human trials would have to take their place. If God did not judge, humans would have to step in. Yet as we saw in chapter 2, instituting a system of human judges was by no means a theologically untroubled business. Judges too spilled blood.

As scholars of the theology of just war have long understood, the abolition of the ordeals drew on the same theology of bloodshed and just killing I traced in the last chapter.[139] As early as the ninth century, Agobard of Lyon denounced the use of ordeals in those terms. Agobard, who was an important advocate of Carolingian ideas of a Christian Peace,[140] based his denunciation of ordeals on the same grounds that were given for the Truce of God by the Council of Narbonne in 1054: ordeals involved the spilling of blood. This was the equivalent of spilling the blood of God himself, declared Agobard, using the familiar formula: "Whoever spills human blood, His blood is spilled as well: For man is made in the image of God."[141] Agobard was only the first such critic. There were many later attacks, too; and by the twelfth century they began to gather great momentum.

Several strands came together in the twelfth-century church attack on the judgments of God. In part the attack was aimed at trial by battle, which the church had viewed with suspicion for centuries.[142] The Second and Third Lateran Councils, dating respectively to 1130 and 1179, condemned jousts and tournaments for "spilling Christian blood." Canons promulgated at these councils denied a Christian burial to anyone who perished in such contests. It is these canons, scholars believe, that constituted the earlier prohibitions on trial by battle to which the Fourth Lateran Council referred: a ban on jousting was by implication a ban on any such violent bloodshed.[143] Combined with a variety of other hostile commentary from the early Middle Ages, they amounted to an important prohibition.[144]

Certainly by the end of the eleventh century the papacy was already applying the established theology of bloodshed to trial by battle. Thus in the 1190s, Pope Celestine III condemned the "depraved" custom by which disputants used trial by battle "when witnesses were not available" to resolve the matter. Combatants in these events were "homicidae," murderers; and so were clerics who participated. After all, "murder can be committed either in fact, or by precept or counsel." The priest who blessed the trial by battle did nothing other than give "precept and counsel."[145] We find, moreover, similar concerns about the low-status ordeals in the same period. A mid-twelfth-century Synod of Reims permitted the ordeal only if no mutilations were to follow upon it.[146] Similarly, the archbishop of Hamburg, writing sometime in the late twelfth century, decreed that clerics could bless the ordeals of hot iron and hot coals — but only if the participants executed a prior guarantee that they would not harm "the human body of those convicted."[147] The twelfth-century Pope Alexander III issued similar decrees.[148] Judgments of God were acceptable — but not if they resulted in blood punishments.

Meanwhile, church leaders were slowly working to create an alternative to traditional forms in adjudication within the church. Disputes between clergy had long been resolved in the same way as disputes between lay people: we have ample records of early medieval clergymen who fought trials by battle and subjected themselves to ordeals just as their lay contemporaries did.[149] Over the course of the twelfth century, though, church reformers developed alternative procedures that would allow clergy to avoid the judgment of God.

These procedures were designed for exactly the same class of cases as the ordeal: they involved cases of fama, of the ill-fame of clergymen. In the case of a cleric who was accused by the voice of the people of a failing such as simony or unchastity, church procedures rejected the judgment of God. Such accused clergy were to clear themselves exclusively through oath or through witness testimony. This was the "purgatio canonica," the "canonical purgation" of the church, which twelfth-century writers contrasted with the "vulgar purgation" or "peregrine purgation" of the lay world.[150] As Winfried Trusen has argued, it was the creation of this purgatio canonica that laid the foundations for postordeal procedure in Europe: clergy were the first to be compelled to swear in order to purge themselves, losing the option of resorting to a judgment of God.[151]

The spread of purgatio canonica meant that twelfth-century clergy were, increasingly, not to avail themselves of the judgment of God. At the same time, a developing body of prohibitions condemned clerical blessings over proceedings that would lead to the shedding of blood. These twelfth-century tendencies set the stage for an intellectual campaign against the judgment of God, and toward the end of the twelfth century, such a campaign began.

Scholars have long recognized that the most important figure in this campaign was the Paris theologian Peter the Chanter. Peter was an influential man — he was, not least, the teacher of Innocent III, the great lawyer pope who presided over the Fourth Lateran Council — and it is Peter's arguments that reappeared in the eventual abolition of the ordeals. Following the old theological tradition of Augustine and Jerome, Peter held that clerics who blessed the ordeal "lent their ministry to the spilling of blood."[152] Both the cleric who "blessed the [hot or cold] element" and "the accused who undergoes the judgment [of God]" committed mortal sin, he declared.[153] The cleric in particular courted great moral danger: when clerics blessed the ordeal, declared Peter, adopting the inveterate language of Augustinian theology, they "were made in a certain fashion into murderers."[154] As scholars have long seen, these were the very arguments that made their way into the canons of the Fourth Lateran Council. Canon 18 applied the theology of bloodshed to the judgments of God. Ordeals were akin to warfare.[155] They were "homicide by precept or counsel."

All of this is well understood. But historians have not quite seen its deeper implication for the theology of judging. We must remember the theology of judicial bloodshed traced in chapter 2 when we considered the law of the ordeals. The great campaign against ordeals was, in effect, a campaign for a kind of changing of the guard — for a transformation in the nature of the officialdom associated with judgment. In the system of ordeals, the official actor was a priest, pronouncing a blessing. Under the new trial systems, the priest was to be replaced by a judge, sometimes himself a clergyman but now serving in what canon lawyers, following their Roman predecessors, called the "officium judicis," the "judicial office." Yet simply substituting the trial for the ordeal could not eliminate all moral danger. The priest who blessed an ordeal associated himself, according to the Fourth Lateran Council, with the shedding of blood. This was unacceptable. But if bloodshed was the danger, suppressing the ordeals was not in itself enough to eliminate it.

After all, the shedding of blood was also an issue for judges. As we saw in the previous chapter, for Saint Augustine and Saint Jerome the office of the judge had to do precisely with bloodshed. Judges, like soldiers, were persons who shed blood. It was this that created the need for a moral theology of judging. In order to avoid becoming a "homicida," a murderer, the judge had to operate only as a "minister of the law." Fully resolving the problems of the ordeal thus required more than their abolition. It also required the establishment of procedures that could shield the judge himself from the dangers of bloodshed.

Canon 18 of the Fourth Lateran Council thus created a moral dilemma for judges, parallel to the moral dilemma it created for witnesses. If the judgments of God were to be abolished, witnesses would have to give sworn testimony. They would have to take the responsibility for judgment upon themselves. The same was true of judges. The abolition of the ordeals meant that clerics could no longer serve, in Peter the Chanter's striking phrase, as "ministers of bloodshed." But it also meant that judges would now have to avoid becoming "ministers of bloodshed" themselves, by becoming "ministers of the law."

Such were the dilemmas of moral responsibility created by the decline of the judicial ordeal. Where at least some of the burden of judgment had been shifted to God, it now fell to two classes of human actors: witnesses and judges. The two chapters that follow discuss how witnesses and judges shouldered that moral burden in two regions of Europe whose law was beginning to grow apart: the western Continent, and England.

*Salvation for the Judge, Damnation for
the Witnesses: The Continent*

Suppose that a man has been incriminated by false witnesses, but the judge knows that he is innocent. The judge must, like Daniel, examine the witnesses with great care, so as to find a motive for acquitting the innocent: but if he cannot do this he should remit him for judgment by a higher tribunal. If even this is impossible, the judge does not sin if he pronounces sentence in accordance with the evidence. For in that case, it is not the judge that puts an innocent man to death. Rather, it is those who declared him to be guilty.

— *Saint Thomas Aquinas,* Summa Theologica

Around 1250, a generation after the Fourth Lateran Council had condemned the ordeals as judgments of blood, an industrious Dominican monk named Vincent of Beauvais set out to compile a compendium of all the wisdom of the world as it was known to his age. Beauvais was a town where medieval Frenchmen were attempting to build the largest cathedral ever erected — an edifice that would collapse disastrously in 1284. Vincent wrote in the same local spirit of magnificent ambition, producing a massive work, known as the *Speculum Majus,* or *Great Mirror,* which surveyed both the whole history of the world and the whole compass of theology. Cribbing from all the leading authors of the day, Vincent vividly summed up the moral theology of law and judging as it had emerged on the Continent by the mid-thirteenth century, after two hundred years of church reform, and in the midst of a gathering effort by the monarchs, princes, and town leaders of Europe to take control of justice.

Dominicans like Vincent were members of a preaching order that had taken up the burden of warning Christians all over Europe against the dangers of sin, and the dangers of sin were Vincent's topic when it came to trial procedure in the era of the declining judicial ordeal. In particular, he addressed the moral predicaments of two actors with whom I closed the previous chapter: the judge and the witnesses. As Vincent presented the theology, these two faced sharply different situations. The soul of the judge was certainly imperiled. Nevertheless, the careful judge could always protect himself. The witnesses, by contrast, were in a treacherous position.

Figure 4. The Roman judge Lampadian, in a fourteenth-century illumination of the popular medieval historian Vincent de Beauvais, dragged off by a demon after unjustly condemning four Christian martyrs. *Judge Lampadian seized by a demon.* Vincent de Beauvais, *Miroir historial dit du roi Jean le Bon.* Paris, Bibliothèque Nationale, Ars MS 5080 RES, f. 214 (1333–1350).

To be sure, it was not the case that the judge faced no spiritual danger, as Vincent explained it. Quite the contrary. The judge, agent of bloody justice, faced a real moral predicament. Vincent began as theologians had begun for centuries, with the Fifth Commandment. No person was permitted to kill. "As the gospels say, 'He who accepts the sword, shall die by the sword.' "[1] Accordingly, judges could expect to approach their task in a state of anxiety. The church forbade the shedding of blood, and so "we desire to avoid killing malefactors." The perils were indeed great. There were, as Vincent explained, repeating standard canon doctrine,[2] four ways of killing: "for justice, out of free will, out of necessity, or by accident." Good judges understood how to kill strictly "for justice." They were "ministers," who did not kill "from spite or the pleasure in shedding human blood." But the judge who killed in any other way, who killed for any reason other than "love of justice," committed a mortal sin. "Peccat mortaliter," declared Vincent more than once, "He commits mortal sin."[3] Indeed, Vincent was fond of stories of judges suffering horrible fates: his *Mirror of History* included a number of tales of ancient judges who had been tempted by demons, carried off by demons, struck dead on the bench by bolts of lightening, and more.[4]

So judges had reason to fear. Yet harsh punishment had to be meted out to criminals. Like other thirteenth-century commentators, Vincent believed it was "a matter of public interest that crimes not go unpunished."[5] The European countryside and the European cities, full as they were of crime and sin, had to be brought to heel. As Vincent put it: "We do not want to neglect to discipline [criminals] by inflicting upon them the punishments they deserve." How, then, could judges punish criminals without danger to themselves? Judges, observed Vincent, might well be tempted to solve their conundrum by avoiding blood punishments entirely, substituting the lash: "Evildoers," they might conclude, "should be flogged, but their limbs should not be cut off, and their bodies should not be put to death."[6] Vincent's modern readers may find this solution quite appealing: Why indeed not simply refrain from mutilating and killing people? Yet Vincent insisted that judges could not escape that easily. Judges were obliged to administer blood punishments. The Old Testament made it clear that flogging was not sufficient: "God said to Moses, 'Thou shalt not suffer evildoers to live.' " Practitioners of bestiality, adulterers, and blasphemers were clearly marked out for a merciless death.[7] Manifestly blood punishments sometimes had to be inflicted.

How, then, was the pious judge to proceed? The answer, Vincent held, was to be found in Saint Augustine. No one was allowed to kill another "by his own authority." But it was not forbidden for a man with "public power" to put the guilty to death "by the rule of the law." A judge, serving in public office, was like a soldier: he acted not for himself but for the benefit of the community. Such a judge was not a "stranger in the celestial fatherland."[8] He remained among the saved. But he had to be careful to function purely as a "minister," acting out of "love of justice." In particular, Vincent concluded, drawing on the learning of his age, the judge could never condemn anyone to death unless he strictly followed the "order of the law": he had to kill "iuris ordine servato."[9]

The judge had to kill iuris ordine servato, strictly following the order of the law. If he scrupulously followed the procedures laid out by canon law, he would not need to "fear the punishments of the Last Judgment" when he "killed malefactors." Rigorous procedure, which the canon lawyers of the thirteenth century were diligently elaborating, would serve as the judge's spiritual armor.

Judges, going out to do war with the evildoers of the world, could thus keep themselves safe. Witnesses, by contrast, faced dangers more difficult to evade. They had, in general, no choice but to testify. "Remaining silent about the truth to the prejudice of another is mortal sin," explained Vincent, "and the church is obliged to correct sinners."[10] To be sure, there were certain situations in which the law was willing to excuse witnesses: if witnesses were old or infirm, they did not need to testify.[11] There was also no need for witnesses if an accuser came forward to make a formal accusation. In that case, the evidentiary burden was entirely upon the accuser, who was obliged to produce proof "clearer than the light of midday," or else take the consequences upon himself.[12] Cases in which such accusers came forward were rare, however. And in all other cases, declared Vincent, canon procedure required that witnesses be compelled to testify. Indeed, they had to be compelled for their own good: if witnesses remained silent, their souls would be damned. In fact, Vincent insisted that witnesses be compelled to testify even against their own relatives.

Vincent made it clear that he understood what a difficult position this rule put witnesses in. "The witness may easily run the risk of death," he observed, and of blood guilt as well.[13] And yet the witness was obliged to testify. Vincent tried to offer the witness a kind of escape route. Witnesses, he noted, could try to shade their testimony in an attempt to protect themselves, speaking in the spirit of loving correction of a fellow Christian: "It is sufficient to escape the fetters of sin if [the witness] just gives evidence by saying things that are more likely to help [his neighbor] than harm him, by correcting him or helping reconcile him to God."[14] How exactly the witness was supposed to manage this rhetorical feat, lovingly correcting his neighbor while "running the risk of death," Vincent did not pause to explain in any detail. In the end, he simply insisted that the witness had to testify.

At the same time, inevitably, Vincent warned witnesses thunderously against the dangers of perjured testimony. Again quoting standard literature, he declared that a "false witness" committed a threefold offense, against God, the judge, and the defendant.[15] Sometimes the witness might commit trivial mistakes, to be sure. In those cases, the witness committed a venial sin. But escape from guilt was not easy. The soul of any witness who knowingly gave false testimony was in peril. Moreover, even witnesses who claimed ignorance might commit mortal sin, declared Vincent, if their ignorance was "crass and supine." And what did that mean? As contemporary canon law explained, it was, in particular, "crass and supine" to claim ignorance about something that "everybody in town knows."[16]

This was not a cheery picture. To be sure, Vincent did not entirely abandon the milder teachings of earlier centuries. In particular, he held that sworn testimony should be a last resort, to be used only if the case could not be decided in any other way.[17] Nevertheless, the picture he painted was grim. Vincent and his colleagues were thrusting witnesses onto the frontlines of the war that was medieval justice, exposing them to multiple dangers: they might be killed; they might find themselves tainted by the blood of the person against whom they testified; and if they tried to equivocate, or even tried to plead ignorance, they might be damned.

Salvation for the judge, damnation for the witnesses. This chapter and the next describe how Western legal systems developed in the face of the moral theology that Vincent presented with such homely ferocity. Unlike their predecessors, thirteenth-century jurists and theologians like Vincent were no longer willing to tolerate a world in which "crime went unpunished," and they had taken up the sword. In this great campaign, judges were to follow certain procedures; and if they did so, they would be safe. Witnesses, by contrast, had to testify in ways that exposed them to potentially deadly peril.

By the time Vincent of Beauvais was finishing his *Mirror,* in the mid-thirteenth century, the two great Western legal systems — the "accusatorial" common law of England and the "inquisitorial" law of the Continent — had begun to take definitive shape. As I shall try to show in this chapter and the next, both took shape partly in response to the pressures of the moral theology of judging; in particular, both were systems effectively designed to protect judges from spiritual danger. Yet in both systems, protection for judges came at the cost of endangering witnesses — among them, the twelve witnesses of the common law jury. On both sides of the English Channel, the law developed in such a way as to shield judges, respectable members of governing classes, from the threat of damnation, while putting an ominous burden on witnesses, most especially ones of low status.

The Judge and the Witness are accordingly the two protagonists of my discussion. In addition to the judge and the witness, though, I shall discuss two other figures featuring in the medieval dramatis personae: the accuser and the accused. To understand the emergence of both the common law and the law of the Continent, we must understand how all four of these figures — accuser, accused, witness, and judge — were treated in the law on either side of the Channel.

The decline of the judicial ordeal brought with it new dilemmas for all four of these figures. In the high age of the judicial ordeal — before 1170 or so — the judge, the witness, the accuser, and the accused were all in a position to avoid considerable moral responsibility. The potential accuser was under no obliga-tion to undertake the perilous business of bringing an accusation. The witness, too, was under no obligation to undertake the perilous business of testifying under oath. As for the accused, he could not be compelled to confess, and he always had some means of attempting to avoid conviction. If an accused man was oath-worthy, he could clear himself through oath or trial by battle. If he was not oath-worthy, he could "take God as his witness" by undergoing an ordeal. An ordeal was certainly painful and frightening, but it frequently re-sulted in acquittal. The judge, finally, was in a favorable moral position as well: to the extent that cases were decided by judicial ordeal, they were de-cided by God — which meant that they were not decided by the judges them-selves. Thus in practice, no legal actor was consistently forced to take full responsibility for the consequences of judgment.

The transformation of Western justice in the late twelfth century changed all that. Beginning about 1170, the positions of all four figures began to shift ominously. In England, as we shall see in the next chapter, the monarchy attempted to create a system that represented a form of compelled accusation. The early common law, traditionally described as an accusatorial system, was indeed a system that involved a certain measure of compulsory accusation.

The Continent did not follow suit in that regard: on the Continent, the accuser was not generally compelled to bring an accusation. But if Continental law went relatively easy on the accuser, it went relatively hard on the accused: by the mid-thirteenth century, Continental law had increasingly moved to-ward a system in which the accused was threatened with torture in order to coerce a confession. In England, by contrast, torture of the Continental sort never established itself. From the point of view of moral theology, we can thus state the contrast between English law and Continental law in straightforward (if simplified) terms: postordeal England became a world of compulsory ac-cusation, whereas the postordeal Continent became a world of compulsory confession.

But both became worlds of compulsory witness testimony. Indeed, in the end, the key innovation of the period 1170–1250, on both sides of the Channel, was the same: the witnesses were forced to talk. The English monarchy took a line different, in this respect, from that taken by Continental law: the common law organized its witnesses into the panel of twelve who made up the jury. On the Continent too, though, witness testimony was compelled, even without any panel system. On both sides of the Channel, meanwhile, procedures were developed that protected judges from danger. As the ordeal declined in importance, trials presided over by judges became the norm; but all over the Western world, judges were shielded from blood guilt.

This chapter traces the changing fates of the accuser, the accused, the witness, and the judge in the law of the thirteenth-century Continent. It also traces the rise of important new developments in law and theology. In the course of discussing the positions of the accuser and the accused, the chapter presents the basic outlines of the inquisitorial procedure of the Continent and describes the system of judicial torture. In the course of discussing the position of the judge, it presents the developed medieval theology of judging — a theology that turned on two key terms, "conscience" and "doubt."

Continental Procedure (I): The Accuser and the Accused

Let us begin with the Continental accuser and accused as they were treated in the new thirteenth-century world of inquisitorial procedure and judicial torture.

As we have seen, European law traditionally held that a proceeding should be initiated, if possible, by an accuser: "Normal criminal procedure in the early Middle Ages hinged upon the appearance of an accuser, who brought the charge, offered to prove it, and took the consequences for failure to do so."[18] Yet bringing an accusation was a perilous business in the age of the judicial ordeal. Accusers might well be obliged to back up their accusations by putting their own lives on the line, submitting to judicial combat with the person accused. Even accusers who did not have to undergo judicial combat might be subject to other legal penalties if the trial did not result in a conviction — and trials often resulted in acquittals. What is more, the relatives of the accused person must often have stood menacingly in the wings. It is no surprise that potential accusers hung back, at least some of the time:[19] "Afraid of having to undergo judicial combat at the request of the accused man, [the accuser] remained silent," as we saw in one ordeal narrative.[20]

With the decline of the ordeal, the position of the accuser in Continental law began to change in some important ways — but it did not change enough to encourage Continental accusers to bring more accusations. The new Continental procedure of the twelfth and thirteenth centuries eliminated the requirement that the accuser engage in judicial combat.[21] But if the canonists dispensed accusers from any obligation to fight a judicial combat, they still subjected them to a heavy burden. As Vincent of Beauvais explained, they required the accuser to bring proof of his accusations that was "clearer than the light of the midday sun." James Brundage explains what this meant for the law of accusations under canon procedure: "[T]he established *ordo iuris* by the late twelfth century required an accuser to bring a charge, so that unless someone was prepared to step forward and make a public accusation, no prosecution could commence. Accusation was hazardous for the accuser, because if he failed to prove his allegations he became liable to punishment himself. Proof of an accusation, moreover, required the accuser to bring forward testimony from two credible persons who were prepared to testify under oath that they had personally witnessed the events or the behavior complained of."[22] Thus if canon lawyers relieved the accuser of the obligation of submitting to judicial combat, they substituted something that was almost as daunting: they required the accuser to produce two eyewitnesses who would accept the dangerous responsibility of testifying under oath. Accusers who failed to meet this stiff burden would suffer criminal penalties for having made their accusation.

This approach created an essentially insoluble dilemma. Canon procedure required an accuser: early twelfth-century canonists like Ivo of Chartres had insisted that there had to be a proper accusation in order to initiate a criminal proceeding.[23] Yet, considering the risks of bringing an accusation, one could be sure that accusers would rarely come forward.

It was in the search for a solution to this dilemma that canon lawyers developed their so-called inquisitorial procedure. Medieval inquisitorial procedure was partly used for tracking down heretics, as my readers will know. But it had a more complex history than that. It developed to deal with cases of *fama*, ill-fame — cases in which the anonymous voice of the people accused someone but no witness or accuser came forward. Brundage explains its origin:

> As early as the late eleventh century, church reformers had become acutely aware that the accusatory procedure . . . made it nearly impossible to prosecute [clerical] 'occult crimes' successfully. The 'occult crimes' that most immediately bothered the reformers were sex offences, especially clerical concubinage, fornication and adultery, as well as simony. . . .
>
> Efforts to mend this obviously unsatisfactory situation began to take shape around 1200 in the form of a new type of criminal process designed to deal more adequately with the 'occult crimes' that escaped successful prosecution

under the accusatory system. The new criminal process was inquisitorial procedure, so-called because it was conceived of as an investigatory process
initiated by public authorities, such as judges, who operated through inquiry
(*per inquisitionem*) into wrongdoing that was a matter of common knowledge
or grave suspicion (*notorium, manifesta* and *fama* were the terms generally
used to describe such affairs. No accuser was necessary under inquisitorial
procedure. In addition the rules of evidence were relaxed so as to make conviction easier to obtain . . .). Inquisitorial procedure did not require 'full proof'
but instead demanded only an accumulation of 'partial-proofs,' such as inferences or presumptions (*indicia*) that pointed to the defendants' guilt, provided that some more-or-less direct evidence was available to confirm them.[24]

Such was "inquisitorial procedure," with its system of "partial proofs." It was
a system intended to deal with exactly the same circumstance previously dealt
with by the ordeal: it was used in cases in which "and the voice of the public is
saying that a person is guilty"[25] but no witness would speak up — cases, that is,
in which the accused was widely suspected, but no one would give testimony.

In the high age of the ordeal, such suspected persons, if of low status, would
have faced an ordeal, and they would have had a fair chance of surviving: the
system of ordeals gave them a chance to "take God as their witness" in order to
prove the veracity of their claim of innocence. By the thirteenth century, the
new inquisitorial procedure no longer permitted accused persons to take God
as their witness in this way. Instead, it threatened something more fearsome,
and more likely to produce a conviction. If the partial proofs produced
through inquisition were weighty enough, inquisitorial procedure would turn
to judicial torture, in order to extract from the accused a confession.[26]

It is important to emphasize that this inquisitorial system, despite its use of
judicial torture, was by no means arbitrary. It was both intellectually sophisticated and highly regulated. The new Continental system was founded on the
so-called romano-canonical practice of proof, which reached its first maturity
during the thirteenth century, and which continued to lie at the foundation of
Continental law for a half-millennium thereafter. This new romano-canonical
procedure grew up largely in the universities,[27] and it breathed their air of logic
and systematicity. It was founded on a carefully worked-out law of proof:
under this Continental system, as it developed in the thirteenth century, the
judge was to apply a set of elaborate rules, following a detailed schedule that
assigned different weights to different pieces of evidence.[28]

And this elaborate system was intended to make it difficult to proceed either
to torture or to punishment. Medieval criminal procedure was by no means
unrelentingly fierce. The romano-canonical rules were applied in any case that
might result in a blood punishment; and following long-standing Christian

traditions, always suspicious of blood punishment, they were designed to set great obstacles in the path of judgment. In particular, the romano-canonical rules used the same standard used for valid accusations: blood punishments could only be administered if the guilt of the accused was documented through proofs that were "luce meridiana clariores," "clearer than the light of the midday sun."[29] But what counted as such proof? Here again canon procedure used the same rule that was used for accusers: it required the testimony of two unimpeachably trustworthy eyewitnesses. Such testimony constituted "full proof" — "plena probatio" in the Latin of the Middle Ages. Inquisitorial procedure thus transferred to the court the burden that fell upon the accuser in accusatory procedure. Under accusatory procedure, the accused was required to produce two witnesses. Under inquisitorial procedure this became the obligation of the court.

So the inquisitorial court was obliged to induce at least two witnesses to talk, if possible. Of course, the testimony of two unimpeachably trustworthy eyewitnesses was rarely available. Some offenses were witnessed by only one person, or none. But even where eyewitnesses existed — as they might well have in cases of heresy or feud killings, for example — it was unlikely that they would willingly testify. To be sure, as we shall see shortly, the new canon procedure called for such witnesses to be compelled. But even the theoretical possibility of compulsory testimony did not guarantee that full proof would always be attained. So what was to be done if full proof was impossible? It was only in cases in which full proof was lacking that Continental law called for judicial torture. Torture could not be ordered in all cases. Persons of high social standing — members of the nobility and the like — could not be tortured at all. Even with regard to lower-status persons, moreover, judges were forbidden to order torture unless there were "half-full proof" — "semiplena probatio,"[30] proof that was the equivalent of the testimony of a single eyewitness. A confession extracted by torture also had to be repeated voluntarily in court. This last limitation is one that John Langbein is surely right to regard as "feeble."[31] Nevertheless, taken together, these restrictions do show that the application of torture was never a matter of wholly uncircumscribed discretion. Continental law treated the decision to torture as weighty and troubling.

We shall return to the regulation of torture shortly, when we pass to the figure of the judge and his moral responsibility. For the moment, let me focus on the relationship of this system of judicial torture to the older system of the judicial ordeal.

It should be obvious that judicial torture of the accused, as it emerged in the thirteenth century, bore a close relationship to its predecessor, the judicial ordeal. Both were brutal and painful proceedings. There is an unmistakable resemblance between the older system, which relied on the pain and fear of hot iron and cold water, and the newer system, which relied on the pain and fear of the rack, the wheel, and the screws. Both were used to deal with low-status persons; respectable people were immune from judicial torture, just as they had been immune from the judicial ordeal. Like so many other procedures in the premodern world, both judicial torture and the judicial ordeal were designed to reflect, and reinforce, the fundamental distinction between high and low in society.[32] Moreover, both judicial torture and the judicial ordeal were used in the same procedural setting: as we saw in the previous chapter, the ordeal was used in cases in which there was fama, but neither accusers nor witnesses came forward to testify, and the accused low-status person did not confess. These were the same circumstances in which Europeans later turned to torture. (We shall see in the next chapter that they were also the circumstances in which the English turned to jury trial.) Not least, both judicial torture and the judicial ordeal were intended, at least in part, to coerce confession. As we have seen, the canon law literature had always declared that the threat of the ordeal could serve to "torture people into confessing."[33] The same is of course true of judicial torture. It may well be the case that torture was rarely inflicted, as scholars have argued — but the *threat* of torture must surely have sufficed to induce a confession often enough.

In all these respects, the new system of judicial torture played much the same structural role that the judicial ordeal played. The critical difference is that the system of judicial torture left less room for an acquittal. Torture was the product of the tough-minded attitude toward crime that we saw in the writings of Vincent of Beauvais, who wrote: "We do not want to neglect to discipline [criminals] by inflicting upon them the punishments they deserve." As we saw in the last chapter, this was the dominant attitude among the churchmen who advocated the abolition of the ordeal: these were men who believed that it was "a matter of public interest that crimes not go unpunished.' "[34] Judicial torture was the creation of such men. It was a physically brutal business, just like the judicial ordeal. But it was a physically brutal business that showed less willingness to allow the guilty to escape.[35] Perhaps, given all its limitations, the system represented only a modest step toward greater severity in the prosecution of crime. Nevertheless, it certainly was a step in that direction.

There is one thing, however, that judicial torture was not: it was not the product of some evolution in the conception of factual proof. Here I must pause to reject, in particular, the influential interpretation of John Langbein. Langbein has treated the relationship between the judicial ordeal and judicial torture as a chapter in the history of factual proof. Following the common line of interpretation, he argues that the judicial ordeal was a factual proof procedure: the ordeal was a kind of oracle, designed to achieve certainty through the intervention of God. Correspondingly, Langbein interprets judicial torture as a device intended to achieve certainty through a different means. As he has recently put it, summarizing work he was done over many years: "The ordeals purported to achieve absolute certainty . . . through the happy expedient of having the judgments rendered by God, who could not err. . . . The new criminal procedure aspired to an equivalent level of safeguard—absolute certainty—for adjudication by mortals."[36]

Yet as we saw in the last chapter, there is little reason to believe that the judicial ordeal was intended primarily as some sort of magical fact-finding procedure. It was not a business by which God did a magical "investigation" in case of factual uncertainty. Instead it was a procedure that served as the equivalent of oath taking for low-status persons, one that frequently allowed them to escape punishment. The basic forms of factual proof in the system of judicial ordeals were no different from the basic forms of factual proof in the system of judicial torture. There was no transition from magical forms of proof to nonmagical forms of proof. Both systems made use of confession and witness testimony. The underlying assumption in both systems was that the accused was, in the ordinary case, clearly guilty. The difference between the two was that accused persons and witnesses were not compelled to talk in the older system, whereas they *were* compelled to talk in the newer one, at least in theory. The right interpretation of the transition from the judicial ordeal to judicial torture is thus not Langbein's. The credit for the right interpretation belongs to Richard Fraher, who has correctly seen that the great transition was simply one to a much tougher approach to the prosecution of crime among the lower orders.

This meant hard times for the accused on the Continent. It also meant hard times for the witnesses, to whom I now turn.

Continental Procedure (II): The Witness

The judicial ordeal was classically used, as we have seen, in cases in which there was no human testimony—cases in which there was fama, ill-fame, but witnesses would not come forward. The new canon law of the twelfth and thirteenth centuries showed a growing unwillingness to tolerate witness recalcitrance, and by the mid-thirteenth century churchmen were insisting that witnesses simply had to speak up.

Gratian's *Decretum* stated the fundamental principle in the mid-twelfth century. There were, the *Decretum* explained, four ways in which human judgment could be perverted by sin: through fear, through greed, through hatred, and through love.[37] Greed, hatred, and love were all emotions that might motivate a person to incriminate another falsely, whereas fear could motivate a person to refuse to speak at all. Such behavior was condemned by the *Decretum:* "Anybody who hides the truth out of fear of the power of someone else, calls down upon himself the wrath of God, because he fears Man more than he fears God. . . . One person may hide the truth, while another utters a lie. Both are criminals, since the former wants to avoid betraying someone, while the second wishes to do someone harm."[38] This passage shows that the canonists understood perfectly well that fear was what prevented witnesses from testifying: testifying was a dangerous business. Yet Gratian's text implied that refusal to testify was no less a mortal sin than leveling false accusations. And leveling false accusations was a deadly sin indeed; on that point, the writings of the theologians and jurists were agreed, as the constant invocation of the story of Susanna in the texts of the period drove home.

If the *Decretum* made it clear that failure to testify was a mortal sin, though, it did not clearly declare that witnesses could be legally *compelled* to testify. Only gradually did canon lawyers arrive at the conclusion that it was desirable to compel testimony. We see canonists reaching that conclusion, possibly for the first time, around 1190, in the realms of the English king. At a time when the English Crown was moving toward a strong program of compelling witnesses to testify, we find the following discussion in a canonist author:

Whether Witnesses can be Compelled

If the witness was present at the events in question of his own free will [sponte interfuit], he can be compelled to testify. . . . Not so if he was there by chance. [It is more appropriate to compel persons who are afraid to testify than to compel persons who say they have no reason to fear. . . .] This is because anyone who does not say he has something to fear, but who still refuses to testify, is presumed to feel doubt about the justice of the cause of the person on whose behalf he would testify. But it is presumed that persons who are afraid would want to testify if they dared to do so. . . .[39]

Only witnesses who had good reason to fear could be compelled to testify. In the analysis of this Anglo-Norman canonist we see the dilemma of the medieval witness in its rawest form. Later medieval governments, with their growing power, aimed to compel witnesses to speak "in order that crimes should not go unpunished." But this landed the witnesses in an extraordinarily difficult position. We shall learn more about how difficult the position of English witnesses was in the next chapter.

Continental authors were slower to come to the conclusion that witnesses could be compelled; and Continental law never assumed that it would be possible to collect adequate witness testimony in every case. Perhaps this is un-surprising: Continental governments, weaker at first than the English Crown, were less able to compel testimony. But by the second quarter of the thirteenth century or so, they had begun to take their own draconian stand.[40] We have already seen Vincent of Beauvais' summary of thirteenth-century Continental views. Fraher has cited one leading canonist, Hostiensis, for the proposition that witnesses should be compelled to speak. Others can be cited as well. "It is a mortal sin to hide the truth," as they often declared.[41] Durand, the great thirteenth-century authority on criminal procedure, insisted that witnesses could be compelled to speak in cases of fama.[42] His later thirteenth-century follower Albertus Gandinus even held that witnesses could be tortured if they "vacillated," declaring at one time that they had been present at a crime while at another denying knowledge of it.[43] Like his Anglo-Norman predecessor a century earlier, Gandinus knew that he had to deal with witnesses who were too intimidated to talk.

Witnesses were to be forced to speak: silence was a mortal sin.

Yet speaking could also be dangerous to the soul. Moralist authors never ceased citing the tale of Susanna. Bearing false witness was indeed a horrible sin; Dante placed false witnesses in the eighth circle of his Hell, almost at the very core of evil.[44] Much lore surrounded the evils of the lying witness: "abun-dant" medieval tales existed "of perjurious oath takers being struck dumb prior to, or collapsing immediately after, their oath."[45] All this played its role in the making of the law: in creating their law of evidence, the canon lawyers drew directly on the tale of Susanna. The very job of the judge was to detect and expose the false witness. If witnesses had to speak, by doing so they entered upon a business of extreme moral peril. We have already seen Vin-cent's summary of the state of the law by the mid-thirteenth century: almost any choice the witness made could lead him into great peril. If he spoke truthfully, he exposed himself to the vengeance of those he incriminated. Yet if he remained silent, he might commit a mortal sin. Above all, if he lied, or even tried to shade the truth, he was damned.

Continental Procedure (III): The Judge and His Conscience

Let us now turn at last to the figure of the judge, and to the moral theology of "conscience" and "doubt" that kept him comparatively safe from danger.

On the face of it, one might imagine that the judge was the figure most directly endangered by the decline of the ordeal. As leading reformers saw it, participating in ordeals tainted the clergy involved with blood; it made them, in Peter the Chanter's phrase, "ministers of bloodshed." Accordingly, reformers denounced the ordeals, holding that trials would have to take their place. Yet substituting the trial for the ordeal did not by any means eliminate the problem of blood guilt. Quite the contrary: theologians had warned for centuries that judges presiding over trials risked making themselves into "murderers," "homicidae." If the ordeal threatened to involve a priest in bloodshed, the trial threatened to do exactly the same thing to the judge. Medieval doctrine brought the connection between judging and blood home in its iconography: The frequently copied opening words of the Book of Wisdom — *Love justice, o Ye who judge the Earth!* — were commonly illustrated with a sword-bearing king, sometimes handing off a sword to a soldier (see figure 3, chapter 3). Law remained a way of making war on the world.

Moreover, judges faced another danger as well, which has been emphasized by Robert Jacob: they took an oath, which by its nature put their salvation at risk.[46]

One would have supposed, in short, that the decline of the ordeals put the judge in exceptional peril. Yet in practice, the judge emerged from the great transition of the period in far less effective danger than any of the other three figures we have discussed: the accuser, the accused, and the witness. Theologians and jurists succeeded in shielding the judge from spiritual risks. They drew on Augustinian theology in order to guarantee that the judge could act merely as a minister of the law: they found ways to permit the judge to declare, in the often-repeated formula of Augustine, *It is the law that kills him, and not I.* They achieved this result partly by drawing on the theology of doubt, as we shall see in the final section of this chapter. But they also protected the judge, as we shall see in this section, by scrupulously distinguishing his role from the role of the witness.

This was indeed the core proposition of medieval moral theology: the roles of judge and witness must be kept strictly separate. The basic tale of this theology was told forty years ago by Knut Wolfgang Nörr.[47] It is a tale of judicial efforts to avoid the moral responsibility for judgment — efforts that often strike the modern reader as bizarre, and ones in which the themes of blood taint and private knowledge played the dominant role. The key formula for medieval canon lawyers read as follows: "Iudex secundum allegata non secundum conscientiam iudicat," "the judge judges according to the evidence presented, not according to his 'conscience.'" What the formula did was to forbid judges to use their independent knowledge of the case — their "private knowledge." It was a formula that led to strange moral paradoxes for the judges of the Continent, and severe moral dilemmas for the criminal jurors of early modern England.

To grasp the theology in question, we must begin by understanding the ambiguities of the *word* "conscience," as well as the character of the *law* of conscience. I begin with the ambiguous word "conscience." "Conscience" has a long history in the West, extending back both to the Stoic philosophers and to Saint Paul. The original form of the word "conscience" is Greek: this is Saint Paul's "syneidesis,"[48] upon which the Latin "conscientia" was modeled. Both terms are built from roots meaning "knowledge of facts" — "eidesis" in Greek, "scientia" in Latin. Literally, "syn-eidesis" and "con-scientia" mean something like "shared knowledge" or, perhaps better, "deepened knowledge." This has important consequences for the meaning of the word "conscience." In Latin (as in modern-day Romance languages) the term is ambiguous, in a way important for the history I recount here. On the one hand, "conscientia" can signify a form of moral apperception — an ability to distinguish between right and wrong. It is in that sense, of course, that we use the word "conscience" in English today. But the Latin "conscientia" — like the modern French "conscience" or the modern Italian "coscienza" — can also mean "awareness of certain facts," or "the state of being informed."[49] This ambiguity matters a great deal for the history of Christian judicial ethics. Both senses of the term played important roles in Christian thinking about the proper role of the conscientious judge: "the conscience of the judge" can refer both to the judge's moral convictions *and* to the judge's knowledge of particular facts — to what canon lawyers would call his "private knowledge,"[50] the knowledge he had as a witness.

"Conscience," this ambiguous word, was the subject of a whole body of law, the law of conscience. The problem of conscience was always centrally important to Christian thought throughout the later Middle Ages and the early modern period. Sometimes it was the problem of "knowledge of facts." But it was first and foremost the problem of "conscience" conceived as an inner moral voice — an inborn sensitivity to the danger of sin, implanted by God. Our conscience was the voice of our "internal forum," the voice, implanted by God, of the "little judge" who sits within us, passing upon the rightness and wrongness of our every act.

In the medieval tradition, though, the governance of conscience was not left entirely to the inner voice. The regulation of conscience was also associated with a particular institutional structure: the conscience of the individual Christian was supervised within the confessional. Confession probably has a long history in the Christian world. But it is especially associated with the same Fourth Lateran Council of 1215 that forbade priests to participate in the shedding of blood. Alongside its ban on clerical association with the shedding of blood, the Fourth Lateran Council promulgated the famous canon "omnis utriusque sexus" — "perhaps the most important legislative act in the history of the Church," as Henry Charles Lea declared in his classic *History of Auricular Confession.*[51] This canon required that "all the faithful of both sexes shall after they have reached the age of discretion faithfully confess all their sins at least once a year to their own (parish) priest . . . otherwise they shall be cut off from the Church (excommunicated) during life and deprived of Christian burial in death." As for the priest taking confession, he was enjoined, upon hearing the sins confessed to him, to administer penance, pouring "wine and oil into the wounds of the one injured after the manner of a skilful physician, carefully inquiring into the circumstances of the sinner and the sin, from the nature of which he may understand what kind of advice to give and what remedy to apply." The priest was also sternly warned never to reveal any of the sins revealed to him in the confessional.[52]

With this, confession, which existed in some form from the early years of the church, became indisputably a major part of Catholic practice. As for the wine and oil of penance, the "remedies" to be applied to the sinner, these became the stuff of the law of conscience. The rules that determined the gravity of various sins, and the proper approach to chastising them, were developed in great casuistic detail by medieval canon lawyers; the law of conscience breathed the same university air as the romano-canonical law of proof. In time, the medieval canon law of conscience was made available to priests through an important species of semipopular legal literature called "confessors' manuals," which instructed priests in great detail on the nature of sins and on the proper punishment for them. Thus in the medieval Catholic tradition the work of the internal forum was not exclusively entrusted to the inner voice of the individual Christian. Instead, the inner voice of conscience was supplemented, or perhaps (as Calvinists would later insist) replaced, by the voice of the confessor; and the internal forum was supervised, or perhaps supplanted, by the bench of the confessional.[53]

Now, within the developing rules of conscience, the problem of judging featured prominently from a very early date. Indeed, the problem of judging appeared in the canon law of conscience contemporaneously with the twelfth-century attack on ordeals. And from the beginning, the problem was approached in a way centrally important for our understanding of jury trial, as a problem of "private knowledge."

As Nörr demonstrated, the ban on the use of private knowledge began to develop over the course of the twelfth century — the same period in which clerical agitation against ordeals was gathering momentum, and the same period in which Ivo and Gratian were exploring the distinctions between the judge, the soldier, and the "murderer." The key text for the lawyers who developed the ban on private knowledge came from the Gospels; and the key example was that of Jesus himself, in the matter of the woman taken in adultery:

> John 8:2–11. Early in the morning he came again to the temple; all the people came to him, and he sat down and taught them. The scribes and the Pharisees brought a woman who had been caught in adultery, and placing her in the midst they said to him, "Teacher, this woman has been caught in the act of adultery. Now in the law Moses commanded us to stone such. What do you say about her?" This they said to test him, that they might have some charge to bring against him. Jesus bent down and wrote with his finger on the ground. And as they continued to ask him, he stood up and said to them, "Let him who is without sin among you be the first to throw a stone at her." And once more he bent down and wrote with his finger on the ground. But when they heard it, they went away, one by one, beginning with the eldest, and Jesus was left alone with the woman standing before him. Jesus looked up and said to her, "Woman, where are they? Has no one condemned you?" She said, "No one, Lord." And Jesus said, "Neither do I condemn you; go, and do not sin again."

As medieval commentators on this famous and beautifully rendered antique story observed, Jesus did not concern himself with his own knowledge of the accused woman's guilt.[54] Instead, he affected a posture that was something like a caricature of the studied indifference of an imperial Roman bureaucrat. Writing unperturbedly with his finger, too busy even to glance up for more than a moment at the crowd of petitioners before him, he asked only whether she had been formally accused — and let her free because she had not been. "The Lord said," read an early text from the twelfth-century revival of Roman law, " 'Go, woman. Since nobody accuses you neither shall I condemn you.' From which it manifestly follows that a judge must never supplement the record with facts from his own knowledge."[55]

The judge, like Jesus, was to confine himself to inhabiting his official role, busying himself with his dossiers while awaiting proper proof of the guilt of the accused. Unless the witnesses or accusers spoke up, the judge was not to act. Such was the ban on private knowledge, the key means by which, in the canon law of conscience, the judge was afforded the chance to avoid the moral responsibility for judgment, maintaining the studied professional distance of a mere minister of the laws, never playing the role of a witness.

Modern readers may doubt that this ban had much practical significance. How often did judges really have private knowledge? Yet to appreciate the authentic impact of the ban, we must begin by recognizing that it was very common indeed for medieval judges to bring private knowledge to the case before them, especially on the Continent. This was in part because Continental judges were local officials who lived and worked in small medieval communities. As scholars have observed, it cannot have been a rare occurrence for judges in a medieval town to have some knowledge of cases before them,[56] and even to have been eyewitnesses. In fact, medieval jurists liked to discuss the problem of the judge who personally witnessed a crime — as the jurists liked to say, "while looking out his window."[57] This was something that they regarded as perfectly possible even in relatively large cities.

Indeed, William Durand, the leading late thirteenth-century authority on criminal procedure, discussed the problem of "private knowledge" on the basis of a real case, on which three of the leading jurists of the early thirteenth century had been consulted: "A judge was looking out his window, and saw a certain nobleman kill somebody in the public square in Bologna."[58] There was nothing improbable about this case: nobles did indeed kill people in the public square in medieval Italian cities, as readers of Italian history[59] (and *Romeo and Juliet*)[60] will know; and an Italian judge's window did indeed typically look out on that same public square.[61] It was entirely likely that a medieval Italian judge might have direct personal knowledge of a vengeance killing. But it was of course in smaller communities that judges must most commonly have acquired knowledge independent of the record in court.

The fact that Continental judges lived in relatively small communities was not, however, the only reason that they were likely to bring private knowledge to their decisions, or even the most important reason. There was another reason, too, which has been emphasized by scholars like Nörr and Antonio Padoa-Schioppa: Continental judges were sometimes clerics, which meant that it was possible that they might have taken confessions that bore on the case they were deciding. Even before the Fourth Lateran Council made confession an annual obligation, cleric-judges were taking confession.[62] This had the inevitable consequence that a judge-confessor might possibly have private knowledge,[63] whether because the accused had confessed to him or because other parties had done so. Indeed, a judge-confessor might know a great deal about the case before him: confessors and penitents shared much of their lives. As John Bossy has observed, "[M]edieval confession . . . was a face-to-face encounter between two people who would probably have known each other pretty well . . . [and] the average person was much more likely to tell the priest about the sins of his neighbours than about his own."[64] This stifling intimacy of the world of confession was also the stifling intimacy of the world of the Continental trial.

So when you appeared before a judge in most small communities during the Middle Ages, there was every chance that he already knew something about your case, and perhaps a lot. Could your judge make use of his private knowledge? Could he act as a witness in your case? If the judge knew the accused was innocent, could he use his private knowledge to acquit? Conversely, if he knew the accused to be guilty, could he use his private knowledge to convict? With regard to medieval English criminal jurors, the answer would be yes: jurors would not only be permitted to use their private knowledge, they would be obliged to do so. But when it came to professional judges, whether in England or on the Continent, the canon law of judging gave exactly the opposite answer.

This was in part because of the peculiar problems of confession. It was a solemn rule that the secret of the confessional could not be violated.[65] But the rule went beyond the treatment of knowledge acquired in the confessional, and it had a purpose different from protecting the confidentiality of matters confessed. Its purpose was to protect the judges themselves. It was by refusing to use their private knowledge, the theologians held, that judges could escape personal moral responsibility for entering judgment, and so escape the threat of "building themselves a mansion in Hell."[66] The ban on private knowledge was a moral comfort rule, a way for professional judges to assure themselves that they had maintained a safe distance from the bloody consequences of the case they were judging. So long as the judge did not comport himself as a witness, he would be safe.

When this ban first began to develop during the twelfth century, jurists did not fully agree on its reach. In particular, they often tried to distinguish between civil and criminal matters. It was, they most frequently held, only in *criminal* matters that the judge was not permitted to make use of his independent knowledge.[67] As Nörr observed, this seems perverse to the modern Continental lawyer, who thinks of the problem of criminal justice as a problem of factual proof. Considering the high stakes in a criminal trial, modern Continental jurists hold that all available evidentiary means must be deployed in order to determine whether the accused is in fact guilty. It is in civil trials, where less is at stake, that there is more room for evidentiary play. So why did twelfth-century jurists take the opposite point of view? As Nörr showed, it is because for them the problem was not a problem of proof at all, but a problem of *conscience*. Medieval jurists were worried about protecting the soul of the judge—a judge who, as Peter the Chanter had worried, might too easily "make himself into a murderer."[68] For such a judge, it was of course criminal matters that presented the gravest threat; for it was criminal matters that involved blood.

Indeed, to feel the full meaning of the ban on private knowledge, we must remember how profoundly the problem of judicial bloodshed mattered in the latter decades of the twelfth century. In chapter 2, we saw the depth of the theological conviction that judges might taint themselves with blood. The same conviction lay behind the theology of private knowledge. We can see this in the first classic formulation of the private knowledge problem — "Is the judge to judge only according to the evidence offered, or according to his conscience?" — probably offered in Paris around 1160, around the same time that the first protojuries were being assembled in England,[69] and about a decade before the first documentation of Peter the Chanter in Paris. This was a period during which the literature of canon law was forming rapidly, after the completion of Gratian's standard *Decretum* around 1140–1150. It was in reliance on Gratian that the anonymous Parisian author attacked the problem of the private knowledge of the judge. The great menace, as this author saw it, was the usual one, the false witness:

> It may happen either in a criminal matter, or in some other transaction, that an innocent person is convicted by false witnesses, while a criminal or wrong-doer is claimed to be innocent. The judge knows the truth of what happened. Query whether he should judge according to his knowledge [secundum con-scientiam], or according to the evidence presented before him [vel potius secundum allegata]. The question permits of little doubt. The guilty person should be absolved, according to the evidence he has offered, if nothing, or only trivial matters, have been offered in proof against him. In doing so I act against "conscience," that is to say contrary to what I know he deserves, but I do not act against "conscience," that is to say what I know I ought to do. After all, any prudent judge must be aware that he is obliged to judge according to the evidence offered before him, if it is unrebutted. It cannot be said that he is the one who acts. Rather it is the law that acts. See *C. XXIII, q. 5, c. si homicidium; et C. XXXIII, q. 2, c. quos.*[70]

This passage deserves to be read closely. Scholars have interpreted it as calling for a complete ban on the judge's use of any private knowledge.[71] But its ban is not clearly quite so absolute. The judge, according to this author, was not to make use of his own knowledge — even if it meant letting the guilty go free. There is no indication in this passage that the author believed the judge should connive in the conviction of an innocent person victimized by false witness. The author's argument, we should note, thus paralleled exactly the argument of contemporary critics of the ordeal: his concern was with cases in which the *guilt* of the accused was clear. It was in those cases that he insisted the judge should not use his own certain knowledge.[72] Just as the ordeal might let the guilty go free, so too should the judge do the same.

And why did the author conclude this? To answer that question, we must read the authority that he cited. If the judge simply followed the dictates of the evidence developed before him, wrote our Paris author, then "it cannot be said that he himself" had condemned the accused. Instead, "the law" had done so.

His citation for this proposition came from Gratian; and it is of course the same passage I have already quoted, the passage on how to avoid becoming a "murderer": "If 'murder' means killing a man, nevertheless sometimes a killing can be done without sin: After all, a soldier can kill an enemy; and a judge, or the judge's minister, can kill a malefactor. Or again a person may unintentionally let his spear fly from his hand. These do not seem to me to sin when they kill a man. Nor indeed are they ordinarily called 'murderers.' When a man is killed justly, it is the law that kills him, not you."[73]

Like Peter the Chanter, the Paris author was worried about the classic danger of judging: that the judge might "make himself into a murderer." His response was to shield the judge from responsibility by insisting that the law make the decision, rather than the judge himself. After all, in that case, as Augustine and Gratian had said, "lex eum occidit, non tu."[74]

So long as you do not use your private knowledge, it is the law that kills him, and not you. Judges were not to use their private knowledge, in order to avoid making themselves murderers and thus endangering their eternal life. If the judge was careful to avoid acting as a witness, he would be safe. In subsequent years, the doctrines banning private knowledge developed rapidly. By the late 1170s, they had taken a classic, and charming, medieval form: canon lawyers declared that judges could judge without peril to their souls because they had more than one "body." In this, the judge was akin to the king: the king had two bodies, his private person and his royal one.[75] The judge went the king one better: *he* was a triple person. The judge might know some things from the confessional. There were things known to him "ut Deus," "as God." Other things were known to him in his professional role as judge, "ut iudex." Finally things were known to him as a witness, as a private person — "ut homo," "as a man,"[76] or (as later canonists would put it) "ut privatus," "as a private person."[77] Of the three, only the judge was permitted to judge.[78] During the twelfth century, there was as yet no general agreement on these doctrines.[79] After the early thirteenth century, though, the law of conscience came into clearer focus: the judge could never deploy his knowledge as a private person.[80]

But with this, medieval moral theologians found themselves facing a paradoxical and disturbing result, famous in the Middle Ages, both on the Continent and (as we shall see) in England. Judges were never permitted to use their private knowledge. To do so would be to confuse their three separate "bodies." But this potentially meant that, in the name of conscience, judges might sometimes end up convicting persons they knew to be innocent. Let me emphasize that, in the social setting of the age, this cannot have been an entirely rare problem.

How could one deal with this quandary? Much of the mature canon law of conscience, as it emerged during the thirteenth century and after, turned precisely on this question. Some writers thought the judge could simply find ways to prod the witnesses toward creating a record that reflected what he knew to be the truth. Most insisted that a judge in possession of private knowledge should refer the case to a judicial superior.[81] Some thought the judge should testify himself publicly, describing what he had seen.[82] Failing these expedients, though, at least some theologians concluded that the judge was simply under an obligation to judge according to the proofs offered by the parties — *even if it meant condemning an innocent person.*[83]

That, in particular, is how no less a figure than Saint Thomas Aquinas saw the matter. In a manner typical of the tradition I have been tracing, Aquinas treated the problem of conscientious judging as part of his larger discussion of murder: the question was precisely how a judge might avoid "making himself a murderer."[84] Aquinas's answer summarized the wisdom of the Continent, while introducing a new variation on Gratian's approach: "Suppose that a man has been incriminated by false witnesses, but the judge knows that he is innocent. The judge must, like Daniel, examine the witnesses with great care, so as to find a motive for acquitting the innocent: but if he cannot do this he should remit him for judgment by a higher tribunal. If even this is impossible, the judge does not sin if he pronounces sentence in accordance with the evidence. For in that case, it is not the judge that puts an innocent man to death. Rather, it those who declared him to be guilty."[85] *It is*, said Aquinas in effect, ringing a variation on Gratian, *the witnesses who kill him, and not you.* The judge was to keep his own soul safe; and if the accused suffered unjustly, that was the fault of the false witnesses — those "rabid dogs."[86] If this sort of argument seems unpalatable, the answer lay to hand for medieval casuists: "multa cum conscientia contra conscientiam fiunt," "doing things in good conscience often requires doing things against one's conscience."[87] It might seem that a judge who condemned an innocent committed a mortal sin, but in fact he condemned the accused not in his private person but in his official person as judge.[88] At any rate, it was necessary at all costs to maintain a strict role separation between judges and witnesses.[89] The alternative was that the judge would build himself "a mansion in Hell."[90] The judge was to be saved; the witnesses were to be damned.

Not every writer agreed with Aquinas. Some of his fellow theologians, like Nicholas of Lyra, disagreed.[91] Moreover, Continental jurists were particularly inclined to reject his conclusion. Unlike the theologian Aquinas, practicing jurists found the idea that judges would condemn innocent persons unpalatable: "No judge is obliged to execute a criminal sentence that he believes to be unjust," wrote one leading fourteenth-century jurist.[92] Specialists in Roman and canon law "seem to feel the contrary" of what Aquinas feels, wrote another.[93] Nevertheless, the jurists too wrestled hard with the problem. They had no choice but to wrestle with it, for the problem revealed a core tension in the moral system of the law. The law had developed in a way intended to protect the judge against the dangers of judgment. Yet inevitably this implied that sometimes innocent accused persons might have to suffer in order to keep their judges safe.

As we shall soon see, this great debate in moral theology too was not confined to the Continent. Max Radin demonstrated seventy years ago that the English were full participants in it from the Middle Ages onward.[94] Indeed, the English moralists of the seventeenth and eighteenth centuries were all still immersed in the same debate; in this, too, English justice did not develop innocent of wider Western trends. But as we shall also see, English justice presented peculiar problems, problems faced by no one on the Continent. The Continental law solved the moral challenge of judging by insisting on a strict role separation between the judge and the witness in cases of blood. Yet this was precisely the role separation that would prove impossible for the common law criminal juror.

Continental Procedure (IV): The Judge and His Doubts

During the great centuries of medieval church reform, the ban on private knowledge thus developed as a fundamental bulwark of the law — but not as a bulwark protecting the accused against false conviction. Instead, it developed as a bulwark protecting the soul of the judge against the dangers of judging. Indeed, so far was the ban from being a protection for the accused that Aquinas expressly condoned the conviction of the innocent. For Aquinas and some other theologians, there was no way to keep the judge safe from damnation other than to allow him sometimes to send the innocent to the gallows. Otherwise the judge might fail in the key moral task of keeping his role distinct from that of the witness.

Keeping the role of the judge distinct from the role of the witness was one way of protecting the judge. There was another as well: the judge was protected through the scrupulous application of the procedure of doubt — the procedure to which I now turn.[95]

As we have already seen, by the early thirteenth century theologians had concluded that the judge's soul was safe so long as he made his decision "iuris ordine servato," "observing correct procedures." This was the formula that brought the ancient teaching of Saint Augustine into the High Middle Ages, the medieval means of guaranteeing that it was the law that killed the defendant, not the judge. As I now want to show, the "correct procedures" of the thirteenth century were framed in terms of the moral theology of "doubt." Long before the rise of the common law reasonable doubt rule, the problems of judging were already being analyzed in terms of doubt both on the Continent and in England.

We have already had a first taste of Continental criminal procedure as it emerged in the thirteenth century. This was the procedure founded on "full proof," "half proof," and so on, the procedure that determined when an accused person was or was not subject to torture. Historians have sometimes described this Continental law of proof as a purely mechanical system, designed to eliminate judicial discretion.[96] Recent scholarship has demonstrated that that is not true. In fact, judges retained considerable discretionary wiggle room under the Continental system.[97] This is particularly so because Continental judges, like common law jurors, had to make their decision "according to conscience." As recent scholarship has emphasized, the obligation to judge according to conscience created an ineliminable residue of subjective evaluation in the task of judging.[98] It is true that the Continental judge was guided by an elaborate law of evidence; but in the end, he had to make an authentic conscientious decision, through what canon lawyers called a "motus animi," a "movement of the mind."[99] Nevertheless, though the system was by no means mechanical, it was certainly highly rule-bound, providing the judge with detailed, scripted guidance every step of the way and carefully delimiting the sorts of evidence he could consider.[100] The law walked the judge step by step through the procedures he was to follow.

As we have already seen, the key question in this law was whether or not there was half proof. If half proof had been attained, the judge could order torture of a low-status accused person. But how was a judge to determine whether there was half or full proof? He was to follow a kind of script for the weighing of evidence. The technical term for such evidence was "indicium," "hint" or "proof," and what judges were commanded to find were "indicia indubitata," "proofs that did not permit of any doubt." Indeed, the carefully elaborated rules of the Continental law of evidence, in their effort to regulate the use of blood punishments, turned precisely on the question of *doubt*, in ways that were intimately bound up with the law of conscience, and that were fateful for the shaping both of Continental judging and of common law criminal jury trial.

Let us turn, then, to the theology of doubt. Within the law of conscience, "doubt" was a term of central importance. Indeed, any reader with a good Catholic education is likely to know this, since "doubt" remains a term of central importance in Catholic moral teaching. The *Catholic Encyclopedia* explains how "doubt" is understood down to this day, in phrases that date back to the Middle Ages:

Doubt

(Lat. *dubium,* Gr. *aporia,* Fr. *doute,* Ger. *Zweifel*).

A state in which the mind is suspended between two contradictory propositions and unable to assent to either of them. . . . Doubt is either *positive* or *negative.* In the former case, the evidence for and against is so equally balanced as to render decision impossible; in the latter, the doubt arises from the absence of sufficient evidence on either side. . . . Again, doubt may be either *theoretical* or *practical.* The former is concerned with abstract truth and error; the latter with questions of duty, or of the licitness of actions, or of mere expediency. A further distinction is made between doubt concerning the existence of a particular fact *(dubium facti)* and doubt in regard to a precept of law *(dubium juris). Prudent* doubts are distinguished from *imprudent,* according to the reasonableness or unreasonableness of the considerations on which the doubt is based.

Every reader of this passage will notice instantly that the question of doubt, in Catholic moral theology, is particularly framed as the question of when doubts are *reasonable.* Every reader will also notice that, according to that theology, unreasonable doubts are imprudent ones, ones we must not follow. With this we have nothing other than a reasonable doubt standard: indeed, we have the very reasonable doubt standard that is still applied in American criminal trials, as I want to show in the balance of this book. But to see how "reasonable doubt" crept from Catholic moral theology into American criminal procedure, we must once again burrow into the history of the Christian theory of adjudication as it developed in the Middle Ages, and especially on the medieval Continent.

The moral theology of doubt began taking shape during the same reformist centuries we have been discussing all along. To understand its place in criminal procedure, we must begin with an oft-quoted principle laid down by the early medieval Pope Gregory the Great: "Grave satis est et indecens, ut in re dubia certa detur sententia": "It is a grave and unseemly business to give a judgment that purports to be certain when the matter is doubtful."[101] That principle was picked up by reforming lawyer-popes of the later twelfth and early thirteenth centuries, in ways that would affect legal analysis for many generations on both sides of the Channel. It also became associated with another intellectual creation of those same reforming popes: the so-called safer path doctrine, which would still be guiding moral theologians in eighteenth-century England.

Let us begin with the safer path. The first statements of the safer path doctrine, like so much of what we have seen, involved efforts to guarantee the ritual purity of clergy faced with possible blood taint. Clement III, pope very briefly from 1187 to 1191, presented the doctrine in a decision involving a cleric and an arguably accidental death: "A certain priest wished to punish a member of his family using the belt that he ordinarily wore, and tried to flog the fellow. However, it happened that his knife slipped out of the sheath that was attached to the belt, and gave the man something of a wound in the back. The wounded fellow lived for a while, and the wound was healing, but then matters took a turn for the worse, and he went the way of all flesh. This created some doubt about whether the priest in question should be suspended from his office."[102] The core question here was one of pollution: it was the question of whether the cleric in question had so polluted himself through a fatal shedding of blood that he could no longer perform his sacramental duties —even though that act of bloodshed was unintentional. The answer to that question was of course doubtful.

Clement responded with the kind of injunction that is common in many legal systems committed to norms of ritual purity.[103] When in doubt, it was necessary to take "the safer path," avoiding any risk of pollution: "Since we ought to choose the safer path in cases of doubt [cum in dubiis semitam debeamus eligere tutiorem], it is proper to tell this priest not to involve himself further in sacred orders; but having done penance he should content himself with ministering in the minor orders."[104] Such was the safer path doctrine: in cases of doubt, "in dubiis," one should act in such a way as to minimize the possibility of pollution. The doctrine was reiterated in famous form a few years later by Innocent III, the lawyer-pope who presided over the Fourth Lateran Council.[105] In a case, like so many cases he dealt with, concerning the fitness of a cleric for his office, Innocent produced the classic formulation of the safer path doctrine: "In dubiis via eligenda est tutior," "When there are doubts, one must choose the safer path." This phrase, which English and American moralists would still be repeating seven centuries later, became standard.[106]

One must choose the safer path, since "doubtful matters" presented a serious danger to the soul. But what was a "res dubia," a "doubtful matter"? And how was one to stay on the safer path? Theologians addressed this urgent moral question by dividing judgment into four famous degrees of certainty. A Christian concerned about the salvation of his soul was enjoined to seek certainty of the highest degree. Certainty of this highest degree was called "moral certainty" — note well the phrase; it still sometimes appears in America jury instructions today. Below moral certainty lay three lower degrees. These were, in order, *opinion*, *suspicion*, and *doubt*. "Doubt" was thus the technical term for the lowest degree of certainty in judgment. Doubt took a variety of forms, of which "practical doubt" — doubt about whether or not to engage in a particular act — posed especially pressing problems. To act when one was uncertain about the rightness or wrongness of the action in question was to engage in an act evil in itself, and so to commit a mortal sin. Thus, with regard to practical doubts the rule of Innocent III held with special force: "In dubiis practicis tutior via est eligenda," "In cases of practical doubt, one must take the safer path."[107]

These teachings came to involve immense and fascinating complications, particularly as the doctrine reached its maturity in the writings of sixteenth-century Spanish moralists[108] and their seventeenth-century French successors.[109] We shall return to those developments in chapter 6. For the moment, let us examine the connection between the theology of doubt and medieval criminal procedure. For indeed, the moral theology of doubt lay at the very foundation of criminal procedure as the Continental jurists developed it, in ways we must understand if we are to understand our own common law history.[110]

To follow the development of criminal procedure as an aspect of the theology of doubt, we must start once again with Ivo of Chartres, the brilliant and influential reformer of the late eleventh century. In his *Decretum,* his compilation of canon texts, Ivo recorded the text of a letter from the second-century Pope Sixtus II. This letter addressed the ticklish question of when one could condemn sinners. The answer Sixtus gave was reminiscent of the theology of private knowledge: God, he declared, was the only judge who could always judge with certainty. For humans it was different. When humans confronted "incerta" — uncertain allegations — they could not condemn an accused person unless it was by "indiciis certis," evidence sufficient to create certainty.[111] The key phrase here, "certis indiciis," was to become a standard in Continental criminal procedure, always associated with the concept of "doubt."

That association was made in particular by Gratian, in a passage that, as scholars have observed, definitively introduced the doctrine of "doubt" into canon criminal law. In two consecutive passages, Gratian echoed first Gregory the Great's declaration on doubt, "ut in re dubia certa detur sententia," and then Ivo:

> C. LXXIV. *A decision that purports to be certain does not resolve a doubtful matter.*
>
> It is a grave and unseemly business to give judgment that purports to be certain when the case is doubtful.
>
> C. LXXV. *Things that are not proved through certain evidence are not be believed.*
>
> . . .
>
> Even though certain things may be true, nevertheless they are not to be believed by the judge, unless they are proved by certain evidence.[112]

Thus were the two key terms — "indicia," "evidence," and "dubia," "doubts" — linked in canon law. By the end of the twelfth century, the connection between the theology of doubt and the technicalities of criminal procedure had been clearly drawn, in ways that linked doubt just as clearly with the moral problems of private knowledge. Thus the late twelfth-century canonist Huguccio analyzed the problems of criminal procedure as follows: A "doubtful matter" was a matter "not proven by witnesses, or documents, or evidence such as a confession." A "doubtful matter" was a matter "known to the judge in some other way."[113] To Huguccio, the question of doubt was thus identical with the question of private knowledge. Conversely, obeying the rules of evidence was no different from declining to use one's private knowledge.

As Continental criminal procedure developed over the subsequent centuries, jurists never lost sight of the connections among "doubt," "proof," and "private knowledge": criminal procedure was about "doubt," and the great task of a criminal justice system was to arrive at "indicia indubitata," evidence that permitted no doubt.[114] By obeying the dictates of such evidence, the judge could judge without slipping into the role of witness. It was precisely in the course of wrestling with doubt, for example, that Albertus Gandinus, a leading thirteenth-century criminal law scholar, developed the basic hierarchy of proofs in criminal procedure, explaining how evidence was to be weighed.[115] Many other medieval proceduralists could be cited. I shall simply summarize the mature version of the law as we find it in the writings of a leading scholar of the sixteenth century, Prosper Farinacci.[116]

As we open Farinacci's standard *Practice and Theory of Criminal Law* and turn to the chapter "de indiciis et tortura," "on proofs and torture," we find a wealth of moral theology of doubt. Indeed, we find that mature Continental criminal procedure adopted the moral theology of doubt as its very framework.[117] The problem of proof, as Farinacci presented the standard learning, was nothing other than the problem of "rei dubiae," "doubtful matters," in the phrase that dated back to Gregory the Great and Gratian.[118] Faced with such doubtful matters, one needed proof. But what was a "proof," an "indicium"? A proof, explained Farinacci, was a kind of probable guess: it was a "conjecture" that was so probable that it "compelled the conscience of the judge to judge according to it."[119] And how was one to evaluate the probability of one's conjectures? Farinacci's answer was drawn in the most straightforward way from moral theology: one was to apply the familiar scale of certainty developed by the moral theologians. Thus some conjectures gave rise to "opinions"; while some gave rise to "suspicions"; and others gave rise to "doubt." Farinacci presented all this in the classic language of the moral theologians. His account paints a lovely picture of the Continental doubting mind, flitting back

and forth from possible conclusion to possible conclusion, until the final decision is seized by a movement of the mind:

> At times the judge, faced with the evidence presented before him, feels doubt,
> now leaning to the one party, now to the other, and his mind is not able to
> come down on one side, as when the proofs are equal or there is some obscu-
> rity about them. Now after this period of doubting, the judge begins to incline
> to one party more than the other. At that point, doubt ends, and suspicion
> begins. And if this suspicion is the result of grave proofs [si ista suspicio oritur
> ex gravibus indiciis], then suspicion ends, and opinion begins. . . . Now
> properly speaking, we say that the judge "doubts," when no reason or cause is
> present [quando nulla adest ratio, nullaque causa], which inclines him more
> to one party than the other . . . and a person is "in doubt" when his mind does
> not incline more to the plaintiff than it does to the defendant. But if after
> doubting, the judge is moved by some piece of evidence or argument to lean in
> the direction of the other party, then he is no longer said to "doubt" but to
> "have a suspicion."[120]

It was in these movements of the doubting mind that the fundamental
decisions of criminal procedure were to be made: only if there were "indicia
indubitata," "proofs permitting no doubt," could the judge proceed to the
next step in Continental justice: ordering torture.[121]

Even once the judge proceeded to torture, though, he was by no means done
with moral theology. For the decision to torture a defendant itself presented
the familiar problem of private knowledge.[122] Already in the thirteenth century it was understood that the problems of private knowledge dictated the
very details of the regulation of torture. As Nörr has shown, medieval jurists
insisted that tortured persons could not be asked leading questions, probably
because doing so would effectively inject the judge's own private knowledge
into the proceedings.[123] Those same problems continued to haunt the understanding of torture thereafter. We can take a summary of the mature position
of Continental law from a seventeenth-century Italian handbook of criminal
procedure. The author cited Farinacci among many others to make the point
that a judge could never use his private knowledge in proceeding to torture:

> *Whether Torture can be ordered on the basis of*
> *the Knowledge [Conscientia] of the Judge.*
>
> *Summary.*
> 1. *Torture cannot be ordered solely on the basis of the judge's knowledge*
> *[conscience], even if the judge is empowered to exercise discretion, & even if*
> *he is of strongest opinion.*
>   * * *

The judge is warned that he must not proceed to torture on the basis of his own knowledge, since it is a well-worn rule, repeated by everyone, that the judge must judge according to the dossier, and evidence properly developed on the record.[124]

Torture was a problem of "conscience" — which, given the ambiguities of the word "conscience," meant that it was a problem of the judge's private knowledge.

In all this, Continental criminal procedure was built on the foundations of the moral theology of doubt. Jurists understood this, and so did moral theologians. Indeed, moral theologians took an active and continuing interest in the dilemmas of the judge throughout the later Middle Ages and early modern period. For example, Leonard Lessius, a leading Flemish theologian of the later sixteenth and early seventeenth centuries, offered the same sort of analysis that Farinacci did. Lessius too used the standard four-part scale of certainty: doubt, suspicion, opinion, and firm judgment. He then explained how the scale of certainty bore on the question of "indicia": "These degrees [of certainty] are so constituted, that greater proofs are required to arrive at suspicion, than at simple doubt, and greater proofs for the definitive determination of guilt ["sententia"] than for a mere judgment."[125] A judge who judged in a state of doubt[126] always committed a mortal sin, Lessius added ominously.[127] Such warnings were found in abundance among the moral theologians, notably the great figures at work in sixteenth-century Spain,[128] and they would continue to be found right to the end of the eighteenth century. We may cite, for example, a standard French "dictionary of conscience," used from the early eighteenth through the early nineteenth century to guide priests: "In every case of doubt, where one's salvation is in peril, one must always take the safer way: *In dubiis via eligenda est tutior,* as Innocent III says. . . . A judge who is in doubt must refuse to judge, whether the doubt has to do with the person, the law or the fact."[129] "A judge may never judge, when he is in doubt." Many other such texts were published during the same decades, at the time the reasonable doubt rule was forming in England: "A judge commits a mortal sin if he embraces a merely probable conclusion, ignoring one that is more probable," writes a German Lutheran in 1702.[130] "Just as no warrant is given for sin in war," writes a Neapolitan Catholic seventy years later, still linking the theology of judging with the theology of war at the end of the eighteenth century, "so the judge must be careful to keep himself safe in perilous matters."[131]

The structure of Continental criminal procedure was thus modeled on the structure of the theology of doubt, in ways that implied that a judge's salvation was at stake in every evidentiary decision he made. Correspondingly, the old theological language rang through some of the leading texts right to the end of the Middle Ages. For example, Aegidius Bossius, a leading authority of the fifteenth century, still spoke about the dangers of "passion," about judges who hastened too merrily to punishment: "Si iudex gloriatur in morte hominis sicut nonulli faciunt nostra tempestate, homicida est," "If the judge glories in the death of a man, as no small number do in our age, he is a murderer."[132]

Despite that, though, it would probably be a mistake to imagine that most Continental judges were terribly worried about the safety of their souls by the sixteenth century. As Nörr observed forty years ago, the real drama in the development of this law was the drama of the emergence of a distinctive professional identity. By the sixteenth century, Continental judges — unlike common law jurors — were hardened professionals, who probably treated ad-judication as a matter of routine, rarely suffering from conscientious qualms or any lesser form of moral indigestion. Scholars have recognized that sixteenth-century Continental jurists took a toughened attitude, displaying more of an interest in proof than in charged moral dramas of the criminal law that had preoccupied the Middle Ages.[133] Indeed, when we browse in the juristic litera-ture of the sixteenth century and after, we do not find the jurists repeating the warnings of their contemporary moral theologians. To be sure, there is plenty of vitriol on the subject of malfeasant judges. Farinacci, for example, declared that judges who tortured without proper proof were "dogs," who should be criminally prosecuted.[134] This is violent language, from a man who thought that the criminal justice systems of his day risked doing evil (despite his own notorious harshness in sentencing). But it is not precisely the language of conscience.

For most professional Continental judges by the sixteenth century, it is undoubtedly the case that the Continental rules had become merely a means of factual proof — as a way of determining what had really happened in cases of uncertainty. The old moral comfort function of the rule probably withered away for most Continental judges after the fifteenth century. Their world was one in which the old anxieties about blood taint had been fully overcome through the development of a professional judicial ethos by the end of the Middle Ages. But for English jurors of the same period, the situation was different.

Before turning directly to English jurors, though, we must review one more aspect of "doubt" in Continental law. This is the famous Continental rule "in dubio pro reo," "in doubt you must decide for the defendant." This celebrated rule represented the Continental form of the presumption of innocence.[135] John Langbein has already noted that it must have some connection with the reasonable doubt standard.[136] And, as we shall see, he is entirely right.

The maxim "in dubio pro reo," whose history was traced by Peter Holtappels forty years ago, is yet another a rule that grew more or less directly out of safer path doctrine. Albertus Gandinus described the rule this way in the thirteenth century: "When there are doubts and the evidence is uncertain [in talibus dubiis et incertis probationibus] it is better to leave the malefactor's misdeed unpunished than to convict an innocent, since in cases of doubt [in dubiis] punishments are better made milder than harsher."[137] This rule was in counterpoise to the rule of private knowledge as theologians like Aquinas interpreted it. Perhaps judges who had private knowledge were obliged sometimes to convict the innocent. But when judges judged on the basis of the evidence produced before them, they were obliged to make the contrary error, leaning to the side of innocence. The in dubio pro reo rule was indeed a rule of moral theology, just like the private knowledge rule: it too offered counsel about how to act when you found yourself, in Innocent III's constantly cited phrase, "in dubiis," "facing cases of doubt." Indeed, as the standard juristic writing of the early modern Continent explained, in dubio pro reo was the other side of the procedural coin that required proof "clearer than the midday sun" before sending a person to blood punishment.[138] Thus it is no surprise that Aegidius Bossius, who was the first to turn the phrase "in dubio pro reo"[139] in the fifteenth century, spoke in terms that echoed the moral theology whose history I have traced: "First of all, you should know that judge must not be quick to punish, but must consider everything carefully: Err in haste, repent at leisure. . . . He must follow proper procedures, and try to determine the truth, only judging after he has done so . . . the judge must be brought to punish only in sorrow . . . if the judge glories in the death of a man, as no small number do in our age, he is a murderer."[140] In dubio pro reo was a rule that created a form of protection for the accused that grew out of the familiar fear that the judge might make himself into a murderer.

This is not the place for a full-scale survey of the Continental literature of in dubio pro reo, which is very rich. It is important, though, to note two of its characteristic themes, both of which would play important roles in later English jurisprudence.

First, Continental jurisprudence framed the question of in dubio pro reo as one involving "benignity" and "mildness": when faced with "doubts," the literature held, the judge must choose the "more benign" and "milder" path.[141] Second, the jurists who created the in dubio pro reo rule were not unaware that their creation presented dangers for the management of public justice. Indeed, Continental jurists understood full well the danger in any rule of lenity: the danger that criminal justice might break down. The demands of conscience were in conflict with "the wellspring of thirteenth-century criminal jurisprudence: 'it is a matter of public interest that crimes not go unpunished.' "[142] As Albertus Gandinus put it, it was perfectly clear that there was a "public interest" that misdeeds should not go unpunished. Yet this public interest was in unavoidable tension with any rule that counseled mildness.[143] This medieval conflict would be fought and refought repeatedly in subsequent centuries, as jurists reflected on the tensions between private conscience and the role of the judge as a "public person."[144] In particular, it was a conflict that English observers would still be fighting out four centuries later, and in urgent tones.

Salvation for the Judge, Damnation for the Jury: England

It is the conscience of the jury that must pronounce the prisoner guilty or not guilty.

And to say the truth, it were the most unhappy case that could be to the judge, if he at his peril must take upon him the guilt or innocence of the prisoner, and if the judge's opinion must rule the matter of fact, the trial by jury would be useless.

— *Sir Matthew Hale*, Historia Placitorum Coronae

We come at last to jury trial at common law, the subject of this chapter and the next two. The previous chapters have dwelt at length on the Christian traditions of antiquity, and on medieval Continental Europe. This may have seemed a strange exercise to most Americans, who generally think of the common law as more or less purely secular, and more or less purely English in origin. Nevertheless, without knowledge of the broader world of Latin Christendom, it is difficult to understand the rise of jury trial at common law, and impossible, as we shall see in these chapters, to appreciate the theological significance of its structures. Common law jury trial is the product not just of England but of the wider Christian world.

The birth of jury trial was forced by a great religious event, the Fourth Lateran Council of 1215. As we have seen, the Fourth Lateran Council, in its famous eighteenth canon, "Judgments of Blood," condemned the use of the judicial ordeal. Participation in an ordeal, the council held, was no different from blood surgery or blood warfare: it polluted any clergyman who took part in it, and therefore no blessings could be pronounced over the ordeal.[1] In most parts of Europe the Fourth Lateran Council had little immediate effect; outside England, the judicial ordeal continued without pause for a long time after 1215. In places like France, we must wait nearly half a century before we can find any clear impact from Lateran IV at all, and the use of ordeals continued long after that. (Indeed, in Continental Europe we still find traces of the ordeal as late as the eighteenth century.)[2]

But in England, the effect of promulgation of the canon "Judgments of Blood" was rapid and dramatic. Four years after the Lateran Council met, in 1219, a directive went out from the new English king Henry III, instructing the English justices to find some new means of adjudicating disputes, "since the

Figure 5. From a fourteenth-century *Book of the Worthless and Vile*, an image of false witnesses, counseled by a demon. *False Witnesses, counseled by demon*. Soester Nequambuch, Stadtarchiv und wissenschaftliche Staatbibliothek, Soest. A. Nr. 2771.

Church has forbidden the judgments of fire and water."[3] Within a year, the justices, drawing on a form of protojury, settled on jury trial. Common law jury trial thus emerged as the first fully realized substitute for the judicial ordeals of hot iron and cold water, decades before Continental law followed suit.

These events are well understood, and historians have accordingly long recognized that jury trial belongs to religious as well as legal history — that jury trial was the English response to a religious spur from Rome.[4] Moreover, during the past two decades legal scholars have succeeded in demonstrating that canon doctrine had a significant influence on the emerging forms of jury trial from the latter part of the twelfth century onward.[5] It is thus well established that the early history of the common law is, at least in part, a chapter in the history of medieval Christianity.

Nevertheless, there remain unanswered questions. Why did the English react so much more rapidly and decisively to the Fourth Lateran Council than did their Continental cousins? What were the precise implications of jury trial for the moral theology of judgment? What, most broadly, was the Christian theological significance of jury trial?

These are the questions this chapter addresses. Jury trial, as I shall try to show, developed its peculiar structures in part in response to the common Western dilemmas of the moral theology of judging; and it did so in ways that eventually placed English jurors under exceptional moral pressure. In the previous chapters, I sketched out the dilemmas of the Christian moral theology of judging. In chapter 1 we saw that anxiety about the act of judging was widespread in the premodern world. In chapter 2, we traced the rise of a peculiarly Christian theology of judging, associated with the infliction of blood punishments. Chapter 3 discussed the medieval European system of judicial ordeals, which offered some means of escaping the spiritual and corporeal dangers of judging in Western European law as it existed before 1170 or so. As we saw in that chapter, ordeals were administered in cases in which no one would come forward to accuse, no one would come forward to testify, and no one would confess — cases in which no one would take responsibility under oath for judgment.

In chapter 4, we turned to postordeal developments on the Continent. As we saw, Continental jurists were eager to guarantee that "crimes should not go unpunished." At least partly in consequence, they tried to move away from the ordeal system, which resulted in frequent acquittals. Instead of relying on ordeals, the newly emerging "inquisitorial" procedure of the Continent called for the testimony of witnesses, which was to be compelled if necessary. In the absence of adequate witness testimony, the inquisitorial law of the Continent threatened torture to force the accused to confess. Meanwhile Continental law also created procedures intended to shield the judge from moral responsibility for judgment: so long as Continental judges scrupulously avoided playing the role of witness, and obeyed the dictates of the moral theology of doubt, they could expect to remain safe from the dangers associated with the infliction of blood punishments.

By the mid-thirteenth century, a system of Continental law had thus emerged that put sharply divergent spiritual pressures on different judicial actors. Judges were generally safe from spiritual danger, under the law of the Continent. So long as they strictly observed the dictates of the law of criminal procedure, they could pursue the prosecution of crime without risk to their own salvation, even to the extent of ordering torture and death. Witnesses, by contrast, faced considerable spiritual (and corporeal) risk, since testifying under oath remained a dangerous undertaking. The accused, of course, faced possible torture.

The common law of the island kingdom of England emerged in the face of the same political pressures, and the same moral challenges, as the civil law of the Continent. England too had the system of ordeals in the eleventh and twelfth centuries. English monarchs too set out to prosecute crime more effectively; the same desire to ensure "that crimes should not go unpunished" found on the Continent could be found in England as well. England also had the same moral theology of judging as the Continent.

Nevertheless, the English royal alternative to the old ordeal system took a distinctive form. Twelfth-century English kings were more powerful than their Continental counterparts, and they were able to begin compelling accusation and witness testimony from an unusually early date. These early English efforts to compel testimony and accusation culminated in the creation of jury trial: early English jurors were indeed nothing other than accusing witnesses, who were legally compelled to give their testimony under oath. Of course, the role of accusing witness had historically been a very dangerous role indeed, and the institution of jury trial thus exposed the jurors to considerable risk. That risk was present from the earliest emergence of protojuries in the mid-twelfth century. The situation became worse for jurors after 1215. With the abolition of the ordeal, jurors were obliged, at least in principle, not only to serve as witnesses but also to render the general verdict of "guilty." This meant that thirteenth-century jurors effectively mixed the roles of witness and judge, which put them in a position that had been vigorously condemned by Christian moral theology.

The common law was thus a system that put uniquely severe pressure on the jurors. At the same time, though, it was a system that went relatively easy on the accused. Unlike Continental law, the English common law never developed a practice of judicial torture — though a good argument can be made that it came close to doing so.[6] While accused persons were compelled to plead either "guilty" or "not guilty" in England, they were not compelled to confess. This absence of judicial torture, about which English authors boasted for centuries, was the other side of the coin of the moral pressure put on the jurors.[7] Continental law introduced torture because it was unable to obtain either a formal accusation or adequate witness testimony. The jury system spared English justice this dilemma. Unlike Continental law, English law guaranteed itself technically adequate accusation, and technically adequate witness testimony, by empaneling a jury to testify and convict. Because it made use of jurors in this way, it had no need to compel confession. By putting a heavy burden of responsibility on the jurors, English law could put a relatively lighter burden on the accused.

The common law thus emerged as a distinctive tradition in the Christian West. Instead of being a system that rested on compelled confession, it was a system that rested on compelled witness testimony and compelled accusation. In one respect, though, English law was close indeed to the law of the Continent. Even as the English monarchy cracked down on crime, English law spared the judge moral responsibility. Indeed, as we shall see, the English judge found himself in an even more favorable position than his Continental *semblable*. Continental judges faced spiritual danger whenever they used private knowledge, and they risked acquiring private knowledge because they lived in the same small communities as accused persons, and because they might sometimes take confession. Ultimately they ran spiritual risks because they were obliged to enter the equivalent of verdicts, deciding questions of guilt or innocence. English judges faced almost none of those dangers. In fact, the common law was a system that could have been designed to spare the judge from moral danger.

English law put all of the moral burden on the witness and the accuser — which is to say, in effect, that it put all the moral burden on the jury. The jury did not feel the full weight of this moral burden in the Middle Ages: medieval law found various ways to shield the jurors, as we shall see in this chapter. The later history of jury trial, however, was different. As we shall see in chapters 6 and 7, in the seventeenth and eighteenth centuries the moral dilemma facing Christian jurors became acute.

The Emergence of Judge and Jury: Ordeals and Trials by Battle

The theological drama of the common law is the drama of the two judicial actors of jury trial, the judge and the jury. We must begin by understanding how these two actors emerged in the decades before and after 1200, before turning to the natures of the moral dilemmas they respectively faced. We must also understand the English fates of two different kinds of judgments of God: ordeals, used in cases of blood, and trial by combat, used in real property disputes.

Why is there a common law? Why did England develop a legal tradition different from that of the Continent? This is a question that has preoccupied — indeed, obsessed — legal historians for two centuries, and they have given a variety of answers. Today, though, many historians lay the greatest weight on one fact in particular: the English monarchy was exceptionally powerful during the critical period from 1000 to 1200.[8] Indeed, as recent scholarship has shown, the common law was the product of perhaps the most powerful monarchy that existed in eleventh- and twelfth-century Europe.[9] There is not perfect agreement about the reasons for the precocious power of the English monarchy, which predated the Norman Conquest of 1066. Perhaps it reflects nothing more elusive than geography. England was a relatively compact and lightly populated region, comparatively easy to dominate. The little island kingdom off the northwestern edge of Europe was a place where rulers could work their will with comparative ease. Whatever the reason, the Anglo-Saxons and Danes who ruled England in the eleventh century already exercised authority that was significantly more imposing than that of their Continental contemporaries, as the leading historian of Anglo-Saxon law has argued.[10]

English government remained unusually strong, moreover, after the Norman Conquest. The Norman kings were exceptionally effective (and exceptionally fierce) rulers. The same was true of their successors, the Angevins, who were a terror to their subjects, dominating by their "ira et malevolentia," their "wrath and malevolence."[11] Most impressive among these wrathful and malevolent Angevin monarchs was King Henry II. It was Henry who presided over the initial stages in the creation of the common law in the decades after his accession to the throne in 1154.

The precocious power of the English island monarchy helps explain a great deal about the peculiar evolution of the common law, contemporary scholars believe. For example, it helps explain the relatively limited role played by the Roman and canon sources in the common law. The English kings had comparatively little need for Roman or canon law. They were capable of imposing a relatively uniform law on their compact realm without drawing on the putatively universal authority of either ancient Rome or the church. Moreover, they had already taken major steps toward the development of a royal common law before university learning had produced its developed romano-canonical law.

Most broadly, the early effectiveness of English government helps account for the character of the common law, which retains an unmistakably medieval cast. To lawyers trained in the civil law tradition, the common law looks like a remarkably archaic system. It is a system based on medieval property law, on medieval concepts of vested rights, on medieval procedures, and more. In the broadest sense, it is a legal system that has preserved a medieval concept of rights and liberties. How has this archaic system survived? The answer may have to do, once again, with the fact that English government developed so precociously. Because the English monarchy ruled with such early relative success in the Middle Ages, English law became fixed in its early form, preserving medieval traditions that are still with us in the modern world. The common law is the product of a successful medieval monarchy, and as a result it has remained medieval law to a remarkable degree.

The same precocious power of the English monarchy, as I want to show in this chapter, can also help us to understand the peculiar moral dilemmas of the English jury.

Let us look more closely at the early emergence of the jury. The uncommonly powerful English monarchs of the eleventh and twelfth centuries, sitting athwart their island kingdom, created, through a process whose details remain the subject of complex scholarly debates, a general law of the realm called the "common law."[12] The scholarly debates about how this happened are complex indeed. Nevertheless, it is fair to summarize the process, following the account of Joseph Biancalana, by describing the common law as the creation of English kings who were powerful by medieval standards, but far less powerful than kings would become after the Middle Ages. Medieval kings, even unusually potent ones, were by no means fully able to displace all rivals for power. In particular, the kings of England were involved in political conflicts both with the church and with a recalcitrant, and sometimes rebellious, feudal nobility.

In the early stages of the development of English law, those conflicts expressed themselves largely as conflicts over jurisdiction — conflicts over whose court would have authority to decide cases.[13] Medieval law laid great weight on jurisdiction. When Italian city states tried to assert their sovereignty, for example, they did so through insisting on the jurisdiction of their courts to try cases.[14] The power to decide cases on one's own court was an important mark of sovereignty, and an important source of income as well. Correspondingly, it was the subject of hard battling. England was no exception: there too the law was shaped by battles over the authority to decide cases.

Consequently, the very early common law was a body of rules intended, above all, to resolve jurisdictional battles — battles between the Crown and the church, on the one hand, and the Crown and the feudal nobility on the other.

Many of the crucial developments came during the reign of Henry II, who took the throne after a nearly twenty-year period of chaos and intermittent civil war. The early part of Henry's reign was consumed by conflict with the church, and his first procedural innovations reflect that fact. The beginnings of the legal reforms of Henry involved efforts to determine when the monarchy could claim jurisdiction over various matters, and when jurisdiction would remain with the church.[15] If jurisdictional conflicts with the church marked the early years of the common law, though, they soon gave way to jurisdictional wars between the king and the feudal magnates.[16] As the common law embarked on its rapid development in the later twelfth century, it aimed, above all, to specify clearly the relative jurisdictional authority of king and feudal lords.

In these conflicts, jury trial emerged over the course of the twelfth and thirteenth centuries as the chief instrument of royal jurisdictional power. From around 1160 onward, its evolution was rapid, and by the middle of the thirteenth century it had largely taken its mature medieval form. It was a creature of the king: cases decided by jury trial were cases decided by the king's authority. Nevertheless, the king's authority to decide cases remained limited; the institutions of jury trial symbolized respect for the traditional prerogatives of nonroyal actors, and respect for traditional procedural practices as well.

The character of symbolic institutional compromise in early jury trial shows in its treatment of two especially important classes of cases: cases involving blood punishments and cases involving real property. Both of these classes of cases had historically been resolved by the judgment of God—either by ordeal or by trial by battle. The monarchy gradually succeeded in bringing both classes of cases into its courts, substituting jury trial for both historic forms of the judgment of God. But this success came slowly, and it required the monarchy to submit to some complex institutional compromises that permanently shaped the common law.

Let us begin with cases of blood. I have talked a great deal about cases of blood in this book, and about the spiritual dangers that attended them. Despite those dangers, medieval lords were eager to bring blood cases into their courts. The authority to inflict blood punishments, spiritually troubling though it may have been to do so, carried immense symbolic weight. It symbolized sovereignty. To vary the familiar maxim of Carl Schmitt, the "sovereign," in the Middle Ages, was not "he who decided upon the exception";[17] in the pre-nineteenth-century world, the "sovereign" was he who put people to death. This was the great symbol of sovereignty that Roman law called the "power of the sword,"[18] and it was much sought after. Powerful persons did not merely wish to have their own courts. They wished to have particular kinds of courts—courts in which they ordered executions. For the nobility, this was an authority symbolically represented by the coveted right to keep a gallows before one's residence.[19] As for the church, it too sometimes wished to bring cases of blood into its own courts—though not, of course, with the purpose of inflicting the death penalty. As we have seen, the church was forbidden to administer blood punishments. The church merely sought to bring its clergy and its other dependents under its own milder jurisdiction. Yet this too represented a challenge to the efforts of rival powers to try blood cases: a person tried and punished in a church court was a person who had escaped the blood jurisdiction of a rival royal or baronial court.

Faced with this rivalry from both feudal magnates and the church, the English kings made sustained efforts to capture jurisdiction over blood for themselves. In this conflict, the Crown had considerable success. Nevertheless, here as elsewhere, the success of the English Crown was inevitably limited. In part, English kings had to yield to the claims of the church. Those were the claims that were at stake in the most famous conflict of the early years of the reign of Henry II. In the mid-twelfth century Henry made a forceful, but unsuccessful, effort to bring "criminous clerks," clergymen charged with crimes, into the royal courts. (It was this effort that ultimately led to his disastrous clash with Thomas à Becket.) The church won that battle, keeping criminal jurisdiction over its own personnel. If the Crown failed to wrest criminal jurisdiction from the church, though, it had considerably more success in the lay world. To be sure, even there its success had limits.[20] Nevertheless, on balance the monarchy succeeded in monopolizing secular cases of blood. Blood cases became, for the most part, royal cases.

At the same time, bringing cases of blood into royal courts required confronting the dilemmas of the moral theology of blood that had dogged the Christian tradition since antiquity. What this meant, in the end, was a heavy burden for the criminal jurors who were charged with the responsibility of serving.

Who exactly were these jurors? In their earliest incarnations, so far as scholars can reconstruct their history, they were witnesses and accusers. Their role as accusers was especially important. In the high age of the ordeals, as we have seen, blood cases were ideally supposed to be initiated by accusers, who would take it upon themselves to prove the accusations through judicial combat. Unsurprisingly, accusers did not always forward. The consequence was that European justice had to accept the use of the ordeal. This system of accusation was of course a real obstacle to any effort to prosecute crime. If accusers refused to come forward, cases could not be brought. As we have seen, it was precisely for this reason that Continental law developed inquisitorial procedure: it was a procedure designed to be used where there was fama, where the voice of the people suspected a person, but no accuser came forward.

Like Continental rulers, the English kings would not tolerate a regime in which the prosecution of known or suspected offenders required officials to await a willing accuser. The English alternative was not, however, inquisitorial procedure. When the English monarchy took its major steps in the direction of what would become jury trial, in the 1150s and 1160s, inquisitorial procedure did not yet exist in its mature form. There were certainly early versions of inquisitorial procedure in use in the church courts, and they do seem to have had some influence on royal justice.[21] Nevertheless, the English monarchy took a different route, developing institutional alternatives to the older system of accusation.

One such alternative was the institution of so-called approvers.[22] These were convicted persons who had themselves been sentenced to death. The king remitted the punishment of these convicts in return for a service: they were obliged to bring accusations, and then to prove those accusations through judicial battle. This represented a clever compromise with the older institutional traditions of private accusation. By using approvers, the monarchy found a way to introduce a prosecutorial innovation without formally abolishing the older practice. The second of the monarchy's institutional innovations for bringing accusation was a similar kind of institutional compromise. This was jury trial. Like the system of approvers, early jury trial was an institution that married institutional conservatism with prosecutorial innovation, introducing a cleverly modified form of accusation into the common law, as we can see from a new kind of twelfth-century accusatorial body called the "jury of presentment."

The role of the "presenting" juror, as it emerged in the juries of presentment of the later twelfth century, seems to have grown out of an older role: the role of the royal witness.[23] The Anglo-Saxon kings had sometimes assembled groups of witnesses in the course of making inquests. So had the Danish kings, and so had the Norman dukes. Early on these inquests had the purpose of gathering information. In later periods, they sometimes they had the purpose of identifying criminals — or at least, persons deemed by the monarchy to be "criminals." Historians today generally view these groups of witnesses as the ancestors of the jury, though they differ sharply over how precisely to trace that ancestry. Indeed, there have been decades of contentious literature about these protojuries. Most of that literature, though, has centered around questions of no importance for us here — questions about whether these early English judicial institutions were Norman, Scandinavian, Frankish, or Anglo-Saxon in origin.[24] The ultimate ethnic origin of English institutions hardly matters for the history I trace here (and, indeed, hardly matters at all). What counts is that English kings were already compelling panels of local witnesses to make accusations from a relatively early date, even if only sporadically.[25] Whatever their origin, the very existence of these early panels testifies to the precocious capacity of the English monarchy to compel some sworn testimony and accusation.

Much of the early practice of compelled testimony and accusation involved homicide. Several factors were at work here. In part, undoubtedly, the monarchy sought jurisdiction over homicides, just as all medieval monarchies sought jurisdiction over all cases of blood; the right to inflict blood punishments was the great mark of sovereignty. But there were also two other factors. First, the English monarchy sought to collect fines for the commission of murders, just as it sought to collect other kinds of fines.[26] In particular, the Normans required Anglo-Saxons to prove "Englishry" — to prove that murdered persons were not Normans who had been done in by the subject population. It seems likely that Danish conquerors had already imposed similar obligations during the eleventh century.[27] In these cases of homicide, English kings were forcing their subjects to levy accusations well before the ordeals went into decline.

Compelled accusation was not limited to homicide, though. A much-discussed law of Aethelred the Unready, dating to 996 or 997, went beyond that. This law, which applied in Danish dominated communities, required twelve "thegns" — twelve high-status persons — to denounce *all* "malefactors" in their community. Scholars differ strongly over the significance of this early royal measure.[28] What seems clear, though, is that by the mid-twelfth century panels were bringing accusations.[29] English kings was thus requiring local inhabitants to name malefactors well before the first appearance of the jury.[30] There was another factor at work as well: the twelfth-century English church too had its own procedures that bore a resemblance to royal "presentment," as R. H. Helmolz has shown.[31]

By the later twelfth century, England was thus already the home of a substantial tradition of compelled testimony and accusation. This tradition culminated in the crucial period in the formation of the common law, the early part of the reign of Henry II. The critical date is probably 1166. This was the date of the momentous Assize of Clarendon, which charged the king's itinerant justices to collect sworn testimony about crimes:

> 1. In the first place the aforesaid king Henry, on the advice of all his barons, for the preservation of peace and the maintenance of justice, has decreed that inquiry shall be made throughout the several counties and throughout the

several hundreds through twelve of the more lawful men of the hundred and through four of the more lawful men of each vill upon oath that they will speak the truth, whether there be in their hundred or vill any man accused or notoriously suspect of being a robber or murderer or thief, or any who is a receiver of robbers or murderers or thieves, since the lord king has been king. And let the justices inquire into this among themselves and the sheriffs among themselves.

2. And let anyone, who shall be found through the oath of the aforesaid, accused or notoriously suspect of having been a robber, or murderer, or thief, or a receiver of them, since the lord king has been king, be taken and put to the ordeal of water, and let him swear that he has not been a robber or murderer or thief or receiver of them, since the lord king has been king, to the value of five shillings as far as he knows.[32]

The king's judges were thus to assemble bodies of witnesses to "present" the offenses that had been committed in the area. This was the so-called jury of presentment, the immediate ancestor of the common law criminal jury.

The Assize of Clarendon was a major step forward on the path to the creation of jury trial. Still, it was only a step, and it is important to note its institutional conservatism. As the text of the Assize suggests, the monarchy issued this directive in the spirit of ostensible respect for institutional custom that characterized all of its innovations. It did not purport to abolish all existing practices: the new presenting jury was not intended to displace the ordeal. Those accused were still put to an ordeal—afterward, if they failed, to be mutilated, losing a foot.[33] This distinguishes the presenting jury decisively from the mature jury of the common law, and it does so in a way that matters immensely for understanding the moral responsibilities of the assize jurors.

What indeed were the moral responsibilities of the presenting jurors of 1166? In effect, they played a kind of intermediate role between compelled witness and compelled accuser. Recent scholarship has demonstrated that they were indeed expected to testify from their personal knowledge about the events in question: They belonged to the tradition of the "self-informing" jury, the jury of twelve witnesses. Recent scholarship has also demonstrated that they were conceived as "witnesses" according to the technical legal canon law reasoning of the day: the jurors were understood to be fama witnesses of the familiar canon law kind.[34] To the extent the assize called for juries of presentment to be gathered in cases of fama, it was making a merely incremental change to the older ordeal system: it was compelling witness testimony while still leaving the ordeal in place.

But if the presenting jurors were thus playing the role of compelled fama witnesses, they could also be thought of as playing the role of compelled accusers. After all, they were obliged to come forward and name malefactors. Indeed, as *Glanvill*, the late twelfth-century treatise, explained it, the presenting jury was to make its accusation only "si nullus appareat accusator certus sed fama solummodo eum publice accusat," "if no particular accuser comes forward but only fama publicly accuses him."[35] This was the classic setting in which an ordeal had always been held. Indeed, *Glanvill* hewed faithfully to the traditional line: if a "particular accuser" *did* appear, there was no need for presentment at all.[36] This is borne out by the early records of presenting jurors, which show them very much in the business of making accusations.[37] The jurors were thus substitute accusers.

Now, in the high age of the ordeals, as we have seen, bringing accusations was a dangerous business.[38] Yet we should see that the Assize of Clarendon was structured in a way that afforded jurors a real measure of protection, precisely through the institutional conservatism it showed in preserving the ordeal.[39] Preserving the ordeal was a measure that lifted much of the threat that faced the presenting jurors.[40] Since malefactors who had been presented were sent to the ordeal, their ultimate fate was in the hands of God.

That said, we should not exaggerate the ease of serving as a presenting witness. It remained a dangerous job. Perhaps presenting robbers and thieves carried no great risk. But presenting "murderers" was presumably a different matter. The local societies in which this institution was used were, in some measure, vendetta societies; and the "murderers" in question must have been, at least some of the time, persons who had committed feud killings. Presenting such feud killers to royal officials would have courted vengeance from those killers' relations. At the same time, though, juries of presentment took an oath to speak the truth—following the practice of the time, on holy relics.[41] Worse yet, they were subject to amercement for omissions.[42] Taken together, these rules, which so closely paralleled the theological rules we examined in chapter 4, put the presenting jurors to a harsh choice. On the one hand, they must have been tempted to lie, whether to protect themselves or to protect their friends and relatives; as was always the case in the Middle Ages, requiring testimony under oath effectively encouraged perjury. At the same time, they ran a real risk to their salvation if they perjured themselves; and a risk to their financial well-being if they refused to cooperate.

The key to understanding the moral structure of jury trial lies in recognizing that the risks for such jurors only grew after 1215. As we have seen, in that year the Fourth Lateran Council forbade clerical participation in ordeals. While this decree had little immediate effect in most of the Western world, in England its effect was momentous. After a few years of uncertainty, the juries of presentment were saddled with a new responsibility in 1220. Since there was no longer any resort to ordeals, English justice restructured the obligations of the presenting jury: the presenting jurors were abruptly obliged not only to make their accusation but also to declare defendants either guilty or not guilty.[43] That is to say, the older juries of presentment were transformed into the first criminal juries of the kind we still have, confronted for the first time with the responsibility for judgment that had hitherto been delegated to God. Where they had earlier been witnesses/accusers, the new petty jurors now assumed a role that was sharply condemned by moral theology: they mixed the functions of judge and witness. Or as Mike MacNair has put it, the developments of this period conspired to "judicialize" the jurors.[44]

It is worth pausing to ask why the Fourth Lateran Council had such an impact on the island of England, and not elsewhere. Scholars have not been able to provide much by way of explanation. The best suggestion they have been able to offer is the following: King John had been obliged to submit to the authority of the pope, making England a vassal state. Maybe, scholars have thought, this explains England's quick acceptance of the Fourth Lateran: as vassals of the pope, the kings of England felt obliged to comply.[45] Perhaps this played some role, but it is hardly a convincing explanation in itself. The relevant canon of the Council was not framed as a directive from a feudal lord to feudal vassals. It was framed as a rule for the maintenance of clerical purity. Nor were other papal fiefs similarly affected.

There is a more satisfying explanation, one that lies to hand once we understand the drama of the decline of the ordeal. Ordeals were inflicted, as we saw in chapter 3, in cases in which no witnesses would come forward to testify. The true alternative to the ordeal, in every part of Europe, was thus to compel testimony. Why, then, did the English monarchy respond so rapidly to the Fourth Lateran Council? The answer, surely, is this: The English monarchy had already made great strides in the creation of a system of compelled testimony, through the use of juries of presentment. Since witnesses were already being compelled to speak in England, the English were in a significantly better position than their Continental cousins to eliminate the ordeal.

At any rate, by 1220 the twelfth-century jury of presentment, as scholars have shown, was converted into a thirteenth-century form of the criminal jury we know today, charged with the duty of declaring accused persons guilty or not guilty. As a result, royal jurisdiction finally displaced divine jurisdiction, at least in some matters of blood. But that was not the only result. The creation of a criminal jury charged with deciding guilt created a whole new kind of frightening moral responsibility for jurors. We shall see at the end of this chapter that the jurors reacted by resisting the duty to give judgments.

Real Property Disputes: From Trial by Battle to Jury Trial

Jurors in blood cases were not the only ones saddled with difficult moral responsibilities by the Angevin reforms. Similar things can be said about disputes over land. Indeed, it is a point of distinctive importance for the history of the English common law that grave moral responsibilities were attached to what we now call "civil" trials involving land, just as they were attached to "criminal" trials involving blood. It was in the context of the jury trial in land disputes that some of the basic disciplinary mechanisms of the common law developed. It was also in that context that one of the most striking common law rules, the rule of juror unanimity, established itself.

It is no surprise that land disputes should have seemed charged with great significance in the early common law. Control of real property lay at the core of the feudal system. Feudal potentates had power only because they had land; more broadly, family wealth was predominantly wealth in land. There was another reason too for the prominence of land disputes in the early common law, one having to do with the political circumstances of Henry II's accession. Henry came to the throne after a period of chaos, and sometimes civil war, during the reign of Stephen (1135–1154). During these nineteen years of disorder, doubts were raised about title to land in many parts of the kingdom. In 1153, Stephen and Henry entered into the Treaty of Westminster, ending the long civil war that had divided their parties. That treaty, which guaranteed Henry's succession, also guaranteed that justice would be done to those who had suffered "exhereditatio," dispossession from their inherited lands.[46]

After Henry took the throne the following year, he moved vigorously to assert royal authority over disputes involving the "dispossessions" of the previous reign.[47] Yet doing so drew him once again into jurisdictional disputes. In the English law of the twelfth century, disputes over land were not normally resolved by the king, unless they involved the king's own immediate vassals, the tenants in chief. Instead they were resolved in the court of the feudal lord to whom homage for that land was owed. Those disputes were also to be resolved, in principle at least, by God, through trial by battle. Henry II did not attempt to eliminate these traditional approaches; as always, he was in no position to claim exclusive powers of jurisdiction. But his reforms did offer a complex set of alternatives and interventions. In particular, they eventually offered two new kinds of protojury, both organized to deal with land disputes: the grand assize and the petty assizes.

The grand assize, probably established in 1179, was intended to settle property disputes between knights. Customarily, such disputes would have been settled in the Norman way, through trial by battle, the classic form of high-status judgment of God.[48] As early as 1133, though, we have a record of a land dispute being decided by "twelve honest men" in a church court.[49] The grand assize took the same tack, permitting the disputants to put their case before a protojury of twelve "lawful knights" of the area instead of submitting to the judgment of God. This was described by *Glanvill*, the important common law treatise written around 1188, as a "great benefit" conferred by the king upon his subjects, since it permitted them to avoid the "uncertain issue" of trial by battle.[50] Perhaps this was true — in which case we can see that early jury trial was succeeding in its competition with the judgment of God partly because disputants resisted the latter. At any rate, we should note that the grand assize put a new and potentially heavy burden on its "twelve lawful knights," who were now obliged both to take the role of God and to risk incurring the enmity of the losing party in the dispute. Like the jury of presentment, the grand assize was taking on a tough responsibility.

The grand assize was not the only such new institution. There were other early protojuries charged with deciding disputes over landholding — so-called petty assizes. Of these, the most important, for my purposes (and indeed for most discussions of early English legal history) was the assize of novel disseisin. The assize of novel disseisin allowed a person recently "disseised" — that is, dispossessed[51] — of his feudal property to challenge his disseisor before a protojury of twelve "recognitors." If the recognitors held that the complainant had been disseised "unjustly and without judgment," he could reclaim possession of his land and chattels. His disseisor would be obliged to pay a large fine to the king, as well as one to the sheriff charged with supervising the matter.[52]

At first glance, it may look like the moral obligations of these recognitors were less daunting than those of the grand assize. In a sense, the duties of the twelve recognitors in the assize of novel disseisin were limited. Novel disseisin was a "possessory" assize, one that did not purport to resolve ultimate questions of right. A successful complainant would be restored to possession of his property. His opponent could, however, still challenge the results in an ordinary feudal court;[53] here, as so often, the twelfth-century Crown did not succeed in laying claim to an unimpaired jurisdictional monopoly. One might think, then, that the moral burden of the recognitors was light, since they did not have make an ultimate judgment of right themselves. They were not really taking over the ultimate power of judgment from God.

Nevertheless, the assize of novel disseisin in fact put its recognitors in a difficult position. Like the other jurors we have seen, they were witnesses, sworn by an intimidating oath; and the evidence they gave was all too likely to earn them deadly enemies. We have discussions both of an oath used in England, and of the particularly intimidating cognate oath used in Normandy. In England, potential recognitors who wished to claim ignorance were compelled to swear in court that they knew nothing.[54] This indicates clearly enough that many witnesses wished to avoid the obligation of testifying. Why else compel witnesses to swear to what they did *not* know? The recognitors who eventually did testify were also sworn. The Norman version of the oath they took is one that I have quoted before; but it deserves to be quoted again: "Know ye by the faith and belief that you have in Lord Jesus Christ, and that you received in baptism, and upon these relics . . . that if you have lied or concealed the truth in this matter, your souls will be damned in perpetuity, and your bodies will be exposed to shameful abuses in a gaping Hell."[55] The fact that such a threatening oath was administered suggests, once again clearly enough, that the recognitors were very much tempted to lie.

Moreover, they faced a legal threat: the losing party could bring a kind of criminal action against them called an "attaint." The attaint alleged that the recognitors had perjured themselves. If prosecuted in an attaint, the twelve recognitors were to be tried by a second, larger jury, and upon conviction for their "perjury," they were to lose their chattels and suffer imprisonment for at least a year.[56]

The attaint is centrally important for my tale: it was the key medieval institution embodying both the legal and spiritual threats that menaced jurors. The attaint was about perjury — which is to say that it was directed at a theme wholly familiar from the literature of theology, the hideous theme of the false witness. So it is no surprise that when the standard common law literature described the attaint, it drew on familiar theological language. Thus to Bracton, the leading treatise of the early thirteenth century, issues of the assize of novel disseisin were the familiar ones of moral theology. Here is how Bracton described the judge's evaluation of the jury in cases of novel disseisin. Everything depended on whether what the jury said was "certum" or "incertum." In cases in which the judgment was certain, explained the treatise, there were two possibilities: either the jurors were correct, in which case their judgment stood, or else they had perjured themselves, in which case they were vulnerable to the attaint. In the second case, though, the case in which judgment was uncertain, matters were different. Then there was "doubt," which was "perilous." Here, explained Bracton, the judge had to examine the jurors carefully: "If however they have said something that is uncertain, the judge must examine them, in order to draw certainty out of uncertainty, clarity out of obscurity, truth out of doubt. Otherwise their oath will be perilous and dangerous, and a fatuous judgment may result."[57] This is the procedure familiar to us from chapter 4:

the judge, following precepts drawn from the tale of Susanna, is to examine the witnesses closely to determine whether their testimony justifies their "perilous oath."[58] The recognitors were thus threatened both with a criminal sanction in this world (the attaint) and with a divine sanction in the next (damnation), as the term "peril" implies. As we shall see at the end of this chapter, the recognitors in the assize of novel disseisin reacted in exactly the way the jurors of presentment did: they refused to enter judgment.

Thus the danger of perjury clung to real property disputes, just as it clung to cases of blood. It is worth noting that we see this not only in the doctrines of the common law but also in the writings of English moralists. The moralists showed a strange, almost comically English, belief that offenses against property were morally objectionable in almost the same way that murder was morally objectionable. Thus Thomas of Chobham, a theologian active in England from about 1190 until the 1230s, could casually lump together killing a person and seizing that person's land: both were offenses heinous enough to be viewed as deserving violent vengeance.[59] Centuries later, too, English moralists would still be warning jurors both against "sentenc[ing] a Thief or Murderer to be punished upon their secret unproved knowledge" *and* "adjudg[ing] either Moneys or Lands to . . . without sufficient evidence and proof";[60] shedding blood was not the only act that seemed morally charged to English observers.

The attaint will occupy much of our attention over the next two chapters. For the moment, I want to emphasize one important feature of the attaint: it is in connection with the assize of novel disseisin, and the threat of the attaint for perjury, that we discover the beginnings of a troubling rule that is still with us — the rule of the unanimity of twelve jurors.

This rule had many antecedents predating the formative years of jury trial. We have already examined the cases of the twelve thegns of Aethelred the Unready and the twelve knights of the reign of Henry I. This old requirement of twelve reappeared in the reign of Henry II. In particular, *Glanvill*, the late twelfth-century treatise, tells us about it in an interesting passage on the requirement of the unanimous testimony of the recognitors.

Let us look at the question of juror unanimity, through a close reading of *Glanvill*'s passage. That passage is about witness testimony. But it is important to observe that it does not treat the fundamental problem as one of factual proof; the treatise does not declare that sufficient testimony should be gathered in order that judges should be able to determine the truth. Instead, it is concerned that sworn testimony be taken from the magic number of twelve persons before legal consequences attach.

Glanvill discusses two different possible cases. In the first, the truth is known to many, though not all, inhabitants of the area, but it is difficult to gather sufficient sworn testimony. In such a case, the treatise explains, testimony must be sought until twelve persons have been found who will swear under oath: "If . . . some know the truth of the matter and some do not, those who do not shall be rejected and others summoned to court until at least twelve can be found to agree to it."[61] This was a form of what was called "afforcing" the assize, in order to obtain the unanimous agreement of twelve. Let me emphasize that the requirement of the magic number twelve, as we see it in this passage, manifestly had nothing to do with the difficulty of uncovering the truth. There is no reason why unknown truths would have to be clarified through the unanimous accord of any number of witnesses, and no reason why twelve in particular should be required. On the contrary, as *Glanvill* imagines this case, it clearly supposes that the truth is, at the very least, widely known in the community. The testimony of twelve recognitors is required for a different reason.

Glanvill also contemplated a second possible case. This was one in which two parties clashed over some claim of right. Such a situation, the treatise held, also called for a rule of twelve. In this case, though, the rule of twelve looked rather different: it resembled the clash of supporting "witnesses" that we examined earlier in the eleventh-century law of the Family of Worms. Let me quote once again that early eleventh-century law: "If any member of the family should have a dispute with another member about any matter, . . . [l]et each side declare their testimonies, and let their witnesses proclaim their approval joyously. Then let two be chosen to represent the aforesaid testimonies by fighting, so as to resolve the dispute through trial by battle. He whose champion succumbs, is the loser, as though his testimony had been false witness given under oath."[62] Under this law, as we saw in chapter 3, the witnesses were not obliged to swear an oath. Instead the issue of trial by battle determined which side had committed notional perjury. *Glanvill*'s account imagined a similar effort to collect "witnesses" for the two sides, again through afforcement. For *Glanvill*, though, there was no possibility of trial by battle. On the contrary, the very purpose of the assize was to replace trial by battle. Instead, the witnesses were compelled to swear under oath: "If some of them declare in favor of one party and some in favor of the other, then further jurors are to be added until at least twelve agree together in favor of one party. Each juror summoned for this purpose must swear that he will not declare falsely nor knowingly suppress the truth."[63] The law of the Family of Worms had used trial by battle as a substitute for oath taking, in order to spare most members of society the danger of perjury. In the England of *Glanvill*, that option was vanishing: the petty assizes were displacing trial by battle, which meant that the witnesses of a given region were compelled to swear oaths, at the peril of their souls.

So it is that *Glanvill* continued by explaining that these recognitors were subject to the attaint for perjury: "If the jurors are duly convicted in court of perjury . . . then they shall be deprived of all their chattels and movable goods which shall pass to the king, by whose great mercy their free tenements are excepted from this forfeiture. They shall, moreover, be cast into prison and kept there for a year at least. In addition they lose their law for ever [i.e., the capacity to testify in court or fight trial by battle], and thus rightly incur the lasting mark of infamy. This penalty is justly ordained, so that the fear of such punishment shall prevent all men from swearing a false oath in such a case."[64] This was meant seriously. We know of a 1202 case of novel disseisin in which one juror dissented from the vote of the twelve. That one dissenting juror was prosecuted for perjury.[65] Here again some commentary is called for. Why prosecute the one dissenter for perjury? It can only be because the law assumed that the vote of the eleven jurors in the majority represented a truth known to all. If the twelfth dissented, it can only have been because he was perjuring himself.

These rules requiring the unanimous judgment of the twelve were enhanced in subsequent centuries in various draconian ways. In particular, there was a second form of "afforcing the assize" in order to extract a unanimous sworn verdict: the jurors were locked away and denied meat and drink until they agreed.[66] Unanimity of twelve witnesses was thus attained through coercion.

Why was all this done? These institutions had nothing to do with the notion that the unanimous agreement of twelve persons was a particularly good fact-finding device. As is the case with so many medieval sources I have cited, the passages I have quoted here show little concern with the problem of unknown facts at all. Their underlying assumption is that the facts are well-known in the community, but that the "witnesses" — that is, the jurors — must be coerced, or at the very least coaxed, into testifying about them under oath.[67] Their underlying assumption is that the key to trial is *not* the determination of uncertain truths but the compulsion of sworn testimony by a certain minimum number of respectable, oath-worthy members of the community.

All this involved land. The law of attaint and the unanimity rule arose in connection with disputes over real property. As we shall see, blood cases raised more troubling issues. The moral dilemmas confronting jurors in cases of blood were more daunting, and they were not subjected to this draconian regime of coercion in the Middle Ages. Only in later centuries would the moral dilemmas of the blood jurors become acute.

The New Common Law Judge

But before we turn squarely to the moral dilemmas of the new common law jurors in cases of blood, we must review the evolution of the second judicial actor of jury trial, the judge.

The king had always had judges, sometimes attached to his person, and sometimes serving as his delegates. At least from the early twelfth century onward, the king also sent royal officials out on "eyre" — the "iter," or voyage.[68] The eyre was an imposing traveling show of royal power, which moved from area to area in England judging cases, as well as exercising other forms of authority. During the earlier twelfth century, royal authority was exercised both by the king in person, by his financial officials in the Exchequer, and by his delegates in eyre.[69] It is important to note, though, that the early eyres did only a limited kind of judicial work. In the early twelfth century, as Paul Brand has shown, the judges of the eyre did not actually enter judgment. Instead, they presided over sittings of local courts, leaving the work of judging to the "suitors," the customary constituency of the court in question.[70] When the king was not personally present, his judges had limited authority, rendering no judgments themselves but simply appearing in court as the shadows of a distant king.

From the later twelfth century on, though, the role of the royal judge underwent a provocative expansion. Probably beginning with a great eyre of 1176, royal judges on eyre took on the role of active judging. This implied that the eyre, rather than merely lending a ghostly royal presence to the courts of others, was itself a fully sovereign royal court.[71] In the later twelfth century, moreover, the eyre became a regular (and much hated) institution, with judges riding one of a number of circuits in England.[72] The later twelfth-century royal judge was thus a new kind of officer — a full-fledged judge, no longer simply a representative of the royal authority of an absent king.

Meanwhile, alongside the traditional eyres, a new kind of judicial institution began to emerge. This was a central court at Westminster. It was one of the demands of Magna Carta that the king's court meet in some fixed place, so that litigants would not have to seek out the king in person in order to receive judgment. In the early decades of the thirteenth century, the Court of Common Pleas became fixed at Westminster, to be followed later by King's Bench.[73] The judges of these central courts, like those of the eyres, were again full-fledged judges, charged with the obligation of deciding cases. Even in the absence of the king, the new judges were clearly empowered to render judgments. The period 1160–1250 thus saw the emergence of a more powerful and more routinized bench — one made of judges who still "represented the person of the King when they judged,"[74] but who exercised the royal power of judgment with at least the beginnings of an independent authority.

The Special Position of the Common Law Judge

By the mid-thirteenth century, the two actors of English jury trial, judge and jury, had thus emerged. How were these actors to be viewed through the eyes of moral theology? The answer is that both were charged with theologically delicate tasks: jury trial was the scene of a complex drama of moral responsibility.

I begin with the moral responsibility of the judge. As we have seen, the Christian theological tradition created elaborate measures intended to protect the judge against the spiritual dangers of judging in cases involving blood punishments. All of those measures can be thought of as ways of giving flesh to ideas originally proposed by Saint Jerome and Saint Augustine in late antiquity: the judge could keep himself safe from the taint of blood so long as he acted strictly as the minister of the laws. This meant that he had to refrain assiduously from deploying his own private knowledge or acting with passion. It also meant that he was to hew to the safer path, carefully following procedures intended to guarantee that his judgment would never be polluted by unvetted doubt.

These theories were known in England, just as they were on the Continent. Indeed, the circle of the Anglo-Norman canonists of the later twelfth and early thirteenth centuries was among the leading schools of thought on the theology of judging.[75] Standard passages on the potential blood guilt of judges continued to be cited in thirteenth-century England. Thus Bracton, like contemporary Continental treatises, quoted Raymond of Peñafort, the leading canon authority: judges courted blood guilt unless they were careful to kill offenders "iuris ordine servato," "observing the procedures of the law."[76] Ralph Turner has demonstrated that thirteenth-century English observers, like their Continental contemporaries, were especially concerned that clerics who served as judges might be tainted by blood.[77] England was thus not by any means outside the circle of Western Christian cultures.

Moreover, by the fifteenth century at the latest, the English had their own body of precedent digesting the fundamental canon teaching on private knowledge.[78] In particular, a much-cited case of 1406 offered an English version of the standard canon learning. The case presented a dialogue between Tirwhitt, J., and Gascoigne, C.J.:

Tirwhitt, J.: Sir, Suppose a man killed another in your presence and actual sight, and another who is not guilty is indicted before you and found guilty. You ought to respite the judgment against him, for you know the contrary, and to inform the King he may pardon (faire grace). . . .

Gascoigne, C.J.: Once the King himself questioned me as to this case which you put, and asked me what the law was; and I told him as you say. And he was well pleased that the law was so.[79]

Despite his private knowledge, drawn from his "actual sight," the English judge, like his Continental counterpart, was to go ahead and enter judgment, seeking to evade the resulting injustice by engineering a pardon for the offender. There is no reason to assume this case describes a real event: Gascoigne was discussing a familiar chestnut, a moral poser known all through Western Christendom, not retailing a personal anecdote.[80] But in any case the precedent was there.

Yet if conscience and canon teaching were around from the earliest date in the history of the common law, they could not possibly have had the same significance that they did in Continental Europe. As we have seen, Continental law declared judges to be at risk when they made use of their private knowledge. This was knowledge they might have had in two ways: either as private persons, through having directly witnessed a crime, or as clerics who had taken confession.

Both dangers were far less pressing for English judges. There was undoubtedly the occasional moment when an English judge brought personal knowledge to a case; and we do have some evidence of such cases.[81] Nevertheless, the dangers that dogged Continental judges could never have been as grave for English ones. In part this was because English judges were less frequently residents of the locality in which events took place; unlike Continental judges, so often local clerics or local royal officials, the judges of the common law sat in Westminster, traveling to an alien and somewhat hostile "country" on eyre or on circuit.[82] When in need of local knowledge, they depended on local jurors. They were thus less likely to have direct exposure to the facts of the cases they judged. During the thirteenth century, to be sure, clerics judged cases, and Turner has shown that the English were consequently quite anxious about the familiar risk that they might thereby be tainted with blood. Nevertheless, by the end of the thirteenth century, common law judging had become a secular calling.[83]

But most important of all, English common law judges were unlikely to face the Continental dilemmas of conscience because they, unlike their Continental counterparts, were not charged with entering verdicts. Indeed, from the point of view of the English judge, it could be described as a special glory of the common law that, by leaving the job of the verdict to the jury, it avoided putting the souls of its professional judges in any jeopardy.

So indeed English judges seem to have regarded the matter, as familiar passages from the later literature of the common law show. One striking statement comes from Sir Thomas More. More was Lord Chancellor from 1529 to 1533. As such, he had charge of Chancery — itself, as English lawyers understood it, a repository of "conscience"[84] — and as Lord Chancellor he granted the occasional injunction against the enforcement of a judgment at common law. The result, his biographer reports, was some revealing conflict with the common law judges. When common law judges complained about interference from Chancery, More offered them the opportunity to take over the job of "conscience" themselves. Here is the report of More's biographer:

> [A]s few injunctions as he granted while he was Lord Chancellor, yet were they by some of the judges of the law misliked. . . .
>
> [H]e invited all the judges to dine with him in the Council Chamber at Westminster. Where, after dinner, when he had broken with them what complaints he had heard of his injunctions, and moreover showed them both the number and causes of every one of them in order, — so plainly that upon full debating of those matters, they were all enforced to confess that they in like case could have done no otherwise themselves. Then offered he thus unto them: that if the justices of every court — unto whom the reformation of the rigour of the law, by reason of their office, most especially appertained — would upon reasonable considerations, by their own discretions — as they were, as though, in conscience bound — mitigate and reform the rigour of the law themselves, there should from thence forth by him, no more injunctions be granted. Whereunto they refused to condescend.
>
> Then said he unto them: "Forasmuch as yourselves, my Lords, drive me to that necessity for awarding out injunctions to relieve the people's injury, you cannot hereafter any more justly blame me!" After that he said secretly unto me, "I perceive, Son, why they like not so to do. For they see that they may by the verdict of the jury, cast off all quarrels from themselves upon *them*, which they account their chief defense. And therefore am I compelled to abide the adventure of all such reports."[85]

Sixteenth-century common law judges were eager to "cast the quarrels upon the jury," since the jury "by its verdict" took the responsibility for judgment — so much so that the judges refused the opportunity More offered them to escape interference from Chancery. Historians have long taken this passage as evidence that common law judges were eager to avoid the "agonies of decision."[86]

Even more telling descriptions of the attitude of English judges come from the

1660s and after—from a time when, as we shall see, the conflict over the moral responsibility for judgment in jury trial was growing intense. First is a quote from Matthew Hale, writing in the 1660s when he was Chief Baron of the Exchequer. Juries, Hale assumed, made use of "their own knowledge"—something that, as we shall see, was still quite possible. And because they used their own knowledge, they relieved the judge of much of the "peril" of judgment:

> [T]he jury are judges as well of the credibility of the witnesses, as of the truth of the fact, for possibly they might know somewhat of their own knowledge ... and it is the conscience of the jury, that must pronounce the prisoner *guilty* or *not guilty*.
>
> And to say the truth, it were the most unhappy case that could be to the judge, if he at his peril must take must take upon him the guilt or innocence of the prisoner, and if the judge's opinion must rule the matter of fact, the trial by jury would be useless.[87]

The advantage of jury trial was precisely that it made it unnecessary for the judge to engage in the perilous business of "rul[ing] the matter of fact" and pronouncing the perilous verdict of "guilty." A few years later John Hawles said much the same thing, in a much less familiar passage, to which I shall return:

> [T]he *Judges* [can put] the *Burthen* ... upon the Jurors, for *we*, may they say, *did nothing but our duty according to usual Practise, the Jury his Peers had found the Fellow Guilty upon their Oaths of such an Odious Crime, and attended with such vile, presumptions, and dangerous Circumstances. They are Judges, we took him as they presented him to us, and according to our duty pronounced the Sentence, that the Law inflicts in such Cases, or set a Fine, or ordered Corporal punishment upon him, which was very moderate, Considering the Crime laid in the Indictment or Information, and of which they had so sworn him Guilty; if he were innocent or not so bad as Represented, let his Destruction lye upon the Jury* &c. At this rate if ever we should have an *unconscionable Judge,* might he Argue; And thus the Guilt of the *Blood* or *ruin* of an Innocent man when 'tis too late shall be *Bandyed* to and fro, and *shuffled off* from the Jury to the Judge, and from the Judge to the Jury, but really *sticks fast to both,* but especially *on the Jurors*. . . .[88]

Like so many other authors, Hawles saw the moral drama of jury trial as a struggle over the "burthen" of the responsibility for judgment—a struggle in which the judges had the upper hand.

Most of these passages are well known indeed to historians of the common law. Indeed, in light of them, it has become part of our orthodox teaching that jury trial seemed advantageous in part because it spared judges the responsibility for judgment. Thus Maitland, the pioneer of the history of the common law, observed that judges sought to avoid not only "moral" responsibility but also the dangers of vengeance. The rise of jury trial had to be seen against the background of the decline of the ordeal; and it had to be seen as part of an effort to avoid the responsibility for judgment. "[T]he justices are pursuing a course," he noted,

> which puts the verdict of the country on a level with the older modes of proof. If a man came clean from the ordeal or successfully made his law, the due proof would have been given; no one could have questioned the dictum of Omniscience. The *veredictum patriae* is assimilated to the *iudicium Dei*. English judges find that a requirement of [jury] unanimity is the line of least resistance; it spares them so much trouble. We shall hardly explain the shape that trial by jury very soon assumed unless we take to heart the words of an illustrious judge of our own day: — "It saves judges from the responsibility — which to many men would appear intolerably heavy and painful — of deciding simply on their own opinion upon the guilt or innocence of the prisoner." It saved the judges of the middle ages not only from this moral responsibility, but also from enmities and feuds. Likewise it saved them from that as yet unattempted task, a critical dissection of testimony."[89]

J. H. Baker recently made much the same observation: "The judges sought refuge from the agonies of decision," as he put it, and they aimed to make certain that "the ultimate responsibility for a conviction rested on jurors' consciences."[90]

The Special Position of the Common Law Juror

Yet if historians have long understood this great advantage of jury trial from the point of view of the judges, they have not fully reckoned with the other side of the coin: the consequent discomfort of the jury. To be sure, historians all know that "juror timidity" must have played some role in the dynamic of English criminal justice.[91] But they have not put this in the context of the moral theology whose history the previous chapters have traced. Historians have not grasped the gravity of the moral challenge faced by jurors, and as a consequence they have not grasped the original sense of the reasonable doubt rule.

Why is this? In large part, it is because historians have been victims of a process of historical forgetting: they have gradually lost the memory of the moral anxieties of judging that haunted our ancestors. James Fitzjames Stephen still well understood those anxieties in the later nineteenth century. Maitland understood them too — though he added another element to the mix: to explain the dangers of judging, he saw the significance not only of moral responsibility but also of "enmities and feuds." But in subsequent decades historians because less and less attuned to the old moral sensibilities. There have certainly always been scholars who understood those sensibilities, including Max Radin.[92] But most historians have tended to explain premodern fears by anything except the fear of damnation. Some scholars have been able to explain the fears of jurors only by calling them fears of vengeance violence.[93] Unlike Stephen and Maitland, these scholars have tended to forget the moral challenges of medieval judging. Other scholars have thought that the fears of jurors were the fears of criminal liability,[94] or a desire to avoid "the perils of undue influence."[95] Most recently, George Fisher has described the fear of judging as a fear of making "false steps" that could end a career.[96] There is undoubtedly some truth in all of these explanations of the dangers of judging. In particular, there is no doubt that fear of vengeance violence was strong in the Middle Ages, though it had faded by the eighteenth century. Nevertheless, in the end all these explanations of the anxiety of premodern judging miss the large story. As we shall see, there is no way to explain "reasonable doubt" unless we focus resolutely on the *spiritual* anxieties of judging, as most historians since Stephen and Maitland have failed to do.

There is another reason, too, why historians have not appreciated the dilemmas of the criminal jury. The moral anxieties of judging are not the only aspect of jury trial that historians have forgotten. There is also a critical institutional fact that has been forgotten or misunderstood: well into the early nineteenth century, jurors were still expected to make use of their private knowledge of the case, at least occasionally.

As we have seen, medieval moral theology rested on a core prohibition: the role of the judge was to be kept strictly separate from the role of the witness. Judges were not to use their private knowledge. Indeed, it was by scrupulously avoiding any recourse to their private knowledge that Continental judges could keep themselves safe from the perils of judgment, speaking in their "body" as judge, never in their "body" as witness, maintaining the cool distance of a mere minister of the laws.

Yet from the earliest period juries were not in a position to affect any such stance. On the contrary, they were expected to serve not only as judges but also as witnesses.[97] Indeed, as Mike MacNair has shown, early jurors were defined as "witnesses" through the technical vocabulary of canon law.[98] As anyone familiar with the canon tradition can immediately see, this created a morally delicate situation: early English jurors, once they were charged with the obligation of entering verdicts, mixed the two bodies, serving both as judges and as witnesses. This deserves some emphasis, since historians have devoted a good bit of energy to debating (misguidedly, I think) whether early jurors were *really* witnesses or *really* judges.[99] The answer, critically important from the point of view of moral theology, is that they were both.

Moreover, and more important, jurors would continue to mix the role of judge with the role of witness for many centuries. This deserves to be underlined, since historians have not got the history quite right.[100] Historians have generally supposed that jurors ceased making use of their private knowledge before the end of the Middle Ages.[101] Thus historians have observed that jurors began to hear witness testimony in court by the fifteenth century, and especially by the sixteenth.[102] On the basis of this undoubted fact, and on the basis of a seriously misinterpreted passage from Saint Thomas More,[103] they have generally concluded that jurors ceased in any sense to be witnesses by the early modern period.

Yet this is clearly false. Even once the jurors started hearing witnesses in court, they were still expected to make use of their own independent knowledge of the case, at least occasionally. Thus in 1768 Blackstone could still declare, matter-of-factly, that "evidence in the trial by jury is of two kinds, either that which is given in proof, or that which the jury may receive by their own private knowlege."[104] If jurors had any independent knowledge of the case, Blackstone explained, they should simply testify to what they knew in open court, so that everyone present could evaluate it.[105] The eighteenth-century moralist literature continued to assume that jurors might have private knowledge. Thomas Gisborne's 1771 *Enquiry into the Duties of Men in the Higher and Middle Classes of Society in Great Britain*, for example, explained how jurors were to treat evidence — including evidence they had from their own private knowledge: "The special juror is not less obliged in conscience than the grand juror to diligence in investigating all the circumstances of the matter at issue; *to promptness and accuracy in disclosing additional facts known to himself;* and to incorruptible integrity in pronouncing upon the whole evidence."[106] This may not have happened frequently in places like eighteenth-century London. But then again it may: we have reports of such cases from both the seventeenth and eighteenth centuries.[107] Even in the nineteenth century there were reported cases in which jurors did make use of the extrinsic knowledge, and were even instructed by the court to do so.[108]

Jurors thus potentially judged on the basis of private knowledge from the beginning, and would potentially do so for centuries to come. No doubt cases in which they did so were rare after the central Middle Ages. Yet the law of conscience made it clear that the safer path for the soul lay in studiously abjuring *any* judgment on the basis of private knowledge. Indeed, from the point of view of moral theology, as we shall see in the following chapter, it did not matter all that much whether jurors only potentially had such knowledge. What moral theology required was a kind of spiritual exercise: a determined effort to keep the body of the judge separate from the body of the witness. The very structure of the office of the juror made this spiritual exercise impossible.

Nor could anxious jurors take refuge in the other spiritual strategy adopted by Continental judges: they could not claim that their decision was dictated by a strictly rule-bound heuristic; they could not assert, with Gratian, that they were mere ministers of the law, and that it was the law that killed the defendant. On the contrary, they were personally charged with entering the perilous verdict of "guilty," and they were charged with doing so "according to conscience." "[S]ay what is right according to your conscience," jurors were told as early as 1185.[109] Or as fifteenth- and sixteenth-century jury instructions put it: "[D]o in this matter as God will give you grace, according to the evidence and your conscience";[110] "[D]oe that which God shall put in your mindes to the discharge of your consciences";[111] or even more simply, "Doe in it as God shall put in your hearts."[112] Everything for jurors rested on whether they had properly heeded the voice of God within them; and if they had not, they risked mortal sin. Indeed, English moralists, like Continental ones, waxed fierce on the dangers of testimony and perjury.[113]

The result was a peculiarly English dilemma. Common law *judges* could feel entirely safe from the spiritual dangers of pronouncing verdicts on the basis of the knowledge and evaluation of facts. Indeed, they were on a far more advantageous moral perch than their Continental counterparts. After all, the common law lodged the power to find facts and enter verdicts not in the judges but exclusively in the jurors. But the jurors, by contrast, were in a difficult position: it was well understood that they might indeed sometimes judge on the basis of their private knowledge as witnesses; and at the end of the trial, taking on the role of judge, they were to pronounce the perilous word of judgment, "guilty."

The Immunity of the Medieval Criminal Jury

By the seventeenth and eighteenth centuries, this resulted in a kind of moral crisis of jury trial—a moral crisis that produced the reasonable doubt standard. The crisis did not in fact arrive until the early modern period, though. It could not arrive until then: during the Middle Ages criminal jurors were not yet rigorously compelled to enter general verdicts in the morally fraught business of inflicting blood punishments.

There *were* important conflicts in the Middle Ages, but they almost all involved the civil jury, not the criminal jury.[114] Indeed, medieval civil juries seemed to have cared a lot about this issue, since they often resisted entering verdicts. As David Seipp has observed, surveying the evidence of the four-teenth and fifteenth centuries, jurors regularly tried to "shift the responsibility [of entering verdicts] to the person of the judge."[115] In particular, civil jurors sought an important privilege: instead of entering the general verdict, they sought to enter special verdicts, making mere findings of fact while forcing the judge to pronounce the perilous judgment on ultimate liability. Civil jurors were very eager to acquire this privilege. Indeed, Parliament petitioned the king in 1348 to allow jurors in all civil cases to enter special verdicts rather than general verdicts.[116] That petition was brusquely denied, though.[117] In most civil cases, with the striking exception of the assize of novel disseisin,[118] medieval jurors were compelled to enter the general verdict, even though they did so, in the language of medieval law, "at their peril."[119] In fact, civil juries that refused to enter the general verdict were subject to harsh measures: as we have seen, they could be prosecuted through the attaint. Indeed, from the fourteenth century onward, the Crown progressively tightened the screws on civil juries, forcing them to enter the general verdict.[120] Only in the sixteenth century did civil juries acquire the privilege of entering special verdicts.[121]

With criminal juries, however, the story was different. Medieval criminal juries were not threatened with the attaint, and they acquired a privilege that they retained until the nineteenth century:[122] the medieval system spared crim-inal juries the "peril" of delivering judgment by allowing them to enter special verdicts.[123]

The medieval criminal jury's immunity to the attaint has always been re-garded as somewhat mysterious.[124] In theory, the attaint did apply to criminal juries, in an asymmetrical form. As Bracton explained it in the thirteenth century, the defendant could not bring an attaint if he was convicted.[125] The Crown by contrast was entitled to bring an attaint, in theory, in the case of an acquittal. However, as James Bradley Thayer demonstrated a century ago, there is essentially no evidence that the Crown ever did so.[126] Medieval crimi-nal juries were simply not attainted. Indeed, the criminal attaint had to be introduced by separate statue in 1534, when the Tudor Crown was beginning to crack down on criminal juries, and even then it was introduced only "in Wales and its Marches."[127]

So why were medieval criminal juries not attainted? Thayer spent many pages on this problem but could only propose an explanation that seems obviously wrong.[128] Yet the right answer is not all that difficult to identify. Thomas Green, a leading authority on the history of jury trial, has offered it: "[T]he fact that the defendant's life was at stake" made the attaint seem some-how inappropriate in criminal cases, Green suggests.[129] Just so: as we have seen, in Christian moral theology the infliction of blood punishments raised special concerns, and criminal trials resulted in theory in blood punishments.[130] If we keep this moral theology in mind, we have no difficulties explaining why the medieval criminal jury would have been treated differently: forcing jurors to enter verdicts in cases of blood would have put the system under intolerable moral pressure.[131]

Cases of blood created moral pressure. This fact also helps account for the second privilege of medieval criminal juries: they were spared the "peril" of the general verdict by being allowed to enter special verdicts. The common law distinguishes between the "general" verdict — verdicts of "guilty" or "not guilty" — and "special" verdicts, by which the jury simply makes certain findings without making an ultimate determination of guilt or innocence. Today, criminal juries ordinarily give the general verdict, but this was not yet necessarily true in the Middle Ages. Green has traced the rise of special verdicts in medieval criminal trials in elegant detail. It was through permitting special verdicts that medieval law dealt with matters of justification and excuse. In cases of homicide, the jury might desire to bring in a verdict of manslaughter or self-defense. Yet the indictment permitted only the verdict of murder. The law of the fourteenth century thus offered jurors a way out: it allowed them to enter special verdicts, often finding demonstrably fictitious facts while avoiding the uncomfortable task of declaring the defendant either guilty or innocent.[132]

Entering special verdicts was a significant privilege, denied to most civil juries; in the equivalent cases, most civil juries were forced to enter the general verdict. Indeed, to understand why criminal jurors had this privilege we must read the history of criminal juries alongside that of their civil counterparts. The leading case permitting criminal juries to enter special verdicts dates to 1329. The date is significant. The early fourteenth century was generally a time of crisis and change for jury trial.[133] The year 1329 in particular came in the midst of a period when the new regime of Edward III was clamping down steadily on civil juries, with one statute enhancing the threat of attaint in 1326–1327, and one further enhancing the attaint in 1331.[134] There is evidence of criminal jurors too being browbeaten when they refused to give the general verdict in 1321.[135] It was thus in an atmosphere of real tension that it was held that the criminal jury could avoid the general issue by entering a special verdict.[136] The fact that criminal juries acquired this privilege at the height of a period in which civil juries were being disciplined suggests the same conclusion suggested by the criminal jury's immunity to the attaint: the English Crown was sensitive to the special moral problems of the criminal jury.

The immunity of the criminal jury to attaint and its privilege of entering special verdicts were perhaps enough to guarantee that medieval criminal jurors would not face any of the worst dilemmas of the Christian law of conscience. The story is not complete, though, without mentioning one further aspect of medieval justice that offered criminal jurors some measure of moral comfort: courts could avoid inflicting blood punishments in some instances by allowing the accused the benefit of clergy. Benefit of clergy was a device by which accused persons were treated as fictive members of the clergy. This meant that they were subject only to the punishments inflicted by the church. Yet the church was forbidden to inflict blood punishments, which meant that defendants accorded benefit of clergy would be neither executed nor mutilated.

Benefit of clergy became "a regular means of escape from the mandatory death penalty" during the fourteenth and fifteenth centuries,[137] especially beginning in 1352[138] — that is to say, within a few decades after criminal juries acquired the privilege of giving special verdicts. This measure too would have eased the moral pressures on the criminal jury; and it too may in some measure reflect a concern about the moral dilemmas of the criminal judging.

It is, in short, difficult to appreciate the medieval criminal jury unless we remember the intensity of the moral pressures felt by anyone deciding cases of blood. To be sure, moral pressures were not the only kind that medieval criminal jurors experienced. There were certainly other pressures as well. As historians have shown, there were the dangers of vengeance.[139] Maitland was not wrong about that. Historians have also amply shown that jurors were susceptible to financial inducements and threats as well — especially jurors who were not themselves persons of substance in the community.[140] Both medieval and early modern legislation show considerable eagerness to keep poor men off juries, so as to keep the trial process safe from corruption.[141] Such concerns were certainly present: it would be quite wrong to explain every aspect of medieval criminal jury trial by reference to the moral dangers of bloodshed.

Nevertheless, there remain fundamental aspects of jury trial that cannot be understood unless we focus on the specifically moral dangers felt by jurors. Financial inducements and physical threats would have been just as much of a danger in civil trials as in criminal ones. Yet criminal matters were treated specially. The threat of juror corruption was especially a threat where jurors were low-status persons: it "varied in inverse proportion to wealth."[142] Yet as the evidence of later centuries will show, there was plenty of anxiety about the pressures felt by even the most upstanding and substantial members of the community; and those pressures were, as we shall see, very clearly moral ones.[143] Criminal trial mattered because it was *criminal* trial, and that meant that it was a moral trial for the Christian juror, as well as a legal trial for the accused.

At any rate, by the end of the Middle Ages the common law had developed mechanisms that effectively shielded criminal jurors from much moral pressure. William Staunford summarized the standard medieval law in his mid-sixteenth-century guide to criminal law. Staunford spoke in the familiar language of moral theology: the key question was whether the verdict in murder cases was "dowtful": "As for the verdict 'not guilty': It is not always necessary to give the general verdict, since if the fact is such, that it is doubtful [dowtful] to the members of the jury, they are permitted to disburden themselves [pour lour mieulx discharge], by giving a special verdict, or as it is known a verdict at large, just as much in cases of felony as in the assize [of novel disseisin] or trespass, and this appears in the verdict that finds that the defendant has killed in self-defense. . . . And just as they can give a special verdict in a case of self-defense, so can they do it in the case of a homicide *per infortunium* . . . [or] chance medley."[144] Death and doubt: these were the great issues. Sir Edward Coke too cited the same doctrine at the end of the century. For him too the need for special verdicts arose in cases where the jury experienced doubt: "[N]ote, reader, in all cases when jurors find the special matter doubtful in law pertinent and tending to the issue which they are to try, there the Court ought to accept it."[145] Death and doubt presented the great challenges for the criminal jury.

The Crises of the Seventeenth Century

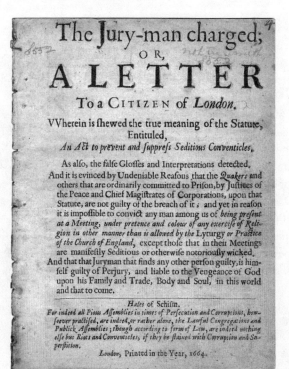

The Jury-man charged;
OR,
A LETTER
To a CITIZEN of *London*.

VVherein is shewed the true meaning of the Statute,
Entituled,
An Act to prevent and suppress Seditious Conventicles.

As also, the false Glosses and Interpretations detected.
And it is evinced by Undeniable Reasons that the *Quakers* and
others that are ordinarily committed to Prison, by Justices of
the Peace and Chief Magistrates of Corporations, upon that
Statute, are not guilty of the breach of it ; and yet in reason
it is impossible to convict any man among us of *being present
at a Meeting, under pretence and colour of any exercise of Religion in other manner than is allowed by the* Lyturgy *or Practice
of the Church of England,* except those that in their Meetings
are manifestly Seditious or otherwise notoriously wicked.
And that that Juryman that finds any other person guilty, is himself guilty of Perjury, and liable to the Vengeance of God
upon his Family and Trade, Body and Soul, in this world
and that to come.

Hales of Schism.
*For indeed all Pious Assemblies in times of Persecution and Corruptions, how-
soever practised, are indeed, or rather alone, the Lawful Congregations and
Publick Assemblies ; though according to form of Law, are indeed nothing
else but Riots and Conventicles, if they be stained with Corruption and Superstition.*

London, Printed in the Year, 1664.

Question: Must a Judge and jury proceed secundum allegata & probata, *according to evidence and proof,* when they know the witness to be false, and the truth to be contrary to the testimony; but are not able to evince it?

Answ. . . . *The Judge must come off the Bench, and the Jury protest that they will not meddle, or give any Verdict (what ever come of it): Because God and the Law of Nature prohibit their injustice.*

Object. It is the Law that doth it, and not we.

Answ. *It is the Law and you: And the Law cannot justifie your agency in any unrighteous sentence. The case is plain and past dispute.*

— Richard Baxter, A Christian Directory *(1673)*

Can you appeal to God with a good conscience, and say before the great and dreadful Judge of Heaven and Earth; Lord, let me suffer Death and Damnation as a Murderer, if these persons be not sufficiently proved guilty?

— H. E., The Jury-Man charged *(1664)*

In the final two chapters, we turn to the seventeenth and eighteenth centuries. These were the centuries of Anglo-American revolutions, during which the core constitutional rights that we associate with American liberty took shape, most prominently in the English Bill of Rights of 1689 and the American Bill of Rights of 1791. These are also the centuries in which jury trial assumed its central place among the political rights associated with the common law. It was, finally, during this period that the reasonable doubt instruction gradually emerged. As we shall see, the emergence of reasonable doubt was directly connected to the constitutional crises of this era — in particular to the crises of the 1660s, 1670s, and 1680s that preceded the Glorious Revolution of 1688. We shall also see that the history of those crises must be read through the lens of the same Christian theology whose history I traced in the previous four chapters. The religion of the Middle Ages was still very much alive in the law of the later English seventeenth century.

This chapter begins by describing briefly the law of jury trial as it developed

Figure 6. From a pamphlet published during the gathering crisis of jury trial in 1664: "The Juryman who finds any other person guilty, is himself guilty of Perjury, and liable to the Vengeance of God upon his Family and Trade, Body and Soul, in this world and that to come." H. E., *The Jury-Man charged; or a Letter to a Citizen of London* (London: n.p., 1664), 1. Beinecke Rare Book and Manuscript Library, Yale University, image 1084188 (1664).

in the sixteenth and early seventeenth centuries. This was a period in which the English Crown worked hard to diminish the right of jurors to resist giving judgments. The modern history of the development of jury trial begins in the 1660s, when this era of royal jury discipline came to an end. After describing these developments, I turn to the two bodies of seventeenth-century literature that allow us to see how the moral theology of the Middle Ages survived in this age of constitutional crisis: first, the Christian literature of conscience, and second, the common law literature surrounding the great jury cases of the later seventeenth century, Wagstaff's Case and Bushel's Case.

In all of this literature, as we shall see, the old moral theology remained alive. It changed in one critical respect, though: in the seventeenth and eighteenth centuries, we find no sense that judges and witnesses faced the danger of vengeance violence. The relatives of the convicted person no longer threatened to step in. The fear of the vengeance of God remained, however, palpably present.

If matters had rested as they were in the Middle Ages, jurors would have faced relatively little of the pressure that eventually gave rise to the doctrine of reasonable doubt. As we saw in the last chapter, medieval criminal jurors were shielded from most of the dangers that might have been caused by pronouncing guilty verdicts. They were not obliged to give the general verdict, and those they convicted often had benefit of clergy. But beginning in the sixteenth and early seventeenth centuries, things changed, and starkly. These were the centuries during which what historians call Renaissance states began to establish themselves in western Europe. Renaissance statecraft involved the assertion of far greater state power than had existed in the Middle Ages. Princes of this era had access to far more powerful weaponry. They made far more aggressive claims for their authority, venturing the claim that they were "absolute." Kings like those of France aimed to eliminate the old representative bodies of the Middle Ages—like the French Estates General, which met for the last time in 1614, to be reconvened only in 1789. This was an era of assertive state power.

The Tudor and Stuart kings of England were monarchs of this era. They too attempted—without success, as it eventually turned out—to build Renaissance monarchies on their own island. Like other monarchs, they worked hard to take firm control of their territories, particularly beginning with what G. R. Elton famously called "The Tudor Revolution in Government."[1] Part of this effort at discipline was directed at criminal jurors, who were subjected to wholly new pressures. Princely governments of the sixteenth century in every part of Europe embarked on tough crackdowns on crime. The Tudors and Stuarts were no exception, and they did not gladly tolerate acquittals. "A virtual revolution was underway from the mid-fifteenth century," as the En-glish Crown set out to bring criminal juries to heel.[2] In particular, this involved harsh discipline for criminal juries that refused to enter the general verdict.[3] By 1516, a new actor came in: Star Chamber, the most notorious instrument of Renaissance royal power in England.[4] Star Chamber took cognizance of crimi-nal jury misconduct for the next century and a quarter. Juries were bound over to Star Chamber for punishment throughout the sixteenth century, and some-times punished by judges as well.[5] Star Chamber actively disciplined recalci-trant criminal juries until it was abolished in 1641. Even after 1641, the judges of the common law courts continued fining and imprisoning criminal jurors,[6] probably with increasing frequency during the 1660s in particular.[7]

The solutions of the medieval common law to the problems of conscience were thus radically rejected during the first period of the rise of the early modern state: no longer permitted to evade giving judgment, criminal juries were subjected to the same pressures that civil juries had been subjected to a few centuries earlier. At the same time, another factor too increased the moral pressure on early modern criminal juries in the sixteenth and seventeenth centuries: the English Renaissance state steadily cut back on the range of offenses for which benefit of clergy was available. In the Middle Ages, as we have seen, juries were sometimes spared the dangers of inflicting blood punish-ments by the institution of benefit of clergy, which allowed defendants to escape unscathed. But especially from the mid-sixteenth-century onward, more and more offenses were exempted from the privilege of benefit of clergy.[8] This too was part of the princely crackdown of the early modern period. Its consequence was that throughout the seventeenth century, criminal juries would face the burdensome obligation of sentencing offenders to blood pun-ishments more frequently than their medieval predecessors did.

The sixteenth and seventeenth centuries were thus moral hard times for English criminal jurors. Only beginning in the later seventeenth century did relief gradually arrive. Over the period from 1660 to 1800, the great period of the solidification and creation of common law "liberties," English government took a critical turn away from the princely practices of the Continent. During this period of slow liberalization, which is my topic in these final two chapters, criminal jurors recovered the privileges they had enjoyed in the Middle Ages. Thus the 1660s saw tense conflict over whether jurors could be punished for refusing to enter general verdicts as directed. Finally, in 1670, Bushel's Case held that they were in principle immune from coercion.[9] This was moreover only part of the shift of the period 1660–1800. In the decades after Bushel's Case, the nature of English punishment changed, too. Benefit of clergy was effectively extended in various ways from the later seventeenth century onward.[10] Between 1706 and 1718, some offenders who pleaded benefit of clergy were subjected to hard labor; and after 1718, offenders were routinely transported to the American colonies. Transportation remained the ordinary punishment until the American Revolution broke out. After a hiatus from 1775 to 1787, it was resumed, with offenders now transported to Australia.

In the decades after the Tudor-Stuart crackdown, mid-eighteenth-century English criminal jurors thus found themselves in a position more like that of their medieval predecessors: they did not generally need to experience moral anxiety over the verdicts they handed down. The only exception came during the period of uncertainty from 1775 to 1787, when it was unclear whether transportation could be resumed as the ordinary nonblood punishment. As we shall see, it was precisely toward the end of that uncertain period, after American victory in the Revolution made it clear that transportation to America was no longer an option, that the reasonable doubt rule introduced itself into English criminal justice.

At any rate, it was during the period 1660–1800, the period during which the sixteenth-century pressures gradually lifted from the criminal jury, that the reasonable doubt instruction slowly emerged. When it did, it emerged in an atmosphere rich in references to the classic moral theology of doubt and blood.

The Cases of Conscience Literature

To follow what happened during the critical decades of the 1660s through the 1680s, we must read two different kinds of literature. One is the familiar literature of the common law itself: in particular, the famous decisions in Wagstaff's Case (1665) and Bushel's Case (1670); the trial of Chief Justice Kelyng before the House of Commons in 1667; the Boston Massacre trials of 1770; and numerous English criminal cases from the Old Bailey dating from 1782 to the mid-1790s. These are all familiar sources to legal historians. But we will not understand these familiar common law texts unless we read them alongside a different body of literature, much less well known to most legal historians — what was called the literature of "cases of conscience." It is in the literature of cases of conscience that we find the old Christian moral theology, with some new English slants, presented to the English reader, in ways that deeply colored the great debates about criminal justice.

The cases of conscience literature is the Protestant, and especially Calvinist, repository of the law of conscience whose history since the twelfth century I have traced.[11] It is indeed a distinctly Protestant literature. In the medieval Catholic world, as we have seen, the law of conscience had a close link with the sacrament of confession. The canon law of conscience, developed by so-

phisticated jurists, was communicated to confessors through so-called confessors' manuals. Following those manuals, confessors were to pour "wine
and oil into the wounds of the one injured after the manner of a skillful
physician," ministering to the souls of their congregants. The Catholic law of
conscience thus supplemented the inner voice of conscience by the trained
voice of the priest.

This historic link between conscience and confession was inevitably shaken
during the Reformation, as confession faded in importance within the Protestant world. In the eyes of leading Protestants — though certainly not of all of
them — the individual sinner did not need the intermediation of a priest in
order to hear the inner voice of conscience. On the contrary, the practice of
confession seemed, especially to Calvinists, a prime example of Catholic perversion of the original Christian impulse — a prime example of an evil corruption by which a priest was interposed between the believer and God. Accordingly, in varying degrees and different ways, the Protestant sects tended to
distance themselves from the sacrament of confession.

That does not mean, however, that the old literature of conscience vanished
in the Protestant world. Even where there was neither confession nor confessors' manuals, there was nevertheless a semi-popular Protestant literature that
purveyed the classic canon law of conscience in its own fashion. This Protestant literature took the form of books of "cases of conscience," of which the
two most famous early versions were produced by two English Calvinists,
William Ames and William Perkins, in the early seventeenth century.

These books differed little in substance from the medieval canon law of
conscience: They contained much the same simplified version of the canon law
of conscience that was found in the old confessor's manuals. But unlike the old
confessors' manuals, Protestant books of cases of conscience were meant to be
read by individual Christians themselves. Indeed, to browse in the cases of
conscience literature is to get a taste of the early modern Protestant experience
in its most astringent form: Protestants who studied cases of conscience books
were Protestants who found themselves alone with their consciences, forced to
act as their own judges, without the supervision of a confessor able to dispense
penance, able to pour "wine and oil into [their] wounds." The cases of conscience literature was the instrument of some of the most anxiety-inducing
aspects of early modern Protestant life. It is within this literature, as I want
now to demonstrate, that we find the key to the origins of the reasonable
doubt standard: in this literature, we find the old theology of doubt, whose
history I traced in chapter 4, applied to the case of English judges and English
jurors.

Here I must pause to say a word about prior historiography. I am not the

first historian to argue that we must look to the literature of cases of conscience in order to explain reasonable doubt. Since a seminal article published
by Theodore Waldman in 1959, a number of important scholars have examined the old books of conscience in the effort to find the origins of the reasonable doubt rule.[12] These include most notably Barbara Shapiro, James Franklin, and Margaret Sampson. These historians have done some superb work;
several illuminating pages in Sampson's work stand out in particular. Nevertheless, they have not quite got the story right, for reasons that have to do
with the remarkable intellectual history of the theology of doubt in the early
modern period.

The theology of doubt underwent striking developments from the sixteenth
century onward. As we saw in chapter 4, the medieval Catholic theology of
doubt established a four-level scale of certainty. The highest of these four levels
was moral certainty, followed by opinion, suspicion, and doubt. Christians
seeking to avoid endangering their salvation were enjoined to transcend the
levels of doubt, suspicion, and opinion in order to attain moral certainty at
last. This theology of doubt provided the framework for a theology of judging
that aimed to safeguard the salvation of the judge by allowing him to achieve
moral certainty before convicting.

The theology of doubt, in the Middle Ages, offered rules for salvation. Yet
its four-level scale of certainty could also be turned to a different purpose, the
purpose of scientific investigation. Exactly that happened during the early
modern period. Indeed, as historians of epistemology and science have shown,
most elegantly Franklin, the theology of doubt was of great importance for the
making of Western epistemology. The famous four degrees of certainty could
be thought of as representing a scale of *factual proof* as well as a scale of *moral
responsibility*. So it was that, in the early modern period, scientists and philosophers concerned with epistemological proof drew directly on the terminology of the theology of doubt. Philosophical programs like Descartes' exercise in "radical doubt" grew out of this theological tradition. So did many of
the basic terms of the scientific search for certainty.[13]

As a result, the old moral theology of doubt influenced early modern science. This undoubted historical fact is at the root of some of the most significant confusion in our literature on the history of reasonable doubt. It is precisely because the theology of doubt worked its way into the philosophy of
science that historians like Franklin and Shapiro could come to a mistaken
conclusion: the conclusion that the reasonable doubt rule had something to do
with the search for scientific certainty—had something to do with an early
effort to create a standard of factual proof at trial. When these scholars,
oriented toward the history of science, investigated the literature of con-

science, they investigated it as a source for the early modern understanding of how to attain factual proof. Shapiro, for example, in her important work, read some of the literature of cases of conscience. But what she read were only the sections on the general theory of "certainty," not the sections on judging and jury trial. Reading the literature in that limited way, she concluded that the reasonable doubt standard was a standard of proof, in which truth was measured by the "satisfied conscience." She concluded that seventeenth-century concepts of the jury grew out of seventeenth-century concepts of epistemology and proof closely related to those of seventeenth-century science.[14] Similar things are true of Franklin's superbly learned book.[15]

Yet if the terminology of doubt could be used for the philosophy of knowledge, it never lost its connection with the moral problematics of judging, and it is a mistake to focus too much on the epistemological puzzles of science if we want to understand the rise of reasonable doubt. The theology of doubt was not just about achieving scientific certainty; it always concerned itself with doubt in moral matters, and indeed with *"reasonable* doubt" in "moral matters."[16] Precisely because it remained a *moral* theology, it applied quite directly to the moral dilemmas of criminal justice. There is no doubt that seventeenth-century jurors were charged to find facts. But from the point of view of moral theology, it was not their task to find facts in the dauntless investigative spirit of a Newton or a Boyle. They were supposed to find facts in a spirit of fear and trembling. As the author of a 1664 pamphlet entitled "The Jury-Man charged" put it, "If they are sworn to give Verdict according to Evidence, may [they] proceed to condemn men without Evidence according to what they believe in their heart?"[17] By no means: "[T]he Juryman who finds any other person guilty, is himself guilty of Perjury, and liable to the Vengeance of God upon his Family and Trade, Body and Soul, in this world and that to come."[18]

Such was the attitude that continued to haunt the theology of judging. If we look past the sections of the cases of conscience literature on certainty and read the sections specifically devoted to judges and juries, we discover that the old moral meaning of the old moral theology was still alive. Perhaps English trial was slowly moving toward a search for factual proof rather than moral comfort in the seventeenth century. Perhaps — though, as we shall, the great English cases of the era do not turn on doubt about the facts at all. But even if there was more mystery about facts in the seventeenth century than in the Middle Ages, the old theology hung on. The prevailing conception of the trial, and of the jury's role, still revolved around the moral responsibility for judgment. The new sciences of the era did indeed make use of a transformed theology of doubt. But when it came to justice, the old untransformed theology of blood was still the order of the day.

It is indeed only by reading the sections on judging, in the cases of conscience literature that we can understand the seminal developments of the late seventeenth century and after.

Let us turn, then, to the sections of the old books of conscience devoted specifically to judging. Throughout the seventeenth and eighteenth centuries, cases of conscience books kept all the traditional canon law problems of the judicial conscience in the English vernacular literature — with certain striking English differences, attesting to a distinctive and somewhat radical English tradition of moral theology. Indeed, English authors were conscious that their thought represented a distinct strain.[19] "We are freed," declared the leading seventeenth-century author Jeremy Taylor, in a most English way, "from the impositions and lasting errors of a tyrannical spirit, and yet from the extravagances of a popular spirit too."[20] They may or may not have been more free; but they were certainly more English.

One such distinctive feature was that English authors did not focus exclusively on blood punishments, as their Continental counterparts did. To be sure, most of the English analysis did concern cases of blood, and we shall see that cases of blood were always the most important in English eyes. Nevertheless, from an early date, English authors also regarded questions of property as raising problems of conscience. Perhaps we can detect in this evidence that property rights mattered more in the English tradition than they did in the Continental tradition. Perhaps it is simply a reflection of the fact that jury trial emerged as a substitute for forms of the judgment of God in two different contexts: both in cases of blood (for which ordeals had been used) and in land disputes (for which trial by battle had been used).[21]

At any rate, the attachment to property rights was only one of the characteristically English aspects of the English literature. The English also regarded themselves as more morally rigorous on the question famously posed by Thomas Aquinas: the question of whether a judge might convict an innocent person in spite of his private knowledge of innocence. As we saw in chapter 4, Aquinas did not shy away from the great moral paradox posed by the ban on private knowledge. Even when a judge's private knowledge told him that the accused was innocent, he had nevertheless to convict if the record developed in court so dictated, and he could not find some way to evade the result. As the paradoxical Thomist conclusion ran: "Many things must be done against conscience for the sake of conscience."[22] Not every Continental moralist followed Aquinas's radical opinion, however. On the contrary: Continental jurists in particular rejected the Thomist assertion that a judge might convict the innocent in order to preserve his own salvation.

The English literature too had a long and unusually aggressive tradition of rejecting Aquinas's argument—a tradition of which English authors, who frequently contrasted themselves with the Spanish, were very proud. Already in fourteenth-century England the fiery reformer Wyclif rejected the Thomist moral paradox.[23] So did Christopher St. German in the early sixteenth century.[24] (Perhaps we can hear an echo in Shakespeare as well: his malfeasant judge Angelo, the protagonist of *Measure for Measure*, defended himself by quoting the Augustinian formula adopted by the canon lawyers, "It is the law not I.")[25] At any rate, Wyclif's and St. German's seventeenth-century successors in the English literature of conscience took the same stand, deeming it unacceptable that judges should contemplate convicting accused persons in the face of their private knowledge of innocence. The English were characterized by a distinctive kind of rigorism, which they proudly contrasted with the Continental/Thomist view. This was, however, a rigorism that would do much to deepen the moral dilemma of criminal jurors.

Thus William Ames, the leading authority of the early seventeenth century, insisted that the judge had to lay down his office rather than convict a person whom he knew from his own private knowledge to be innocent. Ames presented the issue in terms that harkened back to the Middle Ages but resonated with the conflicts over governmental power of his own century. Medieval jurists had distinguished between the body of the "judge" and the body of the "man." Within the in dubio pro reo tradition, they had pointed to the conflict between the "public interest" and the moral requirement of lenity.[26] These were still the terms in which Ames spoke. For Ames, the question was whether it was legitimate to distinguish between the judge as a "public person," the embodiment of the "Common-wealth," and the judge as a man with a "private conscience." Ames held that it was not. In the classic manner of the casuistic literature, Ames presented the arguments for and against:

Of Publique Judgements

Quest 5. *Whether the Judge ought always to give sentence according to the things alleaged and proved?*

20. *A.* 1. The Iudge ought not to passe sentence against the things alleaged and proved, whatsoever there bee in his private knowledge.

For first, the Iudge sentenceth as a publique person, and instead of the Common-wealth. . . . But if the Common-wealth should sentence, it could not proceed, but upon publique knowledge. . . .

If the Iudge could sentence either against, or beside things alleaged and proved, there would from thence follow great discommodities, and the perversion of judgements: when unjust Iudges would easily condemne the innocent, and quit the guilty, under pretext of a private knowledge, which disagreeth from the things alleaged and proved.

Thirdly, there can be no other way, by which the Common-wealth may remaine in quiet.

21. *A.* 2 Yet the Iudge is not so restrained to things alleaged and proved, that he must condemne him to death, whom hee knoweth plainely to bee innocent.

First, Because things alleaged and proved, are onely means of manifesting the truth, and therefore ought not to prevaile with any against the truth which is certainly knowen. . . .

Secondly, Because a Iudge which pronounceth that to bee true which certainly hee knoweth to bee false, would bee a lyer, and sinne against his owne conscience.

22. *A.* 3. Neither is the argument solved by that distinction, betweene the publique and private conscience of a Iudge.

For first, the private conscience ought not to be violated at any time. . . .

Thirdly, Because to slay an innocent, is a fact intrinsecally evill. . . .

23.*A.*4. If the Iudge would but doe his duty in procuring the manifestation of the truth, so much intricatenesse would seldome happen. But if it should happen after hee hath tried all things for the delivery of the innocent, hee is bound to leave his office of Iudge rather than to condemne him.[27]

"Hee is bound to leave office of Iudge" rather than condemn. This was the standard English view, which authors on conscience frequently contrasted with what they insisted was the ugly casuistry of the Catholic world, especially of the Spanish.

As one example among many, we may take Joseph Hall's 1654 *Cases of Conscience, Practically Resolved.* To Hall, the judge who convicted in the face of his exculpatory private knowledge was "guilty of blood"; if such a judge was honest, he would heed the voice of his conscience, "the bird in his bosome," which would tell him that he had made himself a "murtherer":

Case VI. Whether a Judge may upon allegations, proofes, and evidences of others, condemn a man to death, whom he himself certainly knows to be innocent. The question hath undergone much agitation; The streame of all ancient Divines, and Casuists runs upon the affirmative; their ground is, that the Judge, as he is a publique person, so in the set of Judicature, he must exercise a publique authority; and therefore waving his private knowledge and interest, must sentence according to the allegations and proofes brought before him; since he is a Judge of the cause, not of the law; whereof he is to be the servant, not the master: There he sits not to speake his own judgement; but to be the mouth of the law, and the law command him to judge according to the evidence; the evidence therefore being cleare and convictive, the doome can be no other than condemnatory.

For my part, I can more marvell at their judgement herein, than approve it. . . .

It is an evident and undeniable law of God which must be the rule of all Judges; *The innnocent and the righteous slay thou not, Exod. 23.27*. This is a Law neither to be avoided, nor dispensed with: Accusations and false witnesses cannot make a man other than innocent; they may make him to seeme so; in so much as those that know not the cause exactly, may perhaps be misled to condemne him in their judgments: But to the Judge, whose eyes were witnesses of the parties innocence, all the evidence in the world cannot make him other than guiltlesse; so as that Judge shall be guilty of blood, in slaying the innocent, and righteous.

Secondly, the law of judging according to allegations and proofs is a good generall direction in the common course of proceedings; but there are cases wherein this law must vaile to an higher, which is the law of Conscience: Woe be to that man who shall tye himselfe so close to the letter of the law, as to make shipwrack of conscience; And that bird in his bosome will tell him, that if upon what ever pretences, he shall willingly condemne an innocent, he is no better than a murtherer. . . .

Let no man now tell me, that it is the law that condemnes the man, and not the Judge; This excuse will not serve before the Tribunall of heaven; The law hath no tongue; It is the Judge that is *lex loquens;* If he then shall pronounce that sentence which his owne heart tells him is unjust and cruell, what is he but an officious minister of injustice? But, indeed, what law ever said, Thou shalt kill that man whom thou knowest innocent, if false witnesse will sweare him guilty? This is but a false glosse set upon a true text, to countenance a man in being an instrument of evil.

Hall did not deny the difficulties of the matter. He recognized that his world was one of severe disorder, in which the public interest might seem to require loyalty from the public servants charged with carrying out a severe criminal justice. He even struggled to give some credit to the Spanish moral theologians:

What then is in this case to be done? Surely, as I durst not acquite that Judge, who under what ever colour of law should cast away a known innocent, so I durst not advise against plaine evidences and flat dispositions, upon private knowledge, that man to be openly pronounced guiltlesse; and thereby discharged; for as the one is a grosse violation of justice; so were the other a publique affront to the law; and of dangerous consequence to the weale publique: Certainly, it could not but be extreamely unsafe, that such a gappe should bee opened to the liberty of judgement, that a private brest should be opposed (with an apparent prevalence) against publique convictions: our Casuists have beaten their braines to finde out some such evasions as might save the innocent from death, and the Judge from blood guiltinesse: Herein therefore they advise the Judge to use some secret meanes to stop the accusation, or indictment; (a course that might be as prejudiciall to justice, as a false sentence) to sift the witnesses apart, as in *Susanna's* case, and by many subtile interrogations of the circumstances to find their variance or contradiction. If that prevaile not, *Cajetan* goes so farre, as to determine it meet (which how it might stand with their law, he knowes, with ours it would not) that the Judge should before all the people give his oath, that hee knowes the party guiltlesse; as whom he himselfe saw at that very houre in a place far distant from that wherein the fact is pretended to bee done: Yea [citing Dom. à Sot. De Jure, &c. C.l.5.qu.4.] *Dominicus à Soto* could be content (if it might be done without scandall) that the prisoner might secretly be suffered to slip out of the geaole, and save himselfe by flight. Others think it the best way, that the Judge should put off the cause to a superiour Bench, and that himselfe should (laying aside his scarlet) come to the Bar, and as a witnesse avow upon oath the innocence of the party, and the falsity of the accusation: Or lastly, if he should out of malice, or some other sinister ends (as of the forfeiture of some rich estate) be pressed by higher powers to passe the sentence on his own Bench, that he ought to lay downe his Commission, and to abdicate that power he hath, rather than to suffer it forced to a willing injustice.

But despite all that, Hall rejected the view of the Spanish moral theologians, even the best of them:

And truly were the case mine, after all faire and lawfull indeavours to justifie the innocent, and to avoid the sentence, I should most willingly yield to this last resolution: yea, rather my selfe to undergoe the sentence of death, than to prounounce it on the knowne guiltlesse; hating the poore pusillanimity of *Dominicus à Soto*.[28]

Hall's dislike of (and grudging respect for) Spanish moral casuistry was typical of the English world.[29] So was his insistence that judges must rigorously avoid violating their consciences.

This was notably true of the most influential text of the late seventeenth century: Jeremy Taylor's 1660 *Ductor Dubitantium* (The Guide for Those in Doubt). Taylor is indeed a particularly important figure, since he remained highly influential throughout the eighteenth and even nineteenth centuries.[30] Early on in his long text, Taylor turned to the problem of judging. Like other English moralists, he rejected the approach that permitted a judge to condemn the innocent. In his charming baroque style, he decorated his discussion with an anecdote drawn from the literature of classical antiquity:

But then what shall a Judge do, who knows the witnesses in a criminal cause to have sworn falsly? The case is this: *Conopus* a *Spartan* Judge, walking abroad near the garden of *Onesicritus*, espies him killing of his slave *Asotus*; who to palliate the fact, himself accuses another of his servants *Orgilus* and compell'd some to swear it as he affirmed. The process was made, advocates entertain'd by *Onesicritus*, and the poor *Orgilus* convict by testimony and legal proof. *Conopus* the Judge knows the whole process to be injurious, but he knows not what to do, because he remembers that he is bound to judge according to allegation and proof, and yet to do justice and judgment, which in this case is impossible. He therefore inquires for an expedient, or a peremptory resolution on either hand: Since he offends against the Laws of *Sparta*, if he acquits one who is legally convicted; and yet if he condemns him whom he knows to be innocent, he sins against God, and Nature, and against his own Conscience.

That a Judge not only may, but is oblig'd to proceed according to the process of Law, and not to his own private Conscience, is confidently affirmed by *Aquinas*, by his *Master*, and by his *Scholars*, and of late defended earnestly by *Didacus Covarruvius* a learned Man indeed and a great Lawyer. . . .

But if after all this you inquire what shall become of the Judge as a man, and what of his private conscience? these Men answer; that the Judge must use what ingenious and fair artifices he can to save the innocent. . . . [Y]et I answer otherwise, and I suppose, for Reasons very considerable.

Taylor too understood the question as one that opposed the public interest to the private conscience:

Therefore, To the Question I answer, That a Judge in this case may not do any publick act against his private conscience; he may not condemn an innocent whom he knows to be so, though he be prov'd criminal by false witnesses.

And what if Titius be accused for killing Regulus, whom the Consul at that time hath living in his house, or hath lately sent abroad; would not all the world hoot at him, if he should deliver Titius to the Tormentors for killing the man whom Judge knows to be at home, it be dressing of his dinner, or abroad gathering his rents? . . . Of how if he sees the fact done before him in the Court? A purse cut, or a stone thrown at his brother Judge, as it happened at Ludlow not many years since? . . .

I conclude therefore with that rule of the Canon Law, *Melius est scandalum nasci quam ut veritas deseratur*; It is better that a scandal should be suffered, and an offence done to the forms and methods of judicial proceedings, than that truth should be betrayed and forsaken.[31]

By the 1660s and 1670s, then, it was well established in the English literature of conscience that judges must not convict against their private knowledge, despite their status as public persons. Indeed, in the 1650s and 1660s it was presented as a mark of a distinctively high English standard of morality to reject the classic Thomist theology, and most especially Spanish theology. This literature would have been fresh in the mind of every believing Englishman called to serve on a jury; and unless it is fresh in our minds as well, we shall not understand the seminal events of the later seventeenth century.

The Great Cases

With that, let us turn to the crises of the 1660s and 1670s. The most famous conflicts of those years were cases that did not involve blood punishments: these were the prosecutions of Quakers, of whom the most prominent was William Penn. But there were also homicide cases, which cannot be neglected in describing the events of the time. None of these cases, as we shall see, turned on any mystery about the facts.

We begin with the Quaker cases. After the Stuart Restoration in 1660, the Crown attempted to forbid gatherings that might foster political or religious sedition, through the Conventicles Act of 1664.[32] This measure was resisted in particular by Quakers, who continued to gather.[33] The Conventicles Act, importantly, did not threaten any blood punishments; it threatened merely imprisonment, fines, or in extreme cases transportation. Juries in the Quaker cases thus did not face the gravest moral challenges.[34] Nevertheless, when Quakers were prosecuted, conflict arose: jurors sought to deliver "not guilty" verdicts. Indeed, as one 1664 pamphlet insisted, wise jurors had no alternative but to deliver "not guilty" verdicts. As the pamphleteer proclaimed, drawing on the ancient Christian theology that has been my subject throughout this book, jurors who convicted accused persons under the Conventicles Act did so at the cost of their own salvation: "[T]hat Juryman that finds any other person guilty, is himself guilty of Perjury, and liable to the Vengeance of God upon his Family and Trade, Body and Soul, in this world and that to come."[35]

So what could be done to discipline recalcitrant jurors, forgetful of their role as "public persons" and ready to refuse their cooperation in prosecutions in the king's courts? Star Chamber had been abolished. But the judges of the common law had assumed its disciplinary powers, and were fining and imprisoning criminal juries that refused to convict as they had been directed to do in cases in which the evidence of guilt was clear. The question was thus framed as one of whether common law judges could exercise such powers, coercing criminal jurors as they had never been coerced before the seventeenth century. Wagstaff's Case presented a first important test in 1665.[36] That case produced a complex result. Nevertheless, the decision made it clear that King's Bench could make use of its well-established authority to fine jurors who refused to enter guilty verdicts as directed.

Yet a storm of change was gathering, which would end juror coercion within a few years. It was in response to Wagstaff's Case that Matthew Hale, then First Baron of the Exchequer, and a critic of the practice of fining and imprisoning jurors,[37] laid out his important views on the moral responsibility of judges.

Hale was a man knowledgeable in the Continental traditions. His *History of the Pleas of the Crown*, offering his views as of the mid-1660s,[38] presented much of the Continental learning. Margaret Sampson has shown that Hale drew directly upon the Continental law of conscience.[39] Thus Hale cited the hallowed safer path precepts: "[Q]uod dubitas, ne feceris," he wrote, "when you are in doubt, do not act, especially in Cases of Life."[40] This meant, he wrote, in language familiar from the Continental literature,[41] that the judge must err in favor of "mildness" and "mercy."[42] "The best Rule is in Dubiis," he wrote, quoting the famous Latin of Innocent III, "rather to incline to acquittal than Conviction."[43] Hale was a man of his Christian times — not only as a scholar but also in his practical life: his biographer reported that "in matters of Blood, he was always to chuse the safer side."[44]

In responding to Wagstaff's Case, Hale wrote in the same long-familiar vein. The question was whether judges could effectively decide the question of guilt themselves. In the course of arguing against the practice of coercing jurors, Hale insisted that judges should want no such responsibility. After all, as Hale noted, the responsibility for judgment carried with it, in the old language of the medieval common law, "peril." Hale, like all of the moral theologians of his day and of earlier centuries, emphasized the fact that jurors might possibly make use of their private knowledge:

> And although the witnesses might perchance swear the fact to the satisfaction of the court, yet the jury are judges as well of the credibility of the witnesses, as of the truth of the fact, for possibly they might know somewhat of their own knowledge, that what was sworn was untrue, and possibly they might know the witnesses to be such as they could not believe, and it is the conscience of the jury, that must pronounce the prisoner *guilty* or not *guilty*.
>
> And to say the truth, it were the most unhappy case that could be to the judge, if he at his peril must take must take upon him the guilt or innocence of the prisoner, and if the judge's opinion must rule the matter of fact, the trial by jury would be useless.[45]

Hale's argument did not carry the day in Wagstaff's Case, but opposition was growing.[46]

Over the next few years, the opposition centered in particular on Chief Justice Kelyng, who favored fining jurors not only in Quaker cases but also, disturbingly, in cases of homicide.[47] Kelyng was an unbending representative of public power, who showed little patience for supposed English traditions of liberty that interfered with the administration of criminal justice. (He was denounced in particular for having called Magna Carta, quoting Cromwell,[48] "Magna Farta"[49] — words that Kelyng denied having spoken, though he truculently admitted that "it might be possible, Magna Charta being often and ignorantly pressed upon him, that he did utter that indecent expression.")[50] In a number of cases, Kelyng compelled criminal juries not only to convict Quakers but also to enter guilty verdicts in homicide cases.

Kelyng's position on these homicide cases was by no means entirely unsympathetic. To judge from the reports we have, he was especially eager to prevent juries from going easy on masters who brutally beat their apprentices to death:

> [A] smith struck his prentice with a bar of iron, broke his skull, and the prentice died of the wound within two or three days. The jury would not find this murder at the first, whereupon [Chief Justice Kelyng] threatened them and made them go out again, and told them that they ought to find it murder, which accordingly they did. . . .[51]

> [A] man was arraigned for killing a boy; this was the head man to a weaver. The master in his shop gave him power to oversee the rest and correct them if they neglected their work. This boy had neglected to wind some spindles of yarn, and therefore this man beat him about the head with a broomstaff, of which he died within a day or two. The jury found this manslaughter, and because they did not find it murder nor would be persuaded to alter their verdict [Chief Justice Kelyng] told them that if they would not go out again and find murder he would fine them £ 2 a man. The jury for fear went out again and found it murder and the man was hanged.[52]

When we read cases like these, we may find it a little easier to sympathize with the program of the early modern princely states: not all of the "liberties" that Crown officials were attacking were ones that we would approve of. At any rate, Chief Justice Kelyng, who also disciplined jurors who found a homicide to be a case of self-defense,[53] as well as grand jurors who refused to indict in a homicide case,[54] was unapologetic: "I am very strict and severe against highway robbers and in case of blood," he quite simply declared.[55] He was also severe in cases of Quakers: when jurors refused to convict some of them, "he imprisoned and fined some of [the jurors] one hundred marks apiece."[56]

Kelyng was a natural lightning rod for the attacks of those who worried about the liberties of Englishmen. Eventually he was charged by the House of Commons with using "an arbitrary and illegal power, which is of dangerous consequences to the lives and liberties of the people of England; and tends to the introducing of an arbitrary government."[57] What troubled the House, we should note, was not the Quaker cases but the cases of blood: the action against Kelyng was initiated by a report to the House that "there have been some innovations of late in trials for men for their lives and deaths; and in some particular cases, restraints have been put upon juries, in the inquiries."[58] The House called for Kelyng to suffer "condign punishment, lest every sessions produce the like tragical scenes of usurpation over the consciences of Juries."[59] In the end, nothing came of the House's call for Kelyng's punishment; but his denunciation contributed to an atmosphere of gathering crisis over the coercion of "the conscience of Juries."[60]

That crisis came to a head in the famous Bushel's Case of 1670, involving the prosecution of the Quakers William Penn and William Mead for violation of the Conventicles Act. The case is a very famous one. The jurors in Penn and Mead's case, put under severe pressure, insisted in standing upon their "conscience" and rendered a verdict of not guilty[61] — upon which the jurors were fined forty marks, for refusing to acknowledge the "manifest evidence" of guilt. The case was rich in politically charged invective: Penn and Mead's report asserts that the Recorder of London, one of the presiding officials, chose once again to describe Magna Carta as "Magna f——."[62] Their report also claims that the Recorder made a declaration that could have been calculated to scandalize pious Englishmen: "Rec[order]. Till now I never understood the reason of the policy and prudence of the Spaniards, in suffering the inquisition among them: And certainly it will never be well with us, till something like unto the Spanish inquisition be in England."[63] Penn reacted indignantly to this: it was no wonder, he observed, as he was dragged out of court,[64] that the Recorder had no respect for "the fundamental laws of England," "since the Spanish Inquisition hath so great a place in [his] heart. God Almighty, who is just, will judge you for all these things."[65] Spain, as always, remained the home of all things evil in matters of moral theology, for the English.

At any rate, the events of the trial gave rise to Bushel's Case. Juror Edward Bushel, having been imprisoned, brought a writ of habeas corpus. Chief Justice Vaughan discharged him, in a celebrated decision that definitively established that "a juror cannot be fined for a verdict given according to his conscience."[66] Scholars have found Vaughan's decision puzzling: it was founded on the ground, very strange to modern readers, that jurors might use private knowledge.[67] Other arguments were certainly available to Vaughan. For example, he noted that an attaint was technically available against the jurors in the case, since the offense charged was not capital.[68] Yet it was precisely where an attaint was available that fining jurors was unacceptable: "[I]f an attaint lies, and a fine may also be imposed, the jury would be twice punished for the same offence."[69] This was a venerable technical argument, upon which the whole decision might presumably have rested.[70] Yet this technical argument was not sufficient for Vaughan. Nor was it enough for him simply to invoke the jury's "conscience," as he did notably in a phrase added at the last minute to his opinion: "[T]hough the verdict be right the jury give, yet they being not assured it is so from their own understanding, are foresworn, at least *in foro conscientiae.*"[71]

Instead, like Hale a few years before him, Vaughan insisted on focusing upon the classic theological question of the jury's private knowledge. What mattered was that juries might decide upon their "personal knowledge." This meant that they could not be coerced:

> It is true, if the jury were to have no other evidence for the fact, but what is deposed in court, the judge might know their evidence, and the fact from it, equally as they, and so direct what the law were in the case, though even then the judge and jury might honestly differ in the result from the evidence, as well as two judges may, which often happens.
>
> But the evidence which the jury have of the fact is much other than that: for,
>
> 1. Being returned of the vicinage, whence the cause of action ariseth, the law supposeth them thence to have sufficient knowledge to try the matter in issue (and so they must) though no evidence were given on either side in court, but to this evidence the judge is a stranger.
>
> 2. They may have evidence from their own personal knowledge, by which they may be assured, and sometimes are, that what is deposed in court, is absolutely false: but to this the judge is a stranger, and he knows no more of the fact than he hath learned in court, and perhaps by false depositions, and consequently knows nothing.

True private knowledge must decide the case. In particular, because the general verdict mixed findings of fact and law, jurors could never be punished for entering it:

> In special verdicts the Jury inform the naked fact, and the Court deliver the law. . . . But upon all general issues; as upon not culpable pleaded in trespass, 'nil debet' in debt, nul tort, 'nul disseisin' in assize, 'ne disturba pas' in 'quare impedit,' and the like; though it be matter of law whether the defendant be a trespasser, a debtor, disseisor, or disturber in the particular cases in issue; yet the jury find not (as in a special verdict) the fact of every case by itself, leaving the law to the court, but find for the plaintiff or defendant upon the issue to be tried, wherein they resolve both law and fact complicatedly, and not the fact by itself.

Because the jury mixed its fact-finding — partly on the basis of private knowledge — in its general verdicts, it could not be fined or imprisoned.[72]

Why did Vaughan make so much of the jurors' possible private knowledge of the case? John Langbein has derided Vaughan's opinion as "wilfully anachronistic"[73] — "dishonest nonsense," in Langbein's phrase.[74] As Langbein sees it, Vaughan's opinion simply harkened pointlessly back to a long-lost world in which juries were self-informing.[75] Yet this critique is strange. If the opinion was such obvious "nonsense" it is difficult to understand how it could have had the immense impact it had on its contemporaries. Surely Vaughan's audience would have recognized his argument as an irrelevant anachronism, if that is really what it was. The answer, as I hope I have shown, is that the private knowledge question *did* matter to Vaughan and his contemporaries — partly because juror private knowledge had not vanished, as Langbein himself has demonstrated,[76] but more broadly because of the implications of even potential private knowledge for the moral position of the juror. Vaughan was only one of many figures of the time who took the issue very seriously indeed: the moral theologians of the seventeenth century held exactly the same attitude. Because jurors potentially had private knowledge, they faced potential damnation. Vaughan spoke only of the law, to be sure. But what he said must be read against the background of the moral theology of his age. Vaughan's contemporaries could not have heard what he said about the law without hearing theological echoes.

In any case, 1664 to 1670 were watershed years for juror independence. Let us note that the law of those watershed years laid heavy emphasis on the fact that jurors judged according to "conscience," in both older senses of the word: they both exercised a moral faculty in ways that put their own salvations at risk and judged on the basis of private knowledge. In order fully to grasp the significance of the traditions of the moral theology of judging in these cases, though, we must look beyond the narrowly legal literature and bring in the contemporary literature of moral theology.

In the aftermath of Bushel's Case, there was indeed a burst of literature on the moral burdens and moral glories of jury service, which set the terms of a debate that would continue into the 1780s.[77] Three years after Bushel's Case, a new leading cases of conscience text appeared. This was Richard Baxter's *A Christian Directory or a Summ of Practical Theologie and Cases of Conscience*, which appeared in 1673. Baxter was a major figure, a divine whose works would be reprinted for two centuries.[78] Like other authors in the tradition, Baxter analyzed the classic claim, as old as Ivo and Gratian, that the judge could avoid moral responsibility by averring that it was not he himself who made the decision but the law. Writing in the wake of Bushel's Case, he addressed himself directly to jurors:

> Quest. 12 *Must a Judge and jury proceed secundum allegata & probata,* according to evidence and proof, *when they know the witness to be false, and the truth to be contrary to the testimony; but are not able to evince it?*
>
> *Answ.* Distinguish between the *Negative* and *Positive* part of the Verdict or Sentence: In the *Negative* they must go according to the evidence and testimonies, unless the Law of the Land leave the case to their private knowledge.

As for example, They must not sentence a Thief or Murderer to be punished upon their secret unproved knowledge: They must not adjudge either Moneys or Lands to the true Owner from another, without sufficient evidence and proof: They must *forbear doing Justice*, because they are not called to it, nor enabled. But Positively they may *do no Injustice* upon any evidence or witness against their own knowledge of the truth: As they may not upon known false witness, give away any mans Lands or Money, or condemn the innocent; But they must in such a case renounce the Office: The Judge must come off the Bench, and the Jury protest that they will not meddle, or give any Verdict (what ever come of it): Because God and the Law of Nature prohibit their injustice.

Object. *It is the Law that doth it, and not we.*

Answ. It is the Law and you: And the Law cannot justifie your agency in any unrighteous sentence. The case is plain and past dispute.[79]

Any potential juror reading Baxter's text would understand that knuckling under to a figure like Kelyng meant putting his own salvation at risk. Other texts made the same point: it was in 1682, for example, that Gilbert Burnet published his *Death and Life of Sir Matthew Hale*, declaring that the great judge had held that "in matters of Blood, he was always to chuse the safer side."[80]

But such moral rigorism did not settle the whole issue for jurors. As the moralist literature of the time explained to them, there were great spiritual complexities and traps, which could not easily be evaded. Particularly interesting is Benjamin Calamy, a preacher who would still be cited a century later. Calamy was a protégé of the most hated judicial figure of the 1680s: Judge George Jeffreys, the servant of the Stuart king remembered ever after as the most wicked and fearsome enemy of English liberties in the years before the Glorious Revolution. In 1683, Calamy, who had been appointed to the perpetual curacy of St. Mary Aldermanbury through Jeffreys's patronage, published his "Discourse about a Doubting Conscience," subsequently republished as "Discourse about a Scrupulous Conscience."[81] In this discourse, preached as a sermon to great acclaim, Calamy explained the immense public importance of avoiding excessive moral rigorism.

Calamy, a champion of the public interest as understood by the Stuart monarchy, laid out a method for dealing with doubts. In particular, he distinguished between doubts and *scruples*. This was a well-established distinction in moral theology. As Jeremy Taylor had explained in 1660, scruples were dangerously irrational impulses:[82] "Against a *doubting conscience* a man may not work but against *a scrupulous* he may. For a *scrupulous* conscience does not take away the proper determination of the understanding; but it is like a Woman handling of a Frog or a Chicken, which all their friends tell them can do them no hurt, and they are convinced in reason that they cannot, they believe it and know it, and yet when they take the little creature into their hands they shreek, and sometimes hold fast and find their fears confuted, and sometimes they let go and find their reason useless."[83] Calamy seized on this distinction: "Mind your plain and necessary Duty, and trouble not yourselves with scruples about little and indifferent things."[84] "[N]eedless scruples"[85] might easily lead the Christian into a terrible error, the error of sins of omission. In particular, overly scrupulous Christians who did not understand "Duty" might fail to do their part to combat "what is really Evil": "Now our Consciences cannot alter the nature of things: that which is our Duty remaineth so, and we sin by omitting it, notwithstanding we in our Consciences think it unlawful to be done, and what is really Evil continueth such, and is Sin in us. . . ."[86] In particular, one must not allow "Reasons and Exceptions" to stand in one's way: "When I speak of a Scrupulous Conscience, I suppose the Person tolerably well perswaded of the lawfulness of what is to be done, but yet he doth not like or approve of it, he hath some Reasons and Exceptions against it, it is not the best and fittest, all things considered."[87] This bore particularly on the case of public officials like judges: "For all Government and Subjection would be very precarious and arbitrary, if every one that did not approve of a Law or was not fully satisfied about the reasonableness of it was thereby exempted from all obligations to obey it."[88]

The conflict was thus framed as a battle between the moral rigorism of the "safe" conscience, on the one side, and the submission to "Duty" on the other. This was a conflict that mattered a great deal for the administration of justice: there was a real danger that upstanding Christian jurors might resist serving, as indeed they seem to have done;[89] yet the system needed their service. The conflict was fought out through all the literature of the post–Bushel's Case period; the authors of the period clearly felt the need to reconcile conscience and duty. Like Baxter, these authors accepted the severity of the moral challenge facing jurors. At the same time, like their Continental predecessors, they worried over the consequences of this moral theology for the workable administration of justice. Indeed, Baxter himself fully agreed that "scrupulosity" was a danger.[90] Such was the basic dilemma: after 1670 it was impossible to ignore the classic moral theology, in its rigorist English form. Yet at the same time, sensible Englishmen, like Chief Justice Kelyng, still wished to be "strict and severe against high-way robbers and in case of blood."[91]

Thus Zachary Babington, a pamphleteer who addressed himself to grand jurors sitting on "cases of blood," in 1677 invoked moral reasoning that had been familiar since the twelfth century.[92] To Babington, as to Augustine, Gratian, and Peter the Chanter long before him, there was an undeniable danger that any person engaged in judging might "make himself a murderer." Grand jurors must take care "to keep themselves secure from the guilt of Innocent blood."[93] But Babington (like Chief Justice Kelyng)[94] was eager to insist that this should not be taken too far. Did the righteous fear of the guilt of innocent blood mean that the grand jury was to refuse to indict? Not at all: a failure of the indictment in a case of murder would leave the "innocent blood" of the *victim* unavenged, and for that reason, the safer way was to indict. "[I]t is most prudent and safe for every wise and conscientious Grand Jury-man . . . rather to presume it probable, all other Circumstances may be true, as they are laid in the Indictment . . . and so to leave it fairly to the Court to judge thereof, and themselves free from the imputation of Blood by concealment."[95]

Babington was not the only author to say such things. The most important of the texts written along such lines was Sir John Hawles's "The English-mans Right," of 1680. Hawles's much-reprinted pamphlet, to which I have often referred, has been described as disseminating the teachings of Bushel's Case in pamphlet form.[96] This is right, up to a point. Notably, following Bushel's Case, Hawles insisted that juries, "being of the Neighbourhood," might well acquit defendants on the basis of their independent knowledge of the case.[97] Yet, read in its full context, the pamphlet should be seen as more than a rehash of Bushel's Case. It was an attempt to cope with the disturbing implications of Bushel's Case. For, as Hawles understood, the new order that respected jurors' "consciences" was an order that threatened to undermine the workings of criminal justice.

Indeed, like Babington, Hawles was primarily eager to persuade jurors to serve despite their conscientious qualms. His pamphlet took the form of a dialogue between a barrister and a prospective juryman:

> *Barrister*. My old Client! A good morning to you, whither so fast? You seem intent upon some important affair?
>
> *Juryman*. Worthy Sir! I am glad to see you thus opportunely, there being scarce any person that I could at this time rather have wisht to meet with.
>
> *Barr*. I shall esteem my self happy, if in any thing I can serve you. — The business I pray?
>
> *Jurym*. I am summon'd to appear upon a Jury and was just going to try if I could get off. Now I doubt not but you can put me into the best way to obtain that favour.
>
> *Barr*. 'Tis probable I could. But first let me know the reasons why you desire to decline that service.
>
> *Jurym*. You know, Sir, there is something trouble and loss of time in it; and mens Lives, Liberties, and Estates which depend upon a Jury's Guilty, or Not guilty, for the Plaintiff or for the Defendant) are weighty things. I would not

wrong my Conscience for a world, nor be accessory to any mans ruin. There other better skill'd in such matters. I have ever so loved peace, that I have forborn going to Law (as you well know many times) though it hath been much to my loss.[98]

The barrister's response, like that of Calamy, acknowledged the claims of conscience, but opposed to them the claims of public duty:

> *Barr.* I commend your *tenderness* and *modesty*; yet must tell you, these are but general and *weak* excuses. As for your time and trouble, 'tis not *much*; and however, can it be better spent than in doing *justice*, and serving your Country? To withdraw your self in such cases, is a kind of *Sacriledge*, a robbing of the publick of those duties which you justly owe it; the more *peaceable* man you have been, the *more fit* you are. For the office of a *Jury-man* is, *conscientiously to judge his neighbour*; and needs no more *Law* than is easily learnt to direct him therein. I look upon you therefore as a man well qualified with *estate, discretion,* and *integrity*; and if all such as you, should use private means to avoid it, how would the King and Country be honestly served? At that rate we should have none but *Fools* or *Knaves* intrusted in this grand concern, on which (as you well observe) the Lives, Liberties, and Estates of all *Englishmen* depend.

Whatever the dangers of conscience, jurors still had "public" duties that they could not omit. The barrister then offered an argument much like Babington's before him. Avoiding blood guilt required more than just avoiding public service; it meant avoiding sins of omission:

> Your *Tenderness* not be accessary to any mans being wrong'd or ruin'd, is (as I said) much to be commended. But may you not incur it unawares, by seeking thus to *avoid* it? *Pilate* was not innocent because he washt his hands, and said, *He would have nothing to do with the blood of that just one.* There are faults of *Omission* as well as *Commission.* When you are *legally call'd* to try such a cause, if you shall *shuffle* out your self, and thereby persons perhaps *less conscientious* happen to be made use of, and so a *Villain* escapes justice, or an innocent man is ruined by a *prepossest* or *negligent* Verdict; can you think your self in such a case wholly blameless? *Qui non prohibet cum potest, jubet: He abets evil, that prevents it not when he may.*[99]

Thus the troubling picture of the good Christian — one who generally forbore going to law, and who when faced with the task of judgment, worried that he might "wrong his Conscience." Yet this very good Christian, through his laudable qualms, threatened to do injustice by omission.

The rest of the dialogue presented the barrister's efforts to soothe the juryman's moral fears, and to explain the role of jurors in the common law system.

It was true that that role presented authentic dangers to the jurors' souls. In particular, they might be bullied by the court into finding a defendant guilty in cases of seditious libel. Such cases endangered their souls.[100] Yet they could not avoid service:

> *[Barr.]* Thus a **Verdict**, so called in Law, *quasi veritatis*, because it ought to be the **Voice** or **Saying** of **Truth** it self, may become composed in its *material* part of *Falshood*. Thus Twelve men ignorantly drop into a Perjury. And will not every conscientious man tremble to pawn his Soul under the sacred and dreadful solemnity of an Oath, to attest and justifie a Lie upon Record to all Posterity; besides the wrong done to the Prisoner, who thereby perhaps comes to be hang'd (and so the Jury in foro conscientiae are certainly guilty of his Murther) or at least by Fine or Imprisonment) undone with all his Family, whose just Curses will fall heavy on such unjust Jurymen and all their Posterity, that against their Oaths and Duty occasion'd their causeless misery. And is all this think you nothing but a matter of *Formality*?
>
> *Jurym.* Yes really, a matter of *Vast Importance* and *sad* Consideration; yet I think you charge the mischiefs done by such Proceedings a little *too heavy* upon the *Jurors*; Alas good men! They *mean no harm*, they do but follow the *directions* of the Court, if any body ever happen to be to blame in such Cases it must be the *Judges*.[101]

Such were views were understandable, said the barrister. Yet in the end they represented nothing but an effort to "shuffle off the blood guilt," putting upon the judges instead. No such effort could ever succeed:

> *Barr.* Yes, forsooth! That's the Jury-mens *common-plea*, but do you think it will hold good in the Court of Heaven? 'Tis not enough that we *mean no harm*, but we must *do none neither*, especially in things of that moment, nor will *Ignorance* excuse, where 'tis *affected*, and where duty obliges us to *Inform* our selves better, and where the matter is so *plain* and easie to be understood.
>
> As for the *Judges* they have a fairer plea than you, and may quickly return the *Burthen* back upon the Jurors, for *we*, may they say, *did nothing but our duty according to usual Practise, the Jury his Peers had found the Fellow Guilty upon their Oaths of such an Odious Crime, and attended with such vile, presumptions, and dangerous Circumstances. They are Judges, we took him as they presented him to us, and according to our duty pronounced the Sentence, that the Law inflicts in such Cases, or set a Fine, or ordered Corporal punishment upon him, which was very moderate, Considering the Crime laid in the Indictment or Information, and of which they had so sworn him Guilty; if he were innocent or not so bad as Represented, let his Destruction lye upon the Jury* &c. At this rate if ever we should have an *unconscionable Judge*, might he Argue; And thus the Guilt of the *Blood* or *ruin* of an Innocent

man when 'tis too late shall be *Bandyed* to and fro, and *shuffled off* from the Jury to the Judge, and from the Judge to the Jury, but really *sticks fast to both*, but especially *on the Jurors*; because the very end of their Institution was to prevent all dangers of such oppression, and in every such Case, they do not only wrong their *own Souls*, and irreparably *Injure* a particular Person, but also basely betray the *Liberties* of their Countrey in General, for as without their *ill-complyance* and Act no such mischief can happen.[102]

Dismaying advice for a Christian juror, who must fear to "wrong his soul" but must nevertheless serve, inevitably coming perilously close to having "the *Blood* or *ruin*" "*stick fast*" to him.

At the end of the seventeenth century, the basic moral tension of criminal jury trial was thus manifest: jurors were legally free to resist entering judgments and effectively free to resist serving as well. This was one of the consequences of the great English campaign for "liberties" of the late seventeenth century. But in a world of believing Christians, informed about the teachings of moral theology by a widely circulating vernacular literature, this threatened serious difficulties for the administration of criminal justice.

The Eighteenth Century: The Rule Emerges

They do not only wrong their own Souls, *and irreparably* Injure *a particular Person, but also basely betray the* Liberties *of their Countrey in General, for as without their* ill-complyance *and Act no such mischief can happen.*

— Hawles, *The English-mans Right (1680)*

Judge: *[I]n short, if any doubt at all hangs upon your minds, if you feel the least suspicions, any balance at all, you know it is much the safest way, and it must be most pleasant to you, to lean to the merciful side and acquit him.*
Jury: NOT GUILTY.

— *Transcript of trial of Alexander Gregory (1784)*

In a world of believing Christians, inducing jurors to convict could never be entirely easy. This was still true in the eighteenth century, just as it had been true in the thirteenth. To be sure, deep changes had taken place. In the Middle Ages, jurors had to fear vengeance violence. That threat was no longer much present in the eighteenth century. But if the fear of vengeance had vanished, the fear of moral responsibility had not. The risk to the soul still shadowed the trial. As a result, some of the twelve jurors might always be drawn to the safer way, avoiding the spiritual danger entailed by passing judgment. Yet in the common law the unanimous consent of all the jurors was required in order to convict. In consequence, persons whose guilt was clear might escape judgment. It was the resulting tensions that produced the reasonable doubt formula at the end of the eighteenth century: "Reasonable doubt" emerged as a formula intended to ease the fears of those jurors who might otherwise refuse to pronounce the defendant guilty.

The juror fears addressed by Hawles in the seventeenth century were to be found down to the end of the eighteenth. To be sure, eighteenth-century criminal jurors did not by any means always resist convicting. We know that ordinary eighteenth-century Englishmen were eager to serve as jurors, if only for the excitement.[1] The old "peril" of judging was not enough to make them shy

Figure 7. From *The Bloody register: A select and judicious collection of the most remarkable trials, for murder, treason, rape, sodomy, highway robbery, pyracy, house-breaking, perjury, forgery, and other high crimes and misdemeanors* (1764), the progress of justice, from the commission of crime, to the jury's verdict of guilty, to the gallows. Beinecke Rare Book and Manuscript Library, Yale University, image 1022453 (1764).

away from service. Moreover, the eighteenth century was a period during which the old medieval "peril" dissipated considerably. This is primarily because of a fundamental change in punishment practices. On both sides of the English Channel, blood punishments began to fall into disuse, in a process that would eventually culminate in the abolition of the death penalty at the end of the twentieth century in Europe. On the Continental side, various forms of forced labor were slowly displacing execution and mutilation as the normal punishments in the eighteenth century.[2] In England too the criminal justice system was reorienting itself: during most of the eighteenth century, the English system made use of transportation to the American colonies as a substitute for the older blood punishments.[3] Jurors also avoided inflicting blood punishments through the "pious perjury," systematically undervaluing stolen goods in order to allow the accused to escape the most severe penalties of the law.[4]

To the extent that blood punishments declined, all the old bets were off, as John Langbein has rightly insisted.[5] In particular, the old moral theology inevitably mattered somewhat less. That does not mean that the old theology entirely lost its relevance: jurists still framed questions of punishment in the old theological terms. Thus on the Continent the new punishments were known as "Verdachtstrafen," "punishments on suspicion." "Suspicion," as we have seen, was a technical term in the moral theology of doubt: it was the degree of certainty one rank higher than "doubt" but still two ranks lower than "moral certainty." Judges who had a suspicion of guilt had been authorized to order nonblood punishments from an early stage in the development of the Continental system.[6] The new system was thus one in which judges ordered lesser punishments on lesser degrees of certainty.[7] Because death and blood were not involved (at least in principle), the moral stakes in the administration of suspicion punishments were far lower.

In England as well, to the extent that transportation substituted for execution, or other mitigating devices were used, the moral stakes were lower. If blood punishments had been completely eliminated, there would have been much less need for the reasonable doubt instruction. Indeed, it is perhaps not surprising that the reasonable doubt instruction emerged in the Old Bailey (the criminal court of London) in the early 1780s, precisely the years when the system of transportation had collapsed in the wake of the American Revolution.

Nevertheless, these changes in punishment practices were not enough to eliminate all moral concerns. Even though punishment practices were changing in the eighteenth century, there were always at least a few such cases, and the law on the books continued to speak of execution as the normal punishment. So long as Christian jurors knew some moral theology and cared about the risk of "wrong[ing] their *own Souls*," in Hawles's words, something would have to be done to coax them into serving, and into entering the guilty verdict. And Christian jurors knew some moral theology. Christianity was by no means in decline in the Anglo-American eighteenth century: this may have been a century of Deism, but it was also a century of widespread religiosity and occasionally ecstatic revivals. Indeed, for many prospective jurors these were thunderous times of Christian belief; as the 1771 Connecticut *Black Book of Conscience; or God's High Court of Justice in the Soul* proclaimed, "O consider this, all ye that forget God, and make no conscience of your ways, you undermine your own salvation."[8] Judges who wanted to exercise control over jurors—as judges certainly did[9]—thus faced a difficult task: the task of controlling distinctly Christian jurors, whose beliefs could make them a hard herd to ride.

The Eighteenth-Century Moral Literature

Here again, to make clear what was at stake for jurors, we must begin with the popular literature of conscience. The traditions of the literature of conscience were by no means forgotten in the eighteenth century. The texts of Ames, Perkins, Baxter, and Taylor, quoted in chapter 6, continued to circulate. Moreover, the old teachings were presented by a new crop of eighteenth-century moralists and popular legal writers. These men understood perfectly well what was at stake.

For example, we may look at an anonymous 1771 *Guide to the Knowledge of the Rights and Privileges of Englishmen*. The author, cribbing without citation from a 1681 pamphlet,[10] explained law that dated back to the four-teenth century:

> The Office and Power of these Juries [i.e., the "petit-jury"] is *Judicial*, they only are the Judges from whose Sentence the Indicted are to expect Life or Death; upon their Integrity and Understanding, the Lives of all that are brought into Judgment do ultimately depend; from their Verdict their [*sic*] lies no Appeal, by finding Guilty or Not Guilty; they do complicatedly resolve both Law and Fact.
>
> As it hath been the Law, so it hath always been the Custom, and Practice of these Juries, upon all general Issues, pleaded in Cases Civil as well as Criminal, to judge both of the Law and Fact. So it is said in the Report of Lord Chief Justice *Vaughan*, in *Bushel's* Case, that these Juries determine the Law in all Matters where Issue is joined and tried, in the principal Case, whether the Issue be about a Trespass or a Debt, or Disseizin in Assizes, of a Tort, or any such like, unless they should please to give a special Verdict with an implicit

Faith in the Judgment of the Court, to which none can oblige them against their Wills.[11]

From the jurors only was the charged decision of "Life or Death" to be expected; and the common law tradition, as reaffirmed by Bushel's Case, gave them a choice between entering the general verdict or the special verdict. Other moralists also faithfully explained the law of jury duty to their readers —like Thomas Gisborne, who told them of their obligation "in conscience" to disclose their private knowledge, and to exercise "incorruptible integrity in pronouncing upon the whole evidence."[12] Informed Englishmen were supposed to understand the challenges of jury duty, essential to the maintenance of "the *Liberties* of their Countrey."

At the same time, eighteenth-century English moralists repeated all the old lessons of the cases of conscience literature, warning of the danger that an Englishman might "wrong *his Soul*." In particular, they repeated the venerable safer path doctrine. Let me offer two representative quotes. In *A Review of the Principal Quesitons and Difficulties in Morals* (1758), Richard Price wrote: "Our rule is to follow our consciences steadily and faithfully, after we have taken care to inform them in the best manner we can; and where we doubt, to take the *safest* side, and not to venture to *do* any thing, concerning which we have doubts, when we know there can be nothing amiss in *omitting* it; and on the contrary, not to *omit* any thing about which we doubt, when we know there can be no harm in *doing* it."[13] And we find Henry Grove writing in *A System of Moral Philosophy*, published posthumously in 1749, "How is a *good* Conscience to be kept, when the *doubt* lies only on *one* side? I answer, by taking the *other* side of which there is no doubt, and which therefore is the more safe. *In dubiis Pars tutior est eligenda.* 'In all doubtful cases choose the safer side,' is a maxim almost universally agreed upon. He that acts with a doubting Conscience falls under the *Apostolical* censure [citing Rom. 14:23], and needlessly hazards the breach of a divine command, which cannot be done without sin."[14] These moralists were not ready to abjure the English rigorist tradition. Good English Christians serving in positions of public trust must always obey their consciences: there was to be no taking refuge in the concept of a "public conscience." Yet at the same time, they acknowledged that the great challenge remained that of squaring "conscience" with "duty." As Grove put it in his 1749 book:

> They who set up a *publick Conscience*, to which all private Consciences are to submit, must be forced to grant, whether they will or no, that a Man ought not to surrender up his Judgment to the publick Conscience till his private Conscience is satisfied, that the doing so is his duty. Now there are multitudes

who will tell them, that upon the fairest Trial of the pretensions of this publick Conscience, their particular Conscience convinces them that they ought not to be governed by it; whom therefore they must excuse from acting by an implicit Faith, however they may esteem it their own duty to take this method. A public Conscience, that is to subsist by every Man's renouncing his private Conscience, is much like the public Credit in a Community, where all the Members are Knaves and Bankrupts.[15]

Serving in a public capacity was a morally dangerous business, which required every Christian concerned with the salvation of his soul to proceed with extreme care. Yet good Christians must serve.

So it was that the fundamental dilemma of the late seventeenth century hung on, opposing the safe conscience to the claims of public duty. In addressing this dilemma, the eighteenth-century moralists continued to insist on the old provisos. Christians were to stay upon the safer path, which meant that they were to listen to their doubts. But this was not to be taken too far. As Benjamin Calamy had said, a *doubting* conscience was not to be confused with a *scrupulous* conscience. Doubts were legitimate and had to be obeyed; scruples were foolish and had to be ignored.[16] In particular, the moralists held, the good Protestant was always to use his "reason," wherever possible, in order to remove his doubts. We may quote Grove again:

Where the Law is doubtful, and even where there is actually no doubt, the side of example cannot be warrantably taken, till *inquiry* has been first made concerning what the *Law* directs. *To the Law and to the Testimony*, not to Examples, is the rule of proceeding, where the knowledge of the Law is to be had. It will by no means justify a *Roman Catholick* who without consulting his own Reason, or endeavouring to acquaint himself with the doctrine of Scripture, readily gives in to absurdities of belief and practice, that he can plead the Authority of the Church, and follows men of Name for Piety and Learning; neither does his own Conscience make any objections against the way he is in. For no man is privileged from using all the means of informing his Conscience, which God hath put in his power. And much more inexcusable is the person, who swims with the stream when his Conscience is doubting, and he takes no pains to remove his Doubts.[17]

Doubts were, as they always had been, subject to a test of reason — and "Catholicks" remained, as they had always been, the dark examples of unreason.

Doubts were subject to a test of reason. To make this point, it is especially useful to quote one of the most influential of early modern English moralists, Jeremy Taylor.[18] As we have seen, Taylor presented, in a typical English way, a rigorist view on the judge's conscience: a judge was never to "do any publick act against his private conscience."[19] A few chapters later, Taylor went on to address the critical question of the nature of "the doubtful conscience." Here he began by citing the inevitable maxim of Innocent III, that in cases of "doubt" one was to choose "the safer part." The problem of "doubt," explained Taylor, was created by the existence of "reasons on either side":

> When the Conscience is doubtful, neither part can be chosen till the doubt be laid down; but to chuse the safer part is an extrinsecal means instrumental to the deposition of the doubt, and changing the conscience from *doubtful* to *probable*. The Rule therefore does properly belong to the *probable conscience*: for that the conscience is *positively doubtful* is but accidental to the question and appendant to the person. For the reasons on either side make the conscience *probable*, unless fear, or some other accident make the man not able to rest on either side. . . .
>
> If the *conscience* be *probable*, and so evenly weighed that the determination on either side is *difficult*, then the safer side is ordinarily to be chosen.[20]

"This also happens," Taylor informed his readers, "in the matter of Justice very often."[21] Nevertheless, he held, "[i]t is lawful for the Conscience to proceed to action against a doubt that is meerly speculative."[22] And what sorts of circumstances were those? They were precisely circumstances in which there were "reasons" on both sides. In such cases, the doubting Christian was to employ "determination" in the effort to reach a decision:

> Every little reason is not sufficient to guide the will, or to make an honest or a probable Conscience . . . but in a doubting conscience, that is, where there are seemingly great reasons of either side, and the conscience not able to determine between them, but hands like a needle between two load-stones and can go to neither, because it equally inclines to both; there it is, that any little dictate that can come on one side and turn the scale is to be admitted to *counsel* and to *action*; for a *doubt* is a disease in the *conscience*, like an *irresolution* in *action*, and is therefore to be removed at any just rate, and any excuse taken rather than have it permitted. . . . For in a *doubting conscience* the immediate cure is not *to chuse right*, that is the remedy in an *erring conscience*; but when the disease or evil, is *doubting*, or *suspension*, the remedy is *determination*; and to effect this, whatsoever is sufficient may be chosen and used.[23]

Doubts there might be; but one must try somehow to act. Taylor's picture of the doubting mind is indeed much like that of Prosper Farinacci a century before him:[24] the mind wavered, and could not decide. But at last there had to be a decisive movement of the mind. In the end, a reasoned decision would leave the soul of the Christian judge safe.

Such was the eighteenth-century moral literature. It is only if we remember it that we can understand the most revealing passage of all: William Paley's account of jury trial.[25] In 1785, during the very years when the reasonable doubt standard established itself in English justice, Paley, the leading moral philosopher of the day, described the problems of jury trial in the same terms that had been used for more than a century. Paley borrowed the well-established language of the conscience literature, explaining that the reluctance of jurors to convict grew not out of legitimate *doubt* but out of illegitimate *scruples*. He saw particular danger in the tendency of jurors to read too much into the centuries-old maxim requiring that in cases of doubt one choose the safer path. Paley's argument was little different from Calamy's a hundred years earlier:

> I apprehend much harm to have been done to the community, by the over-strained scrupulousness, or weak timidity of juries, which demands often such proof of a prisoner's guilt, as the nature and secrecy of his crime scarce possibly admit of; and which holds it the part of a *safe* conscience not to condemn any man, whilst there exists the minutest possibility of his innocence. Any story they may happen to have heard or read, whether real or feigned, in which courts of justice have been misled by presumptions of guilt, is enough, in their minds to found an acquittal upon, where positive proof is wanting. I do not mean that juries should indulge conjectures, should magnify suspicions into proofs, or even that they should weigh probabilities in *gold scales*; but when the preponderation of evidence is so manifest as to persuade every private understanding of the prisoner's guilt; when it furnishes that degree of credibility, upon which men decide and act in all other doubts, and which experience has shown that they may decide and act upon with sufficient safety; to reject such proof, from an insinuation of uncertainty that belongs in all human affairs, and from a general dread lest the charge of innocent blood should lie at their doors, is a conduct which, however natural to a mind studious of its own quiet, is authorized by no considerations of rectitude or utility. It counteracts the care and damps the activity of government: it holds out public encouragement to villainy, by confessing the impossibility of bringing villains to justice.[26]

The "safety" of the jurors was precisely what was at stake—or so, Paley was convinced, the jurors believed.

The Rule Emerges

All of this should make it completely unsurprising to discover that the reasonable doubt standard grew out of the old safer way moral theology of doubt, and the old fears that public justice would be endangered by the private conscience; and so it did.

Let us turn to the first examples of the use of the rule in the later eighteenth century. To hunt for the first case to use the rule would be misguided; as Barbara Shapiro has argued, the reasonable doubt rule was quite simply in the air in the later eighteenth century.[27] Nevertheless, it is revealing to look closely at the earliest cases in which the formula does turn up. The first examples that scholars have found are from the American colonies, in particular from the closing arguments of John Adams and Robert Treat Paine in the 1770 trial of the soldiers involved in the Boston Massacre — a case in which, let us note, there was once again no uncertainty about the facts. Adams, a man quite familiar with the traditions of Continental law, defending the British soldiers charged in the case, argued that jurors had to take the well-worn safer path. Adams quoted the observations of Hale's *History of Pleas of the Crown*:

> The rules I shall produce to you from Lord Chief Justice *Hale*, whose character as a lawyer, a man of learning and philosophy, and as a christian, will be disputed by nobody living; one of the greatest and best characters, the English nation ever produced: his words are these. 2. H.H.P.C. *Tutius semper est errare, in acquietando, quam in puniendo, ex parte misericordiae, quam ex parte justitiae*, it is always safer to err in acquitting, than punishing, on the part of mercy, than the part of justice. The next is from the same authority, 305 *Tutius erratur ex parte mitiori*, it is always safer to err on the milder side, the side of mercy, H.P.P.C. 509, the best rule in doubtful cases, is, rather to incline to acquittal than conviction: and in page 300 *Quod dubitas ne feceris*, Where you are doubtful never act; that is, if you doubt of the prisoners guilt, never declare him guilty, though there is no express proof of the fact, to be committed by him; but then it must be very warily pressed, for it is better, five guilty persons should escape unpunished, than one innocent person should die.[28]

There was nothing novel about this: we have already encountered many Continental and English moral theologians who had spoken, almost verbatim, in the same terms during the same years, and indeed for centuries. "When you are doubtful, do not act!" Hale is not simply an authority on the law, in this passage. He is an expositor of wholly familiar Christian values.

On the other side, Paine, arguing for the Crown, himself responded by alluding to the moral theological literature. As we have seen, the traditions of moral theology had long resisted excessive radicalism. The Continental tradition had described the dangers of the "benign" view since the thirteenth century. The same was true of the English literature on the problems of justice that had grown up since 1670. That literature held that the doubts that had to be obeyed were those that conformed to "reason." Indeed, the moralist literature had insisted for a hundred years that qualms of conscience not be allowed to prevent the satisfactory workings of public justice. It is in that context that we can understand the words of Paine that were cited by Anthony Morano thirty years ago: "[A] 'Law all Mercy[']] would be an [unjustice] and therefore when we talk of the Benignity of the (*English*) Law We can understand nothing more than what is fairly Comprehended in Coke's Observation on Our Law in General that it is *Ultima Ratio* the last improvement of Reason which in the nature of it will not admit any Proposition to be true of which it has not Evidence, nor determine that to be certain of which there remains a doubt."[29] There was certainly something of Coke in this. But the basic tension between certainty and doubt had been intimately associated with moral theology for centuries, and it continued to be intimately associated with moral theology in the British eighteenth century. The same was true of reason and doubt, Paine's next topic: "If therefor in the examination of this Cause the Evidence is not sufficient to Convince you beyond reasonable Doubt of the Guilt of all or of any of the Prisoners by the Benignity and Reason of the Law you will acquit them, but if the Evidence be sufficient to convince you of the Guilt beyond reasonable Doubt the Justice of the Law will require you to declare them Guilty and the Benignity of the Law will be satisfyed in the fairness and impartiality of the Tryal."[30] The Boston Massacre trial arguments, like everything else we have seen from the period, were framed in the language of safer path theology.

The same is true of the next spate of reasonable doubt cases identified by scholars. These cases come from the Old Bailey in the mid-1780s. John Langbein has emphasized the importance of these cases in his recent, magisterial, work on the "lawyerization" of the common law trial, a book that touches on the problem of the origins of reasonable doubt, along with a host of other questions.[31] Langbein argues that the reasonable doubt rule was, like much of the rest of common law adversarial practice, the result of the introduction of lawyers into the trial. Particularly as defense counsel emerged, he argues, they developed evidentiary and other practices intended to protect the defendant. Langbein has, however, conceded that he is "unable to say how the emergence of the beyond-reasonable-doubt standard was related to the growing lawyerization" that is his theme.[32] The answer, I believe, is that the emergence of the rule is not related to lawyerization, or at least not in any direct way. If anything, these Old Bailey cases show the presence, in the minds of all involved, of safer path moral theology, even more clearly than the Boston Massacre trial. The underlying concern was not with protecting the defendant at all. It was with protecting the jurors.

Again, there should be no surprise in this. Paley, commenting on English criminal justice in 1785, complained precisely that jurors hesitated to convict because they wished to preserve a "safe" conscience. So they did. Our records of what was said in the Old Bailey trials of the time is inevitably spotty. But they make it obvious enough that the moral theology of the safer path was guiding jurors.

The eighteenth century was not the Middle Ages, of course: London at the time was in many ways a modern city, in which anonymous urban crime occurred just as it does today. Nevertheless, if the world was changing, the theology of trial could remain strikingly conservative. Jurists still sometimes spoke of the trial in the way their medieval forebears had done — as an event involving a solemn moral decision to condemn a clearly guilty defendant. As Blackstone described jury trial, for example, its purpose was to guarantee that an accusation should be "confirmed by the unanimous suffrage of twelve of [the defendant's] equals and neighbours."[33] Even in his rapidly changing world Blackstone hung on to inveterate jurisprudential-theological assumptions: a trial was not to solve factual riddles but to *confirm* truths. We find the same assumptions in the reports of the Old Bailey.

For example, we can look to a 1787 trial in which the closing declaration of the judge is framed in the same language used two years earlier by Paley. Paley spoke of jurors who wished to keep their consciences "safe," and so did the judge in this case. He also made it clear that he himself, like public officials for a century, felt the need to compensate for the reluctance of jurors to convict, in order to show proper severity. The guilt of the three accused persons, in the judge's eyes, was "perfectly clear." Yet he acknowledged that he had to bow to juror "conscience":

> Trial of John Ward, alias Spoony Jack, Alexander Bell, Thomas Porter (theft with violence: robbery) (1787):[34]
> The Jury retired for a quarter of an hour, and returned with a verdict
> ALL THREE NOT GUILTY.
> Court. Prisoners, you have been extremely fortunate in the caution that has been used by the Jury in this case, which I am far from blaming: for in a case where any degree of doubt occurs, whatever reason there may be to suspect the guilt of parties, it is always safest to lean on the side of mercy; where any real and substantial doubt occurs: but there are such circumstances proved, that whether you are or are not guilty of the robbery, it is perfectly clear, that you and your associate, that worthless woman there, decoyed this poor man, if not for the purpose of robbing, clearly for that of grossly and cruelly ill-treating him; that is an offence punishable by law, though in a different way; therefore I shall think it my duty, that you should be brought to punishment for that offence; and I shall therefore commit you to Newgate, till you can find bail for assaulting and ill-treating this man; in this case, for the encouragement of those who may have been guilty with their associates, but have shewn some compassion on the person whom they have robbed.

Like English kings centuries earlier, who had insisted on punishing defendants even though the ordeal declared them innocent, this judge refused fully to accept the conscientious acquittal of the jurors. The guilt of the defendant was simply too obvious, even if the jurors were reluctant to take the "unsafe" path of convicting.

Other reports showed the judge taking the same attitude, conceding the right of jurors to take the "surest side" in cases of doubt, but seizing at the least the occasion to admonish the accused:

> Trial of John Shepherd (Theft) (1789):[35]
> [Verdict]: NOT GUILTY.
> Tried by the London Jury before Mr. RECORDER.
> Court to Prisoner. You have had a very narrow escape indeed; the Jury have taken that which is always the surest side, if there is any degree of doubt; as they have spared your life, I hope it will be so conducted by you, as to make this verdict a benefit to yourself.

In yet other reports, judges were more willing to accept the prospect that a jury might acquit because the jurors found the "safest" path, in a case where there was a "balance" of doubt, the "most pleasant" for themselves:

> Alexander Gregory (Theft with Violence; Robbery) (1784):[36]
> [Court]: [I]n short, if any doubt at all hangs upon your minds, if you feel the least suspicions, any balance at all, you know it is much the safest way, and it must be most pleasant to you, to lean to the merciful side and acquit him. . . .
> NOT GUILTY.

The mind in "balance" was a familiar topos from moral theology. So indeed were jurors who, like the jurors described by Hawles a century earlier, were concerned about what was "pleasant" for themselves as well as for the accused.

The search for the safer path showed up in other ways too in the Old Bailey: in some cases, the court coaxed the jury to take the "safest" way by convicting of a lesser charge.[37] As on the Continent, moreover, the language of moral theology also colored the treatment of evidence. Judges commenting on the evidence for the jury also spoke reflexively of "the safer way":

> Trial of Henry Harvey (Deception, Perjury) (1785):[38]
> [G]entlemen, when I call your attention to the circumstance of the case, I am bold to say that her evidence cannot be true, if much of that evidence which has preceded it be true; therefore, wherever there are contradictions as they cannot be both true, the safer way I take it, is to reject such evidence entirely; if the evidence of Goodman be true, the evidence of Brookes is not true; if Brookes's is true, Goodman's is not true; the safer way, and that which has always been taken, as I conceive, by every Jury, is, to reject that testimony entirely.

It is in the same light that we should interpret a 1783 case cited by Langbein, in which the judge told the jury that if "considering the evidence that has been laid before you, and all the circumstances of the case, you should err on the innocent side of the question, I am sure your error will be pardonable."[39] The question, of course, was whether what the *jurors* had done would be "pardonable." The Old Bailey, like the rest of the Anglo-American world, was a world whose conversations casually assumed that wise heads sought the safer way; and judges spoke respectfully of the corresponding anxieties of jurors.

Yet as jurists had recognized since at least the thirteenth century, delicacy of conscience posed inevitable threats to the management of criminal justice. Indeed, the reluctance of jurors to convict could infuriate critics of English criminal justice. Paley was one such critic. Another was Martin Madan, a sometimes eccentric religious polemicist best remembered today for his defense of polygamy.[40] Madan, in his *Thoughts on Executive Justice*, expressed outrage at juries who refused to convict even in cases where there was no meaningful factual uncertainty: "[T]he *petty juries*," he wrote, "who are to stand between the Crown and the prisoners, notwithstanding the solemn *oath* by which they are bound, frequently acquit prisoners, in the very face of the clearest and most indisputable evidence."[41] Worse yet, he continued, the judge "usually takes little further notice of the matter, than to congratulate the prisoner on 'his narrow escape,' and to tell him that 'he has had a very *merciful* jury.' "[42] For commentators like Madan and Paley, who believed, like their medieval predecessors, that crimes should never go unpunished, English criminal jury trial seemed a wayward institution in the latter decades of the eighteenth century — a setting in which unduly "merciful" jurors ignored obvious truths.

So what could be done to induce reluctant jurors to convict? Moral theology had a traditional language for addressing Christians who were reluctant to act — Christians who preferred, in their anxiety, to stay upon the safer path. That language was the language of the theology of doubt. It remained the language of the Old Bailey of the 1780s, as judges spoke of "doubt," in particular of "reasonable doubt." We can see this in a series of cases that begins tentatively in 1782,[43] and more clearly in 1783. In one 1783 trial we find the judge describing once again the classic conflict between private conscience and public duty, as it had been laid out by Calamy a century earlier:

> Trial of John Clarke (Murder) (10 Dec. 1783):[44]
> If from all these circumstances you are clearly satisfied that the wound was the cause of his death, and are also clearly satisfied with the truth of the rest of the evidence, and that the result of that evidence is proved clearly to your

satisfaction, that the prisoner is the man that gave the wound, I am then obliged to tell you that I am of opinion there is nothing in this case that can reduce the crime below that aggravated crime of murder: and it will in that case be your duty to find the prisoner guilty of this indictment: If on the other hand you think there is any room to doubt the truth of the evidence, or that believing the truth of the evidence is not sufficient proof that the prisoner gave the wound, or that the wound was the cause of his death; in that case it is your duty to acquit the prisoner wholly; or if there appears any circumstances that would reduce the crime to manslaughter, in that case you may find that verdict; but there does not appear to me any sort of evidence to take that middle line: Therefore, give your verdict according to your own consciences, you must be clearly satisfied of the fact of a crime so heinous in its nature, and so penal in its consequences, and then it is your duty to the public and to justices, to find the prisoner guilty. If on the other you think there is any reasonable cause for doubt, either upon the fact of his warning the man, or of the wound being the cause of his death, you will acquit him.

Guilty of the wilful murder. Death.

In another trial, we find the judge speaking, as moral theologians had long done, in terms of "moral probability," and of the public interest as well:

Trial of John Higginson (Theft; Embezzlement) (1783):[45]

In almost every case that comes before you, there is a strict possibility where the positive fact itself is not proved by witnesses, who saw the fact, there is a strict possibility, that somebody else might have committed it: But that the nature of evidence requires, that Juries should not govern themselves, in questions of evidence, that come before them, by that strictness, is most evident, for if it were not so, it is not possible that offenders of any kind should be brought to Justice. Where there is reasonable probability, that not withstanding the appearances a man may be innocent, it is very fair to make use of them: But if it goes further, and if there is nothing but absolute possibility, where all the moral probabilities of evidence are against the prisoner, where nothing can save but absolute possibility that he may be innocent, it would be going too far to conclude him innocent from that, that would make it impossible that public Justice should take its course. Therefore, the true question for your consideration is, whether judging of this fact, as you judge of all other facts, that happen in the course of your dealings with mankind, and your correspondence with one another, it appears to you be proved satisfactorily, and to moral demonstration, that this prisoner must have been the person that secreted this letter, and took these notes out of it, if that be the fair result of this evidence, then the prisoner is guilty, and it will be your duty to find him so. If on viewing the evidence any reasonable doubt remains on your minds, that he is the person that secreted this letter, and took the notes out of it, he will be entitled to your acquittal. The public justice of the country is extremely considered, on the one hand, if the charge is fairly brought home to the prisoner, that justice should be done upon him; while on the other hand, if there remains any distant hope of his innocence, he should have the same justice by being found not guilty.

GUILTY. (Death.)

The reasonable doubt language, while hardly yet a fast rule of law, was regularly repeated thereafter:

Trial of Richard Corbett (Arson) (1784):[46]
But you gentlemen will weigh all these circumstances in your minds, in such a case you certainly will not convict the prisoner on a mere suspicion; but if you think his conduct such as can by no possibility be accounted for consistent with his innocence, you will be obliged to find him guilty; I do not mean to say that you are to strain against all evidence, or that if you are clearly and truly convinced of his guilt in your own minds you ought to acquit him, but I say if there is a reasonable doubt, in that case that doubt ought to decide in favour of the prisoner.

NOT GUILTY.

And again:

Trial of Joseph Rickards (Murder) (1786):[47]
If you are satisfied, Gentlemen, upon the whole, that he is guilty, you will find him so; if you see any reasonable doubt, you will acquit him.

Or, for another example:

Trial of George Crossley (Deception) (1796):[48]
The first point, therefore, for you to consider is, whether this is the genuine will of Mr. Lewis, or whether it is a forgery; which, if we should establish beyond any reasonable ground of doubt, for you are not to expect mathematical demonstration in the proceedings of the administration of justice; but you are not to pronounce him guilty of a forgery, if a reasonable doubt can be entertained, by conscientious men upon their oaths, fairly considering the circumstances of the case.

Such was the origin of reasonable doubt.

The question remains why the standard established itself in the Old Bailey when it did, in the mid-1780s. I have already hinted at what I think may be the answer: If we can trust the records that we have, all of these cases—cases speaking not only of "reasonable doubt" but also of "the safer path," "the surer side," and the like—date to the early 1780s, most especially to the years 1783 and 1784. It was in 1785 that Paley addressed himself to jurors who worried too much about keeping their consciences "safe." These years seem to mark the critical moment.

If those were indeed the years in which the old moral theology was definitively introduced into English jury instructions, it is important to note a possible link with the history of punishment. As we have seen, blood punishments were primarily avoided through transportation to America during the eighteenth century. Once the American Revolution began, though, transportation was impossible. For the duration of the Revolution, convicts were put to hard labor, in the so-called hulks on the Thames. It remained unclear, however, what their ultimate fate would be. Only in 1787 was transportation reintroduced, now with Australia as its terminus. Within this period of uncertainty, 1783 is an important date: it was in September of 1783 that the Treaty of Paris was signed, formally recognizing American independence.[49]

Thomas Gallanis has recently argued that this period, in which the practice of punishment was so uncertain, brought with it a real crisis of English justice: unsure what would become of those convicted, the English courts began to experiment with defense counsel.[50] The first cases using the reasonable doubt formula in the Old Bailey crop up during the same period — indeed, they crop up in the year in which it became clear for the first time that transportation to America was an impossibility, while it remained uncertain what was otherwise to be the fate of those convicted. Perhaps — though I offer the suggestion somewhat diffidently — this raised the punishment stakes sufficiently that jurors needed more coaxing to convict than had been the case in previous decades. Seventeen eighty-three was a year when no one could be quite sure where the future of punishment lay.

Conclusion

> *The judge passes judgment on himself as much as on the offender.*
> — *Publilius Syrus,* Sententiae *(first century B.C.)*

When was the rule of reasonable doubt first stated, and by whom? There is no ultimate right answer: the history of this ancient Christian rule is too long and complex to permit us to identify any one date. If we feel that we must credit the earliest statement of the rule to a particular author, we might begin with Pope Gregory the Great, at the threshold of the Middle Ages. It was Gregory who, enthroned in the half-ruined and sadly impoverished city of Rome, admonished a bishop that it was "a grave and unseemly business to give a judgment that purports to be certain when the matter is doubtful."[1] But even Gregory stood only at the endpoint of many centuries of ancient Christian theology on the subject of the moral responsibility of judges and witnesses.

This centuries-old tradition of moral theology was still alive in late eighteenth-century England, when London jurors still sought to take the "safer," "surer," or "most pleasant" path in the face of "doubt," in order to avoid "wronging their souls." It was still alive in the 1770s, when John Adams defended the British soldiers in the Boston Massacre case. And the formulation that emerged in the eighteenth century — "beyond a reasonable doubt" — is still alive in American law today. Indeed, the proposition that guilt must be proven beyond a reasonable doubt has become a pillar of our secular legal system. But we no longer understand it as a principle intended to soothe the anxieties of Christians who fear the responsibility of judgment. Instead, we treat beyond a reasonable doubt as a fact-finding principle, as a heuristic formula that can help guide the individual juror in the effort to achieve sufficient certainty about uncertain facts.

The Supreme Court, per Justice Scalia, recently laid out our modern understanding of the rule and its history. "Beyond a reasonable doubt," declared Justice Scalia in an important 2004 decision on criminal sentencing, is a rule meant to guide the jury in finding "particular facts":

> [The] rule [requiring proof of facts beyond a reasonable doubt] reflects two longstanding tenets of common-law criminal jurisprudence: that the "truth of

Figure 8. The chaste Susanna, spied upon by the elders (along with a mysterious third person). The two elders spying upon Susanna were the medieval paradigms of the false witness, a figure who posed a grave danger to justice, while putting his own soul in peril. *Susanna and the Elders*, from *Prayers to the Saints* (Germany, fifteenth century). British Library, c6536-06, Edgerton 859, f. 31.

every accusation" against a defendant "should afterwards be confirmed by the unanimous suffrage of twelve of his equals and neighbours," 4 W. Blackstone, Commentaries on the Laws of England 343 (1769), and that "an accusation which lacks any particular fact which the law makes essential to the punishment is . . . no accusation within the requirements of the common law, and it is no accusation in reason," 1 J. Bishop, Criminal Procedure 87, p. 55 (2d ed. 1872). These principles have been acknowledged by courts and treatises [for years] and we need not repeat them here.[2]

Once the jury finds the "particular facts" essential to criminal liability, according to our modern concept, guilt has been established "beyond a reasonable doubt." Even the availability of new evidence — even, sometimes, evidence like that of new DNA testing — may not be sufficient to reopen a case, under American law. Once the jury has spoken, the facts are definitively found, and a higher court may no longer retry the case.

Yet is the Court right about the common law traditions it describes? It is certainly true that reasonable doubt is a rule with a very old tradition behind it. It is also true that the common law, in its early stages, deemed the jurors to be the sole "witnesses," while the judge was never to serve as a witness. Finally, it is more or less true, as Blackstone said, that the medieval common law required accusations against a defendant to be "confirmed by the unanimous suffrage of twelve . . . neighbours." Nevertheless, the "relevant authorities" to the contrary notwithstanding, beyond a reasonable doubt was not a rule for the proof of "particular facts" at the time of the framing of the American Constitution, and it has never succeeded in fully functioning as a rule of factual proof. It is a fossil, a misconstrued fragment of the Christian past.

The common law, with its tenacious attachment to tradition, has held on to a rule that emerged in a very different world. The theology of reasonable doubt grew up in ages during which uncertainty about the facts was less common, and less important, than it is today. The paradigmatic case, in this older world, did not involve any great mystery about the particular facts: it was assumed that the guilt of the accused would be more or less clear, much or most of the time, to the "neighbours" who were called upon to judge them. During the long premodern ages that I have discussed, the primary concern of the law was not that it would be difficult to figure out what had happened. The primary concern was that it would be difficult to find neighbors who were willing to cooperate in the process of inflicting punishment. To put it a little differently, the primary role of the "witness," in Christian moral theology, was not to provide factual clues but to take moral responsibility. The law in Blackstone's Christian world did indeed seek out laypeople who were willing to "confirm the truth of the accusation." But as the phrase "confirm the truth of the accusation" implies, the law did not assume that these neighbor-jurors would engage in any complex intellectual operation turning on the determination of particular facts. It asked them to *confirm* a truth, taking responsibility for pronouncing judgment.

As we have seen, from the deep Middle Ages onward, these neighbors sometimes resisted doing so. They did not want to serve as witnesses against members of their community. And it is not hard to understand why. In the Middle Ages, the jurors had to fear possible vengeance, both from human beings and from God. By the time of Blackstone, the fear of human vengeance had probably faded; but the fear of divine vengeance remained strong, for at least some jurors. *[T]he Juryman who finds any other person guilty,* as the seventeenth-century pamphleteer warned, is *liable to the Vengeance of God upon his Family and Trade, Body and Soul, in this world and that to come.*[3] The theology of reasonable doubt was addressed to the anxieties of such jurors. It was designed to help quell fears about the responsibility for judgment, not to resolve factual mysteries. It was designed to coax jurors into acting, in situations in which they felt uneasy about the "perilous" task of condemning others.

That, indeed, is why the common law required the "*unanimous* suffrage of twelve . . . neighbours," as we have seen. There is no reason to suppose that an uncertain fact is more securely established because twelve out of twelve lay-people agree on it, rather than nine out of twelve, or ten out of twelve. The unanimity rule serves a different purpose: it allows the twelve to share the heavy moral responsibility for judgment, and therefore to diffuse it among themselves. The unanimity rule is a moral comfort rule, intended to serve a different purpose from fact-finding. The same is true of "reasonable doubt." That is nothing in that phrase that tells us how to go about determining uncertain facts in any rational or scientific way. The phrase tells us a great deal, though, about how to feel easy in our consciences when we condemn others. And when our ancestors sought to feel easy in their consciences, they drew on a Christian moral theology that did indeed reach back to Gregory the Great, and beyond him to Saint Augustine and Saint Paul.

All this seemed obvious for centuries. Indeed, it probably still seemed obvious in the early nineteenth century. In early nineteenth-century America, courts generally continued to instruct jurors that they should convict only if they had attained "moral certainty." Steve Sheppard has recently traced much of this history.[4] Why did early nineteenth-century Americans speak of "moral certainty"? That phrase is one that we find baffling and troubling today; the Supreme Court in particular has worried over whether invoking moral certainty is appropriate in modern jury instructions.[5] But for the courts of the early Republic, the phrase carried no mystery. The vitality of the old moral theology was not yet sapped, and everyone understood why jurors should seek moral certainty. Thus one of the great figures of early nineteenth-century American law, Chief Justice Lemuel Shaw of the Massachusetts Supreme Judicial Court, still understood proof beyond a reasonable doubt as proof sufficient to attain "moral certainty; a certainty that convinces and directs the understanding, and satisfies the reason and judgment, of those who are bound to act conscientiously upon it."[6] Shaw still lived in a world in which jurors worried about the consequences of their "conscientious" acts. Nor did educated lawyers forget the old anxieties even in the later nineteenth century. As we have seen, the power of the moral drama of judging was still strongly felt by James Fitzjames Stephen in 1883.[7]

By our own day, though, the old anxieties have radically diminished, and we no longer yearn much for moral comfort. Instead, in the modern world we feel a strong need to find ways to resolve *factual* uncertainties; and so we have embarked on the hopeless project of transforming an old moral comfort procedure into a modern factual proof procedure. The result is confusion, and sometimes injustice.

Why indeed is the reasonable doubt instruction so difficult to understand? The answer is easy to give if we know its history. Let us remember how reasonable doubt began. From the old theological point of view, "doubt" was a subjective state of mind. It was something that afflicted Christians when they were anxious, unsure about whether to act, troubled by the possible consequences of their decisions. Jeremy Taylor, the leading English moral theologian of the late seventeenth and eighteenth centuries, gave this old Christian learning a typical early modern expression. What did it mean, asked Taylor, to have *un*reasonable doubts? "[I]t is like a Woman handling of a Frog or a Chicken, which all their friends tell them can do them no hurt, and they are convinced in reason that they cannot, they believe it and know it, and yet when they take the little creature into their hands they shreek, and sometimes hold fast and find their fears confuted, and sometimes they let go and find their reason useless."[8] Eighteenth-century Christians were used to viewing the world in Taylor's way. The issue for them was not whether mysterious "particular facts" could be elucidated through processes of detection, pursued in a detached and calm frame of mind. The issue was whether squeamish qualms about performing an unpleasant duty could be overcome. When they spoke of "reasonable doubt," they had in mind cases in which a person was "convinced in reason" but still felt the urge to "shreek." And their spiritual advisers spent a great deal of time instructing them on how to overcome their squeamish qualms: the eighteenth-century juror came to court well armed with moral advice about how to do his duty. That advice applied regardless of whether there was factual uncertainty in a given case. Indeed, the eighteenth-century theology of reasonable doubt was not designed with the problems of factual uncertainty in mind at all. It was designed to comfort, coax, and prod anxious and reluctant Christians.

And it was well designed for that purpose. Unlike a modern juror, any eighteenth-century juror who was familiar with Christian teachings would have understood what it meant to reflect on whether his "doubts" were "reasonable." If he had been exposed to the large vernacular literature of conscience, quoted at length in chapters 6 and 7, or if he had simply attended Sunday sermons, he would have known that examining his doubts was the right way to deal with the peril to his soul. To him, the question "What is a reasonable doubt?" was not unanswerable. The shelves groaned with books of moral theology that aimed to answer it.

In the modern world, by contrast, jurors are all too likely to be confused by the reasonable doubt instruction. To the modern ear, "doubt" is a term that is both ambiguous and unhelpful. It is ambiguous in the sense that it may be either subjective or objective. Thus it is certainly possible to speak of objective doubt. We can say that facts are "in doubt," speaking of a kind of doubt that all observers might share. This is an intersubjective kind of doubt, doubt that has nothing to do with the inner anxieties of any particular observer. But at the same time, the ambiguous term "doubt" will always carry subjective connotations for some listeners. For some listeners, doubt will remain, at least in part, a subjective state of mind, a condition of fear and trembling, a hesitation to act, an anxiety about unknown consequences, a moral squeamishness. It will remain inward doubt. Jurors may be especially vulnerable to such subjective, inward doubt. After all, they are charged with the momentous business of passing judgment. Faced with that unfamiliar obligation, some of them will always feel uneasiness about their moral responsibility, even if they no longer quite feel the need to "shreek" that their ancestors felt. At best, this will leave some jurors troubled about whether or not they are permitted to heed their inward doubts. At worst, it will leave them baffled about what kinds of doubts are appropriate for them in their roles as fact-finders.

Moreover, even those jurors who understand "doubt" exclusively in its objective sense will find the term unhelpful. Suppose we do experience doubt about the facts—as we are likely to do in the setting of a modern trial. How are we supposed to allay that doubt? What sort of metric do we use to distinguish sufficient doubt from insufficient doubt? When, above all, is a doubt "reasonable"? There is no easy or natural answer to these questions. *Our* shelves do not groan with books of moral theology that could guide us. The term "doubt" is a holdover from an older world, and it does nothing to help us solve the fact-finding problems of a modern trial. Yet in the setting of an American trial, the jurors are told precisely that their job is to serve exclusively as fact-finders, who are to perform their assigned task in as mechanical a manner as possible.

The reasonable doubt instruction does not equip our jurors to perform that task — and modern American jurors really do face a difficult fact-finding task, in which they really do need guidance. Unlike their ancestors, modern jurors routinely decide cases in which there is authentic uncertainty about the facts. In part, as I have argued, this is because we live in much larger, much more anonymous urbanized societies than our ancestors did. In part, it is because of the practice of plea-bargaining, which guarantees that cases in which the accused is patently guilty rarely go to trial. For both those reasons, meaningful factual uncertainty is much more common in modern trials than it was in premodern ones.

Moreover, those modern challenges are exacerbated by the peculiar structure of American jury trial, which puts juror/fact-finders in a strange quandary. It is in the nature of an American trial that the jurors are often not permitted to know some of the facts. American law relies heavily on the suppression and exclusion of evidence. Under the Fourth Amendment, decisive pieces of evidence may be suppressed because of police error or malfeasance. Under the law of evidence, important facts about the case may be excluded because they are deemed "prejudicial" or "irrelevant." These exclusions and suppressions put the jurors in a uniquely difficult position. They are told that their job is to determine the truth, to act as factual puzzle solvers; but at the same time, they are often denied access to the full range of information that would make it possible to do so. Indeed, they may see only a fraction of the information available to the other actors in the case — to the police, to the detectives, to the judge, to the lawyers. Everyone else involved in the trial may know things the jurors are artificially prevented from learning.[9]

Thus the law of evidence and the law of criminal procedure give rise to trials in which American jurors (unlike French or German ones)[10] often receive a strangely fragmentary selection of the pertinent facts in a given case. It is as though the law began by smashing a mirror and discarding some of the shards — only to demand that jurors reconstruct the original image of what happened from the fragmentary reflection that remains. This is a difficult business at best: reconstructing the truth from fragmentary evidence is the sort of challenging, and inevitably uncertain, work that archeologists attempt only after years of training. Yet we tell jurors to do it — while instructing them that facts are best found by paying heed to their "doubts," whatever that might mean. Small wonder that they are sometimes baffled.

To be sure, it is possible to defend American jury trial. The very point of the criminal trial, we can argue, is to throw obstacles in the path of the fact-finder. Excluding and suppressing evidence amounts to a form of systematic protection for the accused: if the fact-finders cannot be sure what happened, it will be extremely tough for the government to win a conviction. According to this reasoning, ours is a system that embodies the ancient moral principle that we associate with Blackstone: "It is better that ten guilty prisoners should escape than that one innocent suffer."[11] We pursue the ends of justice by making it exceedingly difficult to prove that the accused is in fact guilty. The same argument could be marshaled to defend the reasonable doubt formula. It may be true, we could say, that jurors do not understand the meaning of "reasonable doubt." But their confusion can only serve to encourage acquittals. After all, if jurors are not sure how to overcome their "doubts," they can only hesitate to convict.

It is undoubtedly in such terms that most Americans will defend the morality of our criminal justice system; and perhaps the defense is not without some merit: it may indeed sometimes operate to prevent the conviction of the innocent. Still, it is important to recognize that this familiar defense of the common law has real weaknesses. Many leading scholars, both on the left and on the right, are troubled by our approach to criminal procedure.[12] This is not the place to summarize all their arguments, but one deserves some emphasis: despite our belief in the justness of our strange and haphazard system of protections, it *does* result in the conviction of innocent persons. As death penalty opponents have shown, our jurors *do* get the answer wrong.[13] This is hardly surprising, given the strangely fragmentary factual puzzles they are asked to solve; creating artificial mysteries is a weirdly oblique way of pursuing the high moral goal of protecting the innocent.

Indeed, it is fair to ponder whether our modern conception of justice is really more morally justifiable than the old theological conception whose history I have explored in this book. Our contemporary conception imagines that the moral challenge of the criminal law is a *fact-finding* challenge: it is the challenge of distinguishing between those who are in fact guilty and those who are in fact innocent. The great test of the justice of a criminal justice system, according to this conception, is whether or not it results in the conviction of persons who are in fact innocent. If an innocent suffers, the system has failed.

The old moral theology viewed the world differently. It did not start from the assumption that the primary task of the criminal justice system was to sort out those who were in fact guilty from those who were in fact innocent. It recognized that such factual sorting out might sometimes be necessary, of course. In particular, it recognized that innocent persons might be falsely accused. Correspondingly, it developed protections for the innocent, and very significant ones at that, as scholars have demonstrated.[14] Nevertheless, the old theology assumed that, most of the time, the facts would be pretty straightforward — and that most of the time, the accused would be guilty. Because the old moral theology assumed that the facts would typically be pretty straightforward, and that the accused was usually guilty, its moral focus was not on the problems of fact-finding. Instead, its focus was on the morality of punishment itself. The old moral theology enjoined judges to examine their own hearts, asking whether they were right to punish others — even those who were obviously guilty.

To be sure, this did not make the old theology mild. The old theologians lived in a harsh and bloody world, and they endorsed a practice of harsh, often bloody justice. Nevertheless, the old theology was founded on an important and appealing moral belief. Because it focused so squarely on the morality of punishment, the old moral theology did not simply afford protections to the innocent. It also insisted on affording protection to the guilty, by raising doubts about the judge himself. "The judge," as the Roman moralist Publilius Syrus expressed the old wisdom, "passes judgment on himself as much as on the offender."[15]

We have lost touch with that old moral world. Our punishments are no longer as bloody, to be sure. But we have forgotten the old Christian precepts according to which a morally justifiable system must protect *both* the innocent *and* the guilty. Our conception of criminal justice has no obvious place for protection of the guilty at all. The older morality required judges to doubt their authority to punish, demanding that they regard the guilty as human beings like themselves. Our morality demands that we do everything possible to prevent innocent persons from being caught up in the toils of the criminal justice system. But it leaves the guilty to whatever fate the punishment system may hold for them. We organize our justice system to protect the factually innocent, consigning the factually guilty to legal perdition, while tolerating no doubts about ourselves as judges. It is fair to ask whether our view of the morality of a criminal trial is unambiguously superior to that of our ancestors.

So what is to be done with reasonable doubt, and more broadly with the strange, tradition-ridden system of American jury trial?

One answer calls for radical change. This is the answer given by my colleague John Langbein, who has had a career of unmatched distinction as a student of comparative legal history and a forthright advocate of serious reform. Langbein has argued, with deep learning and unimpeachable logic, that common law procedure is simply irremediably flawed. It is not well designed to find facts, and therefore it is not adequate to the task of modern justice —

unlike the procedure of the modern Continent.[16] I have quarreled with some of Langbein's historical arguments in this book, but I believe this great claim of his is incontestable. The most honest and courageous response to the quandaries of jury trial would be to follow the path of our Continental cousins, radically reworking our procedures and our law of evidence so that they are better suited to solving the factual puzzles that the modern world presents. Modern justice requires factual proof. Our procedures should be sensibly ordered so as to provide factual proof, as Continental procedures are. A system founded on evidentiary exclusions and suppressions ultimately serves no morally defensible end. Langbein is right about that.

That does not mean that Langbein is right in saying that Continental procedures have *always* been oriented toward factual proof. As I have tried to demonstrate at length in this book, this is not the case. The strong orientation toward factual proof that we find in Continental law probably dates only to the eighteenth or nineteenth century. When Langbein argues that Continental law was already seeking factual certainty in the thirteenth century, he is projecting a modern reality into a very distant past. Nevertheless, it is true that Continental law has moved energetically toward rational fact-finding over the past two centuries. Some of the old moral comfort rules certainly linger in odd corners of French and German law;[17] but by and large the law of the Continent has succeeded in leaving the premodern world behind, much more so than our own law. If we really wish to have a law that is oriented toward factual proof, we should do the same: we should abandon our system of evidentiary exclusions and suppressions, modernize our law at last, and create straightforward procedures for determining the truth.

For better or for worse, though, we are unlikely to pursue such radical measures. The common law is far too conservative for that. Evidentiary exclusions and suppressions have become much too deeply rooted in our legal culture. Nor are we in any way likely to abandon the reasonable doubt rule. The legitimacy of our common law system depends on its fierce attachment to its traditions, and no quantity of historical learning will change that. So what can we do?

At the very least, we can overcome some of our occasionally credulous, indeed superstitious, attachment to traditional formulas like "reasonable doubt." We can make an effort to understand this ancient phrase (and other ancient phrases like it that haunt our law) in a more historically informed, open-minded, and morally humane spirit.

First, there is no point in trying to be faithful to the original intent of a phrase like "reasonable doubt." This is in part because the phrase has no original drafter: not only does the phrase not appear in the Constitution, it was never crafted by anybody in particular. It emerged in a process of collective European rehashing of the precepts of Christian moral theology that date back to Gregory the Great and beyond. It was created not only by English jurists but also by English moralists — and by Italian and Spanish and French moralists and lawyers as well. There is no original intent to interpret. All that we can do is try to understand the rule in its original context, which is something quite different.

Second, there are better and worse ways to understand the rule in its original context. The worse way is to try to reformulate it in ways that somehow are intended to be faithful to its original purpose. There is more than one way to make this mistake. It would be a mistake, for example, to begin by observing that the original purpose of the rule was to make conviction easier, not harder, and then to draw the nasty conclusion that a modern jury instruction should tell the jury to get over its squeamish qualms and convict. This would make little sense in our world. The problems of our world are not the problems of the eighteenth century, or the thirteenth century, or the fourth century. Jurors today bring relatively few Christian qualms to the process of judgment, and we have little need for a rule intended to coax them into convicting. Moreover, they rarely face cases in which there is no real factual uncertainty. We can no longer instruct jurors that their job is to "confirm" an obvious truth. The very task of the trial has changed in a modern urban world. Saddling jurors with eighteenth-century instructions is neither wise nor kind.

It would make equally little sense to observe that the rule originally had to do with blood punishments, and therefore to restrict it to capital cases. While the rule undoubtedly has a place in capital cases — perhaps the last cases where jurors still fully feel some of the old anxieties — it has a place elsewhere as well, if it has any place at all. It is true that doubt mattered in blood cases in the premodern world. But punishment has changed since then. To return to an example I gave in chapter 2, we are not willing to countenance mutilation, as the Founding Fathers still were.[18] Unlike our ancestors, we no longer think of nonblood punishments as mild punishments. Indeed, in the current American atmosphere, it would be a wholly tragic error to refuse to recognize the harshness of our nonblood punishments, and the correspondingly high moral stakes in inflicting them.

The best lesson to draw from the history of reasonable doubt is not a lesson about how to apply reasonable doubt correctly, either according to its original intent or according to its original context. Those are senseless goals. The real root of our confusion about reasonable doubt has to do with the fact that we have lost the old conviction that judging and punishing are morally fearsome acts. We have a far weaker sense than our ancestors that we should doubt our own moral authority when judging other human beings. There were tough-on-crime programs in the past just as there are now. But in our own tough-on-crime era, we find it easy to forget what Christian jurists remembered during the tough-on-crime era of the late fifteenth century: "[T]he judge must be brought to punish only in sorrow . . . if the judge glories in the death of a man, as no small number do in our age, he is a murderer."[19] We have lost any sense that the challenge facing any humane system of law is to protect the guilty as well as the innocent. That does not mean that we should glorify criminals, of course. The old moral theologians were right: it is a part of our sober public duty to punish. But it is a *sober* duty. Open-hearted human beings condemn others in a spirit of humility, of duteousness, of fear and trembling about their own moral standing. That is what our ancestors, for all their bloodiness, believed; and it is why they spoke about "reasonable doubt."

We cannot return to the moral world of our ancestors: the theology that taught them the lesson of reasonable doubt is lost to us for good. But the lesson is one that we can try to relearn. Most especially, we can try to relearn it in our sentencing practices: we can try to remember that those we convict are humans like ourselves, not to be consigned to prisons until extreme old age, for example.

We can also try to relearn the old lesson of reasonable doubt in conducting jury trial. After all, lay jurors can still find something shocking and fearful in what they do, especially in capital cases, but perhaps in others as well.[20] Indeed, if there is any advantage to jury trial, it is that jurors have not fully come to inhabit the hardened, professionalized attitude of the sixteenth-century Continental judge. Even in capital cases, though, jurors must be reminded of what is at stake. As Theodore Eisenberg, Stephen Garvey, and Martin Wells write, "it would be better to openly and routinely instruct jurors that the decision they are about to make is, despite its legal trappings, a moral one and that, in the absence of legal error, their judgment will be final."[21] It would indeed, and not just where death is involved. Instructing jurors forcefully that their decision is "a *moral* one," about the fate of a fellow human being, is, in the last analysis, the only meaningful modern way to be faithful to the original spirit of reasonable doubt.

Abbreviations

Bl. Comm.	William Blackstone, *Commentaries on the Laws of England*, 4 vols. (repr. Chicago: University of Chicago Press, 1979) (1765–1769).
HEL	William Holdsworth, *A History of English Law*, 17 vols. (London: Methuen, 1903–1972).
Mansi	*Sacrorum conciliorum, nova, et amplissima collectio*, ed. J. D. Mansi, 54 vols., in 57 (Florence: Zatta, 1759–1927).
MGH	Monumenta Germaniae Historica.
PL	Patrologia Latina database, 221 vols. (Alexandria, VA: Chadwick-Healey, 1995).
PM	Frederick Pollock and Frederic William Maitland, *The History of English Law before the Time of Edward I*, 2 vols. (repr. Union, N.J.: Lawbook Exchange, 1996).

Notes

Introduction

1. In Re Winship, 397 U.S. 358, 374 (1970).

2. Id.

3. See e.g. the discussion of People v. Redd, 266 A.D.2d 12, 698 N.Y.S.2d 214 (1st Dep't 1999), cited and discussed in Peter Tiersma, The Rocky Road to Legal Reform: Improving the Language of Jury Instructions, 66 Brooklyn L. Rev. 1081, 1087 (1999).

4. For the views of an eminent federal judge, see Jon O. Newman, Beyond "Reasonable Doubt," 68 NYU L Rev. 979, 982–990 (1993); and for a sharply worded account by a sitting Justice of the Rhode Island Supreme Court, see Stephen J. Fortunato, No Uncertain Terms, Legal Affairs (January/February 2004): 16–18. For an account of the current state of affairs, see John P. Cronan, Is Any of This Making Sense? Reflecting on Guilty Pleas to Aid Criminal Juror Comprehension, 39 Am. Crim. L. Rev. 1187, 1187 (2002).

5. By tradition, the common law condemns efforts to define "reasonable doubt." Wigmore declared "efforts to define more in detail this elusive and undefinable state of mind" to be "ill-advised."; J. Wigmore, A Treatise on the System of Evidence in Trials at Common Law, 3d ed. (repr. Holmes Beach: Gaunt, 2003), 4:3542 (= 2497).

6. See Jessica Cohen, The Reasonable Doubt Jury Instruction: Giving Meaning to a Critical Concept, 22 Am. J. Crim. L. 677, 687–688 (1995). According to Robert C. Power, Reasonable and Other Doubts: The Problem of Jury Instructions, 67 Tenn. L. Rev. 45, 87 (1999), one state has moved out that category since Cohen's study.

7. Cohen, The Reasonable Doubt Jury Instruction, 682–686; Power, Reasonable and Other Doubts, 86.

8. Sullivan v. Louisiana, 508 U.S. 275 (1993).

9. Victor v. Nebraska, 511 U.S. 23–28 (1994) (Justice Ginsburg, concurring in part and concurring in the judgment). For an effort to defend the practice of not defining "reasonable doubt," see Note, Reasonable Doubt: An Argument against Definition, 108 Harvard Law Review 1955 (1995).

10. Miles v. United States, 103 U.S. 304, 312, 26 L. Ed. 481 (1881).

11. Thus my slightly poetic translation of "edificat ad Gehennam." The phrase is quoted and discussed in Knut Wolfgang Nörr, Zur Stellung des Richters im gelehrten Prozeß der Frühzeit: Iudex secundum allegata non secundum conscientiam iudicat (Munich: Beck, 1967), 51 n. 1.

12. Discussed in chapter 4.

13. Collet, Abrégé du Dictionnaire des Cas de Conscience de M. Pontas (Paris: Libraires Associés, 1767), 1:467–468.

14. [John Hawles], The English-mans Right: A Dialogue between a Barrister at Law, and a Jury-Man (London: Printed for Richard Janeway, in Queenshead Alley in Paternoster-Row, 1680) (repr. New York: Garland, 1978), 22.

15. William Paley, The Principles of Moral and Political Philosophy (Indianapolis: Liberty Fund, 2002), 391–392 (orig. 1785). For "innocent blood": Matt. 27:4 (Judas).

16. Id.

17. Trial of John Shepherd (Theft) (1789). The Proceedings of the Old Bailey Ref: T17890603–43.

18. Trial of Henry Harvey (Deception, Perjury) (1785) The Proceedings of the Old Bailey Ref: T17850914–187.

19. Trial of John Shepherd (Theft) (1789). The Proceedings of the Old Bailey Ref: T17890603–43. The same was true on the American side of the Atlantic. As John Adams reminded the jurors in the Boston Massacre trials in 1770, repeating language of moral theology that dated back to the Middle Ages: "Where you are doubtful never act: that is, if you doubt of the prisoner's guilt, never declare him guilty; that is always the rule, especially in cases of life." L. Wroth and H. Zobel, eds., Legal Papers of John Adams (Cambridge, MA: Belknap, 1965), 3:243.

20. Thoughtful historians have long since noticed that the rule must have been designed to make conviction easier, not harder. See Steve Sheppard, The Metamorphoses of Reasonable Doubt: How Changes in the Burden of Proof Have Weakened the Presumption of Innocence, 78 Notre Dame L. Rev. 1165, 1169 (2003); Anthony Morano, A Reexamination of the Development of the Reasonable Doubt Rule, 55 B.U. L. Rev. 507 (1975).

21. Sheppard, Metamorphoses of Reasonable Doubt; Morano, Reexamination of the Development of the Reasonable Doubt Rule; Barbara Shapiro, Beyond Reasonable Doubt and Probable Cause: Historical Perspectives on the Anglo-American Law of Evidence (Berkeley: University of California Press, 1991), 1–41; James Franklin, The Science of Conjecture: Evidence and Probability before Pascal (Baltimore: Johns Hopkins University Press, 2001), 1–101; Margaret Sampson, Laxity and Liberty in Seventeenth-Century English Political Thought, in Edmund Leites, ed., Conscience and Casuistry in Early Modern Europe (Cambridge, U.K.: Cambridge University Press, 1988), 85–87.

22. Especially through the influence of canon law. Javier Martínez-Torrón, Anglo-American Law and Canon Law: Canonical Roots of the Common Law Tradition (Berlin:

Duncker und Humblot, 1998); and e.g. R. H. Helmholz, Origins of the Privilege against Self-Incrimination: The Role of the European *Ius Commune*, 65 N.Y.U. L. Rev. 962 (1990); Charles Donahue Jr., Proof by Witnesses in the Church Courts of Medieval England: An Imperfect Reception of the Learned Law, in M. Arnold, T. Green, S. Scully, and S. White, eds., On the Laws and Customs of England: Essays in Honor of Samuel E. Thorne (Chapel Hill: University of North Carolina Press, 1981), 127–158; Mike MacNair, Vicinage and the Antecedents of the Jury, Law and History Review 17 (1999): 537–590.

Chapter 1. Of Factual Proof and Moral Comfort

1. James Fitzjames Stephen, A History of the Criminal Law of England (repr. London: Routledge, 1996) (orig. 1883), 1:573.

2. Baber Johansen, Vom Wort- zum Indizienbeweis: Die Anerkennung des richterlichen Folter in islamischen Rechtsdoktrinen des 13. und 14. Jahrhunderts, Ius Commune 28 (2001): 11–12.

3. Mathias Schmoeckel, Humanität und Staatsraison: Die Abschaffung der Folter in Europa und die Entwicklung des gemeinen Strafprozeß- und Beweisrechts seit dem hohen Mittelalter (Cologne: Böhlau, 2000), 265 and 265 n. 553 for bibliography.

4. See chapter 7. For a dramatic rendering of the potential liability of judges by a sometimes fanciful common law author, see Andrew Horne, The Booke called, The Mirror of Justices (London: Matthew Walbancke, 1646), 207.

5. For the importance of this theme, see e.g. David Seipp, Jurors, Evidence and the Tempest of 1499, in John W. Cairns and Grant McLeod, eds., "The Dearest Birth Right of the People of England": The Jury in the History of the Common Law (Oxford: Hart, 2002), 91.

6. Vincent de Beauvais, Bibliotheca Mundi, seu Speculi Maioris Vincentii Burgundi Praesulis Bellovacensis, O.P. Tomus Secundus, qui Speculum Doctrinale inscribitur (Douai: Ex officina Typographica Balazaris Belleri, 1624), 839 (= bk. 9, ch. 103), discussed below, chapter 4.

7. For the connection between vengeance and divine retribution, see T. Gorringe, God's Just Vengeance (Cambridge, U.K.: Cambridge University Press, 1996).

8. Adam Smith's Moral and Political Philosophy, ed. Herbert W. Schneider (New York: Harper and Row, 1970), 192–193, 198–199.

9. For reflections by three eminent scholars, see Walter Burkert, René Girard, and Jonathan Z. Smith, Violent Origins, ed. Robert G. Hamerton-Kelly (Stanford: Stanford University Press, 1987).

10. Robert Cover, Violence and the Word, 95 Yale L.J. 1601, 1614–1615 (1986).

11. That the king ruled "justly" (dhammena) is a detail I take from the fuller translation of this tale in Steven Collins, Nirvana and Other Buddhist Felicities: Utopias of the Pali imaginaire (Cambridge, U.K.: Cambridge University Press, 1998), 426, 434.

12. Andrew Huxley, Sanction in the Theravada Buddhist Kingdoms, in Recueils de la Société Jean Bodin pour l'Histoire Comparative des Institutions 58: La Peine (Brussels: Société Jean Bodin, 1991), 4:345. Professor Huxley alerted me to the fact that, as a result of a printer's error, the original passage refers to the "Tenniya" Jataka. Again I have slightly altered this passage to take account of Collins's translation in Nirvana and Other Buddhist Felicities, 426–428.

13. Huxley, Sanction in the Theravada Buddhist Kingdoms, 345, discussing David Richardson, The Damathat, or the Laws of Menoo (Moulmain: American Baptist Press, 1847), 154n. By contrast with Huxley, Collins regards this story as a form of utopia (in the sense, as he puts it, of ou-topia), meant merely as a commentary on the inevitable evils of the world. Nirvana and Other Buddhist Felicities, 434–436. I have no reason to doubt this. The story nevertheless reveals something about the nature of a very widespread kind of human anxiety.

14. See chapter 2.

15. [John Hawles], The English-mans Right: A Dialogue between a Barrister at Law, and a Jury-Man (London: Printed for Richard Janeway, in Queenshead Alley in Paternoster-Row, 1680) (repr. New York: Garland, 1978), 22.

16. Procedure can of course also serve to lend legitimacy to the trial, as famously argued by Niklas Luhmann, Legitimation durch Verfahren (Neuwied am Rhein: Luchterhand, 1969). To some extent legitimation could undoubtedly be analyzed through the dynamic of moral comfort I describe here: one could perhaps argue that the legitimacy of the trial depends on the sense of the participants that they have done no wrong. Nevertheless, the sociology of modern legitimacy involves problems so remote from those I discuss in this book that I prefer to leave this question aside.

17. For Saint Augustine on soldiers, see chapter 2.

18. My guess is that the procedure dates to the seventeenth century. The use of the firing squad may be as old as the sixteenth century. See Claude de Sainctes, Discours sur le Saccagement des Eglises Catholiques par les Heretiques Anciens et nouveaux Calvinistes (Verdun: Bacquenois, 1562), folio version 70(r): "[L]e pendre ou hacquebutter. . . ." In that particular passage, though, the firing squad is presented as an instrument of pure cruelty, used in the course of sacking. Seventy years later, we find the familiar form of the firing squad, for military executions, in Jacques Callot's 1633 series of engravings, "Les misères de la guerre," plate 12, which shows its use in executing deserters. Callot's engraving shows the members of the squad firing in successive ranks, as seventeenth-century infantry did in battle. Presumably this was a mimetic punishment, subjecting deserters to the death in battle that they had fled. While it is easy to uncover subsequent references to the firing squad as a standard military punishment, and in particular as a privileged form of honorable execution, I have not been able to trace the emergence of the use of a blank. Nevertheless, it is easy to imagine something like the practice of blanks being introduced for the execution of deserters, since it was their companions who were obliged to kill them. For the observation that the firing squad was "frequently" ("öfters") used in military justice by the early eighteenth century, see Jacob Friedrich Ludovici, Einleitung zum Kriegs-Proceß (Halle: Im Verlegung des Waysenhauses, 1737), 202. There are nineteenth-century accounts of firing squad procedure that make no mention of the blank, but this silence is difficult to interpret, since there was no reason for commentators on military law to describe customary practices that were not formally part of the regulations. For examples see Thomas Frederick Simmons, Remarks on the Constitution and Practice of Courts Martial, 3d ed. (London: Pinkney, 1843), 406–407; Victor Foucher, Commentaire sur le Code de Justice Militaire (Paris: Firmin Didot, 1858), 569–573. For the example of a Belgian corporal sentenced to die by firing squad rather than by the less honorable penalty of hanging, see Adolphe Bosch, Droit Pénal et Discipline Militaires, ou Code Militaire (Brussels: Tarlier, 1837), pt. 2, p. 96.

19. Critics of American capital punishment, most probingly Laura Underkuffler, have often seized on this example in their efforts to capture what they see as the immorality of American law. Laura S. Underkuffler, Propter Honoris Respectum: Agentic and Conscientic Decisions in Law: Death and Other Cases, 74 Notre Dame L. Rev. 1730–1732 (1999). For this common topos in the death penalty literature, see e.g. Theodore Eisenberg, Stephen P. Garvey, and Martin T. Wells, Jury Responsibility in Capital Sentencing, 44 Buffalo L. Rev. 339, 339 (1996); Underkuffler, Propter Honoris Respectum, 1730–1732; Jonathan Bridges, Hooding the Jury, 35 U.S. F. L. Rev. 651, 658 (2001); and the classic account of Cover, Violence and the Word.

20. United States v. Holmes, 26 F. Cas. 360, 1 Wall. Jr. 1 (C.C.E.D. Pa. 1842), cited and discussed in Regina v. Dudley and Stephens, 14 Q.B.D. 273 (1884).

21. Id.

22. A. W. B. Simpson has expressed doubt that this traditional procedure was really applied honestly. He suspects it was rigged, so that the youngest of the member group was always chosen, or that the perpetrators simply lied after the fact in saying that lots had been drawn. A. W. B. Simpson, Cannibalism and the Common Law: The Story of the Tragic Last Voyage of the Mignonette and the Strange Legal Proceedings to Which It Gave Rise (Chicago: University of Chicago Press, 1984), 65–66, 124, 180. Simpson may indeed be right: like some other moral comfort procedures, this one may have been designed to offer what American politicians call "plausible deniability" as much as, or more than, an authentically randomized method of decision. Nevertheless, I would argue that human psychology is such that people who find themselves in such a situation may be quite capable of successfully fooling themselves into accepting the legitimacy of a procedure that they understand on some level to be dishonest.

23. For example, when an early modern regiment fled the field of battle en masse, military authorities responded by Roman-style decimation, with the victims chosen by lot. See the heart-rending account of the use of this procedure in 1642 in Joachim Burgers, Singularium Observationum Iuridico-Politico-Militarium Centuriae Duae (Cologne: Apud Iodocum Kalcovium, 1651), 364 (= Cent. II, Obs. 65). Burgers's account is directly plagiarized in Ludovici, Einleitung zum Kriegs-Proceß, 203–204.

24. Richard B. Lee, The !Kung San: Men, Women and Work in a Foraging Society (Cambridge, U.K.: Cambridge University Press, 1979), 100.

25. Guido Calabresi and Philip Bobbit, Tragic Choices (New York: Norton, 1978), 57–64.

26. E. Alabaster, Notes and Commentaries on Chinese Criminal Law and Cognate Topics (London: Luzac, 1899) (characters omitted).

27. This was said à propos of Rabelais' famous Judge Bridoye, who decided cases by a throw of the dice. See Rabelais, Le Tiers Livre des Faicts et Dicts Héroïques du Bon Pantagruel (Paris: Garnier-Flammarion, 1970), 191–211 (chaps. xxxix–xliv). The judge, says Pantagruel, "se recommenderoit humblement à Dieu, le juste juge, invocqueroit à son ayde la grace celeste, se deporteroit en l'esprit sacrosainct du hazard et perplexité de sentence definitive, et par ce sort exploreroit son decret et bon plaisir que nous appellons arrest, remueroient et tourneroient les dez pour tomber en chanse de celluy qui, muny de juste complaincte, requeroit son bon droict estre par Justice maintenu, comme disent les talmudistes en sort n'estre mal aulcun contenu, seulement par sort estre, en anxiété et doubte des humains, manifestée la volunté divine." Id., 210.

28. Augustine, Homily on Psalm 30, Sanctii Aurelii Augustini Enarrationes in Psalmos, I–L. Corpus Christianorum Series Latina, vol. 38 (Turnhout: Brepols, 1956), 211: "Sors enim non aliquid mali est; sed res est in dubitatione humana diuinam indicans voluntatem."

29. Stephen, A History of the Criminal Law of England, 1: 573.

30. [Hawles], English-mans Right, 23.

31. Peter Brown, Society and the Supernatural: A Medieval Change, in Brown, Society and the Holy in Late Antiquity (Berkeley: University of California Press, 1982), 313. This point is discussed more fully in chapter 3.

32. See chapters 3 to 5. For similar efforts in Mishnah to create "distance between the judges and the execution," by assigning responsibility to the witnesses, see Beth A. Berkowitz, Execution and Invention: Death Penalty Discourse in Early Rabbinic and Christian Cultures (Oxford: Oxford University Press, 2006), 74 and 120–126.

33. Gratian here quotes Augustine. See the fuller discussion in chapter 2.

34. Discussed in chapter 2.

35. Richard Baxter, A Christian Directory or a Summ of Practical Theologie and Cases of Conscience (London: Printed by Robert White for Nevill Simmons at the Princes Armes in St. Pauls Churchyard, 1673), 149.

36. Plea-bargaining of course features less prominently in Continental Europe, and it may be the case that European trials have, partly in consequence, less the character of fact-finding proceedings and more that of ceremonious condemnation. I do not explore these comparative questions in this book.

37. William Blackstone, Commentaries on the Laws of England (Chicago: University of Chicago Press, 1979) (orig. 1765–1769) (hereinafter Bl. Comm.), 4:343.

38. This is true not only of France or Holland or Germany or Italy. Even countries like Russia (Stephen C. Thamann, The Resurrection of Trial by Jury in Russia, 31 Stan. J Int'l L. 61, 100 [1995]) and China (PRC Crim. P. Law Art. 35 [1979]) declare that uncorroborated confessions are too inherently unreliable to support a conviction.

39. E.g. Richard A. Leo and Richard J. Ofshe, The Consequences of False Confessions: Deprivations of Liberty and Miscarriages of Justice in the Age of Psychological Interrogation, 88 J. Crim. L. & Criminology 429, 455 (1998); Welsh S. White, False Confessions and the Constitution: Safeguards against Untrustworthy Confessions, 32 Harv. C.R. C.L.L. Rev. 105, 111 (1997); Bennett L. Gershman, The Prosecutor's Duty to Tell the Truth, 14 Geo. J. Legal Ethics 309, 346–347 (2001).

40. For the state of American law, see 21A Am. Jur. 2d Criminal Law, 1075; Richard H. Menard, Ten Reasonable Men, 38 Am. Crim. L. Rev. 179, 180 n. 4 (2001).

41. Stephen P. Garvey and Paul Marcus, Virginia's Capital Jurors, 44 Wm. and Mary L. Rev. 2063, 2083 (2003).

42. See the subtle treatment of Continental traditions in Mirjan Damaska, Evidence Law Adrift (New Haven: Yale University Press, 1997).

43. See Code de Procédure Pénal Art. 359, 362 (requiring majority of eight of twelve — nine jurors plus three magistrates — for any decision unfavorable to the accused).

44. See 263 StPO (requiring two-thirds majority).

45. For the contrast between this so-called one witness rule in the common law and the treatment of uncorroborated confessions in other traditions, see United States v. Telfaire,

469 F.2d 552 (1972). Federal constitutional law does require some evidence that a crime has been committed, but no direct corroboration of a confession to sustain a conviction, unless the crime is such that there can be no tangible evidence that it was committed without direct inculpation of the accused. See Smith v. United States, 348 U.S. 147, 153–54 (1954). This is a modern American updating of the widespread premodern rule requiring proof of the *corpus delicti* before a confession can be taken in evidence. For the premodern rule see e.g. Muyart de Vouglans, Les Loix Criminelles de la France (Paris: Barrois/Laporte, 1783), 784. For the history of this rule in the common law, see Wigmore, Evidence, 3:2778–2785 (= 2070). Not all American states accept this rule, though. See Commonwealth v. DelVerde, 398 Mass. 288, 296, 496 N.E.2d 1357, 1362 (1986) (uncorroborated confessions insufficient to support conviction in Massachusetts).

46. See Peter Murphy, Murphy on Evidence, 9th ed. (Oxford: Oxford University Press, 2005), 280; Rosemary Pattenden, Should Confessions Be Corroborated? Law Quarterly Review 107 (1991): 317–339; and for the older common law, William Hawkins, A Treatise of Pleas of the Crown (London: Sweet, 1824), 2:595.

47. See the detailed analysis of Antoine Astaing, Droits et Garanties de l'Accusé dans le Procès Criminel d'Ancien Régime XVIe et XVIIIe siècles: Audace et pusillanimité de la doctrine pénale française (Aix-en-Provence: Presses Universitaires d'Aix-Marseilles, 1999), 242–251.

48. Arlette Lebigre, La Justice du Roi: La vie judiciaire de l'ancienne France (Paris: Editions Complexe, 1995), 204. A similar observation about the pre-execution *amende honorable* is made by Schmoeckel, Humanität und Staatsraison, 206 and 206 n. 134.

49. Quoted in Guy du Rousseaud de la Combe, Traité des Matières Criminelles, 6th ed. (Paris: Humblot, 1769), 462. The same was true of the gallows confessions demanded of English convicts, which allowed everybody present to savor the justice of the execution. For a sampling, see Charles Hindley, Curiosities of Street Literature (London: Reeves and Turner, 1871).

50. Fisher, The Jury's Rise as Lie Detector, 107 Yale LJ 575 (1997).

51. E.g. Richard O. Lempert, Samuel R. Gross, and James S. Liebman, A Modern Approach to Evidence: Text, Problems, Transcripts and Cases, 3d ed. (St. Paul: West, 2000), 228–239.

52. People v. Delira, 2002 Cal.App. Unpub. Lexis 9543, at 5. For the popularity of puzzle analogies, see Peter Tillers and Jonathan Gottfried, Case Comment — United States v. Copeland, 369 F.Supp.2d 275 (E.D.N.Y. 2005): A Collateral Attack on the Legal Maxim That Proof beyond a Reasonable Doubt Is Unquantifiable? Law, Probability and Risk, available at http://lpr.oxfordjournals.org/cgi/content/full/mglo15?ijkey=QtzNTS XHA2VZz6M&keytype=ref&eaf. My thanks to Professor Tillers for sharing his text with me before publication.

53. See the discussions of the writings of Barbara Shapiro and James Franklin in chapter 6.

Chapter 2. The Christian Judge and the Taint of Blood

Epigraph. Agobard of Lyon, Liber contra Judicium Dei, in PL, 104:254: "Notissimum est bonos a malis interfici, nunquam autem malos a bonis, nisi in bellis publicis et legalibus judiciis, pertinet hoc ad occulta judicia Dei, quae sunt sicut abyssus multa, nec est datum hominibus nosse cur omnipotens ita permittat fieri."

1. [Hawles], The English-mans Right: A Dialogue between a Barrister at Law, and a Jury-Man (London: Printed for Richard Janeway, in Queenshead Alley in Paternoster-Row, 1680) (repr. New York: Garland, 1978), 22.

2. Id., 23.

3. Thomas Jefferson to the Abbé Arnoux, 19 July 1789, in The Papers of Thomas Jefferson, ed. Julian Boyd et al. (Princeton: Princeton University Press, 1950–2005), 15:282–283.

4. Antonin Scalia, God's Justice, and Ours, First Things 123 (May 2002), 17–21. Available at http://www.firstthings.com/ftissues/ft0205/articles/scalia.html.

5. For an example, see Paul Hyams, The Strange Case of Thomas of Eldersfield, History Today (June 1986), 12, and the further discussion in chapter 5.

6. U.S. Const. Amend. V. For Jefferson's 1779 scheme of mutilation punishments, see Jefferson, A Bill for Proportioning Crimes and Punishments, in The Complete Jefferson, ed. Saul K. Padover (New York: Duell, Sloan, 1943), 95–96. For a forceful discussion of the use of mutilation at the time of the founding and the challenge it presents for constitutional originalism, see Steven R. Manley, The Constitution, the Punishment of Death, and Misguided "Originalism," Law Review of Michigan State–Detroit College of Law 1999, 913, 942.

7. E.g. Lev. 7:26–27.

8. Lev. 15:19–33.

9. Gen. 4:9–11

10. Num. 31:19

11. For the reasons and sources of the two different reckonings, see e.g. Diarmaid MacCulloch, The Reformation (New York: Penguin, 2003), 145–146.

12. Mary Douglas, Purity and Danger: An Analysis of Concepts of Pollution and Taboo (London: Routledge and Kegan Paul, 1976). It is of course not my purpose in this extremely brief discussion to offer any kind of searching account of the attitude toward blood in the Jewish tradition. That problem is immensely complicated and intricately debated by specialists. Compare e.g. the discussions of Jacob Milgrom, Leviticus 1–16 (New York: Doubleday, 1991), 704–713, 748–758; and Marc Vervenne, "The Blood Is the Life and the Life Is the Blood": Blood as Symbol of Life and Death in Biblical Tradition (Gen. 9,4), in Ritual and Sacrifice in the Ancient Near East, ed. J. Quaegebeur (Louvain: Uitgeverij Peeters en Departement Oriëntalistiek, 1993), 451–470. My purpose is only to highlight the prominence of a taboo orientation in some of the biblical texts in order to set the stage for the later development of later Christian approaches. I am grateful to Professor Calum Carmichael for directing me to this literature and discussing the issues with me.

13. The early development of these doctrines involves complexities into which I do not enter here. See Caroline Walker Bynum, Wonderful Blood (Philadelphia: University of Pennsylvania Press, 2007), 1, with references to further literature.

14. Matt. 7:1.

15. Matt. 27:24–25. For references to this story in the blood guilt tradition, see my discussion later in this chapter (Bracton and Hawles).

16. Petrus Blesensis, Epistola VI, ad Radulfum Bellovacensem, in PL, 207, col. 16c, and generally Alfred Vanderpol, La doctrine scolastique du Droit de Guerre (Paris: Pedone, 1919), 115–124, 180. For a broader survey, see R. Laprat, Bras Séculier — Livraison au, in Dictionnaire de Droit Canonique (Paris: Letouzey et Ané, 1935–1965), 2:981–1060.

17. Isidore of Pelusium, Epistolae, bk. 4, no. 200, Ophelio Grammatico, in Isidore de Péluse, Lettres, ed. Pierre Évieux (Paris: Le Cerf, 1997), 376–377, quoted and discussed in Vanderpol, Droit de Guerre, 116.

18. Council of Valence, IV, Mansi, 3:493.

19. Quoted and discussed in Vanderpol, 118.

20. Isidore of Pelusium, Ophelio Grammatico, quoted and discussed in Vanderpol, Droit de Guerre, 116.

21. Canon XIII, First Canonical Letter (= Epistle 188, in Second Series of the Nicene and Post-Nicene Fathers (Peabody, MA:Hendrickson), 8:223ff.). Available at http://www.ccel.org/fathers/NPNF2–14/7appndx/basil.htm.

22. In PL, 4:631c: "[N]ec post gestatam Eucharistiam manus gladio et cruore maculatur." This tradition survived for many centuries, as the example of the Battle of Hastings shows. After the battle "Norman Bishop laid down an elaborate schedule of penances, carefully geared to the particular actions and attitudes of the participating troops," among them the new king himself. See the discussion, with further citations, in Stephen C. Neff, *War and the Law of Nations* (Cambridge, U.K.: Cambridge University Press, 2005), 62–63.

23. Vanderpol, Droit de Guerre, 110–120, brings together a variety of fundamental passages.

24. Discussion in James Q. Whitman, Harsh Justice (Oxford: Oxford University Press, 2003). As we shall see, there was a great shift in the practice of the application of blood punishments during the early modern period. I leave the fuller discussion to chapter 7.

25. Rom. 13:4.

26. For the general outlines, see e.g. Olga Tellegen-Couperus, A Short History of Roman Law (London: Routledge, 1993), 121–123, 127–130.

27. Councils of Valence and Lerida, cited above.

28. [Damasus] Ad Gallos Episocopos, in PL, 13:1190–1191: "Eos praeterea, qui jus saeculi exercuerunt, immunes a peccato esse non posse manifestum est. Dum enim et gladius exeritur, aut judicium confertur injustum, aut tormenta exercentur pro necessitate causarum." For the authorship see the discussion of Yves-Marie Duval, Ambroise de son élection à sa consécration, in Giuseppe Lazzati, ed., Ambrosius Episcopus (Milan: Università Cattolica del Sacro Cuore, 1976), 261.

29. Paolino de Milano, Vita di Sant' Ambrogio, ed. Marco Nanni (Milan: Edizioni San Paolo, 1976), 60: "[E]gressus ecclesiam, tribunal sibi parari fecit; quippe mox futurus episcopus altiora conscendit; tunc contra consuetudinem suam tormenta personis iussit adhiberi. Quod cum faceret, populus nihilominus adclamabat: 'Peccatum tuum super nos!' 2. Sed non similiter is populus tunc clamavit sicut populus Judaeorum; illi enim vocibus suis sanguinem dominicum effuderunt, dicentes: Sanguis hujus super nos (Matth., XXVII, 25)."

30. Council of Valence I, Canon IV, in Mansi, 3:493 (A.D. 374).

31. Ambrose, Epistola 50, ad Studium, in Sancti Ambrosii Episcopi Mediolanensis Opera (Milan: Biblioteca Ambrosiana, 1988), 20:80–84.

32. Id., 82: "Nam sunt, extra ecclesiam tamen, qui eos in communionem non uocent sacramentorum caelestium, qui in aliquos capitalem sententiam ferendam aestimaverunt." Duval identifies these simply as "heretiques." Duval, *Ambroise, de son élection à sa consécration*, 261.

33. Id., 80: "*Quia non sine causa gladium portat, qui iudicat;* dei enim uindex est in eos qui male agunt."

34. Id., 82: "Excusationem habebis, si feceris: laudem, si non feceris."

35. Id.

36. Commentaria In Hieremiam IV, 35. In *S. Hieronymi Presbyteri Opera*, pt. I, 3, Corpus Christianorum Series Latina, vol. 74 (Turnholt: Brepols, 1960), 201: "Homicidas enim et sacrilegos et uenenarios punire non est effusio sanguinis, sed legum ministerium."

37. Sanctii Aurelii Augustini Quaestionum in Heptateuchum Libri VII, Corpus Christianorum Series Latina, vol. 33 (Turnholt: Brepols, 1958), 221, Quaest. Lev. Qu. 68: "[C]um homo iuste occiditur, lex eum occidit, non tu."

38. This basic teaching is also found in the better-known passage from the City of God, 1: 21, which, however, did not establish itself in the texts of canon law.

39. This argument from ordinary language would be repeated for centuries afterward. Indeed, down to the present day, the law is sometimes framed as the question of who may be called "murderer." For a medieval example, see Agobard of Lyon, quoted and discussed later in this chapter. The fundamental Augustinian attitude can arguably still be seen in the German Criminal Code; StGB 211 (2), introduced during the Nazi period as part of Nazi *Täterstrafrecht,* has never been expunged. It is still concerned, as was Augustine, with defining which persons can be characterized as "murderers." Rather than framing the question as one of defining the offense, it (quite uncharacteristically for German criminal law) focuses on describing who may be called a "murderer": "StGB 211 (2): Mörder ist, wer aus Mordlust, zur Befriedigung des Geschlechtstriebs, aus Habgier oder sonst aus niedrigen Beweggründen, heimtückisch oder grausam oder mit gemeingefährlichen Mitteln oder um eine andere Straftat zu ermöglichen oder zu verdecken, einen Menschen tötet."

40. Augustine, Il "De Libero Arbitrio" di S. Agostino, ed. Franco De Capitani (Milan: Vita e Pensiero, 1987), 246:

> *E.* Si homicidium est hominem occidere, potest accidere aliquando sine peccato: nam et miles hostem, et iudex vel minister eius nocentem, et cui forte inuito atque imprudenti telum manu fugit, non mihi uidentur peccare, cum hominem occidunt.
>
> *A.* Adsentior, sed homicidae isti appellari non solent. Responde itaque, utrum illum qui dominum occidit, a quo sibi metuebat cruciatus graves, in eorum numero habendum existimes, qui sic hominem occidunt, ut ne homicidarum quidem nomine digni sint? *E.* Longe ab eis istum differre uideo: nam illi uel ex legibus faciunt uel non contra leges; huius autem facinus nulla lex approbat.

41. Id., 250:

> Iam uero miles in hoste interficiendo minister est legis; quare officium suum facile nulla libidine impleuit. Porro ipsa lex, quae tuendi populi causa lata est, nullius libidinis argui potest, siquidem ille qui tulit, si dei iussu tulit, id est quod praecepit

aeterna iustitia, expers omnino libidinis id agere potuit. Si autem ille cum aliqua libidine hoc statuit, non ex eo fit, ut ei legi cum libidine obtemperare necesse sit, quia bona lex et a non bono ferri potest. Non enim si quis uerbi causa tyrannicam potestatem nanctus ab aliquo, cui hoc conducit, pretium accipiat, ut statuat nulli licere uel ad conjugium feminam rapere, propterea mala lex erit, quia ille injustus atque corruptus hanc tulit. Potest ergo illi legi, quae tuendorum civium causa uim hostilem eadem ui repelli jubet, sine libidine obtemperari; et de omnibus ministris, qui jure atque ordine potestatibus quibusque subjecti sunt, id dici potest.

Sed illi homines lege inculpata quomodo inculpati queant esse non uideo: non enim lex eos cogit occidere, sed relinquit in potestate.

42. For this theme in Roman Stoic philosophy, see Brad Inwood, The Will in Seneca the Younger, Classical Philology 95 (2000): 58–60.

43. Agobard of Lyon, Liber contra Judicium Dei, in PL, 104:254, Latin text quoted above.

44. See e.g. the texts of Agobard of Lyon, quoted later in this chapter; or e.g. Isaacus Lingonensis, Canones, in PL, 124, 1086b–1086c; Rabanus Maurus, Commentaria in Jeremiam, in PL, 111:971 (quoting Jerome).

45. Eleventh Council of Toledo (675), c. 6, in Mansi, 11:41; cf. Fourth Council of Toledo (633), c. 45 (forbidding clerics to shed blood), in Mansi, 10:630.

46. Vanderpol, Droit de Guerre, 116–117.

47. "Nemo enim clericus vel diaconus aut presbyter propter quamlibet causam intret in curiam, nec ante iudicem cinctum causam dicere praesumat, quoniam omnis curia a cruore dicitur et immolatione simulacrorum." Available at http://www.pseudoisidor.de/html/126_constitutum_silvestri.htm.

48. The contrast of the formerly Carolingian regions with England is emphasized by R. C. van Caenegem, The Birth of the English Common Law, 2d ed. (Cambridge, U.K.: Cambridge University Press, 1988), 10–11.

49. See generally Thomas Head and Richard Landes, Introduction, in The Peace of God: Social Violence and Religious Response in France around the Year 1000, ed. Head and Landes (Ithaca: Cornell University Press, 1992), 1–20.

50. Id., 7–9.

51. Thomas Bisson, The Organized Peace in Southern France and Catalonia, ca. 1140–ca. 1243, in American Historical Review 82 (1977): 290–311, esp. 309; Heinz Angermeier, Königtum und Landfriede im deutschen Spätmittelalter (Munich: Beck, 1966); Bruce O'Brien, God's Peace and King's Peace: The Laws of Edward the Confessor (Philadelphia: University of Pennsylvania Press, 1999); John Hudson, The Formation of the English Common Law (London: Longman, 1996), 83.

52. Council of Narbonne, in Mansi, 19:827–832. Quoted and described as "oft zitiert" in Hartmut Hoffman, Gottesfriede und Treuga Dei (Stuttgart: Hiersemann, 1964), 95. See also Roger Bonnaud Delamare, L'Idée de la Paix à l'Epoque Carolingienne (Paris: Domat-Monchrestien, 1939), 248–249. For an eleventh-century example, see Guibert of Nogent, Moralia in Genesin, in PL, 156:106.

53. For example, Isaacus Lingonensis, Canones, PL, 124:1086: "Quicunque effuderit humanum sanguinem, fundetur sanguis illius, ad imaginem quippe Dei factus est homo."

Agobardus of Lyon, discussed later in this chapter. Hartmut Hoffmann, for reasons that are mysterious to me, denies that this "illius" in this topos refers to God. Hoffmann, Gottesfriede, 95 n. 15. The passages are entirely clear, typically adding the phrase "ad imaginem quippe Dei," and taken directly from Gen. 9:6.

54. Quoted above.

55. Council of Narbonne, chap. II, in Mansi, 19:827.

56. Id.: "Primo ergo omnium institutionum nostrarum, quae in hoc tomo scribenda sunt, monemus et mandamus secundum praeceptum Dei et nostrum ut nullus Christianorum alium quemlibet Christianum occidat, quia qui Christianum occidit, sine dubio Christi sanguinem fundit. Si quis vero, quod non optamus, injuste hominem occiderit, per legem eum emendet."

57. See Bernardus Papiensis, Summa Decretalium, bk. I, tit. 23 (office of judge includes being "in iudicio iustus"); bk. I, tit. 24 (describing office of judge as supervising Peace or Truce). Both in Bernardi Papiensis Summa Detretalium, ed. T. Laspeyres (repr. Graz: Akademische Druck- u. Verlagsanstalt, 1956), 19.

58. For example, James Turner Johnson, Ideology, Reason and the Limitation of War: Religious and Secular Concepts, 1200–1740 (Princeton: Princeton University Press, 1975), 42–46.

59. This is the characterization given by one Web site oriented to a popular audience: http://www.societaschristiana.com/Encyclopedia/T/TruceOfGod.html.

60. Carl Erdmann, Origin of the Idea of Crusade, trans. M. Baldwin and W. Goffart (Princeton: Princeton University Press, 1977), 63, and generally on this theme 62–72.

61. Ivo, Epistle 86, in PL, 162:107. Quoted and discussed in Hoffmann, Gottesfriede und Treuga Dei, 198. For *iudices pacis* see id., 208–209 (Louis VI of France). Moreover, church courts were in principle responsible for supervising the Truce of God, at least as of the late twelfth century. Id., 235 (Huguccio).

62. Robert Jacob, Le serment des juges, in Le Serment, ed. R Verdier, 2 vols. (Paris: CNRS, 1991), 1:439–457.

63. See Susan Reynolds, Kingdoms and Communities in Western Europe, 900–1300, 2d ed. (Oxford: Clarendon Press, 1997), 33–34.

64. Jacob, Le serment des juges, 447–451.

65. Id., 451.

66. In Ph. Godding and J. Pycke, La Paix de Valenciennes de 1114 (Louvain-la-Neuve: Université Catholique de Louvain, 1981), 132, and discussed in Jacob, Le serment des juges, 449.

67. Ernest-Joseph Tardif, Summa de Legibus Normannie in curia laicali (Rouen: Société de l'histoire de Normandie, 1896), 2:232. Discussed more fully in chapter 5.

68. For an authoritative brief survey of the development of canon law in its wider context, see Peter Landau, The Development of the Law, in The New Cambridge Medieval History, IV, pt. 1 (Cambridge, U.K.: Cambridge University Press, 2004), 113–147.

69. Anders Winroth, The Making of Gratian's Decretum (New York: Cambridge, 2000). For a general introduction, see e.g. James Brundage, Medieval Canon Law (New York: Longman, 1995).

70. Burchard of Worms, Decretum 6.31, in PL, 140:772. "Periculose se decipiunt, qui existimant eos tantum homicidas esse, qui manibus hominem occidunt, et non potius eos,

per quorum consilium, et fraudem, et exhortationem homines extinguuntur. Nam Judaei Dominum nequaquam propriis manibus interfecerunt, sicut scriptum est: Nobis non licet interficere quemquam, sed tamen illis Domini mors imputatur, quia ipsi eum lingua crucifixerunt, dicentes: Crucifige eum."

71. Ivo, Decretum, 10.160, in PL, 161:338; Gratian, Decretum Pars Secunda, c. 33, q. 3, dist. 1, c. 23.

72. Ivo, Carnotensis, 10.101, in PL, 161:722–723.

73. Ivo, Decretum, 6.334, in PL 161: 513. For other examples, see Petrus Blesensis, Epistolae, in PL, 207:16; Francius Juretus, Observationes, in PL, 162:413; Isidorus Mercator, Collectio Decretalium, in PL, 130:609.

74. C. 23, q. 5, c. 41: "Si homicidium est hominem occidere, potest occidere [*sic:* modern editions of Augustine give "accidere"] aliquando sine peccato. Nam et miles hostem, et iudex uel minister eius nocentem, et cui forte inuito atque inprudenti telum manu fugit, non mihi uidentur peccare, cum hominem occidunt. Sed nec etiam homicidae isti appellari solent. Idem in questionibus Leuitici: Cum homo iuste occiditur, lex eum occidit, non tu."

75. Summa Decretalium, bk. V, tit. 10, 1., in Bernardi Papiensis Summa Decretalium, ed. E. A. T. Lespeyres (Regensburg: Manz, 1860), 220–221: "Homicidii vero corporalis quatuor sunt species, quia fit quatuor modis, iustitia, necessitate, casu et voluntate; iustitia, ut cum iudex vel minister reum iuste condemnatum occidit. . . . Circa illud homicidium, quod fit iustitia sic distinguendum puto. Cum minister occidit reum, aut condemnatum aut non condemnatum, scil. ad mortem; item ubi condemnatum, aut id facit amore iustitiae aut livore, et ubi amore iustitiae aut est iussus hoc facere aut iniussus. Si occidit non condemnatum, reus est homicidii, quia nimis festinavit . . .; si vero condemnatum occidit livore, similiter est reus homicidii . . .; si autem condemnatum occidit amore iustitiae et iussus, non peccat, alioquin peccat."

76. Raymond de Peñafort, Summula (n.p., n.d.) (= Bibliothèque Mazarine INC 1318), f. 132: "[N]ihilominus incurrit irregularitatem."

77. X. Ochoa and A. Diez, eds., S. Raimundus de Pennaforte Summa de Paenitentia, in Universa Biblitheca Iuris (Rome: Commentarium pro Religiosis, 1976), 1:443:

> Facto [homicidium] committitur quatuor modis, id est iustitia, voluntate, necessitate, casu.
>
> *Iustitia*, ut cum iudex vel minister, reum iustè condemnatum occidit. Hoc homicidium si sit ex livore vel delectatione fundendi humanum sanguinem, licet ille iustè occidatur, iste tamen peccat mortaliter propter intentionem corruptam. Si vero fit ex amore iustitie, nec peccat iudex ipsum condemnando ad mortem, & praecipiendo ministro ut occidat eum, nec minister si iussus occidit condemnatur, peccaret tamen uterque mortaliter si faceret iuris ordine non servato.

78. "Nullus quoque clericus ruptariis vel balistariis aut huiusmodi viris sanguinem preponatur." I believe that this phrase has been mistranslated in the standard texts. The standard translation renders it as "no cleric shall judge cases involving [men of blood]." The nominal form "praepositus" does indeed occasionally refer to persons exercising judicial powers. See Du Cange, Glossarium Mediae et Infimae Latinitatis (repr. Graz: Akademische Druck- u. Verlagsanstalt, 1954), 6:463–464. So far as I can determine,

though, the verbal form did not bear that meaning in the literature of canon law, where it is used in its ordinary and familiar sense of "be put in charge or in command." Since Canon 18 does concern "judgments of blood," it is understandable that scholars have imagined that this passage condemned proceedings in which clerics "sat in judgment" over brigands. (But exactly what proceedings would those have been?) However, this canon also describes practices of bloodshed more broadly; and as we have seen, the theology of judging was always closely linked with the theology of soldiering. Thus I propose that the correct translation is not "judge cases" but "serve as a commander."

79. English translation, with my correction, available at http://www.fordham.edu/halsall/basis/lateran4.html. Latin text in Antonius García y García, Constitutiones Concilii quarti Lateranensis una cum Commentariis Glossatorum (= Monumenta Iuris Canonici Series A, vol. 2) (Vatican City: Biblioteca apostolica vaticana, 1981), 66.

Chapter 3. The Decline of the Judicial Ordeal

1. Mathias Schmoeckel, "Ein sonderbares Wunderwerck Gottes": Bemerkungen zum langsamen Rückgang der Ordale nach 1215, Ius Commune 26 (1999): 123–164.

2. John W. Baldwin, The Intellectual Preparation for the Canon of 1215 against Ordeals, Speculum 36 (1961): 613–636.

3. Schmoeckel, "Ein sonderbares Wunderwerck Gottes."

4. R. C. van Caenegem, The Birth of the English Common Law, 2d ed. (Cambridge, U.K.: Cambridge University Press, 1988), 71.

5. John Hudson, The Formation of the English Common Law (London: Longman, 1996), 74.

6. Jean-Marie Carbasse, Introduction historique au droit (Paris: P.U.F., 1999), 175.

7. Robert Bartlett, Trial by Fire and Water: The Medieval Judicial Ordeal (Oxford: Clarendon Press, 1986), 79.

8. Van Caenegem, The Birth of the English Common Law, 63

9. Esp. Charles Radding, Superstition to Science: Nature, Fortune and the Passing of the Medieval Ordeal, American Historical Review 84 (1979): 945–969.

10. Rebecca V. Colman, Reason and Unreason in Early Medieval Law, Journal of Interdisciplinary History 4 (1975): 571–591.

11. Van Caenegem's Birth of the English Common Law presents at many points a version of the dominant interpretation, oriented toward factual proof, rational and irrational. See e.g. 62–63 and often. My account depends less on that work than on his well-known article Public Prosecution of Crime in Twelfth-Century England, in van Caenegem, Legal History: A European Perspective (London: Hambledon Press, 1991), 1–36.

12. Brown, Society and the Supernatural: A Medieval Change," in Brown, Society and the Holy in Late Antiquity (Berkeley: University of California Press, 1982), 313.

13. Or to put it more in the more technical language of later law, either from knowledge de visu et auditu or knowledge of reputation. See Jean-Philippe Lévy, La hiérarchie des preuves dans le droit savant du moyen-âge depuis la renaissance du droit romain jusqu'à la fin du XIVe siècle (Paris: Recueil Sirey, 1939), 49–53.

14. Esp. Fraher, The Theoretical Justification for the New Criminal Law of the High Middle Ages: "Rei Publicae Interest, ne Crimina Remaneant Impunita," 1984 Ill. L. Rev.

577; van Caenegem, Public Prosecution of Crime in Twelfth-Century England, in van Caenegem, Legal History, 1–36. A similar interpretation is now offered by Finnbar McAuley, Canon Law and the End of the Ordeal, Oxford Journal of Legal Studies 26 (2006): at 475–476 and often. Professor McAuley's learned article is partly framed, strangely, as an attack on an early unpublished version of this book, downloaded from some site on the Internet—although his article attacks me under the name "Whiting," in id., 504–507. I have no way of determining which unpublished version of this book Professor McAuley downloaded: I presented early versions of this project at a number of venues, all of whose organizers posted my drafts. Professor McAuley chose to contact me only at a time when his article was already in proofs, the manuscript of this book was already with the publisher, and whatever early version he read had already been purged from the Internet. He never shared any draft version of his own article with me. At any rate, his attack is odd and misdirected. McAuley declares that I make the "fallacious" claim that the drive to abolish the ordeal grew out of the law of homicide. Id., 505. I never made that claim: the passages that Professor McAuley quotes are efforts to interpret the text of Canon 18 of the Fourth Lateran Council (which, in that now-lost unpublished draft, I characterized, perfectly accurately, as the "ultimate" justification for the abolition), not to offer a thoroughgoing explanation of every factor at work in the decline of the ordeals. As readers of this book will see, my emphasis, like Professor McAuley's, is very much on the campaign to prosecute crime. This was also true of whatever earlier version he read. (My account does, however, differ from Professor McAuley's in focusing more on the difficulty of acquiring sworn witness testimony. I am also more ready than Professor McAuley to credit the interpretation emphasizing the prosecution of crime to the work of prior scholars.) I confess that I do not understand his (rather boisterous) critique at 504–507. I read Canon 18 as directing clerics to avoid contact with blood. Surely that is correct.

15. For a lively rapid survey, see Charlotte Leitmeier, Die Kirche und die Gottesurteile: Eine rechtshistorische Studie (Vienna: Herold, 1953), 9–37.

16. For example, Ian Wood, Disputes in Late Fifth- and Sixth-Century Gaul, in The Settlement of Disputes in Early Modern Europe, ed. Wendy Davies and Paul Fouracre (Cambridge, U.K.: Cambridge University Press, 1986), 18.

17. Examples in Hermann Nottarp, Gottesurteilstudien (Munich: Kosel, 1956), 145–146, and detailed discussion in id., 301–305.

18. The main class of non-low-status persons subjected to the ordeals were women accused of sexual misconduct. Many of these were of very high status indeed.

19. Assizes of Jerusalem, quoted and discussed in Bartlett, Trial by Fire and Water, 30.

20. For example, Leitmeier, Die Kirche und die Gottesurteile, 11–12, 14–19.

21. Bartlett, Trial by Fire and Water, 29.

22. Van Caenegem, Public Prosecution of Crime in Twelfh-Century England, in van Caenegem, Legal History, 1. For an example of a fine for a failed accusation, see Herbert Meyer, ed., Das Mühlhäuser Reichsrechtsbuch: aus dem Anfang des 13. Jahrhunderts; Deutschlands ältestes Rechtsbuch nach den altmitteldeutschen Handschriften (Weimar: Böhlau, 1934), 112.

23. Examples collected in Bartlett, Trial by Fire and Water, 28–29.

24. Ivo, Epistola 252, in PL, 162:258. "Non negamus tamen quin ad divina aliquando

recurrendum sit testimonia quando, praecedente ordinaria accusatione, omnino desunt humana testimonia."

25. Bartlett, Trial by Fire and Water, 29.

26. Gandinus, Tractatus de maleficiis, in Tractatus Diversi Super Maleficiis (Lyon: Apud heredes J. Juntae, 1555), rubr. Quomodo de maleficiis cognoscatur per inquisitionem: "[I]dest quod sit publica vox et fama quod ille sit culpabilis." Quoted and discussed in R. Fraher, The Theoretical Justification for the New Criminal Law of the High Middle Ages, 577, 584 n. 40. Cf. Ivo, Epistle 249, in PL, 162, col. 255.

27. Stephanus V Ludberto Magnuntino Archiepiscopo, in PL, 129:797d; Ivo, Decr. 10.27, in PL, 161:699; Gratian, Decr. Pars Secunda C. 2, q. 5, c. 20.

28. Gratian, Decr. Pars Secunda C. 2, q. 5, c. 20.

29. For example, Thomas of Chobham, cited and discussed later in this chapter.

30. Lodovico Muratori, Dissertazioni sopra le Antichità Italiane (Milan: Società Tipografica de' Classici Italiani, 1837), 4:35; Richard Helmholz, The Early History of the Grand Jury and the Canon Law, University of Chicago Law Review 50 (1983), 620.

31. For examples, see later in this chapter, Family of Worms; Synod of Frankfurt (794), in MGH Leges, sec. II, Capitularia Regum Francorum, 1:75.

32. Bartlett, Trial by Fire and Water, 30.

33. Lex Familiae Wormatiensis Ecclesiae, chap. 31, in MGH Constitutiones, 1:644. Discussed more fully later in this chapter.

34. For example, Synod of Tours (925), Petrus Browe, De Ordaliis (Rome: Pontifical University Gregoriana, 1932–1933), 2, 24; and other examples discussed in Nottarp, Gottesurteilstudien, 262.

35. Morris, Judicium Dei: The Social and Political Significance of the Ordeal in the Eleventh Century, Studies in Church History 12 (1975): 96; also Trisha Olsen, Of Enchantment: The Passing of the Ordeals and the Rise of Jury Trial, Syracuse L. Rev. 50 (2000), 163.

36. For the dating: Joshua Prawer, Crusader Institutions (Oxford: Clarendon Press, 1998), 358–360.

37. Id., generally 358–391.

38. Assises de la cour bourgeois, cap. 286, ed. A.-A. Beugnot, Recueil des historiens des croisades, Lois, 2 (Paris: Imprimerie Royale, 1843), 217. Quoted and discussed in Bartlett, Trial by Fire and Water, 29–30.

39. Id., 218: "Le vescomte det prendre celuy, et metre en prison, et tenir le un an et un jor, por veir se dedens ce terme venra nule persone avant qui le veille apeller ou faire apeller de celuy murtre, ou ce il dedens l'an et le jor en vorreit porter juise. Mais se nul ne veneit dedens l'an et le jor qui de riens le vosist apeller, ny ne vost porter juise en tant, la raison juge qu'il deist estre delivrés de la prison come seluy qui est atant quite de celuy murtre, par dreit et par l'assize." Students of the history of the common law will notice the obvious link to *prison forte et dure*.

40. Hudson, Formation of the English Common Law, 72–73, with citations to further literature.

41. Fuller description in id., 73.

42. Karl Zeumer, ed., Formulae merowingici et karolini aevi: Accedunt Ordines iudici-

eges V (Formulae), e.g. 604, 606, 610, and often. For Christian ritual
arp, Gottesurteilstudien, 242–249.

Kerr, Richard D. Forsyth, and Michael J. Plyley, Cold Water and Hot
l in England, J. Interdisplinary History 22 (1992): 573–595, here

reported, fifty men had committed forest offenses—a crime par-
the king. They were subjected to the ordeal of the hot iron, and all
d. Rufus exclaimed, so it is said: "What is this? Is God a just
no after this believes so. For the future, by this and this I swear it,
my judgment, not to God's, which inclines to one side or the
an's prayer." R. C. van Caenegem, ed., English Lawsuits from
ondon: Selden Society, 1991), lawsuit no. 150, 1:122. This
lence that early twelfth-century observers did not believe that
or example, van Caenegem, English Lawsuits, 1:122; Hud-
Common Law, 74 —though noting that this supposed piece
almost unique." Read closely, the passage does not imply
d "inclines to prayers."
hose who had survived the ordeal, see van Caenegem,
welfth-Century England, 3; for a twelfth-century church
no. 21.

old Water and Hot Iron.
ttarp, Gottesurteilstudien, 111–115.
2, 160–161.
0–122, 138, 181.

o.
teilstudien, 137.

ussing Guibert de Nogent, *De vita sua*, in PL,
iatum, in PL, 205:230.
54, discussed in Nottarp, Gottesurteilstudien,
3, 4; MGH Constitutiones 1:604; Browe, De

mon Law, 74.
20.
ssenschaftlichen Mythologie (Göttingen:

ls. (Königsberg: Borntraeger, 1829).
tingen: Dietrich, 1828), 908–909.
eifelhaft"; 909: "das geschehene oder

65. Grimm, Deutsche Mythologie, 3d ed. (Göttingen: Dieterich, 1854), 1061.

66. In particular, it is more or less directly rejected by Aquinas. Aquinas treats
ordeal as related to oracles by lot, but rejects it on the grounds that it "goes beyond"
practice of casting lots, entering into a different, and forbidden ground. Summa
ologica, 2-2 q. 95 n. 8, available at http://www.newadvent.org/summa/306406.htn

67. For an example of the vitality of Grimm's interpretation in later German liter
see Koestler, Der Anteil des Christentums an den Ordalien, ZRG (Kan) 2 (1912): 21
a particularly subtle scholar, see Adalbert Erler, one of the leading figures of the
German literature, who believed that there were two kinds of ordeals. Some wer
wehrordalien," "defensive" ordeals, which were intended to allow those accused to
their fortitude. But other times, according to Erler, ordeals were "Ermittlungen,"
tigations" intended to ferret out hidden truth with the aid of God. Adalbert Erler, U
der Gottesurteile, Paideuma 2 (1940): 51–53 [44–65]. It is my argument, in eff
Erler's category of Abwehrordalien should feature more prominently in our discu

68. Nottarp, Gottesurteilstudien, 18.

69. Id., 26–27 (discussing Cesare Lombroso).

70. Id., 28.

71. Such was Nottarp's basic argument, which he repeated verbatim in the lo
version of his book, eliminating only one reference to "intellekualistischen en
Juden"; this phrase appeared in the 1949 edition of Nottarp's study, on p. 29
dropped in the 1956 version.

72. Bartlett, Trial by Fire and Water, 29.

73. Quoted above. For the meaning of "accusatio ordinaria" see the discu
Epistle 249, in chapter 4.

74. Nottarp, Gottesurteilstudien, 22 (ordeals "nur Beweismittel").

75. Id., 106.

76. Id., 105.

77. Gratian Decr. Pars Secunda C. 2, q. 5, c. 20.

78. Nottarp, Gottesurteilstudien, 98

79. Id., 320, 346; also 151, 177.

80. See Nottarp's discussion in id., 67, declaring the Rufus "verwarf die
while noting that he did hesitate to continue to make use of them; and 69
Rufus showed "den Skeptizismus der Nordgermanen."

81. For example, Nottarp, Gottesurteilstudien, 165.

82. Id., 350–351.

83. Id., 351.

84. Bartlett, Trial by Fire and Water, 29–30.

85. Id., 79.

86. Id., 158–159.

87. Brown, Society and the Supernatural, 311.

88. Jean Gaudemet, Les Ordalies au Moyen Age: Doctrine, Legis
Canoniques, in La Preuve: Recueils de la Société Jean Bodin pour l'His
des Institutions (Brussels: Société Jean Bodin), 2:100.

89. Olsen, Of Enchantment.

90. Id., 158–159.

91. Davies and Fouracre, Conclusion, in The Settlement of Disputes, 222. For this commonplace observation, see also Hudson, Formation of the English Common Law, 72.

92. Van Caenegem, Public Prosecution of Crime in Twelfth-Century England, 8.

93. The latter emphasized by Bartlett, Trial by Fire and Water, 19–20.

94. For example, Synod of Worms (868), Browe, De Ordaliis, 1, no. 61 (discussing treatment of thefts by unknown perpetrator.); Nottarp, Gottesurteilstudien, 134.

95. Gratian Decr. Pars Secunda C. 2, q. 5, c. 20. For an example in which three women suspected of witchcraft were beaten in order to force them to confess, see Herman quondam Iudaeus, Opusculum de sua conversione, in PL, 170:813–814, and for the connection between ordeals and confession in cases of heresy, the sources collected in Nottarp, Gottesurteilstudien, 170–171.

96. For example, Anonymus Ticinensis (ca. 1320), discussed in Nottarp, Gottesurteilstudien, 146.

97. Bartlett, Trial by Fire and Water, 29.

98. Case of Ailward, lawsuit no. 471, in van Caenegem, ed., English Lawsuits, 2:511.

99. Van Caenegem, Public Prosecution of Crime in Twelfth-Century England, 1.

100. See e.g. Daniel Lord Smail, The Consumption of Justice: Emotions, Publicity, and Legal Culture in Marseille, 1264–1423 (Ithaca: Cornell University Press, 2003); Paul R. Hyams, Rancor and Reconciliation in Medieval England (Ithaca: Cornell University Press, 2003).

101. I do not mean to deny that vengeance can also be sought through litigation, as Smail argues in The Consumption of Justice, 72 and often. Once courts are established, litigants certainly use them in that way. In the early periods of which I speak, though, courts did not have the level of legitimacy they later achieved. I shall return to this theme later.

102. Vincent de Beauvais, Bibliotheca Mundi, seu Speculi Maioris Vincentii Burgundi Praesulis Bellovacensis, O.P. Tomus Secundus, qui Speculum Doctrinale inscribitur (Douai: Ex Officina Typographica Balazaris Belleri, 1624), 839 (= bk. 9, ch. 103).

103. Id.

104. Thomae de Chobham Summa Confessorum, ed. F. Broomfield (Louvain: Nauwelaerts, 1968) (= Analecta Mediaevalia Namurcensia 25), 548–549.

105. Van Caenegem, Birth of the Common Law, 67.

106. R. W. Southern, The Making of the Middle Ages (New Haven: Yale University Press, 1970), 126.

107. Britton: An English Translation and Notes, ed. Francis M. Nichols (repr. Holmes Beach: Gaunt, 1983), 2: 212: "[C]hargé en peril de sa alme de dire verité."

108. "Recognoscite verum per fidem et credulitatem, quam in dominum Ihesum Christum habetis et quam in baptismo recepistis et super sacramentum, quod corporaliter in presentia nostra modo prestistis ita quod, si in aliquo de re ista mendaces fueritis vel veritatem celaveritis, quod anime vestre in perpetuum dampnentur et corpora vestra opprobiose perditioni apertissimae exponantur." In Ernest-Joseph Tardif, Summa de Legibus Normannie in curia laicali (Rouen: Société de l'histoire de Normandie, 1896), 2:232.

109. Van Caenegem, Public Prosecution of Crime in Twelfth-Century England, 6–7.

110. Magnum Rotulum Scaccarii, ed. J. Hunter (London: Record Commission, 1833), 34: "100 Li. ut non amplius sint judices nec juratores." Quoted and discussed, along with

other examples, in van Caenegem, Public Prosecution of Crime in Twelfth-Century England, 5–6 and 6 n. 9

111. Id., discussing Constitutions of Clarendon (1164), in William Stubbs, Select Charters and Other Illustrations of English Constitutional History, from the Earliest Times to the Reign of Edward the First, 9th ed. (Oxford: Clarendon, 1946), 165.

112. Van Caenegem, Public Prosecution of Crime in Twelfth-Century England, 30.

113. Fraher, Theoretical Justification, 582.

114. Honorius, Summa Questionum, D. 1 t. 14 De testibus, q. 15, quoted and discussed in chapter 4.

115. Constitutiones Regni Siciliae 2, 31, de legibus paribilibus sublatis; J. L. A. Huillard-Bréholles, Historia Diplomatica Frederici Secundi, 4, pt. 1 (Paris: Plon, 1854), 102. For another similar case, see Nottarp, Gottesurteilstudien, 143 (dispute of Sessa-Aurunca, 1171, in which sworn witness testimony is taken in place of trial by combat.).

116. Glanvill, 28, ii, 7.

117. Capitula Singillatim Tradita Karolo Magno Adscripta, in MGH Leges, sec. II, Capitularia Regum Francorum, 1:217; see also Leges Burgundionum, ch. 45, in MGH Leges, sec. I, 2, pt. 1, 75–76; further discussion and citation in Nottarp, Gottesurteilstudien, 270.

118. Lex Familiae Wormatiensis Ecclesiae, chap. 31, in MGH Constitutiones, I:644.

119. Glanvill, 34–35, ii, 17, discussed more fully in chapter 5.

120. Gratian Decr. Pars Secunda C. 2, q. 5, c. 20

121. Gaudemet, Les Ordalies, 100.

122. Lawsuit no. 15, in van Caenegem, ed., English Lawsuits, 1:38.

123. For a recent survey, see Schmoeckel, "Ein sonderbares Wunderwerck Gottes."

124. See now the learned survey of primary and secondary sources in McAuley, Canon Law and the End of the Ordeal, 477–481, discussing both the slim scriptural warrant for ordeals and the concern that they had introduced themselves only through custom.

125. Fraher, Theoretical Justification.

126. Bartlett, Trial by Fire and Water, 77–78.

127. For references, see Marcus Jastrow, A Dictionary of the Targumim, the Talmud Babli and Yerushalmi, and the Midrashic Literature (New York: Judaica Press, 1975), 916, s.v. "nasah."

128. Matt. 4:7. I have used the New International Version for these passages, in order to emphasize the original sense of "tentare."

129. Sanctii Aurelii Augustini Quaestionum in Heptateuchum Libri VII, Corpus Christianorum Series Latina, vol. 33 (Turnholt: Brepols, 1958), 10–11: Quaest. Gen. Qu. 26.

130. Baldwin, Intellectual Preparation, 620–621.

131. Id., discussing the Tractaturus Magister.

132. Bernard S. Jackson, Susanna and the Singular History of Singular Witnesses, in Acta Juridica 1977: Essays in Honour of Ben Beinart (1979): 37–54; R. H. Helmholz, The Development of Law in Classical and Early Medieval Europe: The Bible in the Service of the Canon Law, 70 Chi.-Kent L. Rev. 1557, 1573–1574 (1995).

133. Zeumer, ed., MGH Leges V (Formulae), e.g. 641.

134. Case of Ailward, above note.

135. Steve Stern, The Social Significance of Judicial Institutions in an Exploitative

Society: Humanga, Peru, 1570–1640, in The Inca and Aztec States, 1400–1800: Anthropology and History, ed. George A. Collier, Renato I. Rosaldo, and John D. Wirth (New York: Academic Press, 1982), 293–297.

136. Smail, The Consumption of Justice, at e.g. 115–116.

137. John of Wales, Communiloquium [1495] = Harvard Houghton INC 1644, chap. IV: De informatione accusantium: "[S]icut canis rabiosus."

138. Hans Fehr, Gottesurteil und Folter, in Festgabe für Rudolf Stammler (Berlin and Leipzig: de Gruyter, 1926), 231–254.

139. The excellent discussion of Alfred Vanderpol, La doctrine scolastique du Droit de Guerre (Paris: Pedone, 1919), 110–120, deserves more attention from legal historians than it receives.

140. Bonnaud-Delamare, Idée de la Paix, 15, 277.

141. Agobardus Lugdunensis, Liber contra judicium dei, in PL, 104:263: "Sanguinem enim animarum vestrarum requiram de manu cunctarum bestiarum, et de manu hominis: de manu viri et fratris ejus requiram animam hominis. Quicunque effuderit humanum sanguinem, fundetur sanguis illius; ad imaginem quippe Dei factus est homo. Haec prima lex, a Deo data hominibus, prohibet attentissime humanum sanguinem fundere *Non omnis qui hominem occiderit, corporaliter occidetur. Sed secundum illud accipiendum est quod Dominus in Evangelio dicit: Omnis enim qui gladium acceperit, peribit. Et Apostolus ait: Quoniam omnis homicida non habet vitam aeternam in se manentem. Quare autem hunc reatum tanta poena sequatur, haec causa est, quoniam ad imaginem Dei factus est homo.*" For a broader collection of early medieval passages, see Leitmeier, Die Kirche und die Gottesurteile, 44–62.

142. General account in Nottarp, Gottesurteilstudien, 317–319.

143. See Antonius García y García, Constitutiones Concilii quarti Lateranensis una cum Commentariis Glossatorum (= Monumenta Iuris Canonici Series A, vol. 2) (Vatican City: Biliotheca apostolica vaticana, 1981), 66 n. 18 (1). For earlier attacks: Browe, De Ordaliis, 1, no. 9.

144. C. 2, q. 5, c. 7, 15, 20, 26. For the agreement of Henry II in the wake of the Beckett dispute that "clerici non cogantur facere duellum," see Radulphi de Diceto Lundonensis Opera Historica, ed. William Stubbs (London: Rolls Series, 1876), 1: 410.

145. Browe, De Ordaliis, 1, 29.

146. Browe, De Ordaliis, 1, 83, 84.

147. "[N]isi prius accepta non ledendi corporis convictorum plena cautione." Browe, De Ordaliis, 1, 86.

148. Decret. Greg. IX, lib. 5, tit. 14, cap. 1, Browe, De Ordaliis, 1, 24 (trial by battle that results in death or mutilation results in *irregularitas*).

149. For example, Nottarp, Gottesurteilstudien, 241–243.

150. Discussion and references in id., 76–77.

151. See the fuller discussion in chapter 4.

152. Peter the Chanter, Summa, quoted in Baldwin, Intellectual Preparation, 632 n. 113: "[Q]uodam modo homicide efficantur."

153. In PL, 205:226–233.

154. Peter the Chanter, Summa, in Baldwin, Intellectual Preparation, 632 n. 113.

155. Cf. Vanderpol, Droit de Guerre, 119–120.

Chapter 4. Salvation for the Judge, Damnation for the Witnesses

Epigraph. Aquinas, Summa Theologica, 2–2 q. 64 n. 7, available at http://www.newad
vent.org/summa/306406.htm.

1. Vincent de Beauvais, Bibliotheca Mundi, seu Speculi Maioris Vincentii Burgundi
Praesulis Bellovacensis, O.P. Tomus Secundus, qui Speculum Doctrinale inscribitur
(Douai: Ex Officina Typographica Balazaris Belleri, 1624), col. 882 (= bk. 10, chap. 2):
"Utrum occidere liceat alicui. *Gratianus, Ca. 23, q. 5.* Quod autem nulli liceat aliquem
occidere, illo praecepto probatur, quo dominus in lege homicidium prohibuit dicens: *Non
occides.* Item in evangelio. *Omnis qui gladium acceperit, gladium peribit. Item Aug.
Donato. c. unum solum.*" For convenience I use the familiar Catholic numbering of the
Commandment throughout in this chapter.

2. Id., 883 (bk. 10, ch. 3). Vincent was quoting Raymond de Peñafort. For Raymond's
text, see chapter 2 above.

3. Id.

4. For example, Vincent de Beauvais, Bibliotheca Mundi, seu Speculi Maioris Vincentii Burgundi Praesulis Bellovacensis, O.P. Tomus Quartus, qui Speculum Historiale inscribitur (Douai: Ex Officina Typographica Balazaris Beloleri, 1624), 459 (bk.12, ch. 9).

5. Richard Fraher, Conviction According to Conscience; The Medieval Jurists' Debate Concerning Judicial Discretion and the Law of Proof, 7 Law & Hist. Rev. 23, 24
(1989).

6. Speculum Doctrinale, 882–883 (bk. 10, ch. 2): "Ex occasione terribilium iudicium
& legum, ne eterni iudicij penas luant, corrigi eos cupimus, non necari; nec disciplinam
circa eos negligi volumus, nec supplicijs quibus digni sunt coerceri. Sic ergo peccata
eorum compesce, ut sint quos poenitat peccasse. *Item Greg. Pap.* Reos sanguinis defendat
ecclesia, ne in effusione sanguinis particeps fiat. Hinc apparet, quod mali flagellis sunt
coercendi, non membrorum truncatione, vel corporali morte plectendi."

7. Id., 882–883 (bk. 10, ch. 2): "Sed objicitur quod dixit dominus ad Moysen: *Malefi-
cos non patieris vivere.* Item. *Qui coierit cum iumento moriatur.* Item, adulterij & blas-
phemiae crimine notatus, immisericorditer lapidari iubetur. Nonnulli etiam in veteri testa-
menti inveniuntur malos trucidasse, nec transgressores legis, sed defensores appellantur."

8. Id., 883 (bk. 10, ch. 2): "*Prohibetur* ergo illo praecepto [i.e., the Fifth Command-
ment] quique sua auctoritate in necem alicuius armari, non legis imperio reos morti
tradere. Qui enim publica potestate functus, ipsius legis imperios malos perimit, nec illius
praecepti transgressor, nec coelesti patria alienus habetur. *Unde. August. Ad Publicolam.*
De occidendis hominibus, ne ab eis quisque occidatur, non mihi placet consilium; nisi
forte sit miles, aut publica functione teneatur, ut non pro se hoc faciat, sed pro aliis, aut
pro civitate ub etiam ipse est, accepta legitima potestate, si eius conguit personae."

9. Id., col. 883: "Cap. 3. *De diversis causis occidendi. Ex summa de ca.* Homicidium
facto committitur (ut dictum est) quatuor modis, id est iustitia, voluntate, necessitate,
casu. *Iustitia* quidem, et cum iudex vel minister, reum iustè condemnatum occidit. Hoc
homicidium si sit ex livore vel delectatione fundendi humanum sanguinem, licet ille iustè
occidatur, iste tamen peccat mortaliter propter intentionem corruptam. Si vero fit ex
amore iustitie, nec peccat iudex ipsum condemnando ad mortem, & praecipendo minis-
tro ut occidat eum, nec minister si iussus occidit condemnatur, peccaret tamen uterque

mortaliter si faceret iuris ordine non servato." Here again the quote is from Raymond de Peñafort. The same standard passage was quoted by Bracton about the same time. See chapter 4.

10. Id., 714 (bk. 8, ch. 62).

11. Id.

12. Id.: "[L]uce clariores."

13. Id., 839 (bk. 9, ch. 103): "Si prodit eum, forte punietur ille in corpore, vel occidetur à iudice, vel eitam à parentibus illius quem ipse volebat peierare [*sic*, 'perire'], vel ipsemet proditor potest de facili incurrere mortis periculum."

14. Id., 839 (bk. 9, ch. 103).

15. Id., 847 (bk. 9, ch. 114). This topos comes from Isidore of Seville.

16. Id., 835 (bk. 9, ch. 97) (cribbing again from Raymond de Peñafort): "Si vero ignorantia iuris vel facti crassa fuerit & supina, mortale." For the definition of "crassa et supina": X. Ochoa and A. Diez, eds., S. Raimundus de Pennaforte Summa de Iure Canonico, in Universa Biblitheca Iuris (Rome: Commentarium pro Religiosis, 1975), col. 36: "Dicitur autem crassa et supina ignorantia cum aliquis dicit se ignorare quod omnes de civitate sciunt, vel quod publice promulgatum est."

17. Id., 716 (bk. 8, ch. 65).

18. Robert Bartlett, Trial by Fire and Water (Oxford: Clarendon Press, 1986), 29.

19. Fuller discussion in chapter 3 above. In England, at least, accusers apparently did come forward. See John Hudson, The Formation of the English Common Law (London: Longman, 1996), 167.

20. Case of Ailward, lawsuit no. 471, in R. C. van Caenegem, ed., English Lawsuits from William I to Richard I (London: Selden Society, 1991), 2:511.

21. Perhaps this change was inevitable: as Winfried Trusen has shown, the new Continental procedure was the creation of twelfth-century canon lawyers who were primarily concerned with the internal law of the church, in particular with clerics who had committed sins of unchastity or simony. Canonists focusing upon the problem of such errant clerics could hardly have endorsed a procedure that required judicial combat. As we have seen, the church had been opposed to judicial combat for centuries. Twelfth-century canonists would not have created a procedure that required accused clerics to fight battles of blood. Yet the procedures that they developed to deal with clerics became, by the thirteenth century, the procedures applied in all criminal matters. Consequently, judicial combat by accusers fell by the wayside in canon procedure. See Winfried Trusen, Der Inquisitionsprozeß, seine historischen Grundlagen und frühen Formen, Zeitschrift der Savigny Stiftung für Rechtsgeschichte (Kanonistische Abteilung) 74 (1988): 168–230; and the further researches on this theme of Lotte Kéry, Inquisitio—denunciato—exceptio: Möglichkeiten der Verfahrenseinleitung im Dekretalenrecht, Zeitschrift der Savigny Stiftung für Rechtsgeschichte (Kanonistische Abteilung) 87 (2001): 226–268.

22. James A. Brundage, Medieval Canon Law (Harlow: Longmans, 1996), 93.

23. Ivo, Epistola 252, in PL, 162, col. 258: "Non negamus tamen quin ad divina aliquando recurrendum sit testimonia quando, praecedente ordinaria accusatione, omnino desunt humana testimonia."

24. Brundage, Medieval Canon Law, 94–95. This account simplifies some of the issues involved in the treatment of fama, but I leave aside the complexities. For a brief recent

account in English, see Mike MacNair, Vicinage and the Antecedents of the Jury, Law and History Review 17 (1999): 574–578; and the strictures of Charles Donahue, Biology and the Origins of the Jury, Law and History Review 17 (1999): 594–596. The problem of *fama* raises many interesting questions of social history that I cannot discuss. See generally the studies in Thelma Fenster and Daniel Lord Smail, eds., Fama: The Politics of Talk and Reputation in Medieval Europe (Ithaca: Cornell University Press, 2003).

25. Gandinus, Tractatus de maleficiis, in Tractatus Diversi Super Maleficiis (Lugduni: Apud heredes J. Juntae, 1555), rubr. Quomodo de maleficiis cognoscatur per inquisitionem: "[I]dest quod sit publica vox et fama quod ille sit culpablilis." Quoted and discussed in Richard Fraher, The Theoretical Justification for the New Criminal Law of the High Middle Ages: "Rei Publicae Interest, ne Crimina Remaneant Impunita," 1984 Ill L. Rev. 577, 584 n. 40.

26. Brundage, Medieval Canon Law, 94–95, noting that torture was probably rarely used. See the further discussion later in this chapter.

27. For recent studies, see Peter Landau, The Development of the Law, in The New Cambridge Medieval History, IV, pt. 1 (Cambridge, U.K.: Cambridge University Press, 2004), 113–147; Anders Winroth, The Making of Gratian's *Decretum* (Cambridge, U.K.: Cambridge University Press, 2000); Fraher, Conviction According to Conscience.

28. The system is acutely analyzed, on the basis of recent scholarship, in Mathias Schmoeckel, Humanität und Staatsraison: Die Abschaffung der Folter in Europa und die Entwicklung des gemeinen Strafprozeß- und Beweisrechts seit dem hohen Mittelalter (Cologne: Böhlau, 2000), 187–294.

29. Giorgio Alessi Palazzolo, Prova Legale e Pena: La crisi del sistema tra medio evo et moderno (Naples: Jovene, 1979), 3–5; and in the older literature Paul Fournier, Les Officialités au Moyen Age: Etude sur l'Organisation, la Compétence et la Procédure des Tribunaux Ecclésiastiques Ordinaires en France, de 1180 à 1328 (Paris: Plon, 1880), 247.

30. See the fuller discussion in Schmoeckel, Humanität und Staatsraison, 212–213, 219–228. At 212–213, Schmoeckel emphasizes the extent to which Enlightenment critics caricatured this system.

31. John Langbein, Torture and the Law of Proof (Chicago: University of Chicago Press, 1977), 15–16.

32. The comparison is rightly developed by Bartlett, Trial by Fire and Water, 140–142. The use of torture in the early Germanic sources also led Brunner to make this connection for the earliest period. See Heinrich Brunner, Deutsche Rechtsgeschichte, 2d ed. (Leipzig: Duncker und Humblot, 1928), 2:554.

33. Gratian Decr. Pars Secunda, C. 2, q. 5, c. 20.

34. Fraher, Conviction According to Conscience, 24.

35. Cf. the interpretation of Richard Fraher, IV Lateran's Revolution in Criminal Procedure, in Studia in Honorem Eminentissimi Cardinalis Alphonsi M. Stickler (= Studia et Textus Historiae Iuris Canonici 7) (Rome: LAS, 1992), 97–111 (emphasizing bureaucratic nature of system).

36. Langbein, summarizing many years of his research, in The Legal History of Torture, in Torture: A Collection, ed. Sanford Levinson (New York: Oxford University Press, 2004), 94. For his original statement, see Langbein, Torture and the Law of Proof, 7.

37. Decr. Pars Secunda, C. 11, q. 13, c. 78.

38. Decr. Pars Secunda, C. 11, q. 13, c. 80.

39. Honorius, Summa Questionum, D. 1 t. 14 De testibus, q. 15: "Si sponte interfuit, cogi potest. Sibi enim uidetur non imposuisse necessitatem. Si fortuito, secus. Contra decretum tamen potest obici, cum magis uideatur cogendus qui nullum metum allegat quam is qui aliquem cum metu possit excusare, si iustus est, quod tamen non est uerum. Presumitur enim quod qui nullum metum allegant et nolunt testificari, quod diffidant de iustitia ipsius pro quo producendi erant; de aliis autem presumitur quod si auderent uellent, et ita presumitur de iusticia ipsius." I consulted the manuscript of this text held at the Bibliothèque Nationale, Paris, MS Lat 144591. I have relied, however, on the as yet unpublished transcription of this text by Dr. Waltraud Kozur, who very graciously provided me with a copy.

40. A basic account of the law can be found in Carl Groß, Das Beweisverfahren im canonischen Process (Vienna: Becksche Universitäts-Buchhandlung, 1880), 2:26–28.

41. Ordo Judicarius "Scientiam," in Ludwig Wahrmund, ed., Quellen zur Geschichte des Römisch-Kanonischen Processes im Mittelalter, vol. 2, pt. 1 (Innsbruck: Wagner, 1913), 53.

42. Speculum Iuris Gulielmi Durandi (Venice: Bindoni, 1576), 3:47 (= bk. 3, r. de notoriis criminibus v. fama 6).

43. In H. Kantorowicz, ed., Albertus Gandinus und das Strafrecht der Scholastik (Berlin: Guttentag, 1926), 2:157.

44. Inferno, Canto 30.

45. Trisha Olsen, Of Enchantment: The Passing of the Ordeals and the Rise of Jury Trial, Syracuse L. Rev. 50 (2000), 109–196, here 119.

46. Jacob, Le serment des juges, in R. Verdier, ed., Le Serment, 2 vols. (Paris: CNRS, 1991), 1:439–457.

47. Knut Wolfgang Nörr, Zur Stellung des Richters im gelehrten Prozeß der Frühzeit: Iudex secundum allegata non secundum conscientiam iudicat (Munich: Beck, 1967). For other literature on this problem, which is well known to specialists in Continental legal history, see Jacques Delanglade, S.J., Le Juge, Serviteur de la Loi ou Gardien de la Justice selon la Tradition Théologique, 10 Revue de Droit Canonique 141, 151–153 (1960); Domenico Maffei, Il Giudice Testimmone e una "Quaestio" de Jacques de Revigny (MS. Bon. Coll. Hisp. 82), 35 Tijdschrift voor Rechtsgeschiedenis 54–76 (1967); Fraher, Conviction According to Conscience; Laurent Mayali, Entre Idéal de Justice et Faiblesse Humaine: Le Juge Prévaricateur en Droit Savant in Justice et Justiciables, Mélanges Henri Vidal (Montpellier: Faculté de droit, d'économie et de gestion, 1994), 95–103; Antonio Padoa-Schioppa, Sur la conscience du juge dans le Ius Commune Européen, in La conscience du juge dans la tradition juridique européenne, ed. Jean-Marie Carbasse and Laurence Depambour-Tarride (Paris: Presses Universitaires de France, 1999), 95–129; Antonio Padoa-Schioppa, Italia ed Europa nella storia del diritto (Bologna: Il Mulino, 2003), 240–242.

48. Also in Philo of Alexandria: Antonio Padoa-Schioppa, Sur la conscience dans le Ius Commune Européen, in Jean-Marie Carbasse and Laurence Depambour-Tarride, eds., La conscience du juge dans la tradition juridique européenne (Paris: P.U.F., 1999), 105.

49. See G. Krieger, Gewissen, -sfreiheit, in Lexikon des Mittelalters (Munich: Deutscher Taschenbuch Verlag, 1989), 4: cols. 1424–1426.

50. Nörr, Zur Stellung des Richters, 13.

51. Lea, History of Auricular Confession (repr. New York: Greenwood, 1968), 1: 230.

52. Canon 21, at http://www.fordham.edu/halsall/basis/lateran4.html. Latin text in Antonius García y García, Constitutiones Concilii quarti Lateranensis una cum Commentariis Glossatorum (= Monumenta Iuris Canonici Series A, vol. 2) (Vatican City: Biblioteca apostolica vaticana, 1981), 67–69.

53. There is growing literature on the connections between conscience, confession, and law. See Miriam Turrini, La coscienza e le leggi: Morale e diritto nei testi per la confessione della prima Età moderna (Bologna: Il Mulino, 1991); Paolo Prodi, Una storia della giustizia: Dal pluralismo dei fori al moderno dualismo tra coscienza e diritto (Bologna: Il Mulino, 2000); Adriano Prosperi, Tribunali della coscienza: Inquisitori, confessori, missionari (Turin: Einaudi, 1996); Pierre Legendre, Aux sources de la culture occidentale: L'ancien droit de la pénitence, Settimane di studio del Centro italiano di studi sull'alto medioevo, XXII: La cultura antica nell'Occidente Latino dal VII all' XI secolo (Spoleto: Presso la sede del Centro, 1975), 575–595, reproduced in Pierre Legendre, Ecrits Juridiques du Moyen Age occidental (London: Variorum Reprints, 1988).

54. This tale, it should be noted, is not present in the earliest Greek manuscripts, and therefore probably dates to a later period in the development of Christian thought. I am grateful to Professor Bart Ehrman for discussing the textual history of this passage with me.

55. "[D]ominus dixit, 'vade mulier, quia nemo est qui te accuset, nec ego te contempnabo.' Unde manifeste colligitur, quod iudex nequaquam debet de facto supplere." Gloss on C. 2.10 un., quoted and discussed in Nörr, Zur Stellung des Richters, 17–18; Padoa-Schioppa, Conscience dans le *Ius Commune* Européen, 98.

56. Emphasized by Padoa-Schioppa, Conscience dans le *Ius Commune* Européen, 101.

57. For this topos, see Schmoeckel, Humanität und Staatsraison, 192.

58. Speculum Iuris Gulielmi Durandi (Venice: Bindoni, 1576), 2:785 (= Spec. 2.3. de Sententia qualiter sit ferenda), noting that consilia on the case were prepared by Azo, Hugolinus, and Hostiensis. Nörr, Zur Stellung des Richters, 78 n. 53, notes that Hostiensis in the printed version is an error for Accursius.

59. For a fifteenth-century Florentine example, in which a vendetta agreement required the wrongdoer to "sally forth once every eight days, unarmed and unaccompanied, on the streets of Florence and go at least as far as the Mercato Vecchio," see Thomas Kuehn, Law, Family and Women: Toward a Legal Anthropology of Renaissance Italy (Chicago: University of Chicago Press, 1991), 147.

60. Romeo and Juliet, act 3, scene 1 (set in "a public place").

61. Most famously to tourists in Siena, where the Palazzo Pubblico, which housed the Podestà, looks out on the Campo. In Bologna, too, the Palazzo Communale does indeed look out on the Piazza Maggiore.

62. Nörr, Zur Stellung des Richters, 13.

63. Padoa-Schioppa, Conscience dans le *Ius Commune* Européen, 101 (discussing Stephen of Tournai).

64. John Bossy, The Social History of Confession in the Age of the Reformation, Transactions of the Royal Historical Society, 5th series, 25 (1975): 24.

65. Nörr, Zur Stellung des Richters, 39.

66. Id., 51 n. 1.

67. This view was represented in particular by Martinus of Gosia, a famous twelfth-century lawyer whose views often aimed to christianize the doctrines of Roman law. Id., 18–19, 25. "M[artinus] dicit, quod si iudex sciens veritatem negotii, de quo iudex et testis est, quod potest sententiam ferre, secundum quod noverit in civili causa, sed non in criminali, ubi sine accusatore iudicare non potest, exemplo Christi, qui mulierem accusatam de adulterio absolvit, dicens: Mulier, non est qui te accuset, nec ego to condemnabo. Alii contra: dicunt enim et in civili et in criminali causa iudicem secundum quod scit iudicare posse." Dissensio on C. 41.21.13, quoted and discussed in Nörr, Zur Stellung des Richters, 22. Not every twelfth-century jurist, it should be said, saw things the way Martinus did. For a rapid survey of the criminal/civil distinction in later centuries, see Delanglade, Le Juge, Serviteur de la Loi, 151–153.

68. Peter the Chanter, Summa, in John W. Baldwin, The Intellectual Preparation for the Canon of 1215 against Ordeals, Speculum 36 (1961): 632 n. 113. Quoted and discussed in chapter 3 above.

69. Padoa-Schioppa, Conscience dans le *Ius Commune* Européen, 99–100.

70. Quaestiones Dominorum Bononiensium, in Giovanni Palmerio, Scripta Anecdota Glossatorum, 1, additions, 237 (Bologna: Azzoguidiana, 1913): "Tam in crimine, quam in negotio innocens falsis testibus convincitur, et criminosus, vel obnoxius, innocens astruitur. Iudex scit veritatem negotii. Queritur an secundum conscientiam, vel potius secundum allegata iudicare debeat. Solutio: Ultimus questionis articulus non multum habet dubietatis. Solvendum enim puto nocentem, secundum quod allegatum est a parte sua, si nulla vel minus frivola contra ipsum allegantur. Et facio contra conscientiam, idest contra id quod scio eum mereri, non tamen facio contra conscientiam, idest contra id quod scio me facere debere. Debet enim quisque prudens iudex scire secundum testimonia inducta se debere iudicare, si ea nullatenus posit repellere. Nec dicitur ipse hoc facere, sed lex, *ut C. XXIII, q. 5, c. si homicidium; et C. XXXIII, q. 2, c. quos.*"

71. Padoa-Schioppa, Conscience dans le *Ius Commune* Européen, 99–100

72. Cf. the opinion of Pillius, discussed in Nörr, Zur Stellung des Richters, 27.

73. Latin text quoted and discussed above, chapter 2.

74. The author also cited C. 33, q. 2 c. 18.

75. ErnstKantorowicz, The King's Two Bodies: A Study in Mediaeval Political Theology (Princeton: Princeton University Press, 1957). For the comparison: Nörr, Zur Stellung des Richters, 71.

76. Id., 45 n. 37.

77. Id., 50.

78. Id., 40; Padoa-Schioppa, Conscience dans le *Ius Commune* Européen, 103. For civilians like Azo, there were naturally only two persons: ut iudex and ut privatus. Padoa-Schioppa, Sur la conscience dans le *Ius Commune* Européen, 107.

79. Nörr, Zur Stellung des Richters, 28.

80. Id., 32 (discussing Azo).

81. On these and other expedients: de Langlade, Le Juge, Serviteur de la Loi, 143–144; Nörr, Zur Stellung des Richters, 51–84.

82. This was the view of the great sixteenth-century theologian Thomas de Cajetan, Secunda Secundae Partis Summae Theologicae S. Thomas de Aquino, cum Commentariis

(Venice: Apud Juntas, 1638), 163v, marginal commentary bottom right (judge must declare publicly "vidi in tali loco, &c.").

83. There was also a tradition, notably in France, that held that the king was not bound by any such moral dilemma. Only inferior magistrates were bound to judge exclusively on the record. Nörr, Zur Stellung des Richters, 86–88; and the "Quaestio" of Jacques de Révigny published in Maffei, Il Giudice Testimmone, 74–76. It is conceivable that this has some bearing on the English tradition, to the extent juries were conceived as "judges without a superior."

84. Homicide is the general topic of quaestio 64, in which this passage appears.

85. Aquinas, Summa Theologica, 2–2 q. 64 n. 7, at http://www.newadvent.org/summa/306406.htm.

86. John of Wales, Communiloquium [1495] = Harvard Houghton INC 1644, chap. IV: De informatione accusantium, discussed above in chapter 3.

87. Nörr, Zur Stellung des Richters, 52; Padoa-Schioppa, Conscience dans le *Ius Commune* Européen, 100–101 (Summa Colonensis).

88. Nörr, Zur Stellung des Richters, 52–53 (Alanus).

89. Id., 77, with citations to further literature.

90. Id., 51 n. 1.

91. See de Langlade, Le Juge, Serviteur de la Loi, 149–151.

92. Angelus de Ubaldis, In Dig., de re iudici. Miles, a divo pio. Bibliothèque Mazarine INC 727, 41[r].

93. Baptista de Salis, Summa Casuum, Bibliothèque Mazarine INC 506, Fo. CXLIX[r].

94. Radin, The Conscience of the Court, Law Quarterly Review 192 (1932): 506–520.

95. David Powers has observed to me that a doctrine of doubt and blood punishment similar to the one I describe here is found in the Islamic jurists. See Power, Law, Society and Culture in the Maghrib, 1300–1500 (Cambridge, U.K.: Cambridge University Press, 2002), 78–81. As he rightly notes, this raises the question of whether Western jurists were borrowing from Islamic ones. I have no answer to that question.

96. This view was famously presented by John Langbein, Torture and the Law of Proof, 6. See also, in a more extreme formulation, Barbara Shapiro, Probability and Certainty in Seventeenth-Century England (Princeton: Princeton University Press, 1983), 174 (Continental judge "an accountant").

97. See especially the discussions, disagreeing with Langbein, of Fraher, Conviction According to Conscience, 56–64; Schmoeckel, Humanität und Staatsraison, 267–294; and Susanne Lepsius, Von Zweifeln zur Überzeugung: Zum Zeugenbeweis im gelehrten Recht ausgehend von der Abhandlung des Bartolus von Sassoferrato (Frankfurt a. M.: Klostermann, 2003), 167–175.

98. Schmoeckel, Humanität und Staatsraison, 286–287.

99. For discussion of this terminology, and its parallels in the Romanist writings of Bartolus, see Lepsius, Von Zweifeln zur Überzeugung, 169–175.

100. Id., 288–289

101. In Philip Jaffé, ed., Regesta Pontificum Romanorum, 2d ed. (repr. Graz: Akademische Druck- und Verlagsanstalt, 1956), 1779, quoted and discussed in Nörr, Zur Stellung des Richters, 41–42; Schmoeckel, Humanität und Staatsraison, 195.

102. Clemens III, in PL, 204:1486–1487: "Ad audientiam apostolatus nostri ex parte

vestra pervenit quod quidam presbyter volens corrigere quemdam de familia sua eo cingulo, quo cingi solebat, illum verberare tentavit: et contingit quod cultellus de vagina, quae cingulo adhaerebat, elapsus eum in dorso aliquantulum vulneravit. Postmodum vero cum ille vulneratus aliquandiu vixisset, et jam convaluisset a vulnere, graviori, ut creditur, infirmitate perculsus, cum sana mente, ac devotione debita viam est universae carnis ingressus. Quia vero utrum occasione vulneris decessisset dubium habebatur, [eodem presbytero ab omni officio, beneficioque suspenso,] quid super hoc vobis esset agendum apostolicam sedem consultare voluistis."

103. See e.g. Robert Lingat, Classical Hindu Law, ed. and trans. D. M. D. Derrett (Delhi: Oxford University Press, 1998), 40–45.

104. Clemens III, PL, 204:1487. "Nunc itaque vestrae discretionis industriae duximus respondendum, quod, cum in dubiis semitam debeamus eligere tutiorem, vos convenit injungere presbytero memorato, ne de caetero in sacris ordinibus administrare accedat; injuncta tamen poenitentia congruenti potestis ei concedere, ut sit contentus in minoribus ordinibus ministrare. Si vero [vobis legitime constiterit, quod] ex alia infirmitate obierit, de vestra licentia poterit, sicut erat solitus, divina officia celebrare." I have left aside here fuller discussion of the treatment of the possible "alia infirmitas," which, for all its interest, is not important to my argument.

105. Innocent too was concerned, unsurprisingly, with the ritual purity of clerics. The details of the case are not worth repeating here.

106. In Decretalium Gregorii Papae IX, Compilationes, Liber V, TitulusXXVII. De clerico excommunicato, deposito vel interdicto ministrante, chap. V. Available at http: //www.fh-augsburg.de/~harsch/Chronologia/Lspost13/GregoriusIX/gre _ 5t27 .html: *"Quod autem, postquam se novit excommunicatum a nobis, divina sibi fecerit officia celebrari, et fidelium communioni se ingesserat frequenter, id non in contemptum sedis apostolicae vel tanti etiam sacramenti, sed spe veniae asserit se fecisse, ne videlicet induresceret amplius, vel durius eius animus proterviret, si nunquam divinis officiis interesset; licet in diebus solennibus se nunquam celebrationi divinorum ingesserit, sed cum paucis in angulo alicuius ecclesiae occulte non festivis diebus divina sibi fecerit interdum officia celebrari.* Licet autem in hoc non videatur omnino culpabilis exstitisse, quia tamen in dubiis via est tutior eligenda, etsi de lata in eum sententia dubitaret, debuerat tamen potius se abstinere, quam sacramenta ecclesiastica pertractare."

107. For example, Enciclopedia Cattolica (Vatican City: Ente per l'Enciclopedia cattolica e per il Libro cattolico, 1950), 4: col. 1945 (s.v. "dubbio").

108. de Langlade, Le Juge, Serviteur de la Loi, 153–156.

109. James Franklin, The Science of Conjecture: Evidence and Probability before Pascal (Baltimore: Johns Hopkins University Press, 2001), 94–101, 218–212.

110. For a discussion that highlights the moral challenge of judging as medieval jurists saw it, see Palazzolo, Prova Legale e Pena, 41–42 and esp. 110–111 n. 23, which presents the basic connection between the structure of moral theology and the structure of criminal procedure traced here. For an elegant account of the place of "doubt" in medieval juristic culture, see Manli Bellomo, I Fatti e il Diritto: Tra le certezze e i dubbi dei giuristi medievali (secoli XIII–XIV) (Rome: Il Cigno, 2000), esp. 439–528.

111. Ivo, Decretum, 5.247, PL, 161:399. "Justo enim judicio Dei plerumque peccatoribus potestas, qua sanctos ipsius persequuntur, conceditur, ut qui Spiritu Dei juvan-

tur et aguntur fiant per laborum exercitia clariores. Illi tamen qui hoc agunt nullatenus evadunt poenam; quia, ut ait Dominus: *Vae illi per quem scandalum venit (Matth. XVIII). Item. Paulo post.* Incerta non judicemus quoadusque veniat. Dominus, *qui et illuminabit abscondita tenebrarum, et manifestabit consilia cordium (I Cor. IV).* Et quamvis vera sint, non tamen credenda sunt, nisi quae certis indiciis comprobantur, nisi quae manifesto judicio convincuntur, nisi quae judiciario ordine publicantur. Nullus ergo humano potest condemnari examine, quem Deus suo judicio reservavit."

112. Decreti Pars Secunda, C. 11, q .3 c. 74:

> C. LXXIV. Res dubia non diffiniatur certa sententia.
> Graue satis est et indecens, ut in re dubia certa detur
> sententia.
> C. LXXV. Non credantur que certis iudiciis non demonstrantur.
> Item Augustinus in libro de penitencia. [c. 3.]
> Quamuis uera sint quedam, tamen iudici non
> sunt credenda, nisi certis indiciis demonstrentur.

See the discussion in Schmoeckel, Humanität und Staatsraison, 195–196.

113. In Nörr, Zur Stellung des Richters, 42.

114. See the discussion in Schmoeckel, Humanität und Staatsraison, 187–189, beginning from the formula of Azo, "Probatio est rei dubie per argumentum ostensio."

115. See the discussion in Peter Holtappels, Die Entwicklung des Grundsatzes "in dubio pro reo" (Hamburg: Cram, de Gruyter, 1965), 9.

116. For Farinacci as an example of the connection between moral theology and. criminal procedure, see Palazzolo, Prova Legale e Pena, 110–111 n. 23.

117. Specialists in Continental legal history are in the midst of exploring the relationship between theology and law. See most recently the stimulating discussion of Lepsius, Von Zweifeln zur Überzeugung, at e.g. 244–297. I do not attempt to offer any full account here. I simply give the examples in the text in order to set the stage for the discussion of the moral theology of doubt in the common law. A detailed investigation of the relationship between the moral theology of doubt and the structure of criminal procedure on the Continent would burst the bounds of this book.

118. Prosper Farinacci, Praxis et Theoricae Criminalis Partis Primae Tomus Secundus (Lyon: Sumptibus Iacobi Cardon, 1634), 157 (= De Indiciis & Tortura, Titulus V, Quaestio xxxvi, nos. 5, 6, 9).

119. Id., 157, no. 28: "Indicium esse coniecturam ex probabilibus & non necessariis ortam, à quibus potest abesse veritas, sed non versimilitudo, & quae quandoque iudicantis mentem ita perstringit, ut cogat Iudicis conscientiam secundùm eam iudicare."

120. Id., 164, no. 198: "[Q]uando iudex ex deductis coram eo dubitat modò ad unam partem, & modò ad aliam, nec ad unam potiùs quam ad aliam animum applicat, ut est quando probationes sunt aequales vel quando habent aliquando obscuritatis. Et adverte, quòd si post hanc dubitationem Iudex inclinare incipiat in unam partem potiùs, quam in aliam, tunc cessat dubitatio, & intrat suspicio. Et si ista suspicio oritur ex gravibus indiciis, tunc cessat suspicio, & intrat opinio. . . . tunc propriè dubitare Iudicem dicimus, quando nulla adest ratio, nullaque causa, ex qua magis in unam partem quàm in alteram inclinet . . . & dubius is dicitur, quando non magis animum suum ad actorem, quàm an

reum inclinat. At si Iudex post dubitationem aliquo motus indicio, vel argumento in alteram partem flectat, licèt cum dubitatione, & tunc non ampliùs dubitare, sed suspicari dicitur."

121. Id., 158, no. 42.

122. I have quoted before the thirteenth-century scholar Durand, who spoke of the judge who, looking out of his window onto the public square, saw a nobleman committing murder. What troubled Durand in that case was precisely the question of torture. Nobles could not ordinarily be tortured. So could this rule be abrogated, since the judge had certain "private knowledge" of the noble's guilt? Durand held that it could not, Speculum Iuris Gulielmi Durandi, 2:785 (= Spec. 2.3. de Sententia qualiter sit ferenda). Quoted and discussed in Nörr, Zur Stellung des Richters, 78.

123. Nörr, Zur Stellung des Richters, 21 (discussing Placentinus). Indeed, leading questions were frowned upon, for this reason, in all phases of adjudication. Id. The ban on leading questions was older, though, already to be found in the Roman sources. See Schmoeckel, Humanität und Staatsraison, 262.

124. Sebastiano Guazzini, Tractatus ad Defensam Inquisitorum, Carceratorum, Reorum, & Condemnatorum super quocunque crimine (Venice: Apud Bertanos, 1699), bk. 2, 98–99 (= Defensio XXX, Cap. XXIX):

> Tortura an inferri possit ex conscientia iudicis.
> *Summarium.*
> 1 *Tortura non potest inferri ex sola conscientia iudicis, quod procedit etiam in iudice habente arbitrium in procedendo, & si iudex esset optimae opinionis.*
> * * *
> Iudex caveat in ista materia, ne procedat ad torturam ex sola sua conscientia, cum regula sit satis trita, & in ore omnium, quod iudex debeat secundum acta, & allegata iudicare. . . .
>
> Et in specie, ut non possit inferri tortura ex sola iudicis conscientia, Boss. Tit. de indic. Numero 141. Speculat. In tit. de sent..qualiter,versic.item debet ferri, Marsil.d.sing.266.in fin. Iul.Clar.q.8.num.5.vers. & licet, ubi testatur, quod ita teneant Doct.& q.66.num.2. Farin.cons.83.ubi concludunt, quod si iudex viderit Seium committere delictum, & non adsint alia indicia contra eum, non posset iudex illum torquere, licet Dec.d.c.14.num.3.& sub vers.prior opinio videatur isto casu tenere contrarium, & ibi allegat aliquas rationes.

125. Leonardus Lessius, De Iustitia et Iure (Venice: Apud Andraeam Baba, 1625), bk. 2, chap. 29, 6–8. [= p. 275]: "Hi gradus ita se habent, ut maiora indicia requirantur ad suspicionem, quam ad simplicem dubitationem, & maiora ad sententiam quam ad iudicium."

126. Id. ("iudicium temerarium" — defined as judging in a state of doubt at top of column).

127. Id.

128. de Langlade, Le Juge, Serviteur de la Loi, 153–156.

129. Collet, Abrégé du Dictionnaire des Cas de Conscience de M. Pontas (Paris: Libraires Associés, 1767), 1:467–468:

Dans tous les doutes, où il s'agit du péril du salut, il faut toujours suivre le parti le plus sûr: *In dubiis via eligenda est tutior,* dit Innocent III, cap. 3 *de Clerico excomm.* Clément III enseigne la même maxime, ainsi qu' Eugene III, cap. 3 de *sponsalib. & matrim.* . . .

Un juge ne peut jamais juger, lorsqu'il est dans le doute, soit que son doute regarde la personne, le droit ou le fait.

130. Kaspar Ziegler, Dicastice, sive de Judicum Officio et Delictis, Tractatus Moralis, In quo tota Judicis conscientia excutitur (Wittenberg: Sumptibus Christiani Theoph. Ludovici, 1702), 752: "Peccat Judex, qui amplectitur & sequitur opinionem probabilem, relicta & rejecta probabiliori."

131. Johannes Rogerius Trochaeus, De officio iudicis in caussis [*sic*] capitalibus ex bono et aequo decidendis liber singularis ad leges (Naples: Terri, 1774), 54: "Quemadmodum enim in bello peccanti venia non datur, ita si de hominis salute erretur semel, actum est de ejus capite, nec iterum est errori locus. Ergo respiciendum esse Judicandi Marcellus ait, hoc est, cautim, & circumspecte agendum, nec quicquam temere statuendum, cum omnino tutum non sit in rebus periculosis errare, seu labi." (commentary on Dig.48.19.11pr.). For the theological background, see J. M. Harty, Probabilism, in New Advent Catholic Encyclopedia, available at http://www.newadvent.org/cathen/12441a .htm.

132. Aegidii Bossii Patricii Mediolanensis . . . Tractatus Varii (Lyons: Apud Antonium de Antoniis, 1562), 457.

133. See the discussion of sixteenth-century changes in Paolo Marchetti, Testis contra se: L'Imputato come fonte di Prova nel Processo Penale dell' Età Moderna (Milan: Giuffrè, 1994), 27–38 (noting diminished focus both on the soul of the accused and on the relative discretion in decision of the judge); and his discussion of later centuries in id., 169–208.

134. Farinacci, Praxis et Theorica, 183 (nos. 110 and 111).

135. See Peter Holtappels, Die Entwicklung des Grundsatzes "in dubio pro reo" (Hamburg: Cram, de Gruyter, 1965); and for the place of the maxim in modern law, e.g. Jan Zopfs, Der Grundsatz "in dubio pro reo" (Baden-Baden: Nomos, 1999).

136. Langbein, Historical Foundations of the Law of Evidence: The View from the Ryder Sources, 96 Col. L. Rev. 1168, 1199 n. 152 (1996).

137. In Holtappels, 10: "Et in talibus dubiis et incertis probationibus melius est facinus impunitum relinqui nocentis quam innocentem damnare, et quia in dubiis pene sunt potius molliende quam exasperende."

138. For example, Holtappels, Entwicklung, 43 (quoting Gaill).

139. See the article "In dubio pro reo" in Detlef Liebs, Lateinische Rechtsregeln und Rechtssprichwörter, 6th ed. (Munich: Beck, 1998). On Bossius, an unoriginal but faithful reporter of the state of the doctrine of his time, see Palazzolo, Prova Legale e Pena, 81–85.

140. Aegidii Bossii Patricii Mediolanensis . . . Tractatus Varii (Lyons: Apud Antonium de Antoniis, 1562), 457: "1. Et in primis sciendum est, quòd iudex non debet esse manu promptus in puniendo, sed prius omnia cautè considerare, quod enim incautè factum est cautè evitandum est, c.j. & fin. de sacra.non.reiter. nec debet facilè se movere iudex, nec literis in alterius detrimentum adhibere.c.inquisitionis.§j.extrà, de accusat. Sed secundum

iuris ordinem procedere, & veritatem inquirere, & rectè posteà iudicare, ut not.per Ioan.Fab. in rubr.instit.de publi.iudi. ubi dicit quod cum dolore iudex trahi debet ad poenam infligendam & invitus.xxiij.q.v. quasi per totum maximè in c.miles.& in c.cum minister. Et si iudex gloriatur in morte hominis sicut nonulli faciunt nostra tempestate, homicida est, ubi aliâs minister Dei dicitur, ut per Io.Fab.ubi suprà, & per Angel. ibi, & vera iustitia habet compassionem, ut ait Gregor.xlv.distinct.c.vera iustitia."

141. For example, Holtappels, Entwicklung, 42 (quoting Fichard: "in poenis benignior interpretatio facienda"); 50 (quoting Carpzov: "in dubio semper in mitiorem partem sit praesumendum.").

142. Fraher, Conviction According to Conscience, 24.

143. Quoted and discussed in Holtappels, Entwicklung, 11.

144. For example, Cajetan, Secunda Secundae Partis Summae Theologicae S. Thomas de Aquino, cum Commentariis 163r (marginal commentary bottom left) (judge a "persona publica").

Chapter 5. Salvation for the Judge, Damnation for the Jury

Epigraph. Hale, Historia Placitorum Coronae (repr. Clark, N.J.: Lawbook Exchange, 2003) (orig. 1736), 2:313.

1. See the text quoted in full in chapter 2 above.

2. Mathias Schmoeckel, "Ein sonderbares Wunderwerck Gottes": Bemerkungen zum langsamen Rückgang der Ordale nach 1215, Ius Commune 26 (1999): 123–164.

3. In PM, 2:599.

4. Esp. Paul R. Hyams, Trial by Ordeal: The Key to Proof in the Early Common Law, in On the Laws and Customs of England: Essays in Honor of Samuel E. Thorne, ed. Morris S. Arnold et al. (Chapel Hill: University of North Carolina Press, 1981), 90–126.

5. Mike MacNair, Vicinage and the Antecedents of the Jury, Law and History Review 17 (1999): 537–590.

6. The *prison forte et dure* of early English law, whose precursor in the Burgesses' Assizes of Jerusalem was discussed above in chapter 3, was transformed into the far more menacing *peine forte et dure*. It is striking to contrast this English development with developments in Sweden, where the practice of *prison forte et dure* was still to be found, under the name *svårare fängelse*, in the statute of 1734.

7. In HEL, 5:185.

8. Esp. Raoul van Caenegem, Public Prosecution of Crime in Twelfth-Century England, in van Caenegem, Legal History: A European Perspective (London: Hambledon, 1991), 1–36; van Caenegem, Criminal Law in England and Flanders under Henry II and Count Philip of Alsace, in id., 37–60.

9. Patrick Wormald, The Making of English Law: King Alfred to the Twelfth Century, vol. 1 (Oxford: Blackwell, 1999).

10. Id.

11. J. E. A. Joliffe, Angevin Kingship, 2d ed. (London, 1963), 87–109.

12. There has been immense controversy among legal historians over how this took place. One famous view, propounded by S. F. C. Milsom in the 1970s, holds that the English kings never intended to create anything like that common law at all. Instead, the

common law arose as the unintended byproduct of royal efforts to make feudalism function properly. S. F. C. Milsom, The Legal Framewok of English Feudalism (Cambridge, U.K.: Cambridge University Press, 1976); cf. also R. C. Palmer, The Feudal Framework of English Law, Michigan Law Review 79 (1981): 1130–1164. Most scholars today view the Milsom interpretation as extreme. See esp. Paul Brand, *Multis Vigilis Excogitatam et Inventam:* Henry II and the Creation of the English Common Law, in The Making of the Common Law (London: Hambledon, 1992), 78–10.

13. Joseph Biancalana, For Want of Justice: Legal Reforms of Henry II, Columbia Law Review 88 (1988): 433–536.

14. For a nuanced discussion, see Joseph Canning, The Political Thought of Baldus de Ubaldis (Cambridge, U.K.: Cambridge University Press, 1987), 93–158.

15. See the literature surveyed and discussed in MacNair, Vicinage and the Antecedents of the Jury, 580 and 580 n. 187.

16. It may be that even with regard to the real property disputes that stood at the base of jurisdictional conflicts between Crown and nobility, the first conflicts arose between Crown and church. See Mary Cheney, The Litigation between John Marshal and Archbishop Thomas Becket in 1164: A Pointer to the Origin of Novel Disseisin? in Law and Social Change in British History, ed. J. A. Guy and H. G. Beale (London: Royal Historical Society, 1984), 9–26; Biancalana, For Want of Justice, 483–484.

17. Schmitt, Politische Theologie: Vier Kapitel zur Lehre von der Souveränität, 3d ed. (Berlin: Duncker und Humblot, 1979), 11.

18. D. 2, 1, 3.

19. For discussion with citations to further literature, see F. Merzbacher, "Hochgerichtsbarkeit," in Handwörterbuch zur deutschen Rechtsgeschichte 2:172–175; and A. Erler, "Galgen," in id., 1:1375–1377.

20. The medieval Crown did not succeed in depriving the English nobility of all cases of blood. Feudal potentates commonly preserved for themselves the right of "infangthief" — the right to execute thieves caught in the act. This was an unmistakable breach in the royal monopoly of blood, and it embarrassed the publicists of the common law. Thus while Bracton, the leading early thirteenth-century text on the common law, proudly declared that "the lord king has the power of judging in matters of life and members," the author had to admit that in practice there were others who also had the "liberty" of judging such thieves. Bracton f. 122, in Bracton on the Laws and Customs of England, ed. Samuel Thorne (Cambridge, MA: Belknap, 1977), 2:346. Moreover, the kings allowed some offenders to buy their way out of blood punishments. See John Hudson, The Formation of the English Common Law (London: Longman, 1996), 79, and literature cited there in n. 77. Not least, the king also shared in the privilege of inflicting blood punishments. Other persons too had a certain right of participation in the act of punishment — notably the accusers in blood cases. Into the thirteenth century, an accuser might join with the king's officer in horrible acts of mutilation, such as gouging out the eyes of the accused and castrating him. Paul Hyams, The Strange Case of Thomas Enderfield, History Today 36 (June 1986): 12; van Caenegem, Public Prosecution of Crime in Twelfth-Century England, in van Caenegem, ed., Legal History: A European Perspective (London: Hambledon Press, 1991), 20 n. 59; PM, 2:496 n. 7. Perilous for the soul though it was — and we shall see that the English, like other Europeans, were anxious about the peril in inflicting blood punishments — the right to mutilate and execute was sought after.

Hanging people, gouging their eyes out, and cutting off their testicles — those sorts of acts showed one's power over one's dependents, or over one's enemies, and they undoubtedly offered a pleasure difficult to resist. The twelfth-century monarchy did not have enough power to deny this pleasure to all persons and at all times.

21. R. H. Helmholz, The Early History of the Grand Jury and the Canon Law, U. Chicago L. Rev 50 (1983): 613–627.

22. F. C. Hamil, The King's Approvers, Speculum 11 (1936): 238–258.

23. This is the classic view of Brunner, Die Entstehung der Schwurgerichte, as recently defended, with considerable emendation, by Macnair, Vicinage and the Antecedents of the Jury.

24. Ralph V. Turner, The Origins of the Medieval English Jury: Frankish, English, or Scandinavian? Journal of British Studies 7 (1968): 1–10.

25. Rightly emphasized by van Caenegem, Public Prosecution of Crime in Twelfth-Century England, 3.

26. Discussion in van Caenegem, Public Prosecution of Crime in Twelfth-Century England, 6–7. For the pre-Norman period, see Patrick Wormald, Frederick William Maitland and the Earliest English Law, 16 Law & History Review 1, 16–17 (1998).

27. Bruce R. O'Brien, From Mordor to Murdrum: The Preconquest Origin and Norman Revival of the Murder Fine, Spcculum 71 (1996): 321–357.

28. See in particular, Naomi Hurnard, The Jury of Presentment and the Assize of Clarendon, EHR 56 (1941): 379–383; and the doubts expressed by van Caenegem, The Birth of the Common Law, 79–80; as well as the summary of the literature in Helmholz, Early History of the Grand Jury, 614–615.

29. See the discussion of the evidence in Roger Groot, The Jury of Presentment before 1215, 26 Am. J. Legal History 1, 3–5 (1982).

30. For example, Hudson, Formation of the English Common Law, 65, 70–71.

31. Helmholz, Early History of the Grand Jury and the Canon Law.

32. English Historical Documents, 1042–1189, ed. David C. Douglas and George W. Greenaway, 2d ed. (London: Eyre Methuen, 1981), 440–441.

33. Discussion and further references in Hudson, Formation of the English Common Law, 130–131.

34. Daniel Klerman, Was the Jury Ever Self-Informing? S.Cal. L. Rev. 77 (2003): 123–149; MacNair, Vicinage and the Antecedents of the Jury; also the discussion of van Caenegem, Public Prosecution of Crime in Twelfth-Century England, 10–11; and the discussion of the canon parallels in Helmholz, Early History of the Grand Jury, 618–620.

35. The Treatise on the laws and customs of England commonly called Glanvill, ed. G. D. G. Hall (London: Nelson, 1965), 171, xiv, 1; and the discussion in MacNair, Vicinage and the Antecedents of the Jury, 583.

36. Glanvill, 171–173, xiv, 1. See the discussion in Helmholz, Early History of the Grand Jury, 624, emphasizing the identity between Glanvill's analysis and that of contemporary canon law.

37. See the survey of early records in Groot, Jury of Presentment before 1215, 7–24.

38. See chapter 3 above.

39. See generally the discussion in van Caenegem, Public Prosecution of Crime in Twelfth-Century England, esp. 13–16.

40. Cf. MacNair, Law, Politics, and Jury, 605.

41. Bracton f. 116, ed. Thorne 2:329: "[S]ic me deus adiuvet et haec sancta."

42. Hudson, Formation of the English Common Law, 125, citing Bracton, ff. 116, 143, in Thorne 2:329, 403–05.

43. Here I disagree in effect with Groot, who argues that the jurors were already effectively giving verdicts before 1215. Groot, Jury of Presentment before 1215. There is a difference in moral theology between making an accusation followed by ordeal and engaging in the "perilous" business of pronouncing the accused guilty.

44. MacNair, Law, Politics, and the Jury, Law and History Review 17 (1999): 603, with careful general statement of MacNair's claims.

45. Hermann Nottarp, Gottesurteilstudien (Munich: Kosel, 1956), 68; PM, 2:599 n. 6.

46. See English Historical Documents, 2:436–440.

47. Discussion in Hudson, Formation of the English Common Law, 126–129, with citations to further literature.

48. Hudson, Formation of the English Common Law, 111, 201–204.

49. R. C. van Caenegem, ed., English Lawsuits from William I to Richard I (London: Selden Society, 1991), no. 281, discussed in Hudson, Formation of the English Common Law, 113.

50. Glanvill, 28, ii, 7.

51. In using this term, which is convenient for purposes of explication, I do not mean to imply that the feudal of law of seisin was identical with the Roman law of possession. My brief discussion necessarily elides that complex problem.

52. Hudson, Formation of the English Common Law, 197.

53. Id., 198, on continuing availability of writ of right.

54. Glanvill, 34, ii, 17: "Si nulli eorum rei veritatem inde scierint, et hoc in curia super sacramentum eorum testati fuerent."

55. "Recognoscite verum per fidem et credulitatem, quam in dominum Ihesum Christum habetis et quam in baptismo recepistis et super sacramentum, quod corporaliter in presentia nostra modo prestistis ita quod, si in aliquo de re ista mendaces fueritis vel veritatem celaveritis, quod anime vestre in perpetuum dampnentur et corpora vestra opprobirose perditioni apertissimae exponantur." In Ernest-Joseph Tardif, Summa de Legibus Normannie in curia laicali (Rouen: Société de l'histoire de Normandie, 1896), 2:232.

56. For the twelfth-century punishment, see Glanvill, 35–36, ii, 19.

57. Bracton, f. 185b, in Thorne 3:74: "Si autem incertum dixerunt iudex examinare debet, ut de incerto faciat certum, de obscuro clarum, de dubio verum: alioquin anceps et periculosum erit sacramentum et inde sequi poterit fatuum iudicium." The evidence of Bracton suggests that in the thirteenth century criminal inquiries were being conducted in more or less the Continental way. Bracton describes a judge acting very much like a romano-canonical inquisitor, investigating fama, local rumors, and reputation: "Iustiarius igitur si discretus sit, cum propter famam et suspicionem per patriam debeat veritas inquiri an indicatus de crimine ei imposito culpabilis sit vel non, imprimis debet inquirere, si forte dubitaverit et jurata suspecta fuerit, a quo vel a quibus illi duodecim didicerint ea quae veredicto suo proferunt de indictato, et audita super hoc eorum responsione de facili perpendere poterit si dolus subfuerit vel iniquitas. Dicet forte aliquis vel major pars iuratorum, quod ea quae ipsi proferunt in veredicto suo didicerunt ab alio tali, et sic

descendere poterit interrogatio et responsio de persona in personam usque ad aliquam vilem et abiectam personam, et talem cui non erit fides aliquatenus adhibenda." Bracton in Thorne, 2:404. If judges were taking the active role in examining jurors implied by this passage, then criminal juries were not confronted with giving the general verdict in the full sense. The responsibility for finding the facts in such a case would rest with the judge. Indeed, Bracton implied exactly that. If the judge did not carefully examine the jury, he warned, he would be adopting the morally dangerous position of Pontius Pilate: "Et ita inquirat ne dicatur Ihesus crucifigitur et Barrabas liberator." Id. The mid-thirteenth-century judge as Bracton presents him seems to have shared in the task of entering judgment, and therefore in the ominous moral responsibility.

58. As Mike MacNair observes, Bracton's account makes it clear that the canon law of proof could still have established itself in England as of the time the treatise was composed. MacNair, Vicinage and the Antcedents of the Jury, 538.

59. Thomas of Chobham, Summa Confessorum, ed. F. Broomfield (Louvain: Nauwelaerts, 1968), 258: "[S]i tu offendisti aliquem occidendo patrem eius vel exherendando eum." See also the discussion in Paul Hyams, Rancor and Reconciliation in Medieval England (Ithaca: Cornell University Press, 2003), 57. I take "exherendando" to signify dispossession from real property as "exhereditatio" does in the Treaty of Westminster, discussed above.

60. Richard Baxter, A Christian Directory or a Summ of Practical Theologie and Cases of Conscience (London: Printed by Robert White for Nevill Simmors at the Princes Armes in St. Pauls Churchyard, 1673), 149, discussed in chapter 6.

61. Glanvill, 34, ii, 17.

62. Lex Familiae Wormatiensis Ecclesiae, chap. 31, in MGH Constitutiones, I:644.

63. Glanvill, 34, ii, 17.

64. Glanvill, 36, ii, 19.

65. Select Civil Pleas, ed. William Paley Baildon (London: Quaritch for Selden Society, 1890), 96, pl. 241.

66. See J. H. Baker, The Oxford History of the Laws of England, vol. 6 (1483–1558) (Oxford, 2003), 365–369.

67. For a dramatic example involving the coercion of jurors to testify to thefts, see Matthew of Paris's report for the year 1249 in Matthew Paris' English History from the Year 1235 to 1273, trans. J. A. Giles (London: Bohn, 1853), 2:296–297. My thanks to James Gordley for pointing me to this source.

68. For a discussion of the "sparse" evidence for early royal judges, see Hudson, Formation of the English Common Law, 31–34.

69. Id., 33–34.

70. Brand, Making of the Common Law, 80.

71. Id., 77–102.

72. Hudson, Formation of the English Common Law, 123.

73. For example, id., 224.

74. Bracton, f. 108, in Thorne, 2:307: "[R]egis, cuius personam in iudicando repraesentant."

75. Stephan Kuttner and Eleanor Rathbone, Anglo-Norman Canonists of the Twelfth Century, Traditio 7 (1949–1951): 279, 288–290, and later from Italy. Id., 327. This is

not substantially affected by Kuttner's subsequent "retractationes." Texts like the Cologne Summa "Elegantius in iure divino," which included an important discussion of the problems of judicial conscience, Knut Wolfgang Nörr, Zur Stellung des Richters im gelehrten Prozeß der Frühzeit: Iudex secundum allegata non secundum conscientiam iudicat (Munich: Beck, 1967), 52; Antonio Padoa-Schioppa, Conscience dans le *Ius Commune* Européen, in Jean-Marie Carbasse and Laurence Depambour-Tarride, eds., La conscience du juge dans la tradition juridique européenne (Paris: P.U.F., 1999), 100–101, were known to the English. Kuttner and Rathbone, Anglo-Norman Canonists, 298–299. The basic canon formulas continued to be cited into the nineteenth century.

76. Bracton f. 120b in Thorne, 2:340. See Fritz Schulz, Bracton and Raymond de Peñafort, Law Quarterly Review 61 (1945): 286–292, showing Bracton's dependence on Raymond's treatment of homicide. The passage in question is the same as that quoted above, at the end of chapter 2, and transcribed by Vincent de Beauvais, discussed in chapter 4. Maitland mistakenly ascribed the passage to Bernard of Pavia in Maitland, ed., Select Passages from the Works of Bracton and Azo (London: Selden Society, 1895), App. II (pp. 225–235). Helmholz, oddly, follows the error of Maitland on this, also attributing the passage to Bernard of Pavia. Helmholz, Early History of the Grand Jury, 627.

77. Ralph V. Turner, Clerical Judges in English Secular Courts: The Ideal versus the Reality, in Turner, Judges, Administrators and the Common Law in Angevin England (London: Hambledon, 1994): 159–179.

78. Thayer, A Preliminary Treatise on Evidence at the Common Law (Boston: Little, Brown, 1898), 291. Indeed, the familiar canon formulas were known and cited down into the nineteenth century in England. For a mid-nineteenth-century example: Aldridge v. Great Western Railway 3 Man. & G. 516, 521 (1841) (ER 1249). In nineteenth-century cases, though, the formula is used purely to create a rule of evidence, without any notion of the older function of the rule. For a Connecticut example of this use of "secundum allegata" as a purely evidentiary rule, see Treat v. Barber, 7 Conn. 274, 1828 Conn. LEXIS 38 (1828). The rule also mutated into a rule on damages. See The Sarah Ann, 21 F. Cas. 432, 1835 U.S. App. LEXIS 288, 2 Sumn. 206 (Circ. Court D. Mass. 1835); Richard v. Clark, 43 Misc. 6222, 88 N.Y.S. 242, 1904 N.Y. Misc. LEXIS 216 (1904); Wilson v. Kelso, 115 Md. 162, 80 A. 895, 1911 Md. LEXIS 13 (1911).

79. 7 Hy IV, Pasch. Pl. 5 (p. 41):

> Tir. Sir, mittom[us] que un home occist un auter en votre presence vous veiant, & un auter q~ n'est culp~ est endict devant vous, & trove culp~ de m~ la mort, vous duisses respiter le judgement devers luy, p~ c~ vous estes sachant del contrary, & faire ouster relation a Roy p~ fair~ grace, nient pluis deves vous don~ judgement en c~ case, avant c~ q~ ceux p~ q~ maines le Roy fuit pay (ut supra) soient faits venire, & p~ c~ q~ vous estes apris de record q~ le Roy fuit accept Sñr immediate p~ eux, ut supra.

> Gas. Un foits le Roy mesme dda de moy m~ ceo case, que vous aves mis, & moy dda q~ fuit la ley, & jeo luy disoie sicome vous dites; & il fuit bien please q~ la ley fuit tiel.

I have taken the translation given by Thayer, Preliminary Treatise on Evidence at the Common Law, 291.

80. As observed by Radin, The Conscience of the Court, Law Quarterly Review 192 (1932): 507–508.

81. Note the evidence of Jeremy Taylor, Ductor Dubitantium, or The Rule of Conscience in all her General Measures; Serving as a great Instrument for the determination of Cases of Conscience (London: Printed by R. Norton, for R. Royston, Bookseller to the King's Most Sacred Majesty, 1676), 65: "[H]ow if [the judge] sees the fact done before him in the Court? A purse cut, or a stone thrown at his brother Judge, as it happened at Ludlow not many years since?" — evidence not only of what judges might know but also of what the atmosphere in seventeenth-century assizes was like. For a description — including the throwing of a brickbat at a judge — see J. S. Cockburn, A History of English Assizes, 1558–1714 (Cambridge, U.K.: Cambridge University Press, 1972), 110. For private knowledge among jurors see John H. Langbein, The Criminal Trial before Lawyers, 45 U. Chi. L. Rev. 263, 288 n. 74 (1978); id. 290.

82. See generally J. H. Baker, An Introduction to English Legal History, 3d ed. (London: Butterworths, 1990), 14–26. For a broad survey of "the Age of the Travelling Justices," see Alan Harding, The Law Courts of Medieval England (London: Allen and Unwin, 1973), 32–123.

83. Turner, Clerical Judges in English Secular Courts, 159–179.

84. Baker, Introduction to English Legal History, 122–128. For the connection with conscience as administered in the confessional, id., 127 and 127 n. 59.

85. William Roper, The Lyfe of Sir Thomas Moore, Knighte, ed. James Mason Cline (New York: Swallow Press and William Morrow, 1950), 43–44.

86. Baker, Oxford History of the Laws of England, 6:47–48.

87. Hale, Historia Placitorum Coronae, 2: 313.

88. [Hawles], The English-mans Right: A Dialogue between a Barrister at Law, and a Jury-Man (London: Printed for Richard Janeway, in Queenshead Alley in Paternoster-Row, 1680) (repr. New York: Garland, 1978), 23.

89. Frederick Pollock and Frederic William Maitland, The History of English Law before the Time of Edward I (repr. Union, N.J.: Lawbook Exchange, 1996), 2:627.

90. Baker, Reports of Sir John Spelman, 2:43, 138; similarly Baker, Oxford History of the Laws of England, 6: 47.

91. Thomas A. Green, Verdict According to Conscience: Perspectives on the English Criminal Jury Trial, 1200–1800 (Chicago: University of Chicago Press, 1985), 65.

92. Max Radin, The Conscience of the Court, Law Quarterly Review 192 (1932): 506–520.

93. David Seipp, Jurors, Evidence and the Tempest of 1499, in "The Dearest Birth Right of the People of England": The Jury in the History of the Common Law, ed. John W. Cairns and Grant McLeod (Oxford, 2002), 91 (fear of "reprisal" and "vengeful litigant[s]"); Brown, Society and the Supernatural: A Medieval Change," in Brown, Society and the Holy in Late Antiquity (Berkeley: University of California Press, 1982), 313.

94. Morris Arnold, Law and Fact in the Medieval Jury Trial: Out of Sight, Out of Mind, 18 Amer. J. Legal Hist. 267, 268 (1974), and the discussion below.

95. Baker, Oxford History of the Laws of England, 6:47; id., 352.

96. Fisher, The Jury's Rise as Lie Detector, Yale L. J. 107 (1997): 706. J. H. Baker speaks of "pressures [the judges] would sooner avoid" — pressures, that is, from the

interested parties. J. H. Baker, Introduction, in Baker, ed., 2 The Reports of Sir John Spelman (London: Selden Society, 1978), 106.

97. Baker, Introduction to English Legal History, 86–90; Green, Verdict According to Conscience, 3–4; de Groot, Jury of Presentment; Mike MacNair, Vicinage and the Antecedents of the Jury, Law and History Review 17 (1999): 537–590. For further literature and debate on the character of the medieval self-informing jury, see Klerman, Was the Jury Ever Self-Informing?

98. MacNair, Vicinage and the Antecedents of the Jury. Green, Verdict According to Conscience, 11, also makes the important observation that Angevin reforms already put jurors in a more difficult position to the extent it substituted blood punishments for an earlier system of feud compensation.

99. See the exchange between Wormald, Neighbors, Courts and Kings: Reflections on MacNair's *Vicini*, Law and History Review 17 (1999): 597–601; and MacNair, Law, Politics, and the Jury, 603.

100. Thus MacNair, in his exemplary study of the subject, concludes that the roles of witness and judge were already being separated by the time of Bracton. MacNair, Vicinage and the Antecedents of the Jury, 587. I believe this greatly underestimates the ongoing theological difficulties they faced.

101. Notably Langbein, The Criminal Trial before Lawyers, 263, 299 n. 105.

102. Green, Verdict According to Conscience, 108–110.

103. J. H. Baker, for example, writes: "Sir Thomas More stated quite explicitly in 1533 that jurors were not to be regarded as witnesses, but as judges of fact." Baker, Introduction, in 2 The Reports of Sir John Spelman, *109;* also Baker, Oxford History of the Laws of England, 6:361–362. This is a misinterpretation. More's tract, written as a response to Christopher St. German, turned entirely on the question of what sorts of witnesses could properly testify before courts investigating heresy through the use of inquisitorial procedure. See generally the Introduction of the editors to More, The Debellation of Salem and Bizance, in John Guy, Ralph Keen, Clarence Miller, and Ruth McGugan, eds., The Complete Works of St. Thomas More (New Haven: Yale University Press, 1987), 10: lxviii–xciv. The question in particular was whether accused heretics could be compelled to undergo purgation, rather than being tried by juries. Id., liii–lvii. St. German defended jury trial, holding that jurors' "conscience" offered adequate guarantees: "[T]hat al his honest neighburs wene that he were one [i.e., a heretic], and therefor in their conscience dare not swere, that he is any other." Id., Appendix, 356.

More disagreed, and it was in this context that he insisted that jurors were not "witnesses." They were not the sort of witnesses that it was necessary to examine in a case of heresy, for which More viewed inquisitorial procedure as proper. More's passage says nothing whatsoever about whether jurors might have private knowledge. It simply says that they cannot be closely examined with regard to their knowledge of particular facts, as would be the case with witnesses subject to inquisitorial procedure. Instead, their verdict, qua general verdict, must be accepted: "[B]ycause I spake in myne apologye of such witnesses in felonye: thys good man [i.e. St. German] maketh here a doute/ what manner wytnesses I mene/whyther I mene yᵉ .xii. men that are the iury, or other wytnessys that are brought into the court for to enforme them. . . . But veryly as for me, I shal put hym out of that dowt, that I ment not them. For I neuer toke the .xii. men for wytnessys in my lyfe. For why shold I call them witnesses, whose verdycte the iudge taketh for a sure sentence concernynge the facte, without any examynacyon of the cyrcumstaunces, wherby they know or be ledde to byleue theyr verdicte to be trew?" Id., 149. Within the context of More's argument, this had the important implication that jury trial was inappropriate in heresy cases, where close examination of the testimony was, to More's mind, essential. It had minimal bearing, though, on the structure of ordinary jury trial in his time, beyond confirming the point that a general verdict was a general verdict, and that jurors were not individually examined.

104. Bl. Comm. 3:368.

105. It is worth noting that this was the same solution famously proposed on the Continent by Cajetan. See above, chapter 4.

106. Thomas Gisborne, An Enquiry into the Duties of Men in the Higher and Middle Classes of Society in Great Britain, 4th ed., 2 vols. (London: Printed for B. and J. White, and Cadell and Davies, 1771), 2:460. An interesting passage in Gisborne explores the problems of commercial matters in particular: "In deciding on mercantile proceedings, let him be guided by law, and not by what may have been the practice, perhaps the reprehensible practice, of himself or his friends in a similar instance." Id.

107. For the seventeenth century: Bennet and the Hundred of Hartford (1650), in Style, 233 (Mich. 1650); Fitz-James v. Moys (1675), in Siderfin, 133 (Pasch. 15 Car.II); for the eighteenth century: Langbein, Criminal Trial before Lawyers, 263, 288 n. 74 (1978); id. 290.

108. Wigmore was well aware of the "comparative recency" of the insistence that jurors never make use of their private knowledge. See Wigmore, A Treatise on the System of Evidence in Trials at Common Law (repr. Holmes Beach: Gaunt, 2003), 2324, and generally 2325. For American examples of jurors making use of knowledge not based on evidence offered in court: Parks v. Boston, 32 Mass. 198, 1834 Mass. LEXIS 4, 15 Pick. 198 (1834) (court instructed jury to make use of its private knowledge); Sam v. State, 31 Tenn. 61, 1851 Tenn. LEXIS 17, 1 Swan 61 (1851) (juror made use of private knowledge). This is not surprising: most communities were still small enough that it cannot have been unusual for jurors sometimes to possess extrinsic knowledge of the case.

109. The case in question involves an interesting figure, Abbot Samson of Bury St. Edmunds, who, as Susan Reynolds notes, "had studied the liberal arts and scriptures before he become abbot in 1182, [and] was then able to learn enough different kinds of law on the job to serve as a judge delegate, astound an undersheriff by his knowledge, and be labeled a barrator." Reynolds, The Emergence of Professional Law, Law and History Review 21 (2003): 362. Here is the report as it comes down to us: "But when the church of Boxford was vacant and a recognition [i.e., a jury] had been summoned to deal with the matter, five knights came, tempting the abbot and asking him what they should swear concerning it. The abbot, however, refused to give or promise them anything, but said: 'When it comes to making oath, say what is right according to your conscience.' But they retired in indignation, and by their oath deprived him of the advowson of that church." Van Caenegem, ed., English Lawsuits from William I to Richard I, 2:615, no. 568. Discussed in Raoul C. van Caenegem, La Conscience du Juge dans l'Histoire du Droit Anglais, in La conscience du juge dans la tradition juridique européenne, ed. Jean-Marie Carbasse and Laurence Depambour-Tarride (Paris: P.U.F., 1999), 274. An early use of the

word "conscience," in L. J. Downer, Leges Henrici Primi (Oxford: Clarendon Press, 1972), 264 (chap. 87, 3a), is of no relevance. It is not entirely clear whether "conscience" in this passage means "knowledge" (as would have been the case earlier in the twelfth century) or "the exercise of moral judgment." What is clear is that concern with conscience was present from an early date, and that juries were self-informing.

110. Quoted in Baker, Introduction, in Baker, ed., 2 The Reports of Sir John Spelman, 112 (1465).

111. Sir Thomas Smith, De Republica Anglorum, ed. Mary Dewar (Cambridge, U.K.: Cambridge University Press, 1982), 114.

112. Quoted in John Langbein, Prosecuting Crime in the Renaissance: England, Germany, France (Cambridge, MA: Harvard University Press, 1974), 50. The "heart" and the conscience were associated in the language of the day: "[C]onscientia is cordis scientia," wrote William Fulbeck. Fulbeck, Direction or Preparative to the Study of the Law, ed. Peter Birks (Brookfield, VT: Gower, 1987), 87 (1599). For the role of "conscience" in later medieval English Law, see Norman Doe, Fundamental Authority in Late Medieval English Law (Cambridge, U.K.: Cambridge University Press, 1990), 132–154.

113. John of Wales, Communiloquium [1495] = Harvard Houghton INC 1644, chap. IV: De informatione accusantium, discussed above in chapter 3.

114. The conflicts begin in the thirteenth century, and they begin over the assize of novel disseisin. The assize was in a sense a quasi-criminal procedure, since it presumably sometimes involved lawless seizures of real property. Nevertheless, it did not involve blood punishments, and thus did not belong among the classic criminal actions of the premodern world. Despite that, there were intense conflicts over jury verdicts in the assize of novel disseisin during the thirteenth century. Those conflicts involved, in particular, the attaint. As early as 1202, we have a record of jurors in the assize of novel disseisin being subjected to the attaint, Curia Regis Rolls, 2:97–98. And the same happened repeatedly thereafter. H. G. Richardson and G. O. Sayles, Select Cases of Procedure without Writ under Henry III (SS 60) (London: Selden Society, 1941), lxxxvii–lxxxix. Behind this lay some kind of conflict whose terms are not entirely clear to us now: jurors for some reason were giving verdicts unacceptable to the Crown. In 1285, though, the massive legal reforms of Edward I brought relief. The Second Statute of Westminster, in that year, permitted jurors in the assize of novel disseisen to offer special verdicts, finding the facts in the case while praying the justices to arrive at the actual verdict. 13 Edw. I Stat. West. Sec. 30 (1285), in Statutes of the Realm, I:86. After 1285, juries seizing the chance given to them by the Statute of Westminster, repeatedly entering special verdicts in the Assize of Novel Disseisin. Arnold, Law and Fact in the Medieval Jury Trial, 267, 269–271. The coercion of jurors thus took place outside the assize of novel disseisin thereafter.

115. Seipp, Jurors, Evidences and the Tempest of 1499, 90.

116. 34 Edward III, c. 7.:

> *[Petition]*: ITEM prie la dite Commune, q~ en chescun Enquest jurre, & grant Assise, les Jurrours puissent dire la verite du faite si veullent come en Assise de novele disseisine.
>
> *[Royal response]*: Soit tenuz la Lei q'ad estez usez en ce cas cea en arere.

117. Although the king denied essentially all the requests put by the Commons with regard to the management of justice, no other was denied so categorically. The other

formulas of denial were milder, as in petition 12: "Il serroit a faire novelle Ley, dont le Roi n'est pas avys unqore."

118. See above, note 114.

119. The interpretation of this phrase, while not easy, is important for the argument of this book. Nevertheless, in the hope of keeping the text to a readable length, I place the discussion here in the margin.

The language of the Statute of Westminster included a term that would remain at the center of debates for centuries thereafter: jurors in the assize of novel disseisin entered the general verdict, the statute explained, at their "peril": "And also it is Ordained, That the Justices assigned to take Assises shall not compel the Jurors to say precisely whether it be Disseisin or not, so that they do shew the Truth of the [Deed,] and require Aid of the Justices; but if they of their own head will say, that it is Disseisin, their Verdict shall be admitted at their own Peril [sub suo periculo]." 13 Edw. I Stat. West. Sec. 30 (1285), in Statutes of the Realm, I:86. But what "peril" was it that the jurors faced? Scholars generally interpret this passage to refer to the peril that they would be attainted. Arnold, Law and Fact in the Medieval Jury Trial, 268. This certainly may be right: what thirteenth-century jurors feared may simply have been the danger of prosecution. Nevertheless, it is important to observe that "peril" may have had another aspect already in the thirteenth century, as it clearly would later. The "peril" in question may also have been not the peril of attaint in this world but the peril of damnation in the next. Thus Britton, writing of the attaint shortly after this statute, uses "peril" in exactly this sense: the juror is "chargé en peril de sa alme de dire verité." Britton: An English Translation and Notes, ed. Francis M. Nichols (repr. Holmes Beach: Gaunt, 1983), 2:212. There is also evidence for this in Bracton, in the discussion of the attaint quoted and discussed earlier in this chapter. If we read the Statute of Westminster against the background of these passages, we can surmise that the English drama of 1285 was no different from the contemporary Continental dramas. In cases of uncertainty, jurors did not want the peril of judgment. Yet if jurors were dispensed from it, the peril would pass to the judges instead.

The question of "peril" remained particularly associated, as we might expect, with giving the general verdict. Cf. Coke's report of Rawlyns's Case (Mich. 29 & 30 Eliz.):

> And Wray, C.J. said, that it was adjudged in Pleadal's case, in 8 Eliz. that because a jury did not find such a lease by deed indented which took its operation only by conclusion, intending that they being sworn *ad veritatem dicendam,* and that estoppels conclude the parties, but not the jurors, to say the truth, were therefore attainted and had judgment accordingly: for the justices in the same case held, that the interest of the land as to parties and privies was in a manner by such conclusion bound, and no conclusion shall be by such deed indented after the term ended, as Wray, C.J. held; and in such a case the jury ought, if they will not find the special matter, and leave it to the judgment of the law, to find "at their peril" according to law.

4 Co. Rep. 53b. This was also true of Hale, in the passage I quote in chapter 6.

"Peril" remained a standard term thereafter, in ways that may deserve their own history. Baker notes that "[t]he years books are full of references to the 'peril' or 'ambiguity' of the 'lay gents' who constituted the jury." Baker, Introduction, in Baker, ed., 2 The Reports of Sir John Spelman), 103. Baker interpreted the "peril" in question as the peril of favoritism, id. 103–104, and that again may certainly have been part of it. See also Baker, Oxford History of the Laws of England, 6:351–352. There is no reason why such an open-ended term should have had no ambiguity.

120. See Baker, Oxford History of the Laws of England, 6:365–369.

121. Baker, Introduction to English Legal History, 99; Baker, Oxford History of the Laws of England, 6:400–403; S. F. C. Milsom, Historical Foundations of the Common Law (London: Butterworths, 1981), 77 (Slade's Case). The relationship between special and general verdicts raises issues that I do not discuss in this book. Historians recognize that the doctrinal development of the common law depends on the rise of the special verdict, which allows room for the judges to discuss nice questions of law. This too could be related in revealing ways to the problem of avoiding moral responsibility for judgment, but I leave that issue aside.

122. See William Hawkins, A Treatise of the Pleas of the Crown (London: Sweet, 1824), 2:619 ("It is settled . . . that a jury may give a special verdict in any criminal case. . . .).

123. Certainly the jury did sometimes enter the general verdict. Green, Verdict According to Conscience, 17–18.

124. Green, Verdict According to Conscience, 19.

125. There was a technical reason for this: the accused, by "putting himself upon the country," had offered the jurors as his witnesses, and therefore could not subsequently raise doubts about their credibility.

126. Thayer, Preliminary Treatise on Evidence, 156–162.

127. Statute of 26 H. VIII. c. 4.

128. The Crown, argued Thayer, enjoyed overwhelming procedural advantages. In particular, only the Crown could offer witnesses. In light of this procedural leg up, the medieval Crown had no need of the attaint in the Middle Ages; it could be sure of winning anyway. Thayer, Preliminary Treatise on Evidence, 157–162. This explanation is hardly convincing, though. It is not obvious why a party with some legal advantages would refrain from using others. Indeed, there is an odd element of illogic in Thayer's argument: the Crown would only have needed the attaint in cases in which its other procedural advantages had not given it victory at trial. Finally, and perhaps most important, Thayer's explanation cannot account for later developments. As we shall see, the Crown *did* begin prosecuting criminal juries in the sixteenth century, through Star Chamber. Yet its other procedural advantages were no less imposing then. There must have been some other reason why the medieval Crown declined to prosecute criminal juries.

129. Verdict According to Conscience, 20. At 66, however, Green leaves the same question unanswered.

130. Indeed, as Green has pointed out, the introduction of the power of the Crown through the jury of presentment changed the calculus. In earlier periods, homicides could be dealt with through money compensation. But once the Crown became involved, mutilation and execution became the natural consequence of a criminal conviction. Green, Verdict According to Conscience, 9–10. This meant that the stakes were indeed especially high — not just for the defendant but also for the jurors.

131. The same may be true of the rule of juror unanimity. We have seen that jurors in cases of novel disseisin were subject to "afforcement," which compelled a unanimous

verdict of the twelve. Afforcing the assize was an important form of coercion; and like the attaint, it was not clearly at home in blood cases. This may explain a passage in Britton, the late thirteenth-century treatise writer. Britton observed that there was "no matter of greater moment, than that of life and limb." Correspondingly, he held that jurors in criminal matters could not be held to a rule of unanimity: "If they cannot agree in one mind, let them be separated and examined why they cannot agree; and if the greater part of them know the truth and the other part do not, judgment shall be according to the opinion of the greater part." Britton, 1:31. Nevertheless, this passage is self-contradictory and by no means easy to interpret.

132. Green, Verdict According to Conscience, 53–59; Baker, Introduction to English Legal History, 95–96.

133. The early fourteenth century saw "a major readjustment of the Crown's administration of criminal justice." This involved the decline of the eyre and the rise of special commissions of trailbaston and oyer et terminer. See Green, Verdict According to Conscience, 20–21; Richard Kaeuper, Law and Order in Fourteenth-Century England: The Evidence of Special Commissions of Oyer and Terminer," Speculum 54 (1979): 738–742. Alan Harding, Early Trailbaston Proceedings from the Lincoln Roll of 1305, in R. B. Hunisett and J. B. Post, eds., Medieval Legal Records Edited in Memory of C. A. F. Meekings (London: H. M. Stationery Office, 1978): 130–138. By 1352, it also resulted in a clear distinction between the jury of presentment and the trial jury. Stat. 25 Edw. 3, stat. 5, c. 3. Green, Verdict According to Conscience, 21–22.

134. ST. 1 Edw.III c. 6; 5 Edw. III c.7. For the general chronology, see HEL, 1:340.

135. Lacer v. John, servant of Serjeant Cambridge (1321), 86 Selden Society 142, 143. Quoted and discussed in Baker, Introduction to English Legal History, 95 and 95 n. 38.

136. 3. E. 3. Intinere North. Fitz. Coron. 284. The jury found facts that presented a classic case of self-defense. For the pattern of fourteenth-century self-defense cases, see Green, Verdict According to Conscience, 36. The fact-findings in these special verdicts may often have been false, as Thomas Green argued. Id., 35–46. The court accepted the special verdict, then entered judgment for murder. Thereafter the king pardoned the offender. This solution — the king's pardon — was thus the same one offered by Gascoigne seventy years later as a remedy for the case in which the judge convicted despite his private knowledge of innocence.

137. Baker, Introduction to English Legal History, 587.

138. Statute of 25 Edw. c. 4.

139. Seipp, Jurors, Evidences and the Tempest of 1499.

140. For example, Baker, Introduction, in Reports of Spelman, 107; Cockburn, History of English Assizes, 113–114; Green, Verdict According to Conscience, 22.

141. Green, Verdict According to Conscience, 22.

142. Baker, Oxford History of the Laws of England, 6:353–355.

143. See chapter 7.

144. Sir William Staunford, Les Plees del Coron (repr. New York: Garland, 1979), 165:

> Sur lissue de rien culpable: nest touts foits requisit daver un general verdit, quar si le fact est tiel, que il est dowtful a eux del iurre, silsoit felonie ou non: ils posent pour lour mieulx discharge, doner un special verdit, cestascavoir verdit a large,

auxibien in cas de felonie, come in assise ou trespass, et ceo apiert in le verdit que trova que un tuast auter in son defens. Quar cestuy qui est arraigne, ladoit pleder de rien culpable, et unquore in le verdit: le iurie peut exprimer tout le circumstance del fact, & concluder que il luy tuast in son defense, & ceo apiert, titulo Coron in Fitz. P. 226. P. 284. P. 286. & P. 287, & H.44.E.3.P.94. . . . Mesme ley est si un arraine de murder, pleda de rien culpable, et est trove que il luy tua per chance medley, ou in son defense, et nemy de malice prepense, come apiert.T.26.H.8.f.6. . . . Et issint cases home purrost imaginer sauns nomber, in queux special verditz, sur le general issue tendu: serront bons.

145. 9 Co. Rep. 14a. (= English Reports 752).

Chapter 6. The Crises of the Seventeenth Century

Epigraph 1. Richard Baxter, A Christian Directory or a Summ of Practical Theologie and Cases of Conscience (London: Printed by Robert White for Nevill Simmons at the Princes Armes in St. Pauls Churchyard, 1673), 149.

Epigraph 2. H. E., The Jury-Man charged; or a Letter to a Citizen of London (London, 1664), 15.

1. G. R. Elton, The Tudor Revolution in Government: Administrative Changes in the Reign of Henry VIII (Cambridge, U.K.: Cambridge University Press, 1962).

2. Thomas A. Green, Verdict According to Conscience: Perspectives on the English Criminal Jury Trial, 1200–1800 (Chicago: University of Chicago Press, 1985), 105, and generally 113–118.

3. In part, this effort involved raising the property qualifications for jury service, so that jurors would be less subject to pressure. Green, Verdict According to Conscience, at e.g. 114.

4. Michael Stuckey, The High Court of Star Chamber (Holmes Beach: Gaunt, 1998), 49–50; J. A. Guy, The Court of Star Chamber and Its Records to the Reign of Elizabeth I (London: H.M. Stationery Office, 1985), 53.

5. Green, Verdict According to Conscience, 140–143; J. S. Cockburn, A History of English Assizes, 1558–1714 (Cambridge, U.K.: Cambridge University Press, 1972), 123–124; J. H. Baker, Oxford History of the Laws of England (Oxford: Oxford University Press, 2003), 6:372–373.

6. HEL, 1:344–345.

7. Green, Verdict According to Conscience, 209 and 209 n. 31.

8. Generally chronology in J. H. Baker, An Introduction to English Legal History, 3d ed. (London: Butterworths, 1990), 588; Green, Verdict According to Conscience, 117–118, 120–121. The criminal justice of the period also created a growing summary jurisdiction for nonblood cases. See the survey in John M. Murrin, Trial by Jury in Seventeenth-Century New England, in Saints and Revolutionaries: Essays on Early American History, ed. David Hall, John Murrin, and Thad Tate (New York: Norton, 1984), 152–206, here 155–156.

9. Full discussion later in this chapter.

10. 3 and 4 Will. and M. c. ix, x 5 (admitting women to the privilege); 5 Anne c. vi (abolishing the [by then meaningless] requirement of demonstrating literacy.).

11. See Paolo Prodi, Una storia della giustizia: Dal pluralismo dei fori al moderno dualismo tra coscienza e diritto (Bologna: Il Mulino, 2000), 363–370 (the Protestant world), and throughout for the fundamental tension between law and conscience in the Western tradition.

12. Waldman, Origins of the Legal Doctrine of Reasonable Doubt, Journal of the History of Ideas 20 (1959): 299–316.

13. For brief general accounts, see see Pietro Palazzini, Dubbio, in Enciclopedia Cattolica (Vatican City: Ente per l'Enciclopedia cattolica e per il Libro cattolico, 1950), 4: cols. 1944–1948; and J. M. Harty, Probabilism, in New Advent Catholic Encyclopedia, available at http://www.newadvent.org/cathen/12441a.htm.

14. For Shapiro's efforts, see her Beyond Reasonable Doubt and Probable Cause: Historical Perspectives on the Anglo-American Law of Evidence (Berkeley: University of California Press, 1991), at e.g. 14–16, and the discussion of Jeremy Taylor at 263–264 n. 57 (discussing Taylor on knowledge but not on judging). To Shapiro, the questions of law remain those a historian of science naturally asks: questions about fact, epistemology, and assumptions. See Barbara Shapiro, A Culture of Fact: England, 1550–1720 (Ithaca: Cornell University Press, 2000), 8–16.

15. Franklin has lengthy discussions both about the law of evidence, James Franklin, The Science of Conjecture: Evidence and Probability before Pascal (Baltimore: Johns Hopkins University Press, 2001), 1–63, and about "the doubting conscience and moral certainty," id., 64–101. Nevertheless, he does not bring his wide and learned treatment together in the right way with regard to judging. Franklin and Shapiro, upon whose first-rate work I have drawn with real gratitude, have focused too much on the modern concept of reasonable doubt as a standard of factual proof, failing to catch sight of its premodern meaning. The best account in the literature on moral theology that I have seen is in the two pages of Margaret Sampson, Laxity and Liberty in Seventeenth-Century English Political Thought, in Conscience and Casuistry in Early Modern Europe, ed. Edmund Leites (Cambridge, U.K.: Cambridge University Press, 1988), 85–87.

16. For example, Laxity and Liberty, 78.

17. The Jury-Man charged, 12.

18. Id., 1.

19. See generally H. R. McAdoo, The Structure of Caroline Moral Theology (London: Longman's, Green, 1949), 1–13.

20. Quoted in id., 3.

21. Fuller discussion above, in chapter 5.

22. Fuller dicussion above, in chapter 4.

23. Discussed in Max Radin, The Conscience of the Court, Law Quarterly Review 192 (1932): 517.

24. As Christopher St. German put it, judges could "sometimes give judgment against their own knowledge, and also against the truth, and yet no default to be in them, as it is in all trials." However, he denied the applicability of the rule in capital cases. St. German, Little Treatise, cited and discussed in Baker, Oxford History of the Laws of England, 6: 47 and 47 n. 246, without reference to the Continental parallels.

25. Measure for Measure, act 2, scene 2.

26. Above, chapter 4.

27. William Ames, Conscience with the Power and Cases Thereof (London: Printed by Edw. Griffin, for John Rothwell; and are to be sold at his Shop at the Sign of the Sun in Paul's Churchyard, 1643), 281–283.

28. Joseph Hall, Cases of Conscience, Practically Resolved. (London: Printed by R.H. and J.G. and are to be sold by Fr: Aglesfield at the Marigold in S. Paul's Churchyard, 1654), 117–129

29. For an ironic example, see [Anon.], TO 'EN APXH: Or an Exercitation upon a Momentous Question in Divinity, and Case of Conscience, viz. Whether it be lawfull for any Person to act contrary to the Opinion of his own Conscience, formed from Arguments that to him appear very Probable, though not Necessary or Demonstrative (London, 1675), 12:

> In dubiis animae tutior pars est eligenda. . . .
>
> That is is Lawful for a Man to act contrary to the Opinion of his own Conscience, which he judgeth safest, according to the Opinoin of others, which he judgeth less probably true, and less safe. Of this mind besides Vasquez and Medina (before mentioned by us) he saith are Mercado, Velentia, Julier, Suarez, Enriquez, Azorius, Bennes, Navarrus, Arragon, Salon, Lopez, Ledesma, Sala, Sairus and Leonardus. More than a full Jury, were they all good Men and true: But let us hear their Reason.

30. On Taylor's general approach, see McAdoo, Structure of Caroline Moral Theology, 37–57.

31. Jeremy Taylor, Ductor Dubitantium, or The Rule of Conscience in all her General Measures; Serving as a great Instrument for the determination of Cases of Conscience (London: Printed by R. Norton, for R. Royston, Bookseller to the King's Most Sacred Majesty, 1676), 62–67.

32. Stat. 16 Chas. 2, c. 4 (1664).

33. See generally Green, Verdict According to Conscience, 200–264.

34. In this sense, we can certainly see a kind of radicalism in the theology of this period, which seems to push the problem of the moral responsibility of jurors well beyond its traditional place in cases of blood and real property disputes. Nevertheless, the literature of the time does seem to show some uneasiness about this departure from tradition. Thus The Jury-Man charged, 15, went out of its way to insist that persons prosecuted under the Conventicles Act *might* face a blood punishment: "They shall be hanged as Felons if they return without Licence in seven years space; can you appeal to God with a good conscience, and say before the great and dreadful Judge of Heaven and Earth; Lord, let me suffer Death and Damnation as a Murderer, if these persons be not sufficiently proved guilty?"

35. The Jury-Man charged, 1.

36. 1 Keble 934, 83 Eng Rep. 1328; 1 Keble 938, 83 Eng Rep. 1331; Sir T. Raym. 138, 83 Eng. Rep. 75; 1 Sid. 273, 82 Eng Rep. 1101 (1665).

37. Green, Verdict According to Conscience, 210, citing Hale, Historia Placitorum Coronae (repr. Clark, N.J.: Lawbook Exchange, 2003) (orig. 1736), 2:160.

38. Id. The text is dated to 1676 by D. E. C. Yale, Introduction, in Sir Matthew Hale's Prerogatives of the King (London: Selden Society, 1976), xxiv–xxiv.

39. Sampson, Laxity and Liberty, 85–87.

40. Hale, Historia Placitorum Coronae, 1:300.

41. But to some extent possibly coined by Hale himself: see the discussion of Carleton Kemp Allen, Legal Duties and Other Essays in Jurisprudence (Oxford: Clarendon, 1931), 257–258.

42. Hale, Historia Placitorum Coronae, 2:290: "ex parte misericordiae"; id., 2:305: "ex parte mitiori."

43. Hale, Historia Placitorum Coronae, 1:509.

44. Gilbert Burnet, Life and Death of Sir Matthew Hale (London: William Taylor, 1682), 24.

45. Hale, Historia Placitorum Coronae, 2:313.

46. Green, Verdict According to Conscience, 208–221.

47. See the general account in id., 212–220.

48. See Robert Edgar Megarry, A Second Miscellany-at-Law (London: Stevens, 1973), 197–198.

49. Howell, State Trials, 6:995.

50. The Diary of John Milward, Esq., ed. Caroline Robbins (Cambridge, U.K.: Cambridge University Press 1938), 167.

51. Id., 167–168.

52. Id., 160.

53. Id., 160.

54. R. v. Windham, 2 Keble, 180; and the account in Milward's Diary, 168–169.

55. Id., 168.

56. Id., 160.

57. Journal of the House of Commons, 9:35, col. 2.

58. Judge Keeling's Case, quoted in Howell, State Trials, 6:992.

59. Id., 996.

60. Id.

61. Howell, State Trials, 6:961–970; for the imposition of the fine, 968.

62. Howell, State Trials, 6:953.

63. Howell, State Trials, 6:965.

64. So we may conclude from the report that the Recorder said, "Take him away, take him away, take him out of the Court." Id. 969.

65. Id., 969.

66. Bushel's Case, English Reports 84:1123–1125. For a 1680 case in which a judge nevertheless fined a juror, see John Langbein, The Origins of Adversary Criminal Trial (Oxford: Oxford University Prss, 2003), 324 n. 346.

67. For the puzzlement of Langbein and Green, see the discussion below.

68. Howell, State Trials, 6:1009; English Reports, 84:1123–1125.

69. Bushel's Case, English Reports, 84:1123–1125; cf. Howell, State Trials, 6:1009.

70. For this issue in the earlier debates over Star Chamber, see William Hudson, A Treatise of the Court of Star Chamber, ed. Francis Hargarve (Birmingham: Legal Classics Library, 1986), 72: "And first of perjury; wherein I must first meet with that positive opinion 8. *Eliz. Dyer,* that there was no punishment for perjury before the statute of *5. Eliz,* but against jurors only by way of attaint: and I cannot but marvel that so learned and reverend men should light upon so fond an opinion." See the full discussion in id., 72–73.

71. For the addition of this phrase after the manuscript of the opinion had been drafted, see Green, Verdict According to Conscience, 244 and 244 n. 175.

72. Vaughan's reasoning is presented in Howell, State Trials, 6:1009–1019.

73. John H. Langbein, The Criminal Trial before Lawyers, 45 U. Chi. L. Rev. 263, 299 n. 105 (1978).

74. Langbein, Origins of Adversary Criminal Trial, 324 n. 346.

75. Langbein, Criminal Trial before Lawyers, 299 n. 105, though also noting that Old Bailey juries did sometimes bring independent knowledge to the case.

76. Id., 288 n. 74 (1978); id. 290. See also Green, Verdict According to Conscience, 245 (arguing that jurors sometimes had knowledge of reputation). So also Giles Duncombe, Trials per Pais (Buffalo: Hein, 1980) (1682), 274: "They may have other Evidence than what is shewed in Court. They are of the Vicinage, the Judge is a Stranger. They may have Evidence from their own personal Knowledge, that the witnesses speak false, which the Judge knows not of; they may know the witnesses to be stigmatized and infamous, which may be unknown to the Parties or Court."

77. Alongside the sources discussed in the text, see also Anon., The Security of English-Mens Lives, or the Trust, Power, and Duty of the Grand Jurys of England (London: Printed for T. Mitchel, 1681), quoted later in this chapter.

78. For Baxter's fame, see Sampson, Laxity and Liberty, 87.

79. Richard Baxter, A Christian Directory or a Summ of Practical Theologie and Cases of Conscience (London: Printed by Robert White for Nevill Simmors at the Princes Armes in St. Pauls Churchyard, 1673), 149.

80. Burnet, Life and Death of Sir Matthew Hale, 24. For another example from the period, see Anon., The Power and Privilege of Juries Asserted (London: Janeway, 1681).

81. See Jim Spivey, Benjamin Calamy, in Oxford Dictionary of National Biography (Oxford: Oxford University Press, 2004), 9:483–485.

82. For Taylor's place, with regard to this problem, within the larger theological tradition, see McAdoo, Structure of Caroline Moral Theology, 88–97.

83. Taylor, Ductor Dubitantium, 160.

84. Benjamin Calamy, A discourse about a scrupulous conscience, preached at the Parish-Church of St. Mary Aldermanbury (London: Printed for Rowland Reynolds, 1683), 4.

85. Id.

86. Id., 5.

87. Id., 35–36.

88. Id., 38.

89. For the familiar problem of respectable Englishmen avoiding jury service, see e.g. Cockburn, A History of English Assizes, 111–112 (grand juries), 118–122 (petty juries).

90. For "scrupulosity" in the thought of the period, including in the thought of Baxter, see Sampson, Laxity and Liberty, 87–88.

91. Milward's Diary, 168.

92. For Babington in the context of conflicts between judge and jury, see Cockburn, History of English Assizes, 115.

93. Zachary Babington, Advice to Grand Jurors in Cases of Blood (London: Printed for John Amery at the Peacock against St. Dunstan's Church in Fleet-street, 1677) (repr. New York: Garland, 1978), B7r.

94. R. v. Windham, 2 Keble, 180; and the account in Milward's Diary, 168–169.

95. Babington, Advice to Grand Jurors, 112–113.

96. Green, Verdict According to Conscience, 252 (Hawles's pamphlet long influential and "a gloss" on Bushel's Case.) Green interprets Hawles's pamphlet as a defense of the right of the jury to find law. Id., 257. In my view, this does not quite capture the tenor of the pamphlet, which emphasizes all aspects of the jury's responsibility as forms of moral responsibility.

97. [Hawles], The English-mans Right: A Dialogue between a Barrister at Law, and a Jury-Man (London: Printed for Richard Janeway, in Queenshead Alley in Paternoster-Row, 1680) (repr. New York: Garland, 1978), 29.

98. Id., 1.

99. Id., 2.

100. Seditious libel cases raised some significant issues that I do not deal with here. In these cases, the traditional role of the criminal jury was effectively reversed: where criminal juries had taken it as a privilege to enter special verdicts, avoiding the responsibility of the general verdict, in seditious libel cases jurors tried to lay claim to the authority to enter verdicts, while judges tried to compel them to enter special verdicts. See generally the discussion of Green, Verdict According to Conscience, 318–355; Langbein, Origins of Adversary Criminal Trial, 329; and the background in Philip Hamburger, The Development of the Law of Seditous Libel and the Control of the Press, 37 Stanford L. Rev. 661 (1985). Here as elsewhere the relationship between special and general verdicts demands a much deeper treatment than I give it in this book.

101. [Hawles,] English-mans Right, 22.

102. Id., 23.

Chapter 7. The Eighteenth Century

Epigraph 1. [Hawles], The English-mans Right: A Dialogue between a Barrister at Law, and a Jury-Man (London: Printed for Richard Janeway, in Queenshead Alley in Paternoster-Row, 1680) (repr. New York: Garland, 1978), 23.

Epigraph 2. The Proceedings of the Old Bailey Ref: T17840915–10.

1. My thanks to Professor Bruce Smith for making this observation to me in conversation.

2. Langbein has been a pioneer of the comparative study of the decline of blood punishments in the West. See already John H. Langbein, The Historical Origins of the Sanction of Imprisonment for Serious Crime, 5 J. Legal Studies 35–60 (1976). For a survey of liberalizing criminal procedure in eighteenth-century France, see Bernard Durand, Déontologie du Juge et Droits de la Défense: Quelques pistes dans la procédure criminelle d'ancien régime, in Justice et Justiciables, Mélanges Henri Vidal (Montpellier: Faculté de droit, d'économie et de gestion, 1994), 213–237.

3. See generally J. M. Beattie, Crime and the Courts in England, 1660–1800 (Princeton: Princeton University Press, 1986), 500–519, 538–548, 592–601, 619–621.

4. For a general survey of the devices of leniency, see J. S. Cockburn, A History of English Assizes, 1558–1714 (Cambridge, U.K.: Cambridge University Press, 1972), 127–133.

5. Langbein, The Origins of Adversary Criminal Trial, 17, 334–336.

6. Mathias Schmoeckel, Humanität und Staatsraison: Die Abschaffung der Folter in Europa und die Entwicklung des gemeinen Strafprozeß- und Beweisrechts seit dem hohen Mittelalter (Cologne: Böhlau, 2000), 295–359.

7. As Peter Holtappels, Die Entwicklung des Grundsatzes "in dubio pro reo" (Hamburg: Cram, de Gruyter, 1965), 67–74, pointed out more than forty years ago; see also the more detailed discussion of Giorgio Alessi Palazzolo, Prova Legale e Pena: La crisi del sistema tra medio evo et moderno (Naples: Jovene, 1979).

8. Andrew Jones, The Black Book of Conscience; or God's High Court of Justice in the Soul (New London, CT: Timothy Green, 1771), 13.

9. Famously observed by John H. Langbein, The Criminal Trial before Lawyers, 45 U. Chi. L. Rev. 263, 284–287.

10. The passage is taken verbatim from Anon., The Security of English-Mens Lives, or the Trust, Power, and Duty of the Grand Jurys of England (London: Printed for T. Mitchel, 1681), 9–10.

11. [Anon.,] A Guide to the Knowledge of the Rights and Privileges of Englishmen (London: Printed for J. Williams and W. Bingley, 1771), 95–96.

12. Thomas Gisborne, An Enquiry into the Duties of Men in the Higher and Middle Classes of Society in Great Britain, 4th ed., 2 vols. (London: Printed for B. and J. White, and Cadell and Davies, 1771), 2:460.

13. Richard Price, A Review of the Principal Questions and Difficulties in Morals (London: Printed for A. Millar in the Strand, 1758), 311.

14. Henry Grove, A System of Moral Philosophy, 2 vols. (London: Printed and Sold by J. Waugh, 1749), 2:42–43.

15. Id., 2: 15–16.

16. For example, id., 24–25: "With regard to the *Law* there is a *right*, an *erroneous*, a *doubting*, and a *scrupulous* Conscience. A *right* Conscience is that which decides aright, or according to the only Rule of Rectitude the *Law* of God. This is threefold, *well-informed, probable* and *ignorant*. A *well-informed* Conscience in all its decisions proceeds upon the most evident principles, demonstrative if the subject will supply them, or where these fail, on the surest foundation it can get. It is not more a duty to labour after such a Conscience as this, which renders the obedience we pay to God's commandments a *reasonable Service*, than it is a happiness to injoy it. The satisfaction of it being like that of a Traveller who is perfectly acquainted with his way, and though it lies among a thousand other paths, know himself not to be mistaken."

17. Id.

18. For Taylor as "England's last great casuist," see Edmund Leites, Casuistry and Character, in Leites, ed, Conscience and Casuistry in Early Modern Europe (Cambridge, U.K.: Cambridge University Press, 1988), 124–125.

19. Jeremy Taylor, Ductor Dubitantium, or The Rule of Conscience in all her General Measures; Serving as a great Instrument for the determination of Cases of Conscience (London: Printed by R. Norton, for R. Royston, Bookseller to the King's Most Sacred Majesty, 1676), 62–67.

20. Id., 136–138.

21. Id., 138.

22. Id., 139.

23. Id., 142.

24. Quoted above, in chapter 4.

25. Paley's place in the debates of the time is described in Green, Verdict According to Conscience, 303–305, and for the larger context of the desire to crack down on crime, 290–310.

26. Paley, The Principles of Moral and Political Philosophy (Indianapolis: Liberty Fund, 2002), 391–392 (1785).

27. Barbara Shapiro, Beyond Reasonable Doubt and Probable Cause: Historical Perspectives on the Anglo-American Law of Evidence (Berkeley: University of California Press, 1991), 22–25.

28. L. Kinvin Wroth and Hiller Zobel, eds., Legal Papers of John Adams (Cambridge, MA: Belknap, 1965), 3:243. The discussion of Anthony Morano, A Reexamination of the Development of the Reasonable Doubt Rule, 55 B.U. L. Rev. 507, 517 (1975), hid the quotations from Hale behind ellipses.

29. Id., 271. Quoted and discussed in Morano, Reexamination, 517.

30. Id.

31. Langbein, Origins of Adversary Criminal Trial, 261–266.

32. Id., 265.

33. Bl. Comm. 4:343 (1769).

34. The Proceedings of the Old Bailey Ref: T17870523–99.

35. Trial of John Shepherd (Theft) (1789). The Proceedings of the Old Bailey Ref: T17890603–43

36. The Proceedings of the Old Bailey Ref: T17840915–10.

37. Bridget Murphy, Margaret Murphy (Theft, Pickpocketing) (1783). The Proceedings of the Old Bailey Ref: T17830430–44:

> Court to Jury. The circumstance of privacy seems to be personal, to the person that commits the fact, and that of the person who is present, aiding, and assisting, is guilty of the felony, yet as it depends very often upon the personal dexterity, it might not be fit perhaps to punish the person who means to be aiding and assisting in the general offence of stealing, with the same severity therefore the rule has been, to confine it to the individual hand that commits the fact; therefore, if it cannot be said, that both the prisoners were guilty of the private stealing, it is the safest way to acquit them altogether of the criminal charge.
>
> MARGARET MURPHY, BRIDGET MURPHY,
> GUILTY, Of stealing but not privately.

William Snaleham (Theft: burglary) (1784). The Proceedings of the Old Bailey Ref: T17840421–8:

> Court. Gentlemen of the Jury, As to breaking there is a difficulty which is not explained to your satisfaction or mine; nobody knows how they got into the house, there are no marks of violence any where; there is a small circumstance that goes to make it more probable that it should be at the parlour window, but that I rather think falls short of satisfactory proof that they did get in that way; they might have got in by some way which excludes the idea of force used to obtain admission; as

for instance, if a garret window was open, and they got in by the leads, or if they got in at any other open window by a ladder: it therefore seems to me upon the whole evidence, if you should be satisfied that the prisoner was concerned in this robbery, the safest and properest verdict for you to give will be, that he is guilty of stealing the things, but not guilty of breaking and entering the dwelling house.

GUILTY Of stealing the goods, but NOT GUILTY of breaking and entering the dwelling house.

38. Trial of Henry Harvey (Deception, Perjury) (1785). The Proceedings of the Old Bailey Ref: T17850914–187.

39. Cited and discussed in Langbein, Origins of Adversarial Trial, 263.

40. Martin Madan, Thelyphthora: or a treatise on female ruin, 2d ed. (London: Dodsley, 1781).

41. Martin Madan, Thoughts on executive justice, with respect to our criminal laws, particularly on the circuits, 2d ed. (London: Dodsley, 1785), 141.

42. Id., 144. Madan, it should be said, was not addressing the moral anxieties of the jurors in the way that Paley did. Instead, he was convinced that jurors were showing excessive mercy, notably to young offenders. See id., 143. Nevertheless, it is striking that he assumed that the guilt of the offender was frequently obvious in cases in which juries acquitted.

43. Trial of Thomas Hornsby (Theft with Violence, Highway Robbery) (1782). The Proceedings of the Old Bailey Ref: T17820911–56:

> Court. Have you any reasonable doubt—I am partly sure it was the hanger; the lock of the pistol was found in the co next morning.
> NOT GUILTY

44. The Proceedings of the Old Bailey Ref: T17831210–4.

45. The Proceedings of the Old Bailey Ref: T17830430–67.

46. The Proceedings of the Old Bailey Ref: T17840707–10.

47. The Proceedings of the Old Bailey Ref: T17860222–1.

48. The Proceedings of the Old Bailey Ref: T17960217–70.

49. The general history is presented in T. P. Gallanis, The Mystery of Old Bailey Counsel, Cambridge Law Journal 65 (2006): 169–172 [159–173].

50. Id.

Conclusion

1. Quoted and discussed above in chapter 4.

2. Blakely v. Washington, 542 U.S. 296, 301 (2004).

3. H. E., The Jury-Man charged; or a Letter to a Citizen of London (London, 1664), 1.

4. Steve Sheppard, The Metamorphoses of Reasonable Doubt: How Changes in the Burden of Proof Have Weakened the Presumption of Innocence, 78 Notre Dame L. Rev. 1165, 1181–1206 (2003).

5. See the survey of debates in Robert C. Power, Reasonable and Other Doubts: The Problem of Jury Instructions, 67 Tenn. L. Rev. 45, 58–61 (1999).

6. Commonwealth v. Webster, 5 Mass. 295, 320 (1850).

7. James Fitzjames Stephen, A History of the Criminal Law of England (repr. London: Routledge, 1996) (orig. 1883), 1:573, discussed above in chapter 1.

8. Taylor, Ductor Dubitantium, or The Rule of Conscience in all her General Measures; Serving as a great Instrument for the determination of Cases of Conscience (London: Printed by R. Norton, for R. Royston, Bookseller to the King's Most Sacred Majesty, 1676, 160, discussed above in chapter 6.

9. For an aggressive denunciation of this system, see William Pizzi, Trials without Truth (New York: New York University Press, 1999).

10. Mirjan Damaska, Evidence Law Adrift (New Haven: Yale University Press, 1997).

11. Bl. Comm. 4:358.

12. See above all William Stuntz, The Uneasy Relationship between Criminal Procedure and Criminal Justice, Yale Law Journal 107 (1997): 44–45.

13. For example, James Liebman, Jeffrey Fagan, Valerie West, and Jonathan Lloyd, Error Rates in Capital Cases, 1973–1995, Texas Law Review 78 (2000): 1839–1865.

14. For example, Helmholz, Origins of the Privilege Against Self-Incrimination: The Role of the European *Ius Commune,* 65 N.Y.U. L. Rev. 962 (1990); Antoine Astaing, Droits et Garanties de l'Accusé dans le Procès Criminel d'Ancien Régime XVIe et XVIIIe siècles: Audace et pusillanimité de la doctrine pénale française (Aix-en-Provence: Presses Universitaires d'Aix-Marseilles, 1999).

15. Publili Syri Mimi Sententiae, ed. Otto Friedrich (repr. Heidelberg: Olms, 1969), 77: "Tam de se iudex iudicat quam de reo."

16. See in particular his seminal articles, Controlling Prosecutorial Discretion in Germany, 41 U. Chi. L. Rev. 439 (1974), and Land Without Plea Bargaining: How the Germans Do It, 78 Mich. L. Rev. 204 (1979).

17. I do not explore the fate of the older moral theology in modern Continental law here. Let me simply point to some of its Continental vestiges. The old theological phrase "judex lex loquens," which encapsulated the proposition that it was the law and not the judge who spoke, has of course survived in a new guise in the tradition now associated with Montesquieu that the judge should be simply "la bouche de la loi" — i.e., that the judge should act simply as the mechanical implementer of the legislative will. In that respect, the old moral theology has been refashioned into a new doctrine of separation of powers. The old doctrine has also survived in the French insistence that juries should decide according to their "intime conviction," and in the various uses of "doubt" in Continental criminal law. These are topics that deserve a longer treatment than I give them here.

18. Discussion above in chapter 2.

19. Aegidii Bossii Patricii Mediolanensis ... Tractatus Varii (Lyons: Apud Antonium de Antoniis, 1562), 457.

20. This may help explain why Harry Kalven and Hans Zeisel, in their famous study The American Jury (Chicago: University of Chicago Press, 1966), 55–65, found that in 86 percent of those cases in which judge and jurors disagreed, the jurors were inclined to acquit.

21. Theodore Eisenberg, Stephen P. Garvey, and Martin T. Wells, Jury Responsibility in Capital Sentencing, 44 Buffalo L. Rev. 339, 379 (1996).

Index